Bamboo for Gardens

BAMBOO
for Gardens

TED JORDAN MEREDITH

TIMBER PRESS
Portland · Cambridge

Frontispiece: *Chusquea culeou* 'Caña Prieta'. Author's garden.

Copyright © 2001 by Ted Jordan Meredith. All rights reserved.

All photographs and drawings are by Ted Jordan Meredith.

Published in 2001 by
Timber Press, Inc.
The Haseltine Building
133 S.W. Second Avenue, Suite 450
Portland, Oregon 97204, U.S.A.

Timber Press
2 Station Road
Swavesey
Cambridge CB4 5QJ, U.K.

www.timberpress.com

Reprinted 2002, 2003, 2005

Designed by Susan Applegate
Printed in Hong Kong

Library of Congress Cataloging-in-Publication Data

Meredith, Ted.
Bamboo for gardens / Ted Jordan Meredith.
    p. cm.
Includes bibliographical references (p.).
ISBN 0-88192-507-1
1. Bamboo. I. Title.

SB413.B2 M47 2001
635.9'349—dc21

2001035236

Contents

Foreword

BAMBOO DOES THINGS no other plant can. In the human landscape, these abilities are unparalleled. A neighbor's house is constructed too close for comfort, and a living, breathing, moving screen of green is desired to ease the claustrophobia. Bamboos meet the challenge, and within a very short period of time, a new environment is created. Our vision is diverted to the swaying stems, the fluttering leaves, the nesting birds, and the cool shadows. Relieved, the house next door is forgotten. This is what happened to Ted Jordan Meredith, and we are lucky for it. He was introduced to bamboo in just this way, and his research led not only to his successful planting of a privacy screen, but to this book.

On first glance, bamboos arouse curiosity, but with further study, they become completely intriguing, with their myriad shapes and sizes, colors, and growth habits. The often-misunderstood flowering cycles of many bamboos bewilder us, and the newly accepted theories of evolution of these grasses fascinate us. Fear of invasive species keeps bamboo out of some gardens, and yet the fast rates of growth, sheer verticality, erosion control abilities, and colorful variegations make many bamboos excellent choices in many situations. It is a plant of wonder, and of extremes. With the ability to withstand below-freezing temperatures on a university campus in Minnesota, stabilize the earth on a riverbank in Louisiana, or create realistic habitat and food for zoo animals, bamboo can grace almost any landscape. The many attributes of the many bamboos make it absolutely vital to our ever-changing, ever-threatened world around us. This book is a great asset for any landscape architect challenged with site considerations.

It's about time we had a resource such as this book. In addition to our native bamboo species, hundreds of bamboos have been introduced into the United States, starting as early as the first half of the 19th century. Led by Floyd McClure of the U.S. Department of Agriculture, a very active period of introduction occurred between 1924 and 1940. Today, more than 354 kinds of bamboos (species, subspecies, varieties, forms, and cultivars) can be found growing within the United States. And yet only now can we hold in our hands a complete book about growing bamboo in America, written by an American who has actually grown bamboo in his garden.

In February 1928, the USDA published a leaflet (No. 18) entitled *Bamboos and Bamboo Culture*, which stated, "One of the primary objects of this leaflet is to encourage home production of species suitable for the establishment of groves and gardens." Ted Jordan Meredith essentially says the same thing throughout these pages in a way no one has done before. His personal experiences add immensely to the understanding of bamboo. The reader learns exactly how a bamboo grows and why.

The usefulness of bamboo goes far beyond being just another plant in our garden palette. It can be (and is) grown for its utility: poles for building, stems split for weaving baskets and crafts, shoots for culinary nourishment, leaves for animal forage, a vigorous root system for the uptake of wastewater effluent, and stabilization of disturbed soils. The buzzword of "sustainability" is a given when one speaks of bamboo. It gives far more than it takes. It is no wonder that finally now, after a century of growth in the United States, bamboo is gaining attention.

Ted is an accomplished author, but also an accomplished bamboo grower, and his practical experiences weave throughout this book as interesting anecdotes. Stories of success and failure help increase our understanding of how to grow bamboos in our landscapes, and as a result of Ted's insights, the culture section of this book is extremely helpful. As he says, "Bamboo is far more adaptable than once assumed." This book is a resource for anyone, anywhere, who wants to know about bamboo. It tells us how to buy bamboo, how to propagate it, how to harvest edible shoots, how to control its spread, and how to get rid of bamboo when it overtakes its bounds.

These are some of the many questions I have been asked, or posed myself, during the past decade of my interest in bamboo. I have a collection of books relating to bamboo, but not one concise reference that I can refer to when asked the plethora of questions that come my way. My best reference has been through my involvement with the American Bamboo Society, but now, when asked, not only can I suggest membership to our Society, but I can also highly recommend this book.

People want to know more about bamboo, for one reason or another, and the appropriate literature has been lacking. This book constitutes perhaps the most comprehensive assimilation and synthesis of research on bamboos, including the most recent research papers, of any bamboo book intended for non-scientists. The comprehensiveness and technical rigor of the book are a result of this tremendous effort.

With more than 1200 types growing across this planet, there may just be a bamboo for every situation. The past 20 years have brought new introductions into our country; bamboos originating from parts of Asia, Central America, and South America have been imported in hopes of expanding the usefulness and aesthetic qualities of bamboos for our landscapes. And yet, bamboos without names still exist in some habitats around the world. And still, there is so much to learn.

Bamboo for Gardens will help sort out the marvelous world of bamboos for those simply curious, for those who are in need of help, and certainly for those who repeatedly look to bamboo for answers to everyday challenges. Read it and realize bamboo's potential.

SUSANNE LUCAS
President, American Bamboo Society

Preface

I CAME TO THE WORLD OF BAMBOO not because I was attracted to, or even aware of, bamboo's great intrinsic beauty (though that profound enchantment would soon follow), but out of a suburban necessity.

For more than a decade, I had enjoyed, and taken for granted, an expansive greenbelt as an extension of my backyard, and a refuge from an increasingly congested suburban environment. Much to my naive surprise, the expansive greenbelt was suddenly cleared away, along with the hummingbird nests and assorted wildlife.

Space, in the developer's context, is that which should be filled. Unused space is wasted space, and zoning requirements, in the developer's view, already mandate a great wastage of space.

My view was somewhat different. How could the foundation for the new home be laid so impossibly close to my property line? Surely, a mistake—and one that was starkly evident, since all trees and natural vegetation had been eliminated. Of course, it was not a mistake. Nor was it a mistake that the new homes were two stories high, to better make use of the space.

As the builders framed in a large second-story window in perfect position to look down upon me and lay bare my now absent privacy, the certainty of this new, harsh reality had settled upon me. To my great regret, and in spite of obvious appeal, violent and destructive actions seemed neither practical nor productive.

I went looking for a rapidly growing, tall, evergreen screen.

I found bamboo.

Acknowledgments

I LOOK UPON MY ROLE in this book not as one of an expert, for I am surely not that, but as a gatherer and assembler of information from those who are experts, or who have special knowledge or expertise in a given area, whether it be arcane taxonomic issues, or skills propagating difficult bamboos, or the aesthetics and methodologies of landscaping—and all manner of topics beyond and between.

My goal in this project is to assemble, synthesize, and arrange some of this wealth of information so that it is readily assessable to a broad range of garden and bamboo enthusiasts. For much of the world's population, bamboo is an economically and aesthetically compelling plant. For much of the Western world, bamboo is misunderstood, ignored, or reviled. It is my hope that this book will contribute to a better understanding and appreciation of bamboo.

Both directly and indirectly, through written materials and personal communications, many people have contributed to this book. The bibliography reflects the written works by some of these individuals, but the help and assistance goes far beyond what is included in that listing.

In particular, I want to acknowledge the technical reviews that have broadened and deepened my understanding of bamboos, and which greatly benefited the content of this book. Lynn G. Clark, professor of botany and director of the Ada Hayden Herbarium at Iowa State University in Ames, generously and graciously gave her time responding to my inquiries and completing a technical review of the manuscript. The landmark research conducted by Dr. Clark and her colleagues has redefined the origins of the grass family and the origins of bamboos. Among her numerous publications, Clark is co-author of *American Bamboos,* a comprehensive study of the bamboos of the Americas. Previously, relative to Old World bamboos, very little had been written about the bamboos of the New World. *American Bamboos* fills a glaring gap in the literature and is an essential book for the library of any enthusiast or student of bamboo.

Chris Stapleton of the Royal Botanic Gardens, Kew, is a foremost expert on Old World montane bamboos. These beautiful bamboos are a dizzying taxonomic muddle. Stapleton's research and publications have brought a measure of stability and a great deal of clarity to the taxonomy of these bamboos. I want to thank Dr. Stapleton for his assistance with numerous taxonomic issues, and for his review of the sections in the manuscript on the Old World bamboos. Apart from his books and technical papers, Stapleton also writes articles for bamboo enthusiast publications in both Europe and America. He is exceptionally skilled at rendering technically complex issues in a way that they can be readily assimilated by a wide audience.

I also wish to thank the president of the American Bamboo Society, Susanne Lucas, for reviewing the section of the manuscript on the society and for offering helpful suggestions, which I have gladly incorporated.

While it is essential that I acknowledge the careful reviews of the manuscript by Clark, Stapleton, and Lucas, and acknowledge the benefit of the added rigor that has been brought to bear on the work, it is also essential for me to state that the final wording of the manuscript is mine, and that I have sole responsibility for any and all errors that may appear in the book.

In various ways, Ned Jaquith, George Shor, Gib Cooper, and Jesus Mora have assisted me with valuable advice and information. And in a very genuine sense, virtually everyone I have encountered in the American Bamboo Society, and in the bamboo community throughout the world, has contributed insight and information.

I am grateful for the cooperation and assistance of Quail Botanical Gardens, Hakone Gardens, and Bamboo Sourcery nursery in obtaining many of the photographs. I regret that time constraints did not permit me to photographically explore other public gardens, as well as the many excellent bamboo nurseries. Ironically, some of those that I missed are closest to my residence.

I would be remiss not to acknowledge Carol Giberson, who introduced me to the world of plants and gardening. Had I not been so absorbed by this newfound compulsion, I may never have encountered bamboo. Her steadfast support, forbearance, and counsel during this sometimes seemingly interminable book project has been more than welcome.

And I very much want to express my appreciation for my parents, Edward and Nelva Meredith, who encouraged me in my writing efforts from my earliest years. My father also taught me the art and science of photography, and propelled my enthusiasm for the craft. I still recall, quite vividly, my first encounter with the mysterious alchemy of the darkroom, where in the dim red glow, from the photographic paper's white void, images of the world magically appeared.

Thanks!

CHAPTER 1

Bamboo and the Grass Family

IT IS STARTLING TO THINK that giant timber bamboos, up to 1 ft. (30 cm) in diameter and more than 100 ft. (30 m) tall with structural properties that compare favorably with steel, have any kinship with the fine, velvety mat of the suburban putting green—but they do. Like the putting green lawn, bamboo is a grass.

The grass family, Poaceae (Gramineae), is one of the largest and most diverse, consisting of some 650 genera and 10,000 species. Grasses are characterized by a jointed stem called a culm. Leaves emerge alternately, at the joints, in two ranks along the stem. The leaves consist of a leaf sheath surrounding the culm, and a leaf blade growing free of the culm. Leaf veins are usually parallel. The culms are typically hollow, but they can be solid. Each culm section starts and ends with a solid joint called a node. Nodes are usually visible as a swelling encircling the culm. The sections between the nodes are called internodes. The culms of most grasses have high silica content and are shiny. These aforementioned features are characteristic of all grasses. In the case of the giant timber bamboos, we see the typical grass characteristics played out on a grand scale.

Bamboos are members of Bambusoideae, a subfamily of Poaceae. The great diversity of Bambusoideae bespeaks a long period of highly adaptive development. Bamboo forms include delicate, fernlike, tropical, herbaceous plants, perennial groundcovers, shrubs, vining climbers, and arborescent timber bamboos. For our modern world, these enduring grasses offer us great beauty and utility.

At least 90 genera and 1200 species of bamboos are distributed throughout the world's temperate, tropical, and subtropical regions. A highly diverse member of the grass family, bamboos grow from sea level to high mountainous regions. Some groundcover bamboos reach a height of only a few inches and can be mowed like a lawn. At the other end of the scale are timber bamboos that live up to their name, growing like timber and forming towering forests. These giant grasses are harvestable for construction, paper pulp, and food. The uses for bamboo literally number in the thousands.

Bamboo is a principal defining element for many traditional cultures. Bamboo is shelter. It is food, and the means to acquire food. From womb to tomb, bamboo is the source of both physical and spiritual sustenance—the fiber of life.

Bamboo also offers many benefits for modern societies. Among them, bamboo is a prodigious and rapidly renewable source of fiber. Even as the world's forests and habitats rapidly decline, bamboo offers some solutions. As yet, however, this offer is largely unheard, and bamboo itself is at risk in many parts of the world, from unmanaged use by dense populations and from indiscriminate land clearing. The destruction of land and habitats in South America is most heinous. Some species have already disappeared from the face of the earth forever.

Dendrocalamus giganteus, new shoots and culms at the perimeter of the clump. Quail Botanical Gardens.

And of its benefits to modern societies, it must be said that ultimately no amount of conservation or clever use of resources will provide a solution for the accelerating growth and geometric expansion of the world's population. This finite earth will one day run out of resources and space to hold the population, let alone offer a quality of life. Until world population growth is brought to a halt, any "solutions" will, in the end, be as effective as bailing out the ocean with a sieve. Bamboo can play a role in cushioning this confrontation with the finite limits of our earth, and perhaps, one day, play a role in our recovery.

A plant of uncommon beauty, bamboo is extraordinarily strong and extraordinarily delicate. In its mature form, *Phyllostachys heterocycla* f. *pubescens* is the largest temperate-climate bamboo, reaching a height of 90 ft. (27 m) and a diameter of 7 in. (18 cm), with masses of tiny leaves that shimmer in the slightest breeze. Except for the giant oceanic kelp, bamboo is the world's fastest growing plant (Liese 1991). New bamboo culms can grow more than several feet in a 24-hour period, reaching most of their full height in 30 days. It is literally possible to watch bamboo grow.

Bamboos first developed as forest plants, or along the forest margin, evolving into a highly diverse and distributed group. Bamboo is native to all but two of the world's continents—Europe and Antarctica. Although not native to Europe, bamboo is widely grown there as an ornamental. France and Germany have major commercial bamboo nurseries on a scale unknown in the United States.

Not unexpectedly, the bamboos that are native to tropical regions are highly cold sensitive. Many suffer damage with only the slightest frost. Bamboos of the New World genus *Guadua* grow to 100 ft. (30 m) and a diameter of 8 in. (20 cm), yet these giant tree grasses are damaged by even a minor frost. Other tropical and subtropical bamboos are less cold sensitive and can be readily grown in the warmer areas of the United States, or on a small scale as indoor plants where the outdoor climate does not permit.

Most tropical bamboos grow in slow-spreading clumps. In the cooler temperate zones, most native bamboos spread rapidly, with new culms emerging from running rhizomes. There are exceptions. Some species of the tropical *Guadua* can spread rapidly, sending up new culms as much as 20 ft. (6 m) or more away. Some species of the genus *Fargesia,* indigenous to China's mountainous regions, grow in tight clumps, yet they are among the world's hardiest bamboos, able to withstand temperatures of −20°F (−29°C) without damage.

The genus *Phyllostachys* is preeminent among the temperate-climate bamboos. Most of the larger bamboos associated with China and Japan are species of *Phyllo-*

stachys. Comprising some 75 species and more than 200 varieties and forms, the genus offers some of the world's most beautiful bamboos and some of its most useful. In Europe, North America, and other temperate growing regions, species of *Phyllostachys* are the hardiest of the larger bamboos, and the most readily adaptable.

Origin and Distribution

The world's most ancient grasses, antecedents of today's bamboos, were most likely broad-leaved, herbaceous, tropical forest dwellers that may have originated as early as the very late Cretaceous period or early Tertiary period some 65 million years ago. Among the grasses of today, a small, broad-leaved, herbaceous, rain-forest species, *Streptochaeta spicata,* is among those that most closely resemble the ancient grasses. At one time, these earliest grasses were believed to be true bamboos, but molecular analysis reveals that bamboos originated later, probably in the Oligocene or Miocene epochs, some 30 to 40 million years ago (Lynn Clark, personal communication).

Once a matter of controversy, the molecular data now confirm that true bamboos include herbaceous as well as woody species. The woody bamboos that we normally think of as bamboos, members of the tribe Bambuseae, and the herbaceous bamboos, members of the tribe Olyreae, have been shown to be monophyletic; that is, they originated from a common ancestor (Judziewicz et al. 1999). The earliest herbaceous bamboos are believed to have originated in the Southern Hemisphere. Supporting this hypothesis, the oldest lineage of herbaceous bamboos is found in New Guinea. Although much is yet unknown about the evolution of bamboos, it is believed that the divergence between herbaceous and woody bamboos occurred very early in the lineage. It is speculated that, like herbaceous bamboos, woody bamboos originated in the tropical lowlands of the Southern Hemisphere, subsequently radiating into the temperate zone of the Northern Hemisphere. The earliest woody bamboos are believed to have had pachymorph rhizome systems and a branch array resembling that of *Bambusa* or *Guadua.* The leptomorph rhizome systems found in many genera likely evolved later.

The temperate woody bamboos comprise a single lineage. *Arundinaria gigantea* is the only indigenous species of temperate woody bamboos found in the New World. It is uncertain whether or not there were more species in the past.

With the formation of mountain ranges, the tropical woody bamboos diversified and adapted to montane habitats as well as their original lowland domain. Tropical woody bamboos are less well defined than temperate woody bamboos.

Currently available molecular data suggest an early divergence into the woody bamboos of the New World tropics and the woody bamboos of the Old World tropics. However, the morphological similarities between New World and Old World tropical woody bamboo groups suggest just the opposite. Studies already underway may soon shed additional light on the matter.

Most grasses are adapted to open habitats, but most bamboos are adapted to forest environments. Woody bamboos evolved to compete for light with trees and other woody vegetation. Highly effective in this regard, they are important players in forest dynamics. Bamboos may grow in dense thickets or tall forests, dominating and excluding other vegetation, or exist as understory plants in a forest environment. Running bamboos, with their ability to space culms widely apart, are more likely to dominate the understory or overstory of their habitat. Clumping bamboos with closely spaced culms are more likely to coexist with other plants of similar height, though they too may dominate habitats. A few bamboos are climbing or clambering and may overwhelm existing vegetation. In arid areas, bamboos are more likely to be distributed in sites where more moisture is present, such as stream banks, ravines, and gullies.

Europe and Antarctica are the only continents without indigenous populations of bamboo, yet since their introduction into Europe, bamboos have flourished in many areas from the Mediterranean to the Arctic Circle in Norway. Indeed, bamboo may have been indigenous to Europe several million years ago, before disappearing with the Ice Age during the Pleistocene epoch, though this is highly speculative (Liese 1999). If true, this would leave Antarctica as the only continent untouched by this remarkable grass.

Bamboo's broad distribution is rather surprising, especially considering that these are evergreen plants with shallow root systems, and thus structurally are more vulnerable to cold and other climate extremes. Although, not surprisingly, the most concentrated populations of bamboo occur where ample warmth and moisture are available, bamboo can be found in widely disparate regions and climates. Natural bamboo distributions range from the tropics to temperate zones, and from approximately 50°N, where *Sasa kurilensis* is found on Russia's Sakhalin Island, to 47°S, where *Chusquea culeou* grows in southern Argentina. Geologic shifts and climate changes occurring over many millions of years have led to the emergence of some species that are adapted to climatic extremes. In the New World, the genus *Neurolepis* inhabits a higher elevation than any other bamboo genus, with *N. aristata* growing in dense thickets at 14,100 ft. (4300 m) in the Andes in Ecuador. *Neurolepis* is believed to have evolved relatively recently and may have originated during the uplift of the northern Andes about 5 million years ago (Judziewicz et al. 1999).

Although we usually have woody forms in mind when we think of bamboo, approximately 110 species of herbaceous bamboos exist worldwide. Of these, all but two are indigenous to the New World. Most are found in moist forests below 3300 ft. (1000 m) but may occasionally occur at elevations of up to 8900 ft (2700 m). They range from 29°N to 34°S latitude (Judziewicz et al. 1999).

Of the approximately 90 bamboo genera, some 70 are woody bamboos. Of the 70 woody genera, 21 are native to the New World, and some 50 are native to the Old World. The genus *Arundinaria,* as currently constituted, is the only genus native to both the New World and the Old World. The New World has approximately 430 woody species, the Old World approximately 500 to 600 species. When all bamboos, including herbaceous ones, are considered, the numbers of New World and Old World species are roughly equal (Judziewicz et al. 1999). The New World genus *Chusquea* is estimated to comprise more than 200 species, more than any other bamboo genus.

Bamboo distribution can be characterized by its presence in three major geographic regions: Asia-Pacific, the Americas, and Africa. The Asia-Pacific region is the most well known and well developed bamboo region, with some 800 species and varieties and some 45 million acres (18 million hectares) of bamboo. Some of the regions and countries in the Asia-Pacific are China, Japan, Korea, Southeast Asia, India, Australia, New Zealand, and the Pacific Islands. The Asia-Pacific region can be roughly divided into two subregions based on rhizome habit. Bamboos with pachymorph rhizomes and a typically clumping habit are distributed primarily in the warmer areas between the Tropic of Cancer and the Tropic of Capricorn. Bamboos with leptomorph rhizomes and a running habit generally have much greater cold resistance and are distributed at higher latitudes, in such regions as Japan, Korea, and the Huang (Yellow) and Chang (Yangtze) River valleys of China. In China, bamboos with leptomorph and pachymorph rhizomes are distributed in roughly equal numbers. China is one of the world's great centers for indigenous and cultivated bamboo. Some 400 species and 40 genera are native to China. Great forests of timber bamboo flourish in parts of the country, and bamboo is integrated into the modern economy as well as traditional culture. Herbaceous bamboos are absent from China.

The African region is relatively small, with limited extension, nearly entirely in tropical areas, ranging from southern Senegal in the north to southern Mozambique and the island of Madagascar in the south. Although the continent's mainland has fewer than 10 species and only 3 genera, Madagascar is home to some 11 genera and 40 species. Many genera are common to both Africa and the Asia-Pacific.

In the Americas, bamboo occurs naturally from the southeastern United States in the north to the beech forests of central Chile in the south. South America was likely the center of origin for most New World woody bamboos, with subsequent migration to Central America and Mexico after formation of the Panamanian land bridge some 5.7 million years ago. Species indigenous to Central America and Mexico are probably of more recent origin (Judziewicz et al. 1999).

Although the Asia-Pacific region is often assumed to be predominant in the world of bamboo, the Americas are nearly as rich in genera and species, exhibiting a greater range of structural and evolutionary diversity. The Americas have an estimated 41 genera and more than 500 species of bamboos, including both woody and herbaceous types. *Chusquea* is distributed across a wider latitudinal range than any other genus. *Guadua* covers enormous territories of up to nearly 47,000 square miles (122,000 square kilometers) in the Brazilian Amazon and Peru (Londoño 1996).

Except for a few species of the unusual genus *Chusquea,* the only leptomorph bamboos in the New World are *Arundinaria gigantea* and its subspecies, which is also the only bamboo native to the United States. Herbaceous bamboos are nearly exclusive to the Americas, existing primarily as tropical understory plants, and often somewhat resembling ferns or ginger. Most of the New World bamboos, including the woody types, are relatively small, but there are highly notable exceptions, such as the tropical giant, *Guadua angustifolia,* which easily rivals its Old World timber bamboo counterparts in both size and importance to the local economy.

Although some researchers placed bamboo's origins in southern China, other evidence indicates a different origin. A study using chloroplast DNA, and analysis of the cladograms that emerged from the study, placed the origins of bamboo in the Southern Hemisphere, perhaps in South America. Except for recent human introductions, all current South American genera are unique to the region. Although the South American bamboo *Guadua* was once thought to be part of the *Bambusa* genus of India and Asia, it is now known to be a distinct genus.

Southern Asia, arguably the world's greatest bamboo resource, was not bamboo's center of origin, but probably a later, emergent center with highly amenable climatic conditions. As molecular sequence studies become more comprehensive, we may learn much more about the origins and distribution of the world's bamboos. For now, much is a matter of speculation and hypothesis. One such hypothesis, for example, contends that *Arundinaria gigantea,* North America's only indigenous woody bamboo, may be the only New World bamboo of Asian ancestry, perhaps having migrated from Asia across the Bering Bridge during a period of ample warmth and moisture.

The clumping, winter-hardy, montane bamboos of the Sino-Himalayan region were once thought to have originated from bamboos that inhabited the tropical forests of Southeast Asia some 60 million years ago, subsequently evolving as the geologic uplifting gave the tropical bamboos a long, slow ride to elevations of up to 13,000 ft. (4000 m). However, evidence now indicates that the earliest bamboos originated long after this uplifting, and the Old World montane bamboos evolved from the temperate clade of ancestors rather than the tropical clade (Lynn Clark, personal communication).

Human introductions have greatly extended bamboo's distribution, to such difficult environments as arid desert climates and the cold climate extremes of the Arctic Circle. *Fargesia nitida* and *F. murielae* have been growing in Norway for more than 30 years. *Fargesia nitida* has successfully survived winters in Tromsø, Norway, at nearly 70°N latitude, well into the Arctic Circle (Flatabø 1995).

Some of the human introductions occurred sufficiently long ago that the bamboos are fully naturalized. *Phyllostachys heterocycla* f. *pubescens,* for example, was introduced into Japan from China in the 1740s and now covers some 40 percent of Japan's total bamboo acreage. Bamboo was distributed along trade routes, including the ancient maritime spice routes between China, Indonesia, Ceylon (Sri Lanka), and India, cloaking the center of origin for some species. *Bambusa vulgaris* may have originated in Malaysia and Indonesia, but because it is very easily propagated and readily useful, the species is now widely distributed throughout the world's tropical regions as a result of numerous human introductions. *Oxytenanthera abyssinica,* indigenous to Africa, has been introduced into India as a source of pulp for paper.

Some regions without indigenous bamboos have climates that are nevertheless highly favorable to these plants. Southern France, near the Mediterranean, for example, has stands of *Phyllostachys heterocycla* f. *pubescens* rivaling those of their native environments in Asia. The temperature ranges and precipitation patterns of the southeastern United States are highly suitable to many bamboos. The moderate winter climate of America's West Coast, from north to south, is favorable to many species. Most of the rainfall along the West Coast, however, comes primarily in the fall and winter months, while summers are relatively dry. This moisture pattern is just the opposite of the temperate bamboo growing regions of Asia, and supplemental water during the summer months is generally necessary for optimal growth.

Woody and Herbaceous Bamboos

All bamboos belong to the grass subfamily Bambusoideae. The subfamily is comprised of two tribes, Bambuseae and Olyreae (Judziewicz et al. 1999). The woody shrubs and treelike bamboos that we normally think of as bamboo belong to the tribe Bambuseae. Olyreae consists of the herbaceous bamboos. Although the legitimacy of herbaceous bamboos has been accepted for quite some time, recent research has clarified several taxonomic issues. The world's most ancient grasses, once thought to be herbaceous bamboos, are now known to have preceded bam-

Phyllostachys nigra var. *henonis*. Bamboo Sourcery.

boo. Rices are closely related to bamboos and were once thought to be herbaceous bamboos, but molecular analysis has shown that this is not the case.

The woody bamboos are diverse, thriving in many different habitats, from sea level to the high mountains, across a broad latitudinal range. The herbaceous bamboos have a far more limited habitat range, centered primarily in moist forests of the New World. Though not hardy, and with little tolerance for dry conditions, some herbaceous bamboos are very appealing horticultural subjects and can be grown outdoors in a few regions of the United States; many more may be adequately suited to indoor or protected growing conditions, as long as the humidity is sufficient. As of this writing, only a few are available in North America.

The most obvious distinction between woody and herbaceous bamboos is the lignification or "woodiness" of the culm. Herbaceous bamboos have relatively unlignified culms and are unable to support tall growth or heavy leaf canopies. Woody bamboos have complex branching patterns. Herbaceous bamboos either have no branches, or else a simple branching pattern with little or no ramification. Woody bamboos have two growth phases: first, the culm elongates, protected by culm leaves that sheath the new culm but offer little or no photosynthesis, followed by branching and the emergence of photosynthetic foliage leaves. The two phases are not always discrete. In some genera, such as *Phyllostachys,* the second phase begins before the first phase is complete. Herbaceous bamboos, and all other grasses, have a single growth phase, extending photosynthetic leaves as the culm elongates. Woody bamboos have bisexual flowers. Herbaceous bamboos have unisexual flowers (Judziewicz et al. 1999).

The focus of this book, and, indeed, the focus of most gardeners, growers, and landscapers, is on the woody bamboos. Few herbaceous bamboos are currently cultivated, and, in the main, they better fit our conception of little houseplants than they do our conception of bamboo. On the other hand, for the bamboo aficionado, there is considerable appeal in the common ancestry of the herbaceous and woody bamboos. The herbaceous brethren are the world's smallest bamboos. *Raddiella minima* has delicate culms no more than 2 in. (5 cm) tall—contrasting with the culms of some woody timber bamboos that are more than 600 times taller and rival the strength of steel. While not likely to challenge woody bamboos for the hearts and minds of bamboo aficionados, the herbaceous bamboos deserve more attention and cultivation. Many, like the delicate, fernlike *Raddia distichophylla,* are certainly worthy of attention.

CHAPTER 2

Structure and Function

Segmented Structure

The bamboo plant consists of a series of ramifying, segmented, vegetative axes, differentiated, according to function, into rhizomes, culms, and branches. Each axis consists of a series of nodes and internodes. The axes are usually hollow along the internode and always solid at the nodal joint, thus forming a series of segments along the length of the axis, whether the axis is a culm, branch, or rhizome. Roots are the only vegetative axes of a bamboo plant that are not segmented.

Buds, nascent branches, or rhizomes are present at most nodes. During the period of active growth, and sometimes persistently, the segments are covered by leaves or bracts that subtend the bud, protecting it and the internode that arises from the node. Like the buds, the leaves or bracts face alternating sides of the axis along its length. Although the aboveground part of the bamboo plant is differentiated by function from the underground part of the plant, the structures are generally parallel, particularly for bamboos with leptomorph rhizome systems. In some species, roots or root primordia are even present on culm and branch nodes.

The segmented structure plays a major role in giving bamboo its special characteristics. The hollow internodes, common to most bamboos, and solid nodes are fundamental elements in bamboo's notable combination of light weight and great strength.

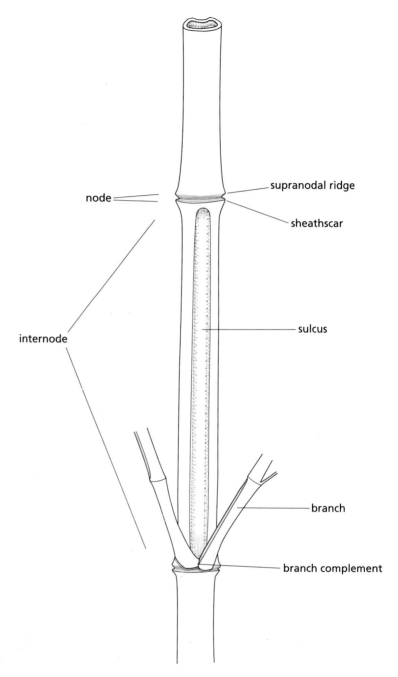

node

supranodal ridge

sheathscar

internode

sulcus

branch

branch complement

Figure 1. Segmented structure and features of a bamboo culm. The pronounced sulcus that runs the length of the internode is characteristic of *Phyllostachys*.

Neck

The neck is usually associated with the rhizome, but it is a structural element of every segmented axis of the bamboo plant. The basal portion of an axis, the neck, consists of tightly compressed segments, usually smaller in diameter than the portion of the axis that follows. Along the neck, the nodes lack buds, and the reduced leaves are small and scalelike. On the branches of many species, the neck is nearly absent. The neck is more obvious at the base of culms and rhizomes, where the structure does indeed more typically resemble a neck.

Structurally, the neck permits creation of a new and larger axis. The highly compressed stacking of progressively larger internodes can create a new axis much larger than the axis from which it originated. This is well illustrated by the rhizomes and culms of leptomorph timber bamboos. The rhizomes are proportionally much smaller in diameter than the culms (new axes) they generate. The highly compressed internodes of the neck progressively increase in diameter to form the base of the culm.

Like other parts of the plant, the neck has developed in specialized ways in response to environmental conditions. The rhizome necks of the pachymorph bamboo *Yushania macrophylla,* for example, are completely hollow, even at the nodes, forming long conduits. This feature may have evolved in response to the seasonally waterlogged conditions of its native environment.

The rhizome neck or culm neck of a leptomorph bamboo is usually short and plays a limited role in the function of the plant. For bamboos with pachymorph rhizomes, however, the neck may serve additional functions, such as establishing support for the culms, and accelerating the spread of the plant. Evident at even the seedling stage, the necks of pachymorph rhizomes typically first turn downward before turning upward to form a rhizome and culm. This initial downward turn serves to establish the new, larger culm more deeply in the soil. The large, tropical pachymorph bamboo *Guadua angustifolia* initiates the neck portions of new rhizomes and culms early, creating feet that penetrate into the soil and help support the towering 100 ft. (30 m) culms. In this species and others, a highly elongated neck allows the bamboo to greatly extend its reach, creating an aggressive spreading habit rivaling that of the larger leptomorph bamboos.

Node

All the jointed axes of a bamboo plant consist of a series of nodes and internodes. The node is always solid and is frequently marked by a swelling of the axis. In early Japanese horticultural texts, the swollen node was said to resemble a crane's knee. All the cells along the internodes are axially oriented—that is, they run along the length of the internode—and are devoid of radial cell elements. Only at the nodes do the cells turn inward across the nodal diaphragm.

New axes only occur at the node, never along the internode. For example, branches are initiated along the culm only at the nodes, secondary branches only at the nodes of the main branches, and so on. Branches, culms, and rhizomes are initiated from buds at the nodes on alternating sides of an axis. On a culm, for example, a bud elongates into a branch or branches on one side of the culm, and the bud and branch complement at the node above it emerge from the opposite side of the culm.

Internode

In bamboos and other grasses, the internode is the portion of the culm, branch, or rhizome between the nodes. Internodes are usually hollow, but they can be solid,

as is the case with most *Chusquea*. If a bamboo shoot is cut in half along its length, a series of compressed nodal diaphragms will be apparent. As the shoot elongates and develops into a culm, the short walls of the diaphragm elongate, form the internode, and give bamboo its height.

The length of a culm's internodes typically (though not always) first increases, then decreases toward the tip of the culm, with the longest internodes found around mid-culm. Severely compressed internodes near the base of some culms is a distinguishing characteristic of *Phyllostachys aurea*. The internodes of some *P. aureosulcata* culms are markedly kinked near the base, an attractive ornamental feature.

Internode length varies among species. The somewhat short internodes of *Phyllostachys hetero-*

Left: A new *Phyllostachys bambusoides* culm. The light-colored rings are the sheath scars, marking the lowermost portion of each node. The slightly raised rings, just above, are the supranodal ridges, marking the uppermost portion of each node.

cycla f. *pubescens* contrast with the relatively lengthy internodes of *P. rubromarginata*. Internode length, however, is not a singular determinant of maximum height. *Phyllostachys heterocycla* f. *pubescens* is the tallest of all running bamboos.

Arthrostylidium schomburgkii, an arcane species found in remote Venezuelan mountains, has exceptionally long internodes extending up to 15 ft. (4.5 m). It was prized by indigenous peoples for use as blowpipes to shoot poisoned arrows.

Sheath scar

A sheath scar surrounds the stem at the node, marking the attachment point of the culm leaf sheath. The sheath scar is the lowermost portion of the node. In some species the sheath scar is inconspicuous. In others, it is prominent and sometimes hairy. The sheath scar may symmetrically encircle the culm, or it may dip conspicuously on the side where the branches emerge. It is an ornamental and distinguishing feature of bamboo.

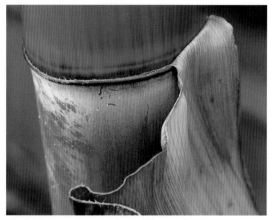

At the lowermost portion of the node, the culm leaf sheath peels away, revealing the sheath scar.

Sulcus

The culm, branch, and rhizome internodes of the genus *Phyllostachys* are distinctive. A pronounced groove throughout the length of the internode is caused by the presence of a developing branch bud at the base of the internode, grooving the culm as it elongates. Other bamboos have only partial grooving, or none at all.

Right: The sulcus, dark green in this example of *Phyllostachys aureosulcata* f. *spectabilis,* is the groove formed when the developing branch bud is held tightly to the extending internode by the culm leaf sheath. The bud has emerged to form a branch, which will reiterate the principal parts of the culm—nodes, internodes, and so forth. The sheath scar is just below the new branch. The supranodal ridge is pronounced in this species and is highlighted here by a brownish red coloration.

The groove is called the sulcus. As with the buds and branches, the sulcus alternates from side to side along the culm's length. The sulcus is distinctively colored in some species and cultivars. For example, it is yellow in *P. aureosulcata* and dark purple-brown in *P. nigra* 'Megurochiku'.

Supranodal ridge

The supranodal ridge delimits the uppermost portion of the node. In some bamboos, the culm is marked by a pronounced ridge at the node, just above the sheath scar. Significant variations can occur among bamboo of the same genus. *Phyllostachys rubromarginata,* for example, has minimal swelling, whereas *P. nidularia* has a very pronounced supranodal ridge.

Rhizomes

For bamboos with a pachymorph rhizome system, rhizomes may appear as little more than the short curved base of the aboveground culm. For bamboos with a leptomorph rhizome system, rhizomes are underground stems that extend the domain of the parent plant and serve as a nutrient storage system for the rapid growth of the culms. Roots emerge from the nodes of bamboo rhizomes.

The aboveground culms in a clump or grove of leptomorph bamboos do not exist in isolation, but are interconnected through an underground system of rhizomes, the primary energy store for the plant. A study based on carbon cycling in *Phyllostachys bambusoides* demonstrated the interrelationships of photosynthetic activity and energy storage and demand (Isagi et al. 1997). When photosynthetic activity creates a surplus, the surplus is stored in the rhizome system. When photosynthetic activity is insufficient for the plant's needs, the plant draws upon the energy stores in the rhizome system. If the rhizome system is unable to meet the needs of the plant, the plant begins killing part of the culms to reduce the plant's needs and reestablish equilibrium.

To the extent that a young grove has developed from a single bamboo plant that has not been divided, the entire grove is a single organism, gathering, storing, and disseminating nutrients for its growth. The rhizomes of leptomorph bamboos are remarkable. The rhizome of a large species from a well-established grove can extend as much as 25 ft. (7.5 m) in a single season of growth. The structure of this underground stem parallels that of the aboveground culm, but the rhizome internodes are much shorter, and the nodes thus more frequent. Arranged horizontally and alternating from side to side, the buds at each node offer the possibility of new culms and new rhizome branches. The rapidly extending rhizomes branch into still more rhizomes, which in turn extend rapidly and branch, quickly establishing an interwoven network. New rhizomes grow close to the surface of the soil, generally on top of older rhizomes, and over and under each other. With each season of growth, the rhizomes form a denser weave. The ground under a well-established grove is an impenetrable mass of roots and interconnected rhizomes several feet thick.

Where erosion and soil stability are a concern, nothing betters bamboo, particularly leptomorph bamboos, for protecting and binding the soil. Bamboos with pachymorph rhizome systems are also excellent in this regard and are often planted for this purpose in tropical environments. It is often written in bamboo literature that Japanese mothers tell their children to run into a bamboo grove in case of an earthquake—"there is no safer place." It is one thing to read such anecdotal tidbits and another to be impressed at how ubiquitous this maternal indoctrination must be. I was in a sushi bar in the United States, talking idly to the sushi chef about bamboo, and he said, "If there is an earthquake, run into a bamboo grove. It's the safest place."

Leptomorph rhizome cell tissue consists of approximately 60 percent parenchyma, or generalized cell tissue, 20 percent sclerenchyma, long-celled structural fibers, and 20 percent conductive tissues in the form of vascular bundles (Ding et al. 1992). Some species, such as *Phyllostachys heteroclada, P. nidularia,* and the native North American *Arundinaria gigantea* ssp. *tecta,* have rhizomes with air canals, suggesting an association with a watery environment during the evolutionary process.

Bamboo rhizomes are segmented, and the leaves are reduced, consisting primarily of a protective sheath, or bract, that surrounds the rhizome, once again paralleling the structure of the aboveground culm. The rhizome's bracts are vital to the growth of a rhizome,

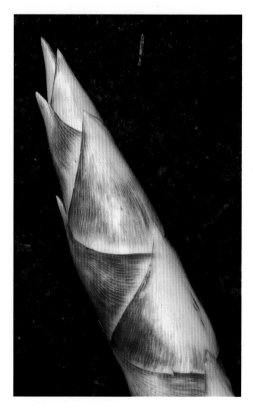

Right: The tip of a *Chusquea* rhizome. The tightly overlapping scalelike leaves, or bracts, protect the rhizome during its elongation and growth. The leaf blades, having no photosynthetic purpose, are highly reduced to a hard, pointed, beaklike structure.

protecting it as it penetrates the soil. The inner surface of the bracts is smooth and polished, allowing the growing rhizome to slide forward as each internode extends. The leaf blade is highly reduced and may be apparent only as the hard tip of the bract. The tip of the rhizome is hard, pointed, and beaklike. Its design protects the critical growing tip from damage and allows ready penetration of the soil. When confronted by an obstruction, the hard, smooth point finds cracks in the obstacle or readily diverts around it. The rhizome tip secretes moisture as it grows, making penetration of the soil easier.

The depth of a new leptomorph rhizome depends on the condition of the soil and the habits of the species. If a layer of moist, loamy soil rests on top of a harder concrete-like base, the rhizome will tend to stay in the loamy soil layer. In poor soils, the internode may vary greatly in length and diameter. Some species, such as *Semiarundinaria okuboi* or some of the larger species of *Pleioblastus*, have highly invasive tendencies, with deep, fast-running rhizomes. Others, such as the large

A rhizome section from a *Phyllostachys* bamboo. A new culm shoot is emerging. The sulcus on the internode, characteristic of *Phyllostachys* culms, is also present on the rhizome internodes. The roots are attached at the rhizome nodes.

timber bamboo species of genus *Phyllostachys,* run close to the soil surface. In general, the new rhizomes of most leptomorph bamboos are within the first foot (30 cm) of soil, and more typically within the first 6 in. (15 cm). In an older grove, the rhizome mass may be much thicker, but the viable rhizomes will remain close to the surface.

Running so close to the surface of the soil, leptomorph rhizomes commonly encounter an obstacle or change in soil depth that causes them to break into the air before penetrating the soil again. Occasionally, and most frequently in a young planting, the tip of a leptomorph rhizome turns up and grows into an above-ground culm. These whipshoots will tend to be more curved, stand less erect, have shorter internodes, and be smaller than culms emerging from buds on a rhizome. Just as a rhizome may break above ground and turn into a culm, a culm may turn downward into the ground and become transformed into a rhizome with the ability to generate new rhizomes, culms, and roots.

How do you know the orientation of an underground rhizome? For *Phyllostachys,* and probably most leptomorph bamboos, the branches emerge from the sides that are roughly parallel to the axis of the rhizome.

Roots

Roots are the only bamboo axes that are not segmented and not protected by a sheathing organ. They grow from rhizome nodes and the nodes of the underground portion of the culm. The roots at the base of the culm are structured differently. They primarily serve to anchor the culm and prevent it from toppling over in the wind, rain, or snow—or the weight of its own leaves. The roots are typical of grasses: fibrous, relatively equal in size,

Right: Usually not as exposed as shown here, the roots at the base of the culm of this new *Phyllostachys decora* shoot are a showy, bright reddish pink. Unlike the roots that grow from the rhizome, which function primarily in the uptake of moisture and nutrients, the roots at the base of the culm function primarily to anchor and stabilize the culm.

without ramified orders. Most roots are concentrated in the upper foot (30 cm) of soil. Bamboo roots can also store starches, though the rhizomes are the chief underground repositories for starches.

Because of their extensive network of rhizomes, leptomorph bamboos are perhaps the world's best plants for erosion control. Pachymorph bamboos lack an underground network of rhizomes, but their root systems extend up to six times the diameter of the clump, making them useful for erosion control as well. In Indonesia, in steep terrain, pachymorph bamboos are planted along the banks of newly bulldozed roads to prevent erosion and slippage.

The roots of some bamboos have become modified in adaptation to environmental conditions. *Thamnocalamus spathiflorus* var. *crassinodus,* for example, has unusually large, succulent roots, which may be an adaptation that permits more effective water storage in dry soils and environments. *Phyllostachys atrovaginata* and *P. heteroclada,* on the other hand, have air canals in their roots as well as their rhizomes, an adaptation to wet or boggy soils that would otherwise not permit growth.

In a few, usually tropical species, root primordia may appear on aboveground nodes of culms and branches. Aboveground root primordia tend to be most evident on the lower nodes, decreasing toward the culm's apex. In *Chimonobambusa quadrangularis,* a moderately hardy running bamboo, the aboveground root primordia dry and harden, giving the appearance of spines or thorns.

Culms

In all but a few species, the culms of bamboo are hollow, except at the node. As in most monocots, the stem does not thicken but emerges from the ground at its final girth. Maximum height is achieved in a single growth period. The culms of most pachymorph bamboos typically require several months or more to attain their full height. Leptomorph bamboo culms race to their full height in five to eight weeks. Most of the growth is accomplished in a three- to four-week period. The most rapid spurt occurs at approximately half the culm's final height. In a mature grove of the larger species of running bamboo, this growth habit can be quite spectacular, as new shoots, a half-foot (15 cm) in diameter, break through the soil and thrust skyward at a rate of a yard or more a day.

The particular species determines the maximum growth parameters, but growing conditions, and the age and size of the grove, determine culm size at a given site. A grove of large leptomorph bamboo requires 10 to 15 years to produce culms of maximum size, pachymorph bamboos typically less. Smaller species generally attain maximum size more quickly. In a developing grove, the largest culms are usually the youngest. Older culms are smaller, reflecting the less mature and more limited capacity of the grove when they were produced.

A new culm rapidly hardens as it emerges from the soil, quickly strengthening to support itself as it thrusts skyward, and to support the branches and leaves that will soon follow. Maximum strength, however, is not achieved until at least the end of the third growing season, or longer for some species. The lifespan of an individual culm varies, but 10 years or less is common. The culms of *Phyllostachys bambusoides,* a leptomorph bamboo prized for the stength and size of its culm wood, can live for at least two decades. Culms of *Chusquea culeou* have been estimated to live up to 33 years. Most bamboos flower at lengthy intervals. When this occurs, the otherwise healthy culms lose strength and become brittle.

Small culms taper from base to tip. Large culms of some bamboo, notably species of *Phyllostachys,* increase in diameter before beginning a long, gradual taper to the tip. Some species taper more rapidly than others. *Phyllostachys rubromarginata,* for example, tapers less rapidly than *P. dulcis.* At a given maximum culm diameter, *P. rubromarginata* will reach a greater height than *P. dulcis.*

Culms are generally green, but the coloration and features are striking and distinctive in many species and forms. The outermost three layers of cells in the developing shoot are normally green but can have other coloration, resulting in bamboos with yellow culms, such as *Phyllostachys bambusoides* 'Allgold', yellow culms with a green sulcus, such as *P. bambusoides* f. *castillonis,* and green culms with a yellow sulcus, such as *P. bambusoides* f. *castillonis-inversa.* Other culm color variations are possible. *Phyllostachys viridis* 'Robert Young' begins a sulfur green with a few darker green stripes along the internode. The stripes remain green, but the culm turns sulfur yellow, then old gold. *Phyllostachys bambusoides* f. *castillonis* does not go through an initial color shift but is already straw yellow with a green sulcus when the culm leaves fall away. Some bamboos with yellow culms, such as *P. aureosulcata* f. *spectabilis* and *Semiarundinaria yashadake* f. *kimmei,* may take on a range of red color tones, helped by exposure to sun and cold, turning a vivid brick red then changing back to yellow again with the changes of seasonal climates. *Phyllostachys nigra* turns a deep purplish black with age. The culms of *P. nigra* 'Bory' become spotted or blotched with dark purple-brown to black areas. The culms of *P. nigra* 'Megurochiku' remain green, except for the sulcus, which turns a chocolate brown.

Shapes vary as well. The culms of *Chimonobambusa quadrangularis* are slightly square, rather than round. Above each node of *Pseudosasa japonica* 'Tsutsumiana',

Phyllostachys viridis 'Robert Young' culms of varying age.

the culm swells and then tapers, in a shape similar to a green onion. The variations in color and shape are numerous and are part of bamboo's beauty and interest.

The exterior surface of a bamboo culm has a hard, protective, waxy finish. In some species, the new culms may be coated with a waxy white powder. The coating is characteristic of the species and can range from a barely visible light powder to a thick white coating. The powder may cover the entire internode or only a portion near the node. The variations in the coating of white powder and the coloration differences of the underlying culm create a range of distinctive looks among the many species. As the culm ages, the waxy bloom gradually disappears. The waxy coatings resist moisture and protect the young culms and branches. Along the culm, only the sheath scars provide any opportunity for the passage of liquids into or out of the culm, and this only to a minimal degree.

The storage of energy reserves in the culm, in the form of starches, is generally associated with pachymorph bamboos that lack the extensive network of a leptomorph rhizome system, but leptomorph bamboos store starches in the culm as well. A study of *Phyllostachys viridiglaucescens,* for example, showed that young, three-month-old culms contained no starch, since all available nutrients were being used, but older culms contained starch, and even culms as old as 12 years continued to have stores of starches and the ability to mobilize them.

Culm cell tissue consists of approximately 50 percent parenchyma, or generalized cell tissue, 40 percent sclerenchyma, long-celled structural fibers, and 10 percent conductive tissues in the form of vascular bundles (Liese 1985). The culm fibers, the sclerenchyma cells, are much longer than similar cells in hardwoods, having a ratio of length to width of up to 250 to 1. The shortest fibers are those nearest the nodes.

Befitting their different functions, the proportions of cell tissue differ significantly from that of the rhizome. Needing to support their own weight and the masses of branches and leaves, as well as to resist the wind and other elements, culms have cell tissue consisting of twice as much fiber as in rhizome cells. Absent the need to provide a conductive architecture for the root system, the quantity of conductive tissue in culms is approximately half that in rhizomes.

Within the culm, the conductive tissues, the vascular bundles, are arrayed distinctively in patterns that can be associated with taxonomic placement at the subtribal and generic levels, and possibly at subgeneric levels in some instances. Vascular bundles, however, are merely one characteristic among an array of characteristics and are not a taxonomically defining feature in and of themselves (Wong 1995b).

The vascular bundles are smaller and more numerous at the periphery of the culm. Toward the interior, they become larger and more widely spaced. These water-conducting tissues are not renewed and must last the life of the culm. As they age, the vascular tissues become partially blocked by deposits, contributing to the loss of vitality and eventual death of an individual culm. During the first several years of a culm's life, the moisture content decreases significantly as the culm matures, and it continues to decrease thereafter, although at a more gradual rate.

Cellulose comprises more than half of bamboo's chemical constituency. Lignin imparts rigidity to cell walls and is the second greatest constituent. Lignification proceeds from top to bottom within the internode. It is initially restricted to the culm walls necessary for mechanical support and to the tissues protecting the delicate vascular system within the culm. Limiting initial lignification to only the essential minimums is likely an adaptive feature that allows bamboo to achieve its extraordinarily rapid culm growth with only minimal resource requirements. In the rapid first month of growth, culm fibers are generally unlignified. Within a year, lignification is essentially complete, though lignin content may increase slightly in older culms.

From a structural standpoint, bamboo is a composite, a material composed of softer, less rigid material and stronger, stiffer material. In bamboo, cellulose is the former, lignin the latter. Structurally, a good composite is superior to its individual components. Although bamboo and wood are chemically similar, bamboo is approximately twice as stiff as wood and possesses far greater shear strength. In certain selected measures of strength, bamboo even exceeds the performance of steel (Janssen 1985). Modern composites, the wonders of science and technology, are emulators of these bamboo grasses.

Branches

Branches emerge at the nodes on alternate sides. Bamboo's branching system is uncommon among monocots and reflects a high degree of specialization. Except in the genera *Chusquea* and *Apoclada,* which have two or more buds present at each node, all bamboo branches at a given node emerge from a single bud. *Chusquea* is quite unusual; in some species, the number of branch buds can number as many as 80 or more (Clark 1989). For bamboos other than *Chusquea* and *Apoclada,* the appearance of multiple branches emerging from a node arises because bamboos often bear lateral buds so close to the primary bud that it appears many branches are emerging independently from the culm. In these instances, the internode of the primary branch is so compressed it is barely distinguishable from its base.

In bamboos, the bud or branch grouping is called a complement. The number of branches in the complement and the nature of their array is an identifying characteristic. The most typical branching pattern of a species is found in the middle of the culm. Lower branches are not always fully developed. Upper branches do not always maintain the branching pattern that distinguishes the species.

Some genera have only a single branch per node. The single branches are usually somewhat smaller than the culm and emerge at a narrow angle to the culm. The lower branch nodes are budless. Branching buds occur only at the higher nodes. Single-branching bamboos are typically shrubby, often with large leaves. *Sasa* and *Pseudosasa* are examples of genera that usually have a single branch at each node, though most *Pseudosasa* bamboos are less shrublike, with a more erect, treelike stance.

A complement of two branches per node is characteristic of *Phyllostachys*. Although the primary and lateral buds elongate simultaneously, the primary branch remains dominant. Occasionally, a much smaller middle branch will also appear. The angle between the branches and culms and between the branching pair ranges from 60° to 80°. The erect culms and branching pattern help give *Phyllostachys* species their imposing treelike stature.

New branches emerging from multiple buds on a *Chusquea* culm.

Branches emerging from a new *Phyllostachys glauca* culm. Both branches arise from a single bud.

In bamboos with three main branches per node, two lateral buds emerge from the first and second nodes of the principal branch. As with culm branches, the secondary branches emerge at the nodes on alternating sides. In this pattern, the spacing of the first and second nodes is so close that the branches appear to emerge from a common base. The three branches elongate nearly simultaneously, but the central, principal branch remains dominant. Species of *Sinobambusa* usually have this type of branch complement.

A branch complement of multiple branches per node has many variations. Some genera, such as *Bambusa,* have a dominant branch surrounded by several or many smaller branches. In the genus *Shibataea,* the branches are relatively equal in size. In some species of *Arundinaria,* the lower nodes of a narrow-angled, three-branch array are budless, followed by strong branching at higher nodes. Other *Arundinaria* species have numerous branches emerging from an apparent common base.

In some species, the number of branches is determined by the maturity of the bamboo or the position on the culm. Lower culm nodes may have none or a solitary branch, middle culm nodes three to five, and the upper nodes may have numerous branches.

Thorns are modified branches. Most bamboos have no thorns, but those that do can be quite formidable. Several *Bambusa* species have thorns, as do nearly all species of *Guadua,* the only New World genus with thorny species.

Leaves

A bamboo leaf consists of the sheath, blade, and ligule, and it may include auricles and fimbriae as additional appendages. Leaves are associated with every segmented axis of the bamboo plant—rhizomes, culms, and branches. The leaf and its parts are modified according to the function required. The prominence of the sheath and the blade varies. On the leaves or bracts that protectively encase the underground rhizome, the sheath dominates, and the blade is all but absent, sometimes appearing as no more than a hard pointed area at the tip of the sheath. With no photosynthetic function, the blade plays little role. For the culm leaves, the sheath clearly predominates, reflecting its primary role in protecting the new culm. The blade plays only an incidental role. On the foliage leaves, however, the blade predominates, reflecting its primary function as the plant's photosynthetic engine.

The terminology regarding bamboo leaves and sheaths has varied over time. Sometimes sheaths are described separately, as sheathing organs, rather than as part of a leaf (McClure 1966), but since the sheath itself may be green and photo-synthetic, it can be properly included as part of the leaf. Given this standing, the term "culm leaf" has gained legitimacy (Judziewicz et al. 1999).

All bamboos have a similar leaf anatomy and characteristics in leaf structure that set them apart from the rest of the grass family. Though these distinguishing characteristics are not readily visible, the foliage leaves with their pseudopetioles overtly differ from most of the rest of the grass family. The pseudopetiole is the stalk at the base of a leaf blade that connects the blade to its sheath. It is sometimes called simply a petiole, although this omits the distinction between the structural element of the monocotyledon bamboo and the true petiole of the dicotyledons. Apart from bamboos, most grasses do not have pseudopetioles.

The sheath connects the blade and pseudopetiole to the branch. The foliage leaf sheath is wrapped so tightly around the branch that it is hardly distinguishable from it on casual viewing. This gives the impression that the pseudopetiole is at-tached directly to the branch, but it is not. Foliage leaf sheaths are much longer

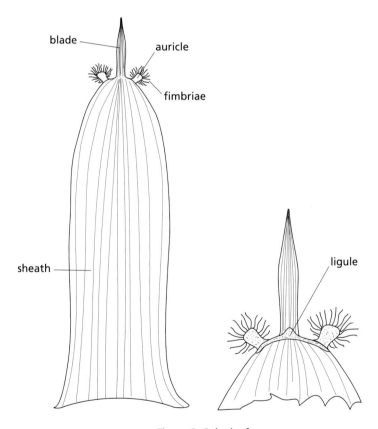

Figure 2. Culm leaf.

than their associated branch internodes and overlap each other. New leaves, tightly rolled along their length, emerge from the preceding leaf sheath, unrolling as they encounter the light of day.

The foliage leaves are not deciduous in most herbaceous bamboos, but they are deciduous in all woody bamboos. Unless in reaction to damaging cold, leaf fall does not occur all at once, but partially and gradually, so that bamboo is always evergreen. In some genera, such as *Phyllostachys,* individual leaves are replaced by branchlets and more leaves, making older culms denser with foliage. The duration and rate of replacement varies. In one study of *Chusquea,* foliage leaves remained for two or more years, but none remained longer than six years.

The culm and branch leaves of some bamboos, including *Phyllostachys,* are immediately deciduous, abscising as soon as the internodes have completed their extension. As each succeeding internode of the rapidly growing culm completes its extension, its leaf turns tan, falls back, and drops away from its last attachment point at the culm. Even on a fairly small bamboo, the culm leaves are quite large, creating a significant spring and early summer leaf fall.

In many bamboos, however, including some in the genus *Arundinaria,* the culm leaves persist, contributing to a tattered look as the culm leaf and its promi-

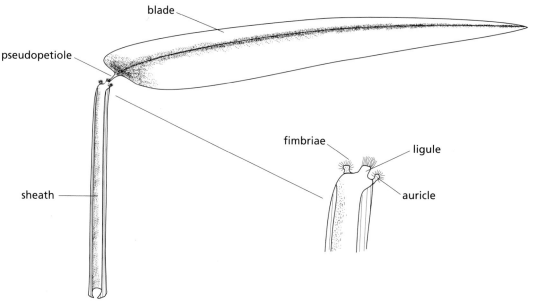

Figure 3. Foliage leaf.

nent sheath weather. *Sasa* culm leaves persist, but the size of the foliage leaf blades so overwhelm the size of the culm that the culm leaves are not particularly conspicuous. *Semiarundinaria fastuosa* rapidly begins to slough off its culm leaves, but they remain connected for a brief time at the center of the sheath's base before finally abscising. Other bamboos, such as some species of *Chusquea*, burst their branches through a persistent culm leaf and its tightly attached sheath.

For most woody bamboos, culm leaves offer a ready basis for identifying species. *Phyllostachys*, among other genera, has highly distinctive culm leaf colors and patterns. Colors, including red, purple, yellow, brown, green, and tan, are patterned in spots, stripes, and veins of various widths, combinations, and graduations, often offering a dramatic display. The overt distinguishing characteristics of color and pattern are helpful for field identification. Other, less overt leaf characteristics also provide excellent keys for identifying bamboos. Such features include persistence of the culm leaf; absence or density of surface hairs; posture of the blade; shape and size of the auricles; presence and size of the fimbriae; shape and size of the ligule; color, pattern, and surface texture of the sheath; and so on. Culm leaves vary from the base to the tip. The culm leaves from mid-culm most prominently display the distinguishing characteristics and are the most representative of the species.

The distinctive culm leaf of *Phyllostachys decora*.

Removal of the culm leaf stops growth of the corresponding internode. A dwarfing technique for bamboo in the garden, and, more typically, for bonsai, calls for early removal of the culm leaf, thus compressing the internodes, increasing branch density, and limiting height.

Blade

On culm leaves, size of the blade relative to the sheath is not uniform on a given plant, ranging from nearly absent at the base of the culm to much more prominent toward the top of the culm. Near the culm tip, the blades develop into true foliage leaves that are as large as, or sometimes larger than, the blades of the foliage leaves on the rest of the plant. Only the foliage leaf blade consistently dominates its associated sheath and looks like a leaf in a conventional sense. Unlike culm leaf blades (except those near the tip of the culm), foliage leaf blades are attached to their sheath by a pseudopetiole, giving the customary appearance of leaves on stems.

The foliage leaf blades are the "leaves" we see when looking at a bamboo plant. They are the most complex and highly differentiated of the leaf blades on bamboo. The upper leaf surface is typically smooth and glossy, glistening when moistened. The lower surface has a dull, matte finish, caused by the numerous projections from the lips of the stomata. The underside is also sometimes covered with minute hairs. This surface prevents moisture from adhering to the leaf and ensures that the air passageways remain unblocked. A leaf blade can be submerged in water for an indefinite time. The upper surface will typically be wet, but the lower surface will essentially be dry, covered by innumerable air bubbles. When applying insect or other foliar sprays to bamboo leaves, it is good to keep in mind that they will not normally adhere to the lower leaf surfaces. Insects that reside on the underside of the leaf may be subject to contact with the spray, but the leaf surface will not, unless measures are taken to inhibit formation of the protective air pockets—measures which defeat the leaves' natural protective system.

All bamboos have parallel veins in the leaf blades. Transverse veins are present as well, and in some species, the transverse veins are prominent and visible, creating a rectangular vein pattern called tessellation. Tessellations are fewer, weaker, and less visible in tropical species, but generally very prominent and greater in number in hardy species. Although some species without tessellated leaf blades are hardy, there is nevertheless a general correlation between tessellation and cold hardiness. Why this is so is subject to speculation. Bamboos that have a greater frequency of tessellation, and tessellation that is more prominent, are inherently more capable of sap circulation within the leaf blade, which is likely a factor in cold hardiness. Within given species, tessellation is greater on leaf blades from older culms. Bamboos with less prominent tessellation also tend to have transverse veins that are thin and S-shaped, whereas bamboos with more manifest tessellation tend to have transverse veins that are prominent, protruding, and much straighter.

Leaf blade size and culm height or width are not directly correlated or, if anything, are sometimes inversely correlated. Mature culms of the largest hardy bamboo, *Phyllostachys heterocycla* f. *pubescens,* are up to 90 ft. (27 m) tall, with a diameter of 7 in. (18 cm), yet they have among the smallest leaf blades of any woody bamboo. Conversely, *Indocalamus tessellatus* is typically no more than 4 ft. (1.2 m) tall with a culm diameter of barely ½ in. (1.25 cm), yet it has leaf blades that are 24 in. (60 cm) long by 4 in. (10 cm) wide, among the largest of any commonly cultivated bamboo. The largest bamboo leaves belong to the New World genus *Neurolepis,* up to 12 ft. (4 m) long in some species, the largest known leaves in the entire grass family. Arborescent tropical bamboos generally have much larger leaf blades than arborescent hardy bamboos, but the general rule does not always hold. The foliage plumes of the delicate-leaved, tropical *Thyrsostachys siamensis* is a case in point.

Young plants often have larger leaf blades than mature plants. A young plant's spindly culms are already out of proportion with the leaf blades, and the larger leaf blades only accentuate an ungainly stature. In one instance, some leaves of a young *Phyllostachys bambusoides* of mine measured 9 in. (23 cm) by 1 ¾ in. (4.4 cm), looking more like a large-leaved *Sasa* than a *Phyllostachys.*

The delicate, finely shaped leaf blades of the small-leaved species define much of the look of bamboo in Asian art and poetry—delicate beauty, seen backlit and jewel-like, or as shadows painted on a white wall, or their sound, rustling, shimmering in the smallest breeze. The larger-leaved varieties create a bold, lush, tropical effect. Together in the landscape, the small- and large-leaved species offer a splendid display of contrast and texture.

It is said that the weight of the leaves in a grove is roughly equal to the weight of the year's new culms. The health and vigor of a grove is dependent on a large and healthy leaf canopy. When establishing a grove, preserving maximum sun-exposed leaf area (except for bamboos that require shade) encourages the most rapid growth. Employing this strategy may mean keeping aesthetically deficient culms for the first years of the grove. Such a strategy, however, does not mean that all culms should be preserved indefinitely. A crowded grove keeps much of its foliage in shade and diminishes vigor. Routine thinning ensures healthy culms and foliage canopies with good exposure to sunlight.

Some species and forms have variegated leaf blades. Variegation is more unusual in larger species, but common among the dwarf and shrub species. In many dwarfs, variegation intensity fades in sunlight and as the season progresses. *Sasa veitchii* exhibits a sort of pseudo-variegation. Toward the end of their first season, the dark green leaf blades wither at the margins, giving the appearance of beige variegation rimming a dark green leaf.

Under certain stress conditions, a plant may develop variegated leaf blades that subsequently return to solid green. When plants are grown from seed, the spontaneous appearance of variegation can be a source of excitement and confusion. You may think you have discovered a new and attractive cultivar, only to find that the variegation does not repeat in succeeding years or in plants propagated from the original. Variegation should be observed over several seasons, and in plants vegetatively propagated from the original, before firmly concluding that it is a stable, variegated cultivar.

The foliage leaves of some tropical herbaceous bamboos are arrayed such that they have a fernlike appearance. A few exhibit nocturnal "sleep" movements, in which the leaf blades change shape with the coming of night. The leaf blades of *Raddia* fold upward along the culm, while those of *Lithachne* fold downward. This curious phenomenon begins at sunset and progresses over a four-hour period, reversing itself at dawn.

The variegated leaf blades of *Sasaella masamuneana* 'Albostriata'.

Another style of variegation in *Pleioblastus akebono*.

Sheath

The sheaths tightly surround and protect the internodes as they lengthen. In the case of the rhizome, this occurs unseen, underground. Although observable in the growth of the branches, the role of the sheath is most visible and dramatic in the growth of the culm. The inner surface of the sheath has a hard glossy finish, allowing the internode to elongate rapidly, while still retaining a tight, protective grip. The white powder visible on new culms of some bamboo species is a waxy substance that helps the internodes extend rapidly. The relatively unlignified, emerging new culm is structurally weak and highly vulnerable to breakage and other damage. The culm leaf sheaths provide structural rigidity and a shield against impact, disease, and pest attack. The sheaths of some species are equipped with additional deterrents to protect the emerging culm. *Gigantochloa apus* and *Guadua angustifolia,* for example, are covered with hairs that irritate the skin and the digestive system.

Bamboo sheaths are sometimes green and may be photosynthetic, though this is hardly their primary role. The ridges that run lengthwise on the outer surface of the sheath are caused by the vascular strands that eventually extend into the leaf blade, providing the vascular connection with the rest of the plant.

Ligule

The ligule, or "little tongue," extends upward from the tip of the sheath proper. Depending on the species, the ligule can be prominent or inconspicuous in size, and it may bear cilia or bristly hairs. The ligule helps keep moisture away from the newly forming culms and branches and prevents moisture from run-

Right: Two culm leaves from a new *Phyllostachys vivax* shoot. The sheath comprises nearly the entire leaf. The blade at the tip is barely noticeable. The top culm leaf shows the exterior of the sheath. The culm leaf underneath shows the hard glossy finish of the sheath's interior surface.

ning down the culm or branch and collecting at the node. The woody bamboos, unlike herbaceous bamboos, also have an outer ligule, but it is always much smaller than the inner ligule and is almost always scarcely visible.

Auricle

The auricles, or "ears," are located at the upper part of the sheath, on both sides of the blade. Depending on the species, they may be prominent or entirely lacking, and present on both sides of the sheath or only one side. Auricles may be deciduous with age and are best observed on young leaves. Regardless of species, auricles are entirely absent from rhizome leaves or bracts.

Fimbriae

Fimbriae, also called oral setae, are the bristly, fringelike hairs that extend from the margins of the auricles. They may be either prominent or lacking, depending on the species. Although usually associated with the auricles, they may be present even when the auricles are absent, extending from the uppermost margins of the sheath.

Flowers and Flowering

Grass flowers are seldom showy. As with most perennial grasses, bamboo seed set is often poor or infrequent, making vegetative reproduction an important means of propagation. Largely because traditional taxonomy was centered on the flowering parts of plants, and the inflorescences of bamboos are evolutionarily quite primitive, bamboos were thought to be the most ancient grasses. With modern molecular techniques, however, it is now known that bamboos are not the most ancient of grasses, even though their inflorescences retain ancient ancestral features (Clark 1997a).

Like most grasses, bamboos are generally wind

Left: A new *Phyllostachys nigra* shoot showing the pronounced auricles and fimbriae. The crinkly leaf blades of the culm leaves cluster at the tip of the shoot.

pollinated, and the flowers are structured accordingly. Petals are absent or highly reduced to scales called lodicules. Bamboo flowers lack nectaries for producing insect-attracting sugary secretions, but pollen is produced abundantly, and stigmas are feathery to readily catch the pollen in the wind. Some tropical herbaceous bamboos that inhabit the rainforest floor may be exceptions to the wind-pollination rule. On the rainforest floor, breezes are all but absent, but these herbaceous bamboos are routinely visited by insects and are likely pollinated by them.

Bamboo flowering is the subject of much mystery, controversy, and confusion. Although a few woody bamboo species flower continuously or annually, most flower rarely. Many species remain in a vegetative growth period for decades without flowering. Some species have never been known to flower, except for a few isolated plants. In well more than a century of observation, *Bambusa vulgaris* has never had a general flowering period. The few isolated *B. vulgaris* plants that have flowered failed to produce viable seed, yet the species is vigorous and apparently undiminished by the lack of genetic diversity.

Flowering is said to occur in great cycles, unique to each species, frequently spanning many decades, or more than a century in some instances. The cycles are said to occur simultaneously throughout the world, independent of local climate and growing conditions. Species of *Sasa,* for example, are purported to flower in roughly 60-year cycles, although some sources indicate a cycle of 100 years or more. Kawamura's 1927 study, using local records and folklore, traced the flowering of Japanese timber bamboo, *Phyllostachys bambusoides,* back to 800 A.D. The study concluded that *P. bambusoides* has a flowering cycle of 120 years, predicting that the next gregarious flowering of the species would occur in 1960, 120 years after the last great flowering in 1840. The prediction proved largely true, when a wave of flowering spread from northern to southern Japan from 1959 into the 1970s, and the species flowered as well in America during roughly that same period.

In spite of such dramatic examples, evidence of flowering cycles is largely anecdotal in nature, absent empirical rigor, and subject to wide variation. It is true that many bamboos of the same species have been observed to flower gregariously throughout the world within a several-year period, after decades of no flowering. Yet, not all plants of a species flower at once. It is more likely that vegetatively propagated cohorts with the same genetic source, and of the same age, are more likely to experience simultaneous flowering. Assuming that this is the case, then over time, particularly with human intervention, the flowering interval may spread over an increasingly extended time span, to the point that flowering periods may begin overlapping. For example, a bamboo plant or grove may flower and produce seed over a period of several years. The earliest plants from the flowering will be several years older (and potentially flower sooner) than the plants from the very end of the flowering cycle, and even more so if the seed at the end of the flowering cycle is "saved" and germination is delayed. If the process is repeated at the next (now extended) flowering cycle, the span of flowering and seeding increases yet again. Combine this with the free-flowing exchange of seeds and plants among growers throughout the world, the diminished instances of isolated and undisturbed natural stands of bamboo, and the likely existence of multiple cohorts, the predictability of flowering cycles diminishes even further. Indeed, every year, *Phyllostachys heterocycla* f. *pubescens* is in flower somewhere in China. Nevertheless, this does not compromise the assertion that plants of the same age from the same cohort will flower at extended intervals and at the same time. Traditionally, we have attempted to track species in order to formulate some sort of understanding of flowering cycles. More appropriately, perhaps, we should be tracking cohorts, or seedlings of the same age from the same plant, or even more accurately (but even more impractical), we might track vegetatively propagated plants from the same seedling, ruling out genetic variation among seedlings. Given the extended length of bamboo flowering cycles, sometimes exceeding a century, the general practicality and accuracy of such measures would be rather dubious.

The mechanism or mechanisms that trigger flowering remain largely unknown. Various hypotheses attempting to explain the synchronized and extended flowering cycles include predator satiation, parental competition, drought, sunspots, earthquakes, and other environmental factors. In his paper, "Why Bamboos Wait So Long to Flower," Daniel H. Janzen (1976) exhaustively studies reports of bamboo flowering dating back more than a millennium, and he offers the hypothesis of predator satiation. He theorizes that seed is produced in such abundance that it exceeds the ability of seed predators to consume or destroy all the seed, thus leaving enough viable seed to become the succeeding generation. Janzen argues that the long vegetative period before flowering is necessary for the plant to accumulate sufficient reserves for the massive flowering and seed production. He and others estimate that the recovery and rebuilding reserves for the next cycle would take some 15 years. If this is the case, the typically more extended flowering cycles are not explained without additional supporting hypotheses such as the suggestion that doublings of the internal clock might arise from mutation or changes in the chromosome count. Neither the predator satiation hypothesis nor others have gained broad acceptance. Clearly, when it comes to explaining bamboo flowering, we are rich in arcane hypotheses and impoverished in knowledge.

Apart from the larger picture of flowering cycles, chemical triggers and associations with flowering are also the subject of study. When flowering is induced *in vitro,* cytokinins are present. Cytokinins are growth-regulating substances associated with delayed senescence, promotion of cell division, breaking dormancy, and flowering. Their role and the reasons for their association with flowering in bamboo is yet to be determined. One study found that flowering was associated with oxidation stress and the presence of hydrogen peroxide, superoxide, and other active oxygen species (AOS). AOS can damage biological molecules such as DNA, proteins, and membranes and cause cell death. The weakened, brittle culms of flowering bamboo may be related to AOS. This study suggests that research on bamboo flowering has been hindered by emphasizing the genetic component rather than physiology, postulating that the flowering of *Fargesia murielae* in Europe in 1994, 1995, and 1996 was linked to hot summers and high ozone concentrations, generating oxidative stress and flowering in bamboos (Gielis et al. 1997). However, *F. murielae* flowered in other parts of the world during that same time period, under widely varying environmental conditions, suggesting that oxidative stress may exacerbate a preexisting disposition toward flowering, but is not itself the causal element. As more becomes known about the physiological associations with flowering, the actual causal factors may reveal themselves more clearly.

Various environmental factors can influence flowering. In India, for example, *Dendrocalamus strictus* flowers erratically in drier regions, but more periodically in wetter regions. Apart from "normal" flowering cycles, stress can bring on flowering. When a grove has been damaged by fire, the rhizomes of pachymorph bamboos have been known to initiate flowering. Drought and winter damage can also bring on flowering, although success in attempting to induce flowering by introducing these factors is far from certain. Winter damage to bamboos of the genus *Phyllostachys,* for example, does not typically elicit a flowering reaction.

Oxidative stress exacerbated by high light intensity and drought may contribute to the onset and rapidity of flowering. Conversely, the absence of stress may delay or fully circumvent flowering. Providing ample water and nitrogen fertilizer may prevent, delay, or minimize flowering, though none of this is certain. If flowering has begun but is not desired, immediately remove the culms that have begun to flower, generously apply nitrogen fertilizer, and water heavily. Bamboo groves in the rich soils of China's Zhejiang Province have reportedly maintained vigorous growth for more than two centuries by controlling flowering behavior (Wang and Shen 1987).

Befitting the mysterious nature of bamboo flowering, it is little surprise that seemingly contradictory conditions are associated with flowering. Stress is generally thought to contribute to the onset or rapidity of inflorescence, but disturbance or stress may also disrupt a bamboo's ability to accumulate sufficient energy reserves to flower. When *Bashania faberi* gregariously flowered in Wolong, China, in 1984, some patches did not flower. Those patches were not random, but were concentrated at elevations above roughly 10,000 ft. (3000 m)—or below roughly 10,000 ft. (3000 m) in clearcuts, or on steep north-facing slopes. This suggests that bamboo plants that have been stressed in a way that prevents them from accumulating adequate energy reserves may have retarded flowering.

Except for those species that flower yearly or are in continuous flower, most bamboos with pachymorph rhizome systems are monocarpic and die after flowering. Some plants, such as beeches, flower and fruit heavily at intervals, and other plants, such as many grasses, die after flowering, but a prolonged vegetative period lasting years or decades, followed by flowering and death, is a distinctive and peculiar characteristic of bamboo. For monocarpic bamboos, the viability of the seed and success of the new seedlings are critical for ongoing survival. Since the mother plant will die, seed offers the only option for continuation.

Most bamboos with leptomorph rhizome systems are typically severely weakened from flowering but eventually recover, though a decade may pass before a large, mature grove is fully restored to its former stature. Mortality is more likely when growing conditions are less than optimal and when there is a heavy seed set from the flowers. Gregarious flowering and seed set consumes all the energy reserves stored in the parenchyma cells of the culm and rhizome. The culms die and become brittle, bending or breaking easily.

Sometimes it seems that there are more exceptions to the flowering rule than followers of the rule—whatever the rule may be. In contrast the genus's normal flowering pattern, at least one clone of *Phyllostachys elegans* has flowered sporadically, every year, for more than a decade, while continuing to grow with moderate vigor. Bamboo nurseryman Ned Jaquith reports acquiring divisions of flowering *P. vivax* and *P. bambusoides* to conduct hybridizing experiments, only to have both cease flowering and regain normal vegetative vigor. Jaquith also reports that a grove of *P. vivax* began to flower after he provided it with ample water and fertilizer. The grove continued to flower gregariously for about a decade before even-

This clump of *Drepanostachyum sengteeanum,* a species with a pachymorph rhizome system, has completed its monocarpic flowering and is now all but dead.

tually dying. During that time, there were two periods of new culm growth with no flowers, but flowering returned the following season.

In many species, reduced plant vigor, early shooting, deformed growth, and weak culms and branches mark an impending period of gregarious flowering. Occasionally, a single culm or branch may flower in response to stress. Such flowering does not necessarily indicate a period of gregarious flowering. The bamboo may return to its vegetative growth cycle without any further flowering.

From a commercial and aesthetic standpoint, gregarious flowering can be devastating. In general, neither a commercial grower nor a gardener would want to rely on a single species or, at minimum, on the same vegetative clone of the same species for risk of losing an entire grove to flowering. In China, *Phyllostachys heterocycla* f. *pubescens* overwhelmingly dominates the vast commercially vital bamboo forests, but the plants are by no means all of the same vegetative clone. Every year, some *P. heterocycla* f. *pubescens* is flowering somewhere in China, but given the infrequency of flowering, and the great clonal diversity, the flowering bamboos are only a tiny fraction of the total bamboo forest. A grower intending to focus on a single species should ensure that the groves are made up of diverse clones. Obtaining plants started from seed, and from flowerings that occur years apart, is one way to ensure diversity. In the United States and Europe, many plants originate from very few clones, so diversity is inherently less likely.

In addition to the impact on commercial production and the health of the grove itself, the generalized flowering of a grove made up of a single species can have significant ramifications on the health and well being of human communities. For cultures that rely on a bamboo grove for shelter, tools, and food, the death of the grove from flowering can be devastating.

The importance of clonal diversity was graphically demonstrated in Thailand in the 1990s. In the early 1900s, *Dendrocalamus asper* was brought from China and extensively vegetatively propagated. By the early 1990s, some 28 factories annually produced 68,000 tons of bamboo shoots. In 1994 to 1995, *D. asper* flowered gregariously in Thailand, devastating the industry. Some 94,000 acres (38,000 hectares) of *D. asper* were eliminated from production, and more than 35,000 farmers lost their livelihood (Muller 1996b). In all, some 70 percent of Thai *D. asper* flowered.

Diversity of species or clones is critical to the avoidance of a precipitous devastation such as befell Thailand. At least five other known clones of *Dendrocalamus asper* did not flower during this same period. A mixture of clones would have avoided disaster. Diversity would mean only a temporary reduction in productivity as a portion of the plants flowered, rather than the devastation of an industry.

Dendrocalamus asper is said to have a flowering cycle of more than a hundred years, and plants generated from seed of the recent flowering should not flower again for more than 100 years. From one point of view, these plants would be ideal for establishing a plantation, but a plantation or forest consisting of mixed clones on differing flowering cycles may be the better prospect for ongoing stability. Adding another twist to this particular example, there is some indication that the Indonesian clones of *D. asper* may not undergo a gregarious flowering cycle. If true, a selection of these clones might be the best choice of all.

Flowering is both a threat and an opportunity. The threat is the death and total loss of the plant, or grove, or forest. The threat may also be the loss of a unique cultivar that may not be readily reproduced from seed. When *Phyllostachys bambusoides* f. *castillonis* gregariously flowered, the form virtually disappeared from America and Europe. Occasionally, an opportunity arises when a sport from a stressed flowering bamboo produces a new cultivar. A highly variegated *P. bambusoides* was discovered as a sport growing from a flowered-out *P. bambusoides* f. *castillonis* that was in demise. The original *P. bambusoides* 'Kawadana' was a sport from a flowering *P. bambusoides*. The *P. bambusoides* 'Kawadana' currently in circulation in the United States originated in England, as a sport from a recovering *P. bambusoides* f. *castillonis* that had flowered. Stressed and recovering bamboos may occasionally produce sports that become new and interesting cultivars or replicate existing cultivars.

So what should one do when bamboo flowers? Try to save the existing plant, particularly if it is a bamboo that is capable of recovering after a gregarious flowering—typically leptomorph bamboos. If the bamboo is a cultivar, variety, or form that may not readily reproduce from seed, saving the flowering plant is all the more important. Also, be on the alert for sports that may arise from the stressed condition. Secondly, harvest the seed and, if possible, grow the seed in a controlled environment rather than in the ground under the flowering plant, in order to ensure maximum survival.

Various practices can be employed to save bamboo once it has begun to flower, but there are no guaranteed methods. A common practice calls for cutting the flowering culms to the ground and fertilizing heavily. A. H. Lawson, former head gardener of the gardens at Pitt White in southern England, recommends against this practice, and instead suggests lessening the strain on the plant by removing the flower spikes as soon as they appear, much as one would remove the plumes from a grass stem. According to Lawson, this method allows the foliage leaves to continue to produce food stores for the plant, prolonging its life. Others argue that

This clump of *Otatea acuminata* ssp. *aztecorum* at Quail Botanical Gardens has flowered and set seed. Although some of the seed has been harvested to grow in a controlled environment, the rest has been left alone as in the wild. Some of the seeds have fallen to the ground, germinated, and generated new seedlings, as seen on the lower left.

this method alone has little effect, and advocate cutting off any culms that are flowering, then dividing the plant into smaller plants by cutting the rhizomes with an ax or specialized rhizome cutting tool, followed by fertilizing and watering. Any new culms that start to flower are removed as well. Results vary. Even though all the culms may be removed, and all the new culms as well if they flower, enough foliage may have been on the plant long enough to augment the energy reserves of the rhizomes, permitting yet another new set of culms. These may be exceptionally spindly and weak, but eventually, if enough culms remain that do not flower, the bamboo can be saved. If just one plant can be saved, it can be vegetatively propagated, and the existing generation can be restored.

When a bamboo gregariously flowers, it is in a highly stressed and weakened condition. As a general rule of thumb, reduce stress to the plant as much as possible. Provide ample water and nutrients (but do not compound the stress by waterlogging the soil or overfertilizing) and shelter the plant from dehydration and climate extremes.

Seeds

Typical of most grasses, bamboos generally produce seed grains (caryopses), but there are variations. In *Schizostachyum,* the caryopsis has a hard, thick pericarp that is easily separated from the seed. Some tropical bamboos, such as species of *Melocanna,* produce a large fleshy fruit. *Dinochloa* is a berrylike fruit, with a thick fleshy pericarp enclosing a large embryo. In general, fruits are not regarded as a key element in taxonomy, but it is an important identifying factor for *Dinochloa.*

The size of the seed also varies widely. *Bambusa bambos* yields approximately 41,000 seeds per pound (90,000 seeds per kilogram), *B. tulda* approximately 12,000 seeds per pound (26,000 seeds per kilogram), and toward the extreme ends of the spectrum, *Dendrocalamus longispathus* about 68,000 seeds per pound (150,000 seeds per kilogram) versus *Melocanna bambusoides* at a mere 32 seeds per pound (70 seeds per kilogram) (Rao and Zamora 1996).

Although the generalized flowering of a grove can create great difficulties for cultures that rely on the grove for shelter, food, and other resources, the bamboo seed can also be a major windfall, such as for the grain produced by those species with abundant and large seed. Historical accounts from India tell of bamboo seed providing relief from famine during the 19th century. In Orissa, in 1812, a general flowering of bamboo produced an abundance of seeds that were cooked and eaten like rice. In 1864, an estimated 50,000 people made their way to the Soopa jungles to collect seed. After about two weeks of collecting, they left with enough to last them through the monsoon season, as well as extra to sell. In another part of India, records show that, in 1866, abundant bamboo seed sold on the market for about 20 percent less than the price of rice.

Similar accounts from China and Japan tell of hunger relief and abundant seed harvests. In 1843, bamboos surrounding the town of Takayama for a distance of many miles flowered and produced an abundant crop of large seed. If the historical accounts can be believed, more than a million bushels of bamboo seed were harvested for food and consumed in various ways, including ground into flour for dumplings, noodles, and gruel. A kind of sake produced from the seed was said to taste a bit sharp, but otherwise similar to sake made from rice. The nutritional qualities of bamboo seed are somewhat superior to rice and wheat (Janzen 1976). In Japan, the bamboo seed has been called natural rice, bamboo rice, and bamboo corn.

Bamboo can produce extraordinary quantities of seed. The fallen seed beneath the mother plant can be as much as 5 to 6 in. (13 to 15 cm) deep. In one study, a 40 square yard (33 sq. m) clump of *Dendrocalamus strictus* produced 320 lb. (145 kg) of seed. Although most bamboo seed is relatively small, *Melocanna bac-*

Bamboo seeds. Clockwise from the upper left, *Bambusa tulda, Fargesia murielae, Phyllostachys heterocycla* f. *pubescens,* and *Dendrocalamus strictus.*

cifera, a bamboo native to India, Pakistan, and Bangladesh, produces a fruit the size of a pear. In 1867, a surveyor reported that, over a 6000 square mile (16,000 sq. km) area, *M. baccifera* plants dropped their fruit so thickly that his surveying instruments were damaged, forcing him to stop work.

In spite of these remarkable occurrences, relatively few bamboo species produce abundant edible seed. Some species produce very few seeds, and they may be too small to bother harvesting except in desperate situations. In the same historical recounting of Takayama's large seed harvest, the seed of hachiku (*Phyllostachys nigra* var. *henonis*), madake (*P. bambusoides*), and medake (*Pleioblastus simonii*) are described as too small and not sufficiently abundant to harvest for food.

Bamboo seed is subject to damage and decimation from insects, birds, and rodents. Just as bamboo seed can be a windfall source of food for humans, so too it is for rats and other rodents. In Brazil, *Merostachys multiramea* flowers and sets massive quantities of seed three to four times a century. The seeds are sometimes baked into breads or used as feed for poultry, but the great abundance of seed also engenders a dramatic increase in the local rodent population and a corresponding increase in poisonous snakes that feed on the rodents—neither of which are particularly beneficial to human inhabitants.

Seeds of tropical pachymorph bamboos such as *Bambusa* and *Dendrocalamus* typically ripen in two to four weeks. Temperate leptomorph bamboos such as *Phyllostachys* require 7 to 10 weeks for the seed to ripen. The ripe seeds are then easily released and drop to the ground. Most bamboo seed is not widely dispersed and is usually not a factor in the expansion of bamboo's range. Seedlings generally arise in very close proximately to the mother clump, though there are occasional exceptions. The large, fleshy fruits of *Melocanna baccifera* can roll downhill and establish new colonies at more distant locations.

Rhizome Morphology and Clump Habit

For many, the following discussions of rhizome systems and clump habit will be more than you may want—and less. After well more than a century, and many attempts at systematically describing rhizome systems and clump habits, the terminology (and the underlying understanding) is still not entirely satisfactory. The subject remains somewhat of a muddle for scientist, grower, and hobbyist alike.

Traditionally, bamboos have been loosely divided into two broad types according to the visible spatial relationships of their culms: caespitose (tightly grouped or clumped) and diffuse (spread about or scattered). More popularly, these two types are termed clumping and running, or clumpers and runners. The two types are associated (rather imprecisely, as we shall see) with the rhizome form as well as with the branching habit of the rhizomes.

The two growth habits illustrate alternate survival strategies. Clumping bamboos spread slowly, but present an impenetrable phalanx against invasive growth. Running bamboos present an alternate strategy, being the essence of invasive growth. They spread rapidly into new territory, finding gaps in the forest canopy, penetrating the root systems of existing plants with sharp rhizome tips, using the energy stores and photosynthetic activity from the established portions of the bamboo plant to rapidly send new culms above the competing foliage, then building an impenetrable mat of rhizomes.

Because this book is intended primarily for an audience of gardeners, growers, and landscapers, the terms clumping and running are sometimes given license, as it is the customary vernacular of bamboo users and enthusiasts, myself included. As we shall see, however, the terminology is reasonably practical within a limited context, but imprecise. As gardeners, growers, and landscapers, we are concerned with the way bamboo extends its territory. Its characteristics in this regard determine what we need to do to control its spread, or increase its spread, or how it will fit and interact with the other plants and features in the landscape. For these purposes, the terms clumping and running serve us sufficiently well, particularly those of us who live in temperate rather than tropical or subtropical climates and thus are not confronted by as many of the exceptions to the rule. However, we may also want to concern ourselves with propagation or with a greater understanding of structure, function, and habit, or we may want to contend with one of the many exceptions. For these purposes, greater precision is warranted. We will explore this more precise terminology and employ it in this book as required.

Terminology

In the sections that follow, the use and misuse of terminology will be further detailed, but as a point of reference, the terms and what they describe can be summarized as follows:

> **Rhizome morphology:** pachymorph, leptomorph, amphimorph
> **Branching habit:** sympodial, monopodial, amphipodial
> **Culm and clump spacing (formal terminology):** caespitose, diffuse, pluricaespitose
> **Culm and clump spacing (informal terminology):** clumping, running

Various terminologies are encountered in bamboo literature. Although the terms sympodial and determinate properly refer to branching habit rather than rhizome morphology, they are often encountered in the literature as referential to rhizome morphology. In this (inauthentic) context, they are broadly synonymous with the term pachymorph. Similarly, in the literature, the terms monopodial and indeterminate are broadly synonymous with the term leptomorph.

Because of variations in rhizome habit and culm initiation within the broad categorizations of clumpers and runners, terminology satisfying the more precise requirements of science has been troublesome. As a practical observation and inclination, we may note distinctive clump habits of various bamboos and look to draw distinctions on that basis. That is, we may note that the culms of different bamboos have distinctly different spatial relationships, some caespitose (tightly grouped or clumped), some diffuse (widely spaced), and perhaps some pluricaespitose (multiple groups or clumps with wide spaces between them). Making just these sorts of observations, Rivière and Rivière, in 1879, were perhaps the first to publish the distinctive growth behaviors, noting that *Gigantochloa* and *Phyllostachys* exhibited distinctly different growth habits, which they identified as "caespitose" and "spreading."

Both taxonomically and otherwise, the morphology and physiology of the rhizome had largely been ignored until 1925, when F. A. McClure published a proposal for the terms sympodial and monopodial to describe the branching habit of the rhizome rather than the clumping habit of the plant. In sympodial branching, each succeeding branch, or axis, becomes dominant. In the context of rhizomes, each new rhizome turns upward and becomes a culm. In monopodial branching, a single, dominant stem, or axis, gives rise to secondary branches, or axes. In the context of rhizomes, each rhizome runs laterally, usually without turning upward to become a culm. This rhizome gives rise to secondary axes that either turn upward to become culms, or constitute new laterally running rhizomes that will, in turn, give rise to secondary axes of their own. Although the rhizome branching types often correlate somewhat with the spatial relationships of the culms—sympodial with caespitose (clumping) and monopodial with diffuse—the correlation is far from perfect, hence McClure's choice and definition of more specific and less ambiguous terminology for the rhizome.

In 1948, the Chinese botanist P. C. Keng promulgated an additional term, amphipodial, to describe bamboos, such as *Shibataea kumasaca*, that have monopodial rhizome systems but are also capable of generating new culms by tillering from the base of existing culms, in the manner of a sympodial system. The term itself, as originally conceived, suggests that a single species may have both rhizome types, but it is questionable whether the base of the tillering culms should be considered rhizomes at all, as they are not generally thickened, nor do they have the initial horizontal or subhorizontal growth habit characteristic of sympodial rhizomes. It can be argued that, once again, although in a more subtle fashion, the description of branching, clump habits, and rhizome forms have been intermingled and muddled. However, if the term amphipodial is applied more narrowly and authentically, to refer only to branching habit, then it is both useful and valid. Bamboos such as *S. kumasaca* have rhizome systems with monopodial branching and tillering culms that exhibit sympodial branching. Since both branching patterns are present, the species can be said to have amphipodial branching.

Over time, the use, misuse, and subsequent confusion of the terms sympodial, monopodial, and amphipodial rendered them increasingly ambiguous, sometimes referring to the spacing and manner of culm initiation rather than to the morphology of the rhizome. In 1966, to rectify the ambiguous terminology, McClure proposed the terms pachymorph and leptomorph to characterize the two basic types of rhizome morphologies. In this context, although *Shibataea kumasaca* exhibits amphipodial branching, its rhizome system is strictly leptomorph.

Most authorities have generally adopted the terms pachymorph and leptomorph to describe rhizome types, although some still regard the terms as synonymous and superfluous, preferring the earlier terms sympodial and monopodial. This point of view, however, merely plunges us back into the muddle. Separating branching habit (sympodial, monopodial, and amphipodial) from rhizome morphology (pachymorph and leptomorph) is a step forward in clarity. With the change in terminology and concept to pachymorph and leptomorph, the term amphimorph is sometimes employed as a convenient replacement for amphipodial, but as such, it is typically misapplied. Authentically, the term amphimorph indicates the presence of both rhizome types: pachymorph and leptomorph. So, are there species that have amphimorph rhizome systems—that is, both pachymorph and leptomorph rhizomes? Although this is also somewhat a matter of debate, in part because of a misapplication of the terms, the answer is "yes," but the occurrences are rare. Although there are probably more, the only three species with confirmed amphimorph rhizome systems are from the New World. They are *Aulonemia fulgor, Chusquea fendleri,* and *C. scandens* (Judziewicz et al. 1999).

Confusion continues because of the persistent inclination to use the same terms to describe several different but interrelated aspects: branching habit, rhizome type, and culm spacing. With respect to culm spacing and clump habit, bamboos with leptomorph rhizomes are usually "running bamboos" with widely spaced culms. In temperate climates, bamboos that have pachymorph rhizomes are typically "clumping bamboos" with closely spaced culms. Yet, although this is usually the case, it is also sometimes far from true. Confusion is not just confined to the casual gardener. In a recent study, researchers believed they had failed in their attempt to demonstrate a difference in the DNA of genera with sympodial and monopodial rhizomes. In their study, the researchers had incorrectly grouped some bamboos with pachymorph rhizome systems (and sympodial branching), including *Melocanna* and *Yushania,* with bamboos that have leptomorph rhizome systems (and monopodial branching). Although *Melocanna* and *Yushania* have pachymorph rhizomes, the rhizomes have very long necks and, thus, diffuse culm spacing. The researchers had confused culm spacing and clump habit with rhizome type (and the rhizome type was also incorrectly characterized by terms that should have been used to describe branching habit rather than rhizome morphology). In this instance, the ambiguities in terminology led to erroneous conclusions.

Rhizome morphology

Pachymorph systems. A pachymorph rhizome always turns upward and becomes a culm. It is nearly always curved and, at its maximum width, is slightly thicker than the aboveground culm it becomes. Rhizome nodes are not prominent. The internodes are wider than they are long and usually solid. New rhizomes emerge from lateral buds on an existing rhizome. As with the original rhizome, these new rhizomes always turn upward and become culms. The neck of the rhizome can be either long or short.

Most pachymorph bamboos are tender plants that thrive in tropical or semitropical environments and tolerate little or no frost. In America, they typically initiate new shoots and culm growth in the summer or fall, sometimes triggered by a period of heavy rain or moisture following a period of relative dryness.

Some pachymorph bamboos, such as a number of the New World *Chusquea* species, are adapted to temperate climates. Although pachymorph bamboos are generally associated with tropical and semitropical environments, some of the world's hardiest bamboos have pachymorph rhizomes. *Fargesia nitida* and *F. murielae,* for example, both delicate montane bamboos with pachymorph rhizomes, are extraordinarily cold hardy. These bamboos are shrublike rather than arborescent. With rare exception, arborescent bamboos with pachymorph rhizome systems are tropical or semitropical.

Leptomorph systems. The structure and growth habit of a leptomorph rhizome differs from a pachymorph rhizome. Although a leptomorph rhizome can turn upward and become a culm, it most typically runs laterally without becoming a culm. A leptomorph rhizome is usually hollow and smaller in diameter than the culms that originate from it. The rhizome neck is always short. Internodes are longer than wide. Nodes are sometimes prominent. Buds are arranged horizontally, and most remain dormant, but those that germinate may produce either culms or new rhizomes.

Most researchers regard leptomorph rhizomes as a later evolutionary development, although this is subject to debate. In one scenario, the leptomorph rhizome may have evolved through prostration of the culm, subsequently becoming more specialized and developing its own season of growth.

Most leptomorph bamboos are frost-hardy plants that thrive in temperate environments with warm summers and distinct winters that provide a period of dormancy. Some species are able to tolerate temperatures below 0°F (−18°C) without sustaining damage. In North America, leptomorph bamboos thrive in the temperate climates of the coastal states and provinces, although they have proven sufficiently hardy to be grown in the interior of the continent. Leptomorph rhizomes typically grow during late summer and fall. New shoots and culm growth typically occurs in early spring through early summer (some, such as species of *Chimonobambusa,* are exceptions and initiate shoots in the fall). Rising temperatures rather than moisture is typically a factor in shoot initiation. Leptomorph bamboos range in size from the smallest of the woody bamboos, the groundcovers and shrubs such as *Pleioblastus pygmaeus* var. *distichus,* to the giant arborescent species such as *Phyllostachys heterocycla* f. *pubescens.*

Amphimorph systems. Bamboos with amphimorph rhizomes are rare. Their rhizome systems include both pachymorph and leptomorph rhizomes. So far, amphimorph rhizome systems have been confirmed in only

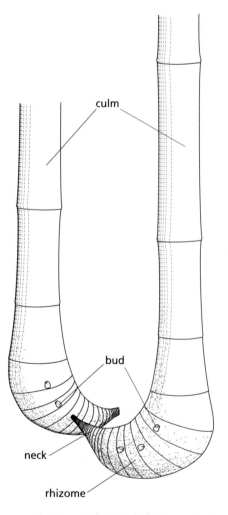

culm

bud

neck

rhizome

Figure 4. Pachymorph rhizome system.

three species, *Aulonemia fulgor, Chusquea fendleri,* and *C. scandens.* Bamboos with tillering culms, such as *Shibataea kumasaca,* have amphipodial branching—rhizomes with monopodial branching, and tillering culms that exhibit sympodial branching—but they do not have amphimorph rhizome systems. The rhizomes are strictly leptomorph.

Culm spacing and clump habit

A system that separately describes culm and clump habit in conjunction with rhizome form is now in place at Britain's Royal Botanic Gardens, Kew. It is employed in conjunction with Kew's World Grasses Database and used for the morphologi-

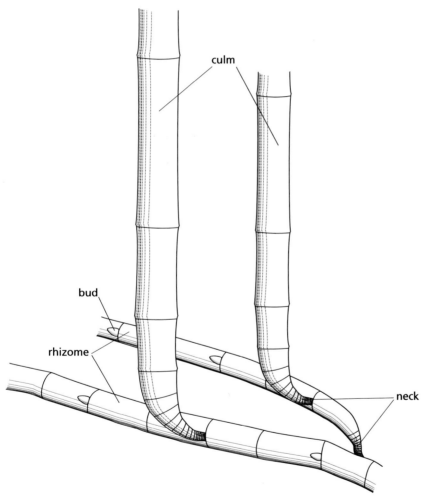

Figure 5. Leptomorph rhizome system.

cal and cladistic analyses conducted at Kew. As with any and all such systems, there are limitations and inevitable ambiguities, but this system makes another positive step in effectively describing rhizome morphology and culm and clump spacing.

Culm and clump terminology addresses the spacing of culms and clumps, independent of the rhizome morphology. Bamboos with pachymorph rhizomes and bamboos with leptomorph rhizomes can have the same clump habit. Conversely, bamboos with the same rhizome morphology can have different clump habits. For example, *Guadua angustifolia* has pachymorph rhizomes and *Phyllostachys vivax* has leptomorph rhizomes, but the culms of both are diffuse (widely spaced). *Bambusa multiplex* has pachymorph rhizomes like *G. angustifolia,* but its culms are caespitose (tightly spaced).

Environmental conditions can play a role in the clump habit. In general, if heat, light, and moisture approximate the ideal for a species, growth will be more vigorous and diffusion more exaggerated.

Diffuse. The term diffuse refers to culms that are widely spaced, arising singly rather than in groups. This growth habit is commonly synonymous with "running bamboos." It is also commonly, but erroneously, associated solely with leptomorph bamboos. In the United States and other temperate climates where bamboo is grown, most bamboos with a diffuse habit have leptomorph rhizomes—but not all. Some temperate-climate *Chusquea,* for example, have pachymorph rhizomes but a diffuse habit. Some species of *Guadua,* a genus of the New World tropics with pachymorph rhizomes, can have exceptionally long rhizome necks that extend 20 ft. (6 m) or more before turning upward to form a culm. *Olmeca reflexa,* a Mexican bamboo with pachymorph rhizomes, has greatly elongated rhizome necks, and new culms can be spaced as much as 26 ft. (8 m) apart. Both *Guadua* and *Olmeca* have exceptionally diffuse culm habits that easily outrun most leptomorph bamboos.

Caespitose. Caespitose culms are spaced closely together in a tight clump. This growth habit is sometimes termed unicaespitose and is commonly synonymous with "clumping bamboos." Although bamboo species with leptomorph rhizomes can display this habit as seedlings, when first planted, or when grown in problematic conditions, such as heavy shade or in cold summer climates, a normally vigorous leptomorph bamboo does not have a caespitose clump habit. Within the context of a normally vigorous bamboo, only pachymorph bamboos with short rhizome necks have caespitose clump habits. Some species of *Bambusa* and *Dendrocalamus* are examples of pachymorph bamboos with short rhizome necks and a caespitose clump habit.

Pluricaespitose. In a pluricaespitose clump habit, culms arise in dispersed clumps. This clump habit is sometimes termed multicaespitose or compound-caespitose. Because new culms can appear far from existing culms, this growth habit is also commonly associated with "running bamboos." Some species with pachymorph rhizomes that have a combination of short and long rhizome necks display this culm and clump habit. *Yushania,* for example, has rhizomes of varying neck lengths. New rhizomes arising from the lower buds closer to the rhizome neck have long rhizome necks. New rhizomes arising from the upper buds closer to the culm have shorter rhizome necks. In succeeding years, this growth habit produces widely dispersed small clumps.

Some species with leptomorph rhizomes and tillering culms also have this culm and clump habit. The culms arise spaced widely apart along the leptomorph rhizome, but new culms tiller off the base of existing culms, forming small clumps spaced widely apart from other small clumps. Bamboos with leptomorph rhizomes and tillering culms that generate a pluricaespitose growth habit are also called amphipodial, or (incorrectly) amphimorph, in some systems. Species of the genera *Pleioblastus, Pseudosasa, Indocalamus,* and *Shibataea* are examples of bamboos with leptomorph rhizomes and a pluricaespitose habit as a result of tillering culms.

Descriptions and limitations

Although broadly referring to bamboos as either clumpers or runners is often all that is needed to meet the communication needs of the average gardener, grower, or landscaper, descriptions of greater precision are sometimes warranted. In these instances, both the rhizome form and clump habit would be described separately. For example, *Phyllostachys bambusoides* would be described as having leptomorph rhizomes and a diffuse habit; *Melocanna baccifera* as having pachymorph rhizomes and a diffuse habit; *Bambusa multiplex* as having pachymorph rhizomes and a caespitose habit; and so on.

We have come a long way in accurately and unambiguously describing bamboo's branching, rhizome morphology, and culm and clump spacing. Still, our terminology and concepts are far from complete, and we are still some distance from ridding ourselves of ambiguities.

How far apart do culms need to be before they should be termed diffuse rather than caespitose? A rhizome neck length of 20 in. (50 cm) is one rule of thumb (Stapleton 1994a). Growing conditions and the size and maturity of the bamboo help determine the rhizome neck length, and thus the distance between culms. How should these factors be considered in the association of a culm and clump habit with a species? Perhaps using the maximum length under optimal endemic growing conditions would best satisfy the needs of the taxonomist—though not the needs of the typical gardener, grower, or landscaper.

As discussed earlier, the species *Olmeca reflexa* is a pachymorph bamboo with what one would readily concede is a diffuse clump habit. Its culms may be spaced as far as 26 ft. (8 m) apart. In the common vernacular, this is certainly a running bamboo. In my small suburban landscape, I grow *Fargesia nitida* and *Chusquea* aff. *culeou*. Both have pachymorph rhizome systems. The *F. nitida* clearly has a caespitose habit. The culms are tightly clumped and offer no threat of unexpected intrusion. But, what about my *C.* aff. *culeou?* Although the clump is no more than 6 ft. (1.8 m) in diameter at the base, the culms are sometimes spaced up to 16 in. (41 cm) apart. In optimal growing conditions, or if the clump were larger, the rhizome neck length and culm spacing might well exceed 20 in. (50 cm). While it is nowhere in the league of *O. reflexa,* it is nevertheless sufficiently spreading that I

Like *Fargesia nitida* (shown in the facing photo), *Chusquea* aff. *culeou* has a pachymorph rhizome system, but the distance between culms is far greater.

The tightly spaced culms in a *Fargesia nitida* clump.

The pachymorph rhizomes of *Chusquea* aff. *culeou* have elongated rhizome necks, giving the clump a more diffuse growth habit. Other bamboo species with pachymorph rhizome systems have rhizome necks that are far more elongated, with distances between culms of up to 26 ft (8 m). Clearly, pachymorph rhizome systems and a clumping (caespitose) habit are not synonymous.

Phyllostachys viridis 'Robert Young' with a caespitose clump habit in cool growing conditions.
In a warmer, sunnier climate, the clump habit would be diffuse.

need to treat it quite differently from the *F. nitida*. Unfortunately, I placed the *C.* aff. *culeou* in a relatively confined area near smaller plants. A new 1 in. (2.5 cm) culm penetrated a nearby dwarf rhododendron, causing a bit of a surprise. Is the clump habit caespitose or diffuse? I am not sure—caespitose, perhaps, if one accepts the 20 in. (50 cm) rule of thumb. My gut feeling on the matter changed somewhat after the rhododendron encounter. Sometimes, distinctions are not a matter of discrete categories, but rather shades of difference along a continuum, or perhaps manifold shades of differences along manifold continuums.

Also in my garden, I have several *Phyllostachys viridis* 'Robert Young' plants that have been in the ground for nearly 10 years. 'Robert Young' has a leptomorph rhizome system and a diffuse clump habit—at least in the textbook context. In my growing conditions, the clump habit is caespitose, certainly far more so than the *Chusquea* aff. *culeou*. The culms are two stories high, but they are spaced no more than 6 in. (15 cm) apart, and typically much closer, often less than 1 in. (2.5 cm). I would like the clumps to spread much faster, but they have not. I live in a fairly cool area of the Pacific Northwest. In far warmer Texas, the culm and clump habit would be greatly different, spreading aggressively with indisputably diffuse culm spacing. In the same cool Pacific Northwest climate, many other *Phyllostachys* species clearly exhibit a diffuse clump habit. Culm and clump habit is a function not only of the species, per se, but also a function of the species' response to environmental conditions. Some species respond more dramatically to variations than others.

It appears that, yet again, the terms and categories relating to rhizome morphology and clump habit are attempting to describe multiple and sometimes conflicting aspects with the same term. The words of F. A. McClure (1966), at an earlier juncture in this conceptual journey, might well again apply here, when he states that the terms "all eventually break down in ways that leave either the original concepts or the distinctive features of associated variables somewhat blurred." Common vernacular is not helpful either. I would hesitate to describe *Chusquea* aff. *culeou* as a clumper without additionally qualifying the description—or as a runner, either, for that matter. Everyone knows (or at least bamboo aficionados know) that *Phyllostachys* is a genus of leptomorph bamboos, and that all phyllostachys have a running habit. Neither I nor most bamboo growers or enthusiasts I know would typically refer to *P. viridis* 'Robert Young' as a clumper. Yet, in my backyard, it is—or rather, it does. As with many things of nature, bamboo does not always lend itself to our attempts at convenient categorization.

CHAPTER 3

Culture

Growth

The yearly cycle

Leptomorph bamboos have two distinct growth periods. After shooting, the culm grows to its full height. For most leptomorph species, culm growth generally ends in early to late summer, depending on growing conditions, followed by growth of the rhizomes. New rhizomes emerge from the buds of existing rhizomes, completing their growth and extension by late fall.

Unlike leptomorph bamboos, pachymorph bamboos do not have a network of underground stems, and thus do not have similar, overtly distinct growth periods. After the shooting and growth of new culms, pachymorph bamboos begin building the energy reserves needed for the following season's shooting period, storing starches in the existing culms and rhizomes.

Shooting. The shooting season is a time of great excitement, particularly in the case of the spring-shooting leptomorph bamboos. After what may have been a long and dreary winter, shooting bamboos are an emphatic shout that spring is here. Emerging from the ground at the full diameter of the new culm, the shoots thrust skyward at an astonishing rate—more than 3 ft. (1 m) in a 24-hour period for some species in an established grove. Even in a small suburban plot, a growth rate of 1 ft. (30 cm) a day is not uncommon. The branchless, rapidly elongating culms invite convenient Freudian comparisons. Such vigor is a dramatic affirmation of spring's renewal.

In an immature grove, and especially in a planting only a few seasons old, shooting shows how much the bamboo has grown. How big are the new culms relative to last year's? How far has the bamboo spread? How many new shoots are there? Are there enough to harvest a few for the table? Unlike other plants, leptomorph bamboos do not indicate how much they have grown by incrementally increasing throughout the year or a growing season, but demonstrate their growth and increase all at once, in a several-week shooting period in the spring.

Reading about the shooting season may bring interest and curiosity, but it does not bring understanding. Only after planting bamboo one summer, waiting through winter, then experiencing the shooting season, can the enthusiasm of bamboo aficionados be appreciated. A rapidly growing timber bamboo such as *Phyllostachys vivax* helps heighten the drama.

A new *Phyllostachys vivax* shoot.

In preparation for shooting, the buds on the nodes of the rhizomes begin swelling. As the shoot breaks ground, its tapered tip does not fully disclose the diameter of the new culm until the shoot is several inches (8 cm or so) above ground —or a foot (30 cm) or more above ground in the case of a huge shoot from a mature timber bamboo. The first culms to shoot are usually the largest and most vigorous. Growth is slow at first, the rate increasing toward mid-culm, and then slowing again. The time of rapid growth is called the "grand period of growth."

Warm weather and moisture encourage shooting in leptomorph bamboos. Unusually high soil temperatures during the shooting period may cause damage rather than forcing new growth. In one study, a soil temperature of 77°F (25°C) caused the shoots to decay and rot. In an area of Japan where the maximum production of *Phyllostachys heterocycla* f. *pubescens* shoots occurs during the month of April, the average soil temperature for the month is about 60°F (16°C).

If late winter or early spring are unseasonably warm, shooting may begin early. If the shooting is significantly outside the normal shooting time or if the weather turns cold, shooting may slow, or the shoots may fail to fully develop, forming compressed internodes or aborting altogether. Rhizomes have an abundance of buds and can produce more shoots in accordance with the needs of the plant. Unseasonably cool weather may extend the shooting season.

Varying periods of warmth and coolness may compress or exaggerate the differences in shooting times among the species. For example, a cold early spring will delay shooting of *Phyllostachys heterocycla* f. *pubescens,* and if the cold period is followed by a period of very warm temperatures, this species may shoot only slightly before *P. vivax.* If early spring is unusually warm, however, followed by an extended period of coolness, *P. heterocycla* f. *pubescens* may shoot early and *P. vivax* will be delayed, exaggerating the difference in relative shooting times.

Mature, stable groves shoot with more regularity within a more tightly defined interval than new or stressed groves. Some species, such as *Phyllostachys aurea,* have a tendency to continue shooting until fall, particularly if spring and summer have been cool. Late-season shoots rarely have the vigor of shoots initiated in the spring, and frost and winter cold may claim them before they are able to harden off.

Occasionally, an unseasonably early shoot may emerge. Unless other shoots soon follow, the shoot is probably aberrant and not a good measure of the start of the bamboo's shooting season. Early shoots often fail to develop properly in the out-of-season coolness. A bamboo's shooting season truly begins when multiple shoots emerge simultaneously or within a few days of each other. Depending on the bamboo and the season, additional new shoots may later follow.

Like temperate-climate leptomorph bamboos, tropical and semitropical pachymorph bamboos shoot during warm, moist conditions. In their native environments, the shooting period for these pachymorph bamboos is not so much associated with the seasons of the year, but with environmental conditions, such as moderating temperatures and the onset of a rainy period. In the regions of the United States where these bamboos can be grown, the environmental conditions conducive to shooting typically occur in midsummer to early fall, but the times vary. In southern California, shooting can begin as early as April, although late June is more common, continuing through October until the cooler November nights bring an end to shooting. The late-shooting culms remain branchless until the spring. Tropical and semitropical bamboos that have been severely damaged by winter cold may attempt to regenerate new culms with the onset of spring. Tropical bamboos grown indoors or in other artificial environments may exhibit all manner of shooting characteristics, as the plants try to adjust to myriad fluctuations in heat from summer sun or winter heat registers, combinations of natural and artificial light, watering patterns, and so on. In general, the shooting period for tropical and semitropical pachymorph bamboos is less tightly defined than the shooting period for leptomorph bamboos.

Not all pachymorph bamboos shoot in the fall, nor do all leptomorph bamboos shoot in the spring. Species of *Fargesia,* temperate-climate pachymorph bamboos, for example, shoot in the spring through midsummer. Species of the leptomorph genus *Chimonobambusa* shoot in the fall. Cycles are altered if mandated by survival needs. If bamboos that normally shoot in the fall are damaged by winter cold, they will send up replacement shoots in the spring.

Shooting times vary among species within a genus. Two timber bamboos of similar appearance, *Phyllostachys vivax* and *P. bambusoides,* shoot weeks apart. *Phyllostachys vivax* shoots moderately early, *P. bambusoides* very late. Although a bamboo's shooting period is usually intense and brief, planting a variety of species with different shoot-initiation periods can extend the shooting season.

When planting bamboo for the edible shoots, selecting species with different shoot-initiation periods can extend the harvest season for choice fresh shoots. Many such combinations are possible. One example might include *Phyllostachys heterocycla* f. *pubescens, P. nuda, P. vivax, P. glauca, Semiarundinaria fastuosa, P. rubromarginata,* and *P. viridis.*

The short internodes of a leptomorph rhizome provide an abundance of buds for new culms and rhizome branches. Many remain in reserve, only becoming active when warranted by the needs of the plant. Toward the end of the shooting season, some of the new shoots may stop growing and wither. This is normal, self-regulating behavior. The bamboo has expended its allocated reserves for new culms, and the shoots that have survived and are continuing toward maturity meet the current capacities and needs of the plant.

A new *Dendrocalamus giganteus* shoot.

Culm development. In the fall, leptomorph bamboos store carbohydrates in their rhizomes in preparation for the next season's growth. The size potential of the new culms is largely determined before they emerge from the soil, by the stored nutrients in the network of rhizomes. Unfavorable conditions such as cool weather, nutrient deficiencies, and insufficient moisture work against achievement of maximum potential. In general, the first shoots that emerge will produce the largest, most robust culms. The last shoots that emerge will tend to be smaller and weaker.

Culm growth is slow at first, with the maximum growth rate coming when the culm has reached approximately half its final height, and then slows progressively as the culm nears the end of its growth. Growth rate is also temperature sensitive. Cool days bring noticeably slower growth. Warm days with ample moisture accelerate growth. Culm growth also can correspond to time of day. Two-thirds of the growth of a *Phyllostachys* culm occurs during the day, whereas some tropical bamboos grow more at night and less during daylight hours.

The major growth period of a leptomorph bamboo culm ranges from 30 to 80 days. A *Phyllostachys* bamboo in a favorable growing climate can reach 90 percent of its final height in 30 days or less. Tropical or subtropical pachymorph bamboos typically require 80 to 110 days, though the final 10 percent of growth may take up to a year. The intervals of rapid growth and duration of the shooting period vary among species. The shooting period for the tropical pachymorph bamboo *Guadua angustifolia,* for example, begins with a three-month period of relatively slow growth, followed by three to six months of rapid development.

Before a new shoot emerges from the ground, the nodal diaphragms are already formed, awaiting elongation of the internodes as the culm sequentially telescopes each section. Anyone who has purchased large *Phyllostachys heterocycla* f. *pubescens* shoots for the table will have seen a good example of the nodal diaphragms (also shown in the photos of the *Phyllostachys vivax* shoot in chapter 6). Each compressed chamber is a future internode.

The extending culm is protected by the culm leaves. As discussed in the previous chapter, prematurely removing a culm leaf stops the growth of the internode. This technique is used in bonsai, when culm leaves are purposely removed early as part of the dwarfing process.

Branching and leafing. For most bamboos, branching is delayed until the new culm reaches most or all of its full height—or the branching may not take place until the following growing season, as in some species of *Fargesia.* The separate branching period enables the new culms to extend rapidly without additional demands on energy reserves, and to begin hardening before bearing the burden of branches and foliage. In some genera, however, such as *Phyllostachys,* branching begins even as the upper internodes of the new culm continue to extend.

In *Phyllostachys,* branch buds are immediately active, with the newly forming branches nestling in the groove (the sulcus) along each internode. *Phyllostachys* branches emerge from the lower culm nodes first and then progressively up the culm as each succeeding internode completes its growth. In other genera, branching may begin at the top of the culm, progressing downward, or at mid-culm, progressing upward and downward. For most bamboos, branches either emerge after the culm leaf has dropped, or they push the culm leaf away from the culm, even as it remains attached at its base. In some bamboos, such as many species of *Chusquea,* the branches burst through the culm leaf's sheath while it is still tightly attached to the culm, in a pattern known as extravaginal branching.

The branches of this *Phyllostachys aureosulcata* f. *spectabilis* are developing rapidly. The culm leaf has previously dropped away.

Immature bamboo has branches on nearly all the nodes. The branch buds at the lower nodes of mature bamboo may remain dormant indefinitely. In industry and craft, *Pseudosasa amabilis,* or Tonkin cane, is prized for its strong, straight culms without prominent nodes. Mature culms of the species may be branch free for as much as three-quarters of their length, thus eliminating the branch "knots" at each node.

Leaf fall is associated with the emergence of secondary branching. In a typical spring scenario, the leaves nearest the branch axis gradually yellow and drop, new branchlets emerge, and new leaves appear on the branchlets. In the spring, a mixture of green leaves and yellowing and dropping leaves is normal and not a cause for concern. In subsequent seasons, the branches increasingly ramify and the leaf canopy becomes denser.

Rhizome growth. The growth of leptomorph bamboo rhizomes begins soon after the new culms of spring and summer begin to photosynthesize. Growth is slow at first. The time of most rapid growth varies according to the yearly climate and regional growing conditions, but typically, growth accelerates rapidly after a leisurely growth period in June and July. Approximately half of the rhizome growth occurs in the months of August and September, and a third of the growth in October, before tapering to a stop in November. Rhizome growth can be dramatic. In a fertile, mature forest of *Phyllostachys heterocycla* f. *pubescens,* rhizomes up to 2¼ in. (6 cm) in diameter readily grow 12 ft. (4 m) or more in a single year.

Through the end of September, photosynthesis primarily supports the growth of the new culms and rhizomes and the grove's heightened rate of respiration. With the cooler, shorter days of fall, rhizome growth slows and respiration diminishes. The carbohydrates produced by photosynthesis are stored as insoluble starches in the rhizomes, awaiting the following spring when the starches are converted to sugars, and another cycle of shooting and dramatic culm growth begins anew.

The branches of this *Chusquea* are bursting through the sheath, a pattern known as extravaginal branching.

Growth of a clump or grove

As the yearly cycles repeat over multiple seasons, clumping bamboos expand their radius and develop into mature clumps. Running bamboos develop into a grove—or, in the case of timber bamboos with sufficient space, a forest. An individual culm attains its maximum diameter and maximum height in a single spurt of growth. In subsequent years, the culm may gain more branches and leaves, but it will neither grow taller nor increase in diameter. As a bamboo clump or grove matures, however, it generates new culms of increasing diameter and height every year. In a healthy, developing clump or grove, the newest culms are always the largest.

The maximum size of the culms is determined by the species and growing environment. Given excellent growing conditions, a small bamboo may be capable of attaining its maximum size in a limited area typical of a suburban plot. A medium-sized bamboo may be capable of attaining maximum size only in larger areas with excellent growing conditions. Giant timber bamboos with a running habit require a large area and ideal growing conditions to achieve their potential, typically attaining maximum size only in native or long-established forests. Although timber bamboos may reach maximum size only in large, old forests, they are nevertheless capable of attaining impressive size and presence even when confined to a relatively small area typical of a residential property. Giant clumping timber bamboos may be too large for many residential landscapes, but given the appropriate climate and growing conditions, they can achieve their maximum size in a relatively small area, perhaps not much larger than the space occupied by a large deciduous tree with a spreading leaf canopy.

The larger the bamboo, the longer it takes to approximate its maximum size. Ten years is a general rule of thumb for a grove of a large leptomorph running bamboo to reach maturity, although achieving a total forest environment and the maximum size of the largest bamboos would take longer. In a study based on carbon cycling in stands of the large leptomorph timber bamboo *Phyllostachys bambusoides,* the projected recovery period after a 99 percent decimation of culms, simulating a period of mass flowering, was 20 years. This matches the recovery period observed in Japan. Under ideal conditions, medium-sized pachymorph bamboos can achieve maximum height within four years, larger species within seven years. For all bamboos, growth gains are most dramatic in early and middle years, slowing as the bamboo approaches the maximum that the species and growing conditions allow.

The shape and spread of a developing clump or grove depends on rhizome type and growth habit. The section "Rhizome System and Clump Habit" in the previous chapter details the factors behind growth habit differences. The temperate-climate, shrubby Himalayan bamboos, such as *Drepanostachyum* and *Himalayacalamus,* have a caespitose growth habit. A developing clump of these bamboos increases gradually and more or less symmetrically. In America, the many tropical and semitropical species of *Bambusa* are the most familiar arborescent clumping bamboos. They have pachymorph rhizomes and many typically exhibit a caespitose growth habit, forming a generally symmetrical, tightly spaced clump. Other arborescent tropical bamboos, such as *Guadua* and *Melocanna,* also have pachymorph rhizome systems, but a diffuse and spreading growth habit, forming open and less symmetrical clumps or groves. Because these are uncommon in America, and only grown in the very warmest locales, tropical and semitropical bamboos are commonly regarded as "clumpers." Although technically incorrect, this conception generally matches what one encounters. Some bamboos, such as *Yushania,* have a pluricaespitose habit. A grove of this type of bamboo spreads somewhat irregularly, forming diffuse clumps over a broad area.

A developing grove of running leptomorph bamboo, prototypically the genus *Phyllostachys,* evolves in a more dramatic and less predictable fashion. In the first year or two, a newly planted bamboo will display a generally clumping, caespitose habit. Unseen above ground, the underground rhizomes will have spent the years extending a considerable distance from their origin. Initially growing in the direction their tips were pointed, the rhizomes adjust their path in the direction of favorable moisture and soil conditions, modifying direction to avoid obstacles. The rhizomes branch into other rhizomes, which in turn branch again. In a mature grove, culms are more or less uniformly distributed, but in a developing grove, new culms are quite diffuse and may appear in asymmetrical patterns at considerable distances from the mother plant.

A saying that may be attributed to other plants, but seems particularly descriptive of leptomorph bamboos, goes like this: "The first year it sleeps. The second year it creeps. The third year it leaps." The saying fairly accurately portrays the behavior of newly planted leptomorph bamboos, initially manifesting a clumping habit before aggressively spreading. A young leptomorph bamboo plant often develops mixed axes, sending forth rhizomes that grow underground for some distance, then turn upward to become culms. These culms are sometimes called whips or whipshoots. In their first years of growth, bamboo plants often generate whips in addition to, or sometimes instead of, culms from buds. Whips are less erect than culms generated from rhizome or basal culm buds, and they are more prone to tip from side to side. Although less stately than a "normal" culm generated from a rhizome bud, a whip's foliage generates food and energy for the rapidly developing plant and spreads its aboveground presence. Whipshoots may appear earlier in the season than shoots from the same plant that are generated from rhizome buds.

If desired, the newly emerging whips can be turned back to the soil to resume their growth as rhizomes. A small trench can be dug underneath the rhizome whip. The whip shoot is then placed in the trench and covered with soil. Sometimes it is also necessary to weight the whip to prevent it from emerging again from the soil.

Leptomorph rhizomes cease growing in the fall. Typically, at least with the genus *Phyllostachys*, the growing tip of the rhizome dies, then the following summer, new rhizomes branch from buds near the end of the living part of the rhizome. Rhizomes rather than culms tend to develop from the buds near the tip of the rhizome. In a young system, rhizome branching is often numerous. In older systems, rhizomes may continue for several seasons without the tip of the rhizome dying. When the tip of a rhizome does die in an older system, only one or two rhizome branches may develop, or a single rhizome branch may simply carry on in the general direction of the original tip.

In the first years of a maturing system, leptomorph rhizomes retain the capacity to turn upward and become culms. Rhizomes in a mature system no longer have this capacity, and a rhizome will die if it does turn upward. In a mature system, a rhizome tip can continue living and extending for several years. As long as the tip continues growing, no branching occurs.

Bamboos with pachymorph rhizomes and a tight clumping habit tend to have the newest culms on the perimeter, and the oldest culms in the center of the clump. To the extent that new rhizomes and culms spread inwardly, they tend to grow on top of the existing mass of rhizomes and roots, forming a raised mound. The center of an old clump will tend to have culms that are fewer and older, sometimes making way for the growth of other vegetation.

Although a culm attains its maximum height and diameter in its first year of growth, its branches may continue to ramify. Bamboos may have a spring period of leaf fall, as the lower leaves on a branch drop away, replacing the leaf with a new branch with leaves or branches at each of its nodes. Each succeeding year can bring increasing ramification, creating a profusion of branches and leaves.

Alternate-year cycles. Some Chinese bamboo forests are classified as either odd-year or even-year forests. Most natural forests are odd-year forests. Newly matured culms shed and replace their leaves at about the end of their first year, and every other year thereafter. In an odd-year forest, most culms replace their leaves in the same year. Thus, in a given year, the culms in an odd-year forest will replace most of its leaves, followed by a year when most culms do not replace their leaves. Shoot production and leaf replacement are related. Many more shoots are produced during years when the leaves are not replaced. In an odd-year forest, shoot production varies widely from year to year. For commercial shoot production, an even-year forest is generally desirable. In an even-year forest, roughly half the culms replace their leaves each year, thus shoot production is relatively uniform from year to year.

A new grove may exhibit either an even- or odd-year shooting and leafing pattern depending on the cycle of the plants used in establishing the grove. In the suburban landscape, a "grove" is often established from a single plant, and thus may exhibit a distinctive odd-year cycle, producing many shoots one year and relatively few the next. The cycles are subject to considerable modification, however, depending on yearly variations in water, nutrients, and other climatic conditions. In a developing grove, the size and productive capacity typically increases significantly from one year to the next, thereby muting the effects of odd-year cycles.

Diseases, pests, unusual weather, insect defoliation, and poor management practices that cause stressed conditions can transform an even-year forest into an odd-year forest. The tendency to harvest a higher percentage of the sparsely available shoots in an off year of an odd-year grove only serves to exaggerate the odd-year effect. By the same token, an odd-year forest can be transformed into an even-year forest by retaining a higher percentage of shoots and new culms during the off year.

Dynamic equilibrium. Once established, commercial groves are maintained in a state of vigorous equilibrium. Old culms are thinned to make way for new culms on a replacement basis. The most robust new culms are selected for the replacement culms. A typical shoot-producing *Phyllostachys heterocycla* f. *pubescens* forest, for example, is thinned to a density of approximately 800 culms per acre (2000 culms per hectare). The culms may be topped so that sun can better reach the soil and promote earlier shoot emergence and shoot harvesting. Old culms are harvested when they are about seven years old, at a rate of about 115 culms per acre (285 culms per hectare). Each year, approximately the same number of new culms is allowed to grow to replace the harvested culms. The new culms are marked with the year of their emergence so that they can be cut at the appropriate age. A grove intended primarily for culm production can be maintained with a greater density of culms per acre, promoting straight culms that support themselves in strong winds with little or no topping. The replacement cycle will typically be shorter, since culms attain maximum strength in about three to five years.

A bamboo grove maintains a dynamic equilibrium by generating new shoots and killing excess culms. If the grove is unable to sustain the culm biomass, excess culms are killed until food consumption no longer exceeds food production. The grove may kill shoots if it can no longer sustain their growth. This often occurs toward the end of the shooting period, when the last shoots that emerge from the ground are aborted. The grove may also generate new shoots outside of the normal shooting season, if new culms are necessary to maintain the grove. *Chimonobambusa,* for example, normally shoots in late summer or fall, but if the aboveground growth experiences severe damage, such as winter kill, the plant will generate replacement culms in the spring.

A general flowering of a bamboo clump or grove is an infrequent, major event—one that can mark its death. Refer to the "Flowers and Flowering" section in chapter 2 for a more detailed discussion of flowering.

Excess shoots are aborted to maintain the grove's equilibrium. In this *Bambusa* clump, the old, aborted shoots are a ghostly white.

Forest ecology

Forest ecology is an extraordinarily complex and vital topic, made all the more so as human populations and technology have become major and sometimes defining factors in their evolution, and sometimes in their demise. The treatment of the topic in this book is very modest, merely offering a flavor of the complex interactions among forest species.

Many bamboos are monocarpic. After a period of gregarious flowering, recovery is mostly or exclusively by seedlings. Bamboos frequently dominate the understory or overstory in forests. The sudden demise, brought about by gregarious flowering, of what had been a dominant plant in the forest understory or overstory creates a dramatic shift in the forest ecology.

The flowering cycle of *Sasa* has been variously placed between 60 to 100 years or more. Dominant in many grasslands and forest understories, the flowering and demise of the monocarpic *Sasa* afford the opportunity for the invasion and establishment of many new species. The *Sasa* seedlings compete with other invading vegetation and require 15 to 25 years before the plants attain full size and regain dominance (Makita 1992). An understory plant, *Sasa* is a determining factor in the growth cycles of the forest overstory and understory.

Sasa flowering cycles are important dynamics in Japanese beech forests. A *Sasa* understory inhibits the establishment of beech seedlings. The lengthy vegetative state of *Sasa*, followed by flowering, death, and a lengthy recovery cycle, allow beech seedlings to establish and grow above the competition in the understory. The mass flowering of *S. kurilensis* in 1995, covering some 2500 acres (1000 hectares) in the beech forests in northern Japan, is providing researchers across a broad range of disciplines the opportunity to study the effects on the ecologies of these forests. Similar cycles are observed in New World beech forests as well, though instead of *Sasa*, these cycles are played out with *Chusquea*. Certainly not exclusive to beech forests, similar cycles are repeated in evergreen forests in the Himalayas and elsewhere.

Flowering cycles affect the forest understory as well. In the Hira Mountains of central Japan, *Sasa tsuboiana* flowered gregariously in 1977. In one area of the mountains, *Miscanthus sinensis*, an herbaceous grass, became dominant in the understory after the gregarious flowering of *S. tsuboiana*, suppressing the regeneration and vigor of the bamboo. After about 10 years, *S. tsuboiana* regained dominance, and the shade-intolerant *M. sinensis* declined rapidly. In other regions of the mountains, 13 years after the gregarious flowering of *S. tsuboiana*, other shrub species remained more widely distributed than they had been before the gregarious flowering—and remained so even after the general recovery of *S. tsuboiana*. In this instance, the predominance of *S. tsuboiana* is likely to continue a gradual increase over the years.

Human intervention can also cause precipitous changes in forest ecologies. In a typical scenario, repeated with many different species in many parts of the world, burning, logging, and land clearing eliminate the overstory, enabling colonizing plants that thrive in the sun to rapidly dominate. Typically, where it is native, bamboo wins the contest. In these situations, bamboo may form vast, dense thickets, excluding other vegetation and earning an unfortunate reputation as a weed.

On a more pleasing note, a dominant forest of timber bamboo substantially creates its own environment, in which it then thrives. For example, in a *Phyllostachys heterocycla* f. *pubescens* forest, the towering culms and masses of foliage form a dense canopy that shades the forest floor and shelters it from drying winds and extremes of heat and cold. The forest floor is covered by dense mulch built up from decades, or perhaps centuries, of leaf fall. The mulch prevents the soil from drying, moderates temperature extremes, and inhibits the growth of other vegetation. The mulch provides an ideal medium for many mushrooms. In China, harvesting a bamboo forest may include gathering edible mushrooms as well as bamboo shoots.

Growth habits under adverse conditions

Like most plants, when faced with adverse circumstances, bamboo adjusts its growth habits to best ensure its chances of health and survival. If bamboo is unable to supply its leaves with adequate moisture, the plant attempts to preserve moisture by reducing the leaf surface area exposed to the air and sun. Bamboo under moisture stress begins to curl its leaves. A severely stressed plant will tightly roll its leaves into the shape of needles, reducing the leaf surface area to an absolute minimum. This phenomenon is made possible by the collapse of large cells near the leaf's surface, called bulliform cells, that cause the curling and rolling effect. If this mechanism proves inadequate, some leaves will turn brown, die, and drop from the plant. Some bamboos, such as species of *Yushania,* curl their leaves in direct sunlight, but this is an adaptation and not necessarily indicative of a problematic condition.

When confronted with abnormally low light, bamboo will drop leaves until the plant is in balance with prevailing light levels. It is common for a bamboo to drop many leaves when brought indoors from an outdoor environment. If the indoor conditions are not extreme, the plant will gradually adjust to the reduced light. Although bamboo grown in less than optimal light will not be as vigorous as bamboo grown under optimal conditions, the ability of bamboo to adjust permits a healthy and attractive plant to be grown in a wider range of environments.

Depending on the species, a leptomorph bamboo will grow less vigorously and spread less in situations of low light. A shaded environment will not deter the running habit of a *Sasa* bamboo that prefers shade, but the same conditions will engender a clumping habit from a *Phyllostachys* bamboo that otherwise would have displayed a strong running habit in sunny, optimal conditions. The *Phyllostachys* bamboo in shaded conditions would also exhibit a general reduction in vigor and much smaller culms.

Growth is also inhibited by conditions that are either too warm or too cool. Many temperate-climate bamboos need a period of cool weather dormancy, or else the subsequent year's growth will be weak and the plant will continue to lose vigor. Winter cold damage can progressively affect the plant. First the leaves brown and wither, then drop, followed by death of small branches, then death of the larger branches, death of the culm top, then death of the entire culm. Under severe conditions, bamboo can be killed to the ground, then grow back again the following spring. If the rhizome system is killed, however, the plant dies.

Every bamboo has a normal shooting season, but under adverse conditions, shooting may occur at any time during the year. Temperate-climate bamboos grown in subtropical conditions or subtropical bamboos grown in temperate conditions may shoot outside their normal season. When grown in America, many subtropical bamboos initiate shoots in late summer or fall, but if cooling weather inhibits shooting, or if the tender shoots are killed by winter's cold, new shoots may be initiated the following spring, as the bamboo adapts to ensure its vigor and survival.

For leptomorph bamboos, culm and rhizome growth normally occur sequentially during the course of a season. A stressed bamboo may forego culm growth during a season, generating rhizome growth only. A new rhizome ensures that there will be viable buds to generate both new culms and new rhizomes. Without viable buds, the plant cannot generate either new culms or new rhizomes, and it will gradually weaken and die.

Although most bamboos normally flower at lengthy intervals, with the entire plant bursting into flower, a plant may generate a few flowers on isolated branches if growing under stressed conditions. This is presumably a protective reaction to produce flowers and seed in the event that the mother plant dies.

Cultural Requirements

Natural bamboo distributions range from tropical to temperate zones, from sea level to more than 14,100 ft. (4300 m) in the equatorial highlands of South America, and from approximately 47°S latitude in southern Argentina to 50°N latitude on Russia's Sakhalin Island. In spite of this broad distribution to widely varying growing regions, the cultural requirements of bamboo are remarkably similar among the manifold genera and species. Bamboos differ most in their preference and tolerance of heat and light.

Bamboo achieves its full growth potential only under ideal conditions, yet this enduring grass can adapt and survive in environments that are far less than ideal, and thrive in good, if not ideal conditions. For the gardener, grower, and landscaper, this means that a relatively wide range of species can be successfully grown in a relatively wide range of environments. On the other hand, if achieving maximum growth potential is the essential goal, only a few bamboo species will be ideally suited to any given environment. In general, bamboos are highly adaptable and easy to grow. Bamboos are also highly responsive plants that generously reward the grower who favorably augments their growing conditions.

Soil

Although bamboo is a tenacious survivor under adverse conditions and is not particularly fussy, the best soils promote rapid growth and the most attractive and productive groves. Bamboo prefers fertile soils rich in organic nutrients. Ideal soils for most bamboos are slightly acidic, loosely textured, and well aerated. They should drain freely, yet retain moisture. Water-saturated, soggy, heavy soils exclude air from the root system, keep soil temperature low, and can cause rhizomes to rot. Tolerance of less-than-ideal soil conditions varies among bamboos. Like most bamboos, *Phyllostachys* prefers loose, well-drained soils that are rich in organic matter, but many in the genus are also tolerant of heavy clay soils. By contrast, species of *Fargesia* are generally exceptionally sensitive to soil drainage and may not survive in heavy clay soils.

An example of an excellent bamboo soil is a slightly acidic, sandy loam with a pH of 5.5 to 6.5. Highly alkaline soil impedes the availability of water to the bamboo, a particularly critical concern during the intense period of shooting and culm growth. Growing regions where alkaline soils are prevalent are also typically hotter, drier areas where adequate water is already a concern. Soils in these areas are typically deficient in organic material and may be deficient in sulfur that would otherwise be generated from organic material. Chlorosis may be a result from sulfur deficiencies, lack of iron, or other causes.

Some bamboos tend to prefer more acidic soil. *Shibataea kumasaca* is exceptionally sensitive to leaf burn from alkaline soils and does best in quite acidic soils. Somewhat unusually, a few bamboos, such as *Otatea acuminata* ssp. *aztecorum*, reportedly prefer a slightly alkaline soil. Certain bamboos are more tolerant of a range of soils. *Semiarundinaria fastuosa* is typically grown in moderately acidic soil but is reportedly very tolerant of alkaline soils with a pH of 8.0 or above.

Even within the same genus, tolerance for soil acidity varies. *Phyllostachys nigra* and *P. nigra* var. *henonis* are reportedly more tolerant of acidic soils than *P. heterocycla* f. *pubescens*. If the soil is too acidic, *P. heterocycla* f. *pubescens* foliage will readily become chlorotic. Curiously, *P. heterocycla* f. *pubescens* is more particular about growing conditions than others of the genus, and it is also intolerant of alkaline soils.

Sandy soils benefit from additions of organic materials. Clay soils can be improved with additions of sand as well as organic materials. A wide range of materials are suitable for organic additions, availability often being among the principal reasons for choosing one over another. Some examples include chipper material, composted nonwoody plant refuse, sawdust, fir bark, hay, apple or grape pomace, composted manure, leaf humus, bark chips, peat, and so on. The woody materials deplete nitrogen as they decompose and so necessitate nitrogen augmentation, a matter easily addressed during normal fertilizer applications. Composted manures make an excellent soil amendment when preparing an area for planting, contributing texture along with fertilizer and organic nutrients. Manures that have been reduced to a fine powder hinder rather than help soil aeration and permeability. The best manures for soil augmentation have some texture.

Although the soil should be well cultivated and loose, it does not need to be cultivated very deeply. Even in Japan's giant *Phyllostachys heterocycla* f. *pubescens* forests, soil was traditionally cultivated only to a depth of 2 ft. (0.6 m) in clay soils, and only to about 1⅓ ft. (0.4 m) in sandy loam soils or soils rich in humus. Although rhizome depth reaches 3 to 4 ft. (1 to 1.2 m) in the giant forests, viable rhizomes typically grow much closer to the surface, and ideal rhizome depth is generally considered to be no more than 1½ ft. (0.5 m).

Mulch

Bamboo benefits greatly from a top mulch. A layer of mulch keeps the rhizome and root system warm and moist, protects it from excess heat or cold, and cycles nutrients back to the soil. In areas with very severe winters, a winter layer of mulch 1 ft. (30 cm) or more deep may be essential for health and survival. For most situations, a layer of mulch one to several inches (2 to 10 cm) deep will suffice. In a controlled test on the effectiveness of mulch, the greatest soil temperature increases occurred in December and January, often the most critical months for cold protection. Mulching promoted the early emergence of new shoots and prolonged the shooting period. In the study, the shooting period, and thus the harvest period for shoots, was increased from one and a half to as much as three months (Cao et al. 1996).

A mature grove provides its own mulch from leaf fall, but a new planting will benefit from augmentation. Leaves, leaf humus, and composted manure work particularly well. Straw, hay, lawn clippings, pine needles, wood chips, and bark, among others, are additional possibilities that can be used alone or in conjunction with other materials.

In general, regardless of the climate or the particular requirements of a given species, a good top mulch is highly desirable. A top mulch tempers the effects of the environment and protects the bamboo from extremes of heat, cold, and drought.

Fertilizer

Ideas regarding fertilizer regimens have varied over the years. A 19th-century book called *The Cultivation of Bamboos in Japan* (Satow 1899) recommends the following:

> The dead bodies of dogs, sheep, cats, rats and other animals, the skins, bones and hoofs of cattle and horses, are the best for this purpose. Decayed rice and wheat plants, rice and barley bran, and other vegetable matter, ashes, the contents of the dust-bin, rotten compost, stable litter, the dung and urine of men and horses, and lime where the soil is not sandy, may all be used.

Confronted by the lack of a ready supply of horse hoofs and dead sheep, the modern suburban gardener is forced to turn to other fertilizer sources. In general, a fertilizer mix suited to growing grass in a given area should also do well with bamboo. A full-range fertilizer of phosphorus, potassium, and a relatively higher amount of nitrogen is generally suitable. Bamboo also responds very favorably to organic manures. One method calls for a generous top dressing of organic manure one year, followed by non-organic fertilizers the following year. Had I the resources, conditions, and time to permit it, I would probably use only organic fertilizers. As it is, I use a combination of the two. There are probably as many favorite fertilizer regimens as there are bamboo growers.

The most important time to apply fertilizer is when the new shoots are forming underground. Depending on the local climate, February, March, or April are the prime times to begin the new year's fertilizing regimen for most leptomorph bamboos. For pachymorph bamboos, the time of the year will depend on the species and the growing conditions, but the same principles apply. Except for the winter months, bamboo is actively growing most of the year, producing and extending new culms, branches, and leaves, or producing and extending rhizomes. The best regimen calls for fertilizing just prior to shooting, and then continuing periodically throughout the active growth period. More frequent fertilizing is appropriate where heavy rainfall leaches the nutrients from the soil.

Where winter freezing is a danger, caution must be exercised not to overfertilize in the fall and winter. While it may be tempting to incorporate organic fertilizers in with winter's protective mulch, this could subject the bamboo to severe winter damage. Slower acting, organic fertilizers can be applied in late winter or early spring after the danger of hard freezing has passed.

Bamboos, particularly the vigorous timber varieties, are nitrogen-loving plants. Like lawn grass, bamboo responds to generous fertilizer applications. Some degree of caution and common sense must be exercised, however. A large, vigorous, timber bamboo may not immediately show the typical effects of excessive fertilization. As an experiment, I once applied massive quantities of nitrogen to a small grove of *Phyllostachys vivax*. New culms shot prolifically, grew vigorously, and the grove appeared healthy. The weight of heavy summer rains, however, revealed the weakened state of the culms, bending and splitting them beyond recovery. The following year yielded very few new shoots and no advancement in size. Bamboo is a heavy feeder, but common sense must prevail.

The fertilizer regimen can also be adjusted in accordance with the grove's intended use. Heavy fertilizer applications are desirable for maximum shoot production. If high-quality culm wood is the principal aim, however, more moderate fertilizer applications would be in order, to ensure the strongest culms.

Water

Although most bamboos are relatively drought resistant, they only thrive with ample water. The roots, however, must not become waterlogged. Except for a very few species that have air channels in their rhizomes, such as *Arundinaria gigantea* ssp. *tecta* and *Phyllostachys heteroclada,* bamboo will not grow in water-saturated, swampy, or boggy conditions. Ideally, the soil should always be moist, but never soggy. For most bamboos, overwatering is not a concern as long as the soil is well aerated and free draining.

A once-a-week watering regimen is a good starting point, but actual watering needs and frequencies will vary widely—from not at all during rainy periods, to every day in exceptionally hot, dry conditions with poor soils and little or no mulch. In drier climates, bamboo benefits from misting, which creates a more locally humid environment and discourages bamboo mites, aphids, and the like.

Proper soil and mulching make watering easier. Many soils shed water when they are dry. Soils containing sand and organic materials help encourage water penetration and absorption even when dry. Peat moss is a notable exception, which, unless moist, tends to shed water. A layer of mulch helps keep the soil moist, diffuses incoming water, and helps it penetrate the soil.

Ample soil moisture is one of the principal triggers that initiates shooting in many tropical bamboos, because it signifies the beginning of the wet season and the period of active growth. All bamboos benefit from ample water during active growth periods. For most leptomorph bamboos, this period begins just prior to shoot initiation in the spring and continues through the succeeding stages of culm growth, branching, and leafing, through midsummer, followed by rhizome growth from midsummer through fall. These bamboos are well matched to their native Asian climates, where the periods of active growth coincide with the wet season. America's West Coast and Mediterranean European climates, however, receive most of their yearly precipitation during periods when the bamboos are dormant or not actively growing. In these regions, even when the temperatures during the growing season closely match those of the native Asian environments, the lack of moisture during the active growing periods limits growth. In these climates, maximum growth is not achievable without irrigation, siting in riparian zones, or some other supplemental water source.

Rhizomes, and subsequently their culms, can be encouraged to grow in certain areas, and discouraged in other areas, by ensuring that the desired areas are generously fertilized and watered. Withholding water and nutrients from an area during the period of rhizome growth is one method of guiding and limiting the spread of running bamboo. It is most effective when the natural growing conditions are dry and nutrient poor. Control and encouragement is only a matter of degree, however, and this method of controlling growth is generally insufficient on its own.

Bamboo leaves curl when the plant is water stressed, and so leaf curling is usually a sign that watering is quickly needed. In severe circumstances, the leaves will roll so tightly that they begin to resemble needles. With a newly propagated bamboo, however, leaf curling may indicate that the bamboo is carrying too much foliage for its root system. Some species naturally curl their leaves when exposed to sunlight, even when they are not water stressed. For the most part, however, leaf curl is a reliable indicator that the bamboo needs water.

Large bamboos in containers becomes water stressed more quickly than bamboos grown in the ground, and they should be monitored more closely during hot, dry periods. A bamboo that is becoming root-bound in a container will need watering more frequently. If a bamboo in a container is drying out more quickly than other bamboos in containers, this is an indication that it needs to be divided or needs a larger container.

Heat and light

With respect to their cultural requirements, bamboos differ most in their preference and tolerance of heat and light. The chapter on the genera and species of bamboo (chapter 9) describes the general requirements for each bamboo, but more factors are at play than can be readily summarized in a listing.

The temperate-climate groundcover bamboos are generally understory plants that prefer some shade. This is especially true in a climate like that of southern California, but in maritime climates, such as those in parts of the Pacific Northwest, the same groundcovers may thrive in full sun. Even more than the groundcover bamboos, many *Fargesia* need shade, yet in parts of cool, cloudy England, they thrive in full sun. Unlike most of the groundcover bamboos, however, most *Fargesia* are intolerant of heat. In hot southern climates that groundcover bamboos could readily tolerate, *Fargesia* may grow poorly—if at all.

Unlike most *Phyllostachys*, *P. nigra* prefers less than full sun in hot, sunny climates. In the maritime Pacific Northwest, however, *P. nigra* not only thrives in full sun, but also achieves a diameter and height that, for the species, is among the largest in the world. On the other hand, these same parts of the Pacific Northwest are much cooler than is ideal for warmth-loving species like *P. makinoi*. Both *P. makinoi* and *P. vivax* prefer full sun, but *P. makinoi* needs much more heat to achieve its growth potential. In the maritime Pacific Northwest, *P. makinoi* never achieves a size that approximates its growth potential, yet it readily does so in Texas. *Phyllostachys vivax* is more tolerant of cooler conditions and grows rapidly and large in the Pacific Northwest. In parts of cool, cloudy England, *P. bambusoides*, the large timber bamboo, may only achieve a diameter of ¾ in. (2 cm), and the warmth-loving *P. heterocycla* f. *pubescens*, even less.

Many leptomorph bamboos will thrive in environments with the same hot, sunny summers that benefit the pachymorph semitropical and tropical bamboos. But unlike the tropical genera, most leptomorph bamboos, including most species of *Phyllostachys*, need a period of cold and winter dormancy, or else future growth will be scraggly or severely limited—if the plant survives at all.

Some of the montane bamboos, such as species of *Drepanostachyum* and *Himalayacalamus*, are only moderately winter hardy, sometimes little more so than the more robust semitropical species of *Bambusa*, yet these relatively cold sensitive montane bamboos still need a period of winter cool. Over an extended period of time, the montane bamboos seldom do well as houseplants under normal, warm, in-home winter temperatures. By contrast, *Bambusa* and other semitropical and tropical bamboos are accustomed to year-round warm temperatures and can make good houseplants if humidity and light are sufficient.

The rate of photosynthesis varies with temperature, available daylight, and seasonal changes in the bamboo plant. A study of *Phyllostachys bambusoides* (Koyama and Uchimura 1995) showed that the maximum rate of photosynthesis occurred between early July and November. The least photosynthesis occurred in May, coinciding with seasonal leaf fall and the rapid growth of the new culms, a period when the bamboo requires a great deal of water for the new shoots. Photosynthesis also decreased when temperatures rose above 80°F (27°C), as the need for rapid respiration limited photosynthetic efforts. Specific responses to seasonal and temperature changes are likely to vary somewhat from this example, particularly for tropical bamboos, with their different seasonal environments and climatic adaptations.

Winter hardiness

Cold hardiness varies widely among bamboos. Some tropical species suffer damage as soon as the temperature drops to 32°F (0°C). Other bamboos can withstand cold to –20°F (–29°C) without damage. In general, most pachymorph bamboos are semitropical or tropical and are far less hardy than leptomorph bamboos, but there are exceptions. Some species of *Fargesia,* a genus of pachymorph bamboos, are among the most hardy of all bamboos. One needs to keep in mind that the minimum temperatures cited in this book and elsewhere are only approximations. Wind, humidity, sun, duration of low temperatures, soil moisture, and so on, all play a role in determining whether or not a bamboo will be damaged. Also, some varieties and ecotypes may exhibit different cold hardiness characteristics than others of the species. *Arundinaria gigantea* ecotypes, for example, vary significantly in cold hardiness.

By convention, the minimum temperatures cited in this book refer to the point at which leaf damage begins to occur. If cold temperatures are persistent rather than brief, the damage will be more severe and will begin at higher temperatures than those cited. In general, if continuing low temperatures at or near the minimum are expected, a more cold-hardy bamboo may be preferable.

Bamboos can, however, be grown in climates with colder temperatures than their cited minimums if one is willing to understand and accept limitations in size and seasonal appearance. Although far from ideal, bamboo can even be grown in areas with severe winters and treated like a renewable perennial, cutting away all the aboveground growth each year, then enjoying the fresh new culms and leaves in the spring, summer, and fall. If not all of the aboveground growth is killed in a given year, growth the following spring will tend to be more robust, and the culms larger. Winters that bring total aboveground mortality will tend to engender a regression in vigor and culm size the following spring.

A few bamboos are naturally deciduous in winter. More markedly, some of the Himalayan bamboos act as herbaceous perennials in their native environments, dying to the ground in winter's cold, then sending up new growth in the spring. They continue to flourish, but will grow much larger and take on a different character when cultivated in an environment with milder winter conditions.

Many bamboos can be grown with little or no winter protection in parts of the United States, but where winters are severe, or when one wants to grow species that normally require warmer conditions, cold protection methods are warranted. Bamboo is commonly regarded as a plant suitable only for southern and coastal zones, but with careful species selection and winter protection, bamboo can be successfully grown, with limitations, throughout the country, including the northern interior (Hawke 1992) and Alaska.

Various reports by growers confirm that bamboo can be grown even in climates with severe winters. *Sasa senanensis* reportedly suffered only moderate leaf damage after a New York winter with little snow cover and occasional temperature drops to −30°F (−34°C). In the same report, *Phyllostachys bissetii* was bent to the ground and covered with mulch, and it was able to retain its green leaves. In another report, approximately 50 species of bamboos were subjected to temperatures that dropped to −31°F (−35°C). The bamboos had about 10 in. (25 cm) of snow cover. All the species were killed to the snowline, but none were killed completely, and all generated new culms in the spring.

Because hardiness ultimately depends on so many factors, experience is likely to vary widely. One report from Tennessee cites twig damage to *Fargesia nitida* and *F. murielae,* reputedly among the hardiest bamboos, at −5°F (−21°C). A grower in Norway reports that the same bamboos experienced a temperature drop to −20°F (−29°C) with only loss of leaves (which were replaced in the spring), but no other damage. Snow cover, or a mulch that covers the entire plant during severe cold, greatly enhances the winter hardiness of bamboo. Note, however, that if the mulch is dense and does not permit air circulation, the bamboo's green leaves may themselves become "mulched," necessitating the generation of replacement leaves in the spring.

Drying winds can severely damage foliage and may cause or contribute to even more extensive damage. In one report from New England, mild fall weather was followed by sudden Arctic winds. All species that were exposed to the winds suffered total leaf kill. Specimens of the same species that were protected in a woodland environment remained green. Preventing winter desiccation is critical to bamboo's health and survival, particularly when temperatures approach the minimum limits for a given bamboo. Rain, snow, watering, misting, plastic tenting, mulching, and anti-desiccants can all help prevent winter damage from desiccation.

In addition to harsh winds and persistent periods of cold, radical fluctuations in temperature can also contribute to further damage even if low temperatures are not that extreme. In the Pahrump Valley of Nevada, September temperatures can drop below freezing one day and be immediately followed by temperatures reaching 95°F (35°C). In January temperatures may climb to 70°F (21°C) for two weeks, creating budding situations in deciduous plants and initiating growth in bamboo, followed by a week or more in February when temperatures drop to 10 to 15°F (−12 to −9°C). The Pahrump Valley climate also includes drying desert winds and high pH clay soils. In this relatively hostile environment, bamboo cannot be said to flourish, yet a number of species, such as *Phyllostachys decora* and *Semiarundinaria fastuosa,* are reportedly viable and rewarding.

Although bamboo may only truly flourish in climates that mimic a species's native environments, bamboo is far more adaptable than once assumed. If one is able to accept smaller culms, or a deciduous habit, or perhaps even a perennial growth habit of winter culm death followed by regenerative growth in the spring, bamboo can be grown successfully throughout most of the world. Careful species selection and cultivation will greatly enhance the opportunities.

Types and degrees of cold damage. Cold damage has a progressive pattern of severity, ranging from leaf browning and damage, leaf drop, damage to branches and culms, culm death, partial death of the rhizome system, and complete death of the plant. Each stage of damage has a progressively negative effect on a bamboo's vigor and growth potential. If all the rhizomes die, the plant dies.

Bamboo with minor leaf damage will look a bit tattered, but any effect on vigor and growth potential will be negligible. Dropped leaves will be replaced with new leaves in the spring, or new branches and leaves, but the bamboo will incur a period of lost or reduced photosynthetic capability. Bare branches detract from aesthetics and may mean a lost or reduced screen from neighbors or passersby.

Branch and culm damage, and especially culm death, seriously impact vigor, aesthetics, and screening. It is usually best to wait until late spring before removing leafless branches and culms. After winter defoliation, the branches and culms are sometimes able to generate new leaves from reserve buds. Damaged and dead culms can be removed, and the rhizome system will generate new culms, but the vigor and growth potential of the bamboo will be severely affected. Even if the culms are killed to the ground each year, it is still possible to grow marginally hardy bamboos in areas with difficult winters. Although the bamboos will never approach their maximum size potential, many of their attributes can still be appreciated. If some of the rhizomes are routinely killed, however, long-term survival will be in doubt.

Preventing and reducing damage. Thick mulch is essential for severe winter areas. Above all, the rhizome system must be protected. Even if culms are killed to the ground, a healthy rhizome system will be able to generate new replacement culms in the spring. A layer of mulch 6 to 12 in. (15 to 30 cm) deep is often sufficient, but if extreme conditions are expected, much deeper mulch may be warranted.

If possible, protect bamboo from the wind. Spraying the leaves with an anti-desiccant can help prevent moisture loss and leaf damage in areas where cold, drying winter winds are a problem. In some instances, culms can be bent to the ground and covered with insulating material, such as evergreen tree boughs, straw, burlap, or any combination of materials that will keep the culm weighted down and provide insulation. Snow protects bamboo from cold and drying, but it can also break branches and culms. Small bamboos can be protected by water-filled, plastic, topless tents of the sort sold for protecting tomato plants in the spring.

Bamboos in containers are most vulnerable to cold damage. The soil should be kept moist, and the bamboo may require watering even in the winter. Grouping containers tightly together creates a larger mass that resists freezing. Tightly clustered foliage also has an insulating effect. More vulnerable species can be placed nearer the center of the grouping. Pile mulch, bark, wood chips, and other such materials around the sides of the container or group of containers, or cover with a tarp, creating a pocket of air connected to the ground or heated building. A greenhouse greatly expands the range of bamboo that can be grown in cold winter areas.

Warmth and moisture help determine when bamboos shoot. Warmth is more of a factor for temperate-climate species, moisture more of a factor for tropical

Borinda fungosa in late winter. The leaves, branches, and upper portions of the culms have sustained cold damage.

The same *Borinda fungosa* plant in midsummer of the same year. The winter-damaged culms were pruned back. The new growth is lush and attractive.

and subtropical species. These shooting tendencies can be a factor in cold damage in some climates. Warming sun and a period of elevated temperatures can stimulate early shooting species. If this is followed by frost and freezing, the new shoots can be damaged or killed. In parts of the American Southeast, for example, bright sun, pronounced temperature variation between summer and winter, and erratic early spring weather put early shooting bamboos at risk. The risk can be minimized by planting on sites that are not heavily exposed to late winter and early spring sunlight (such as slightly north-facing slopes), by covering the new shoots with mulch if a return to cold temperatures is expected, and by planting later shooting varieties. Planting bamboo so that the foliage is in sun but the ground and rhizomes are in shadow is another way to delay shooting.

In parts of the Pacific Northwest, as another example, the concern is often the opposite. Spring weather is less erratic, but cool summers mean that some late shooting varieties may not shoot early enough to allow the new culms to leaf out and harden off before the onset of winter. The rhizome growth period that follows shooting may also be delayed, thus impairing the development of a clump or grove. In this type of climate, later shooting varieties should be planted in warmer, sunnier growing sites. Clay soils can be amended so they warm faster. Mulch can be pulled aside so the soil warms more quickly, or various black or darkly colored warming tarps or cloths can be placed to warm the soil.

In American growing environments, some bamboos, particularly semitropical and tropical species, naturally shoot in late summer or early fall. If late summer and early fall are dry, shooting may be delayed and still be in progress when the colder temperatures of winter begin to intrude. Keeping these varieties well watered during summer and early fall will encourage them to shoot earlier and establish their growth before the onset of colder temperatures.

When choosing a site for bamboo, or a place to cluster containers of bamboo for the winter, remember that cold air flows downhill and pools in low-lying areas or in front of objects, such as buildings, that block or impede the continued flow of cold air downhill. If winter hardiness is a concern, low-lying areas, and other areas that will pool cold air, should be avoided. Forgetting this basic rule, and not paying attention to the lay of the land, cost me the loss of several bamboos one winter.

Environmental stresses and extremes

A variety of environmental factors affect the health and vigor of bamboo. Generally, low humidity is a potentially greater concern than high humidity, exaggerating the effects of excess heat or excess cold. A humidity-loving, tropical or semitropical bamboo will likely suffer greatly when grown in a dry desert environment, particularly when desiccating winds exacerbate the effect. Even though daytime temperatures may be similar to the plant's preferred condition, the cool nighttime temperatures typical of desert environments will greatly reduce the vigor and health of the tropical and semitropical bamboos. Although not generally a concern to the American gardener, many tropical herbaceous bamboos require high humidity levels of 70 percent or more, curling their leaves or showing other abnormal leaf movements when stressed.

What constitutes an environmental stress or extreme depends on the species of bamboo. A temperature of 25°F (−4°C) may be extreme for a tropical bamboo such as *Guadua angustifolia,* but not at all extreme for a temperate bamboo like *Phyllostachys heterocycla* f. *pubescens.* Indeed, most temperate bamboos need a period of winter cold in order to grow and thrive. There are exceptions, however. *Phyllostachys aurea,* for example, is commercially cultivated in Costa Rica and grows well without the benefit of a period of winter cold. Some temperate bamboos, such as *P. heterocycla* f. *pubescens,* thrive in climates with hot, sunny summers, providing there is ample moisture and humidity. Other temperate bamboos, notably the "mountain bamboos," such as *Fargesia nitida,* cannot tolerate strong sun, high summer temperatures, or hot nights. Many chusqueas can tolerate strong sun and hot daytime temperatures, but require cool nights for their health and survival.

Wind, particularly in conjunction with low humidity, exaggerates the effects of excess heat or cold. In the Hira Mountains of central Japan, varying degrees of wind exposure help shape the growth of *Sasa tsuboiana.* Where the wind is strong, the bamboos grow more densely, but are less tall, and longevity is decreased.

Like most plants, bamboos generally prefer conditions free from saltwater in the soil or air. Some species, however, are reportedly quite tolerant of saltwater exposure and do well even when planted near coastal beaches. These include *Pseudosasa japonica, Pleioblastus hindsii, P. gramineus, P. linearis,* and *P. simonii. Semiarundinaria fastuosa, S. okuboi, S. yashadake,* as well as some of the hardy chusqueas, which are also reportedly relatively tolerant. In general, phyllostachys are less tolerant of saltwater, but *Phyllostachys aurea, P. bambusoides, P. bissetii,* and *P. vivax* are reportedly among the better.

Pests and diseases

Bamboos in the tropics are under constant assault by a rich spectrum of insects, including various borers, defoliators, and sap suckers. They threaten the plant from the developing seed through the harvested and cured culm. Fortunately, for the

American gardener, the threat of bamboo pests and diseases is generally minimal and usually confined to disfigurement or moderate damage. Even those growing bamboo commercially on acreage, for the most part, suffer minimal risk. In his 1992 work describing the risks to bamboo plantations in India, Tewari cites the threat of devastation by rats, deer, livestock, porcupines, rabbits, squirrels, and goats, but adds that the greatest risk comes from humans, monkeys, and elephants. In suburban America, the latter are of little concern, except for the risk of humans, perhaps in the form of fraternity brothers acquiring decorations for a tropical-theme kegger (a documented source of devastation).

Aphids. In the tropics, aphid infestations can weaken and kill new shoots. In the United States, aphids are not a significant threat to the health of bamboo, but their excretions foster an unsightly, black, sooty mold. Aphids are not robust and can be killed easily, but their ability to regenerate populations at a stunningly rapid rate makes control problematic. Without mating, they are capable of producing live young that can, in turn, reproduce again within a week. Natural predators, such as the ladybug, can be obtained from commercial supply houses and introduced in large numbers, but they will generally disappear along with their food source, allowing reemergence of the aphid population. Aphids are also active and happily building their populations both early and late in the growing season, times when their natural predators are scarcely present. In some parts of the country, during late fall, when neither the energies of the gardener nor the weather lend themselves to keen vigilance, the aphid's desecration is at its peak, decorating the leaves with the sooty black muck that remains prominent until the leaves are refreshed the following spring.

Soap sprays and chemical sprays are effective in controlling aphids. Simply spraying periodically with a strong jet of water will also help keep the aphid population in check. Persistent chemical sprays should be avoided if natural predators are to be a part of the control regimen. A combination of control methods is often desirable, aiming for suppression rather than eradication.

Beetles. In preparation for the coming season of shooting and culm growth, tropical bamboos store energy reserves in their culms in the form of starches. These accumulated starches are highly attractive to the dreaded powder post beetle in harvested culms. Traditional cultures learn to harvest the culms when the starch content is lowest. Some bamboos are inherently higher in starch than others, and thus inherently more vulnerable to attack. Except perhaps for areas like

Hawaii or southern Florida, powder post beetles are of little concern in most of the United States.

Earwigs and other leaf-eating insects. Earwigs, thrips, and other leaf-eating insects can damage tender new leaves as they are about to unfold. As the leaves mature and toughen, the threat of damage lessens considerably. Even on young leaves, however, damage from these insects is usually trivial.

Mealybugs. Mealybugs are warm-climate aphid relatives. An infestation may appear as cottony deposits. The powdery wax coating that gives them their name also makes them somewhat resistant to insecticides. Soap sprays, chemical sprays, or simply spraying with a strong jet of water will help keep the population in check. Natural predators, such as green lacewings, can be used to control them. Mealybugs are more unsightly than threatening.

Mites. Mites are tiny arachnids. For bamboo growers, the severity of mite problems ranges from a never observed hypothetical to a dreaded scourge with associations akin to that of a social disease. A dozen or more species of mites can afflict bamboo, including the two-spotted spider mite (*Tetranychus uriticae*), but in America, only one, the bamboo mite (*Schizotetranychus celarius*), threatens pervasive disfiguration and impaired photosynthetic capability. Heavy mite infestations can diminish the vigor of the plant. In China, a heavy mite infestation reduced the following year's shoot harvest by approximately 180 lb. per acre (approximately 200 kg per hectare).

The bamboo mite prefers some bamboo species to others, thriving on *Phyllostachys*, but also finding a happy home on species of *Sasa, Indocalamus, Fargesia,* and *Pseudosasa,* among many others. Bamboos with densely pubescent lower leaf surfaces, such as *Semiarundinaria okuboi,* are highly resistant to mite infestations. Members of the same genus without densely pubescent lower leaf surfaces, such as *S. fastuosa,* are readily afflicted by mite infestation.

The bamboo mite inhabits leaf sheaths for eight to ten months, and then emerges in the spring to infest foliage leaves. Bamboo mite colonies form a white protective web on the underside of foliage leaves. Individuals with keen vision can observe the tiny mites moving about within the web, but a magnifying lens may be required to see them. The mites feed by sucking fluid from the leaf cells and assimilating the sugars and proteins, leaving large yellowed areas on the leaf to mark their progress. On bamboo with pronounced leaf tessellation, such as

Phyllostachys, the infested leaves have pronounced rectangular areas of yellowing. As the colonies prosper and expand, more and more of the leaf area becomes splotched with yellowed rectangular sections, eventually covering all or a major portion of the leaf, if conditions are favorable. The mites migrate to other leaves, similarly afflicting them.

As the mites feed, they eliminate excess water by exuding it from their bodies, relying on evaporation to assist in the removal process. High temperatures and low humidity greatly speed evaporation and help mites thrive and spread rapidly. Studies of a species related to the bamboo mite showed that the mite doubled its population in only 36 hours in a high-temperature, low-humidity environment. Under ideal and unchecked conditions, an infestation can rapidly afflict an entire grove, yellowing all the leaves, impairing growth, and destroying aesthetics. Although photosynthetic capability is impaired, the bamboo's survival is very rarely threatened. Degraded aesthetics and, for commercial nurseries, loss of value are the principal concerns.

Mite damage on *Fargesia* leaves.

An insignificant or unknown problem in many parts of the United States, bamboo mites are a plague in other areas. Regions with warm, dry summers, such as much of the West Coast, are most affected. Regions with humid summers, such as much of the East Coast, are less affected. Yet, once resident in an area, the mite will persist, waiting for a hot, dry spell to become rampant. As bamboo is bought, sold, and traded, the mite spreads to previously uninfested sites and may thrive and spread further if conditions are hospitable. Once established, the bamboo mite is extremely difficult to eradicate completely. Their webbing helps protect the mites from predators, climatic extremes, and contact sprays. If only a few survivors or eggs escape eradication, the population can quickly regenerate during a period of hot, dry weather.

Insecticidal soaps, sometimes in combination with oil sprays, can be somewhat effective in controlling bamboo mites, but both soaps and oils can cause severe damage to the foliage and even to new branches and culms, particularly during warm, sunny conditions when control and eradication are most urgently needed. Some advocates suggest spraying with insecticidal soap during a cloudy day, then washing off the soap after a period of several hours. The threat of damage to the plant may be alleviated, but the degree of mite eradication remains less than optimal.

So far, predator mites have proven only partially effective, but more trials are warranted. In Japan, the bamboo mite is reportedly only a minor pest, perhaps held in check by *Typhlodromus bambusae,* an aggressive predator mite that is not native to America.

On a small scale, afflicted leaves can be removed by hand, but the likelihood of leaving some mites behind is high. In certain situations, removal of all aboveground growth and burning or careful disposal of the debris may be an effective, though radical approach.

A systemic miticide, to the extent that any effective ones even exist, would likely be inappropriate if one intends to harvest shoots for the table. A miticide that is absorbed into the leaves but does not migrate throughout the plant is arguably the best mechanism for control and eradication. The miticide is absorbed by the leaves and then kills the mites as they feed. Additional applications at periodic intervals may be necessary to kill subsequent generations of mites as they hatch. Some miticides are ineffective against eggs, whereas others may be effective against eggs, but less effective for live mites. A successful regimen may include periodic application of a single miticide, or application of two different miticides, or application of a persistent miticide. The availability and legality of the different miticides varies widely. Check local sources for what is available and permissible for your area.

Total eradication may be possible if one has only a few, small plants, but if one has large plants, or a grove, total eradication may not be a feasible goal. Rampant infestation can reoccur if even a few mites or eggs are allowed to remain. For most gardeners in mite-afflicted areas, ongoing, periodic treatments are inevitable.

Many bamboo nurseries, resigned to the inevitability of some level of infestation in their primary groves, isolate the containers of bamboos that are for sale and treat them thoroughly for mites. This is a good practice for all who intend to trade or sell bamboos to others. If you live in an area where mites are a problem, or if you obtain a new bamboo plant from such an area, the plant should be temporarily isolated and treated for mites. Only after the new plant is proven mite free should it be removed from isolation.

Scale. Scales are aphid relatives that typically appear as bumps on the culms and branches of semitropical and tropical bamboos. They are unsightly, but generally do relatively little harm. Winter chill usually eliminates them, and they have many natural predators. Their exterior armor makes them resistant to insecticides except when immature. Mature scales are immobile. Scales can be picked off or scrubbed off with a plastic scouring pad.

Slugs and snails. The tough, unappealing culm leaves protect young culms from slug and snail attack, but as soon as the culm leaves drop away, the young culms are vulnerable for the short period of time before they harden sufficiently. Although rarely a significant problem, a new culm disfigured by a slug or snail can be an unpleasant surprise. Bamboo seedlings, however, are vulnerable and can disappear in a single night's rampage. The standard garden remedies for these pests apply to the protection of bamboo as well.

Sooty mold. An unsightly mold that forms a black coating on leaf surfaces, sooty mold lives on the secretions of aphids and related insects, thriving in cool, moist conditions. The mold blocks light from reaching the leaves, thus diminishing photosynthesis. It is controlled by controlling the sucking insects that provide the secretions it feeds upon.

Mammals. Various mammals pose a potential threat to bamboo. Bamboo shoots and foliage are attractive food sources for many animals, but circumstances vary, and the same mammal may present a major threat in one situation and no threat at all in another.

For some mammals, such as mice, chipmunks, squirrels, and deer, eating bamboo is a learned response. When I introduced bamboo to my suburban neighborhood by planting it around my home, the ubiquitous gray squirrels did not bother the new shoots. Presumably, casual exploration led the squirrels to discover that the new shoots were worth gnawing. Now that the pattern has been learned, new shoots and young culms are threatened each spring. Some growers report severe problems with deer that eat foliage as well as new shoots, yet other growers report the presence of heavy deer populations in and around their groves, but no deer damage to bamboo.

Voles and gophers can cause major damage at or below soil level, sometimes eating tender new shoots and rhizomes before they emerge from the ground. Voles, sometimes called field mice or meadow mice, are especially vexing in some areas. Unfortunately, thick mulches, generally beneficial for bamboo, only help shelter and encourage the beasts. Other mammals may also be sources of damage. Even dogs and cats have been known to chew on new shoots and culms, and their scratching and digging can cause inadvertent damage. Livestock usually regard bamboo foliage as a highly desirable browse.

Although not likely a problem in Boston or the suburbs of Los Angeles, kangaroos and wallabies can decimate new growth with their penchant for new shoots and leaves. Giant pandas consume between two and four metric tons of bamboo each year, but they too are seldom a problem in the American residential garden.

Different control methods may be appropriate depending on circumstances. They include providing ready availability of a preferred food source; commercial repellents that are painted or sprayed on new shoots and young culms; shavings from aromatic deodorant soaps that are scattered about or hung from branches; hunting and trapping; poisoning; sound generators for the air or ground; fencing; wire or plastic screens for individual shoots; and underground mesh or surrounding gravel trenches for tunneling animals.

In some instances, methods can be combined to control the spread of bamboo as well as damage to it. A fence separating livestock from a bamboo grove, for example, keeps the livestock from the grove, while effectively limiting unwanted spread of the grove as the livestock consumes the new shoots and foliage along the fence line.

Buying Bamboo

Those who live in the heart of bamboo country have the best choices of sources and methods for obtaining bamboo. Extensive selections of bamboo are available through specialist mail-order nurseries, however, so even individuals without a local source can still enjoy the beauty of this exotic plant.

Quantity and spacing

Quantity and spacing guidelines can only offer a basis for decision. The question, "How many plants do I need?" elicits the return inquiry, "How big of a hurry are you in, and how much do you want to spend?"

The number of plants that should be purchased to fill an area is a basic information need that does not lend itself to a ready answer. The type of bamboo, growing conditions, and the goals of the grower are all factors. If rapidly establishing a hedge is the principal goal, and the extra cost of additional plants is not a limiting factor, then plant spacing of 2 to 3 ft. (0.6 to 1 m) may be desirable. If the grower can wait an additional season or two, growing conditions are optimal, and bamboos with a diffuse growth habit are being planted, then spacing of 6 ft. (2 m) or even more might be reasonable. Ornamental groundcover bamboo is typically planted at a spacing of 1 to 3 ft. (0.3 to 1 m), but like planting for a hedge, the plants may be spaced much further apart if the grower prefers to save costs and wait the extra seasons.

A small grove of medium to timber-sized leptomorph bamboo can be effectively started with plants spaced at 6 to 10 ft. (2 to 3 m). A commercial grove would typically be planted with a wider spacing. Experiments in Alabama concluded that a spacing of 15 to 20 ft. (5 to 6 m) for small nursery plants was satisfactory for establishing a commercial grove over 10 to 15 years, and that little would be gained by closer spacing. By definition, semitropical and tropical pachymorph bamboos with a caespitose habit spread slowly. One might think that a much closer spacing would be desirable to more quickly "fill in the gaps," but their rhizome and root clumps are more subject to the limitations of overcrowding than leptomorph bamboos. Particularly if large, mature clumps are the goal, sufficient spacing must be allowed so the gradually expanding clumps do not crowd each other and their expansive root system has room to develop.

Because each plant develops its own system of rhizomes, roots, and culms, which requires a decade or so to fully mature, radically increasing planting density does not establish a mature grove that much more rapidly. However, since the grove's canopy helps create its own beneficial, moderating environment, provides its own carpet of mulch, and so forth, there is some benefit in planting somewhat more densely to create this environment more quickly. Plants that are larger than common nursery stock will fill the gaps faster and more rapidly establish mature rhizome and culm systems, thus reducing the time to grove maturity.

Other factors can also affect decisions on planting density. For example, if the grove will be harvested prior to achieving full maturity, it may be desirable to increase the planting density so that the gaps between the plants are filled by the time of the first anticipated harvest. Some applications require an "instant landscape," in which no time is allocated for development and growth. The plants are installed like pieces of turf (which they essentially are), abutting each other. Most leptomorph bamboos, whether dwarf or timber, lend themselves to such treatment, creating an instant ground carpet, screen, or grove.

Sources

The American Bamboo Society (ABS) produces a yearly list of all species and forms of bamboo for sale in the United States, including brief descriptions, names and addresses of the bamboo nurseries that sell them, and notes on whether the plants are available by mail or locally. New members automatically receive a copy of the listing. The listing is also available on the ABS web site at http://www.bamboo .org/abs/. For membership information, see the ABS web site or the section on the American Bamboo Society in chapter 7 of this book.

Bamboo plants are available in a wide range of sizes from a variety of sources. Larger plants are often available from local bamboo nurseries and non-specialist nurseries. An extensive selection of species and forms are available by mail through specialist bamboo nurseries, but the plants are necessarily smaller than what might be available locally.

Local nurseries. The bamboo plants available through non-specialist nurseries are typically the more commonly available varieties, such as *Phyllostachys aurea* (golden bamboo), or a generic groundcover bamboo, often a species of *Pleioblastus,* sometimes generically labeled *Sasa pygmaea, Arundinaria pygmaea,* or perhaps even labeled (sometimes correctly) *Pleioblastus pygmaeus.* Prices at non-specialist nurseries are often substantially higher than prices at specialist bamboo nurseries. A search of non-specialist nurseries can, nevertheless, be worthwhile. Although the more commonly available bamboos may be of less interest to the hobbyist or collector, they are still beautiful and rewarding plants.

A much greater variety of bamboo may be available through local bamboo nurseries. Groundcover and small bamboos are commonly sold in 1- or 2-gallon containers. Medium-sized and timber bamboos are typically sold in 3- to 10-gallon containers. Ideally, the plants will be large enough to immediately look good in the landscape, sufficiently robust to rapidly generate new growth, and small enough for relatively easy vehicle transportation. Some bamboo nurseries specialize in large specimen plants and can deliver and install them as part of their sales and service.

Although a single timber bamboo seedling can eventually produce a towering forest, several decades may be required. Bamboo grows very rapidly, but small plants may still require many years to fill a landscaping need. If cost and transportation concerns are not prohibitive, larger plants can have an immediate landscaping impact and may be capable of generating substantial new growth.

Local nurseries may also sell field-dug plants wrapped in burlap. If plant quality is good, this can be an economical way to obtain many new plants for rapidly establishing a grove or large landscape planting.

Mail order. Mail-order bamboo nurseries are excellent sources for acquiring less common or hard-to-find species and forms. In general, however, the plants are smaller, and when shipping is added, the prices may be higher than for locally purchased plants. For the hobbyist or collector, or where bamboo is not readily available locally, mail-order nurseries are a welcome source.

Because some destinations require plants to be shipped soil free, some nurseries may ship all plants without soil. Plants shipped in this manner weigh less, but are less stable than plants shipped in the same container and soil in which they have been growing. Plants acquired from mail-order nurseries cannot be examined and evaluated before purchase. The nursery's reputation and past experience are the only guides to quality. As might be expected, some nurseries are better than others. I have purchased many excellent plants from mail-order nurseries and have only occasionally been disappointed in the quality of the material.

Sales and auctions. The American Bamboo Society and its local chapters hold bamboo auctions and sales. Species new to the United States and other less common bamboos are often first available at the auctions. The plant sales are a good place to find a wide variety of bamboos at a moderate price from enthusiastic and knowledgeable growers. Plant sales are also an important source of revenue for the American Bamboo Society and its chapters, funding new bamboo introductions, publications, workshops, and research.

Evaluating plants for purchase

When buying plants locally, careful examination will help you choose the best stock. For best growth potential, the rhizomes, roots, culms, and foliage must be in balance. If one element is weak, new growth will be diminished or delayed.

Appearance. Unlike many other plants, the current aesthetics of a bamboo plant are much less important than its ability to generate new growth. A tree, for example, generally retains its basic shape for many years, perhaps throughout its life. When purchasing a tree for the landscape, its shape and aesthetics are a prime consideration. New bamboo culms, however, are generated every year. In a developing grove, the new culms will be larger and more attractive than the previous year's culms. Older culms are periodically removed from the grove. In most instances, a buyer will want to choose a bamboo plant based on growth potential rather than current aesthetics. Ideally, of course, a plant with maximum growth potential that also looks good is the best of all.

Rhizome and root system. If feasible, look at the rhizome and root system. Particularly for leptomorph bamboos, but for pachymorph bamboos as well, the rhizome system is an excellent indicator of potential growth. Large, vigorous rhizomes with a healthy creamy yellow coloration (where not covered by sheathing) and similarly colored, healthy, bright creamy yellow buds indicate a robust plant capable of generating vigorous new growth. Healthy buds look bright and plump; avoid plants with rhizomes and buds that are dull brown. Plants with a large, vigorous rhizome system will be capable of generating larger and more numerous culms, and supporting the dramatic growth for which bamboo is known, whereas a plant with a feeble rhizome system will be incapable of generating vigorous growth.

Beware of large culms with small rhizome and root systems. These plants may be newly dug, less stable, and incapable of sustaining growth commensurate with the size of the existing culms. On the other hand, the larger culms may be immediately useful in the landscape. If the plant has been in the container for several weeks or more and looks healthy, it may be a good choice, depending on cost, buyer needs, and expectations. For leptomorph bamboos, a root ball that fills the container, and rhizomes circling the perimeter, indicate a plant that is well established and easily capable of sustaining existing culms and generating vigorous new growth.

If soil readily falls away from the roots and rhizomes, the bamboo may have been recently dug and potted. Such a plant may be excellent stock, but its stability will not yet have been established. Keep in mind, however, that some soil mixes for container bamboos are purposely coarsely textured and

Right: A healthy, vigorous, bright creamy yellow rhizome bud. Dull brown rhizome buds are usually not viable and are incapable of generating new growth. This healthy rhizome bud has already begun shooting.

loose. This type of soil will have a tendency to fall away more easily even for established plants.

Culms. Look at the culms, particularly the newest ones. A large, field-dug bamboo may have impressive looking culms, but its rhizome and root system may be incapable of generating culms of equal size. New shoots or culms that have been generated since the bamboo was potted show the plant's current capability. New, fully extended culms are the best indicators. A shoot with an impressive diameter may not develop fully if the reserves in the rhizome system are exhausted before growth can be completed. If this is the case, the shoot may abort and not develop into a culm (also common and normal in established groves for some of the later emerging shoots) or the culm may have compressed internodes and rapidly taper to a short final height. If new growth is modest or weak, look for a better plant.

Judging the capability of a bamboo plant is easiest after the bamboo has been potted and the period of new culm growth has been completed. If the ability to generate new, vigorous growth is paramount, seek out plants that have generated the most vigorous new culm growth since the plant has been potted. In this context, the size and number of the older culms is largely irrelevant, unless they fulfill an immediate landscaping need.

Foliage. If a plant is being selected for its growth potential, foliage is much less of a concern than the rhizome system or the number and vigor of new culms, but as the energy-generating mechanism for the plant, foliage leaves should not be completely ignored. Rhizomes (and culms, particularly for pachymorph bamboos) are the food-storage repositories that make the intense period of dramatic culm growth possible, in addition to fulfilling other immediate needs of the plant, including the generation of new foliage leaves, but it is the foliage leaves that generate the food and energy for ongoing needs and for storage of any reserves.

Usually, adequate foliage comes automatically with the other factors in the selection process. For example, if a plant is selected because of its many vigorous new culms, a vigorous and extensive foliage canopy is already assured. For maximum growth potential, if there is a choice between two plants with equal rhizome systems (and new culm growth, depending on the season), choose the plant with the most leaf area.

If an immediate landscaping need must be met, however, a different choice may be warranted. For example, if one plant has the most foliage area, but is bushy in form, and a statelier look is immediately needed, a taller plant may be a better choice even though it may have less leaf area.

Inability to generate new growth. Although uncommon, particularly when purchasing from reliable sources, it is nevertheless possible to have a healthy looking plant that is incapable of generating new growth. One typically encounters this when a bamboo plant has been propagated, and the propagule does not have viable rhizome buds to generate new rhizomes or culms.

If the shooting season is over but no new culms have been generated, the plant may never be capable of generating new culms—or the plant may still shoot late in the current season, or may be directing growth to the rhizome and root system. In any case, the plant is, at best, diminished in its ability to generate new growth rapidly, and a different plant should be selected, if available.

Examine the rhizome system for plump, bright creamy yellow buds that indicate the ability to generate new growth. A new rhizome also indicates that the plant is viable and will be capable of generating new culms during the next shooting season (or, sometimes, delayed culms during the current season). If both the shooting season and the season for new rhizome growth have passed, and there are neither new culms nor new rhizomes, avoid the plant. It may never be capable of generating new growth.

Harvesting

Harvesting shoots

Harvesting methods vary widely. Ideally, one would employ a method that would, with the most rapid speed, least effort, and without waste or damage, garner the highest quality, best tasting shoots. In practice, these elements are somewhat in conflict, and some degree of compromise is required. Speed is clearly a factor if one is harvesting a grove commercially. On the other hand, if you are a gardener and have decided to "sacrifice" a precious shoot or two for your table, high-speed harvesting methods are hardly a concern.

So, when and how should you harvest a shoot? Shoots become increasingly tough and less sweet tasting the longer they are out of the soil and the taller they grow. The better bamboos for shoot harvesting are excellent when young and tender, and they still remain good even if they are somewhat tall or have been out of the ground for some time. The least good species are marginal from the start, and stretching the limits with them will not likely result in a fine culinary experience.

Some cultures, however, prefer astringent shoots for some cuisine, so in this context, the preferred species and harvest times would be different. The maximum preferred shoot height for tender, sweet shoots is not a constant but is proportional to the diameter of the shoot. Yet, a strict ratio of height to diameter is not appropriate either, as what would be a suitable ratio for a tiny shoot would be out of line for a giant timber bamboo.

For the commercial producer, economics plays a role in determining when to harvest, since yields are higher when harvest is delayed. When harvesting shoots from the garden or landscape, compromise is also the rule, balancing quality with yield. For practical purposes, shoots are typically harvested after they have emerged from the ground, but before they are out too long and have toughened. If a new shoot would provide a desired new culm for expansion or increased density of a screen or hedge, it may be best to resist its role at the table. On the other hand, smaller shoots, or those that appear where a culm is not needed in the landscape, are excellent candidates for harvest.

The best way to get a feel and understanding for harvesting shoots is to do it. As a very broad rule of thumb, unless you are harvesting giant timber bamboos, harvest shoots when they have been out of the ground for no more than a week or so, and when they are no more than 8 in. (20 cm) tall (preferably shorter). This is just a starting point. Explore freely with the species in your grove or garden. Sometimes, premium shoots are harvested before they emerge from the ground, or soil or mulch is mounded on top of the emerging shoot to keep it "in the ground" longer. These may be regarded as specialized techniques, rather than general harvesting practice.

Shoots grow rapidly and should be checked often to make sure they are harvested at the optimal time. If you are harvesting a grove, the shoots should be checked and harvested daily, if possible. Shoots can be harvested by grasping the shoot at its very base, penetrating the

A *Phyllostachys vivax* shoot ready for harvest.

soil with your fingertips slightly, then rocking the shoot back and forth and twisting a bit until the shoot snaps free. Although this works well enough, some of the edible portion of the shoot is left behind. Severing the shoot below ground to get more of the edible portion is usually a better idea. If the shoot is small, a knife, a sharp digging tool, or other similar instrument can be used. Except for the protective culm leaves, the shoot should be quite tender. I have used a cheap, stainless steel kitchen knife for the purpose, as well as a sharpened cultivating knife of the kind that is sold at garden stores for digging in the soil. The shoots of pachymorph bamboos are generally severed just above the buds that will produce the new culms. Leptomorph bamboo shoots should be severed at the base of the shoot, above the neck, where the flesh is tender and not tough.

Larger shoots are best harvested with tools that one uses standing up, using two hands and possibly a foot to plunge the tool into the soil. This is also the preferred method when speed in harvesting a grove is a factor. In traditional bamboo shoot harvesting cultures, the tool may take the form of a rectangular blade that is a linear extension of the handle, or a narrow triangular blade affixed similarly. A narrow, western garden spade with a square blade is an alternative. Narrow-bladed tools that can be plunged into the soil are particularly useful with tightly clumping pachymorph bamboos, where the digging space may be quite confining. Another traditional alternative is a hoe-like tool with a long narrow blade. This is best suited to leptomorph bamboos where there is sufficient space to dig, and where damage to nearby rhizomes and buds is less of a threat.

See the section "Eating Bamboo" in chapter 6 of this book for information on how to prepare shoots for the table.

Harvesting culms

Culms should be harvested with a saw, never with a hatchet or ax. A hatchet or ax will

A large *Dendrocalamus asper* shoot. Quail Botanical Gardens.

damage the culm that is being harvested, risk damage to nearby culms and rhizomes, and leave jagged stubs that are unaesthetic and threaten injury. The culms of leptomorph bamboos should be sawed, flat across, near their base, minimizing "stumps" that are not only unsightly, but also troublesome or even dangerous protuberances that can trip a worker or damage machinery. To guard against rot, culms of tropical pachymorph bamboos are usually sawed higher, always above a node, at up to 8 in. (20 cm) or more above ground. Any medium- to fine-toothed saw is suitable for the task. Very narrow blades work well when the culms are crowded close together, but the narrow blades tend to bend and kink more easily. Somewhat wider blades are preferable when one has the space to use them.

There are many schemes for determining the proportion and age of the culms to be harvested. In general, clear-cutting is not recommended for either pachymorph or leptomorph bamboos, as it weakens the bamboo and inhibits re-growth.

Dendrocalamus giganteus. Quail Botanical Gardens.

In Orissa, a state in India where clear-cutting *Bambusa bambos* is a common local practice, the groves are incapable of producing full-sized culms again until 10 years after clear-cutting, a significant loss of productivity (Tewari 1992). Culms less than three years old should not be harvested when quality culm wood is desired. For some bamboos, additional age, up to seven years or so, may yield even stronger culms. Most commercial harvesting practices target culms that are not much more than three years old.

Although culms can be taken at any time during the year, some seasons are better than others. In traditional cultures, harvesting regimens have evolved based on practical experience with native bamboos. In Java, culms are harvested in the "old season," a period roughly corresponding to the months of January through June. During this period, particularly in May, the starch content of the Javanese bamboos is at its lowest. This is important for two reasons. The dreaded powder post beetles are less likely to attack the culms when the starch content is low. Secondly, the new culms, having depleted the starch reserves in the mother culms for their rapid period of growth, are no longer dependent on the (now nearly nonexistent) energy stores of the mother culms. If the mother culms were harvested during the shooting and growth period, energy stores would be diminished, and growth would suffer.

In general, the culm harvest period is more critical for tropical pachymorph bamboos than for temperate leptomorph bamboos. The tropical bamboos are at great risk of powder post beetle attack, and bamboos with a pachymorph rhizome system are generally more dependent on starch reserves in the culms to support new growth; leptomorph bamboos have a network of rhizomes for energy storage. Bamboo culms are best harvested after the period of new growth has been completed. Leptomorph bamboos have a period of rhizome growth that follows culm growth. For most leptomorph bamboos, the period of rhizome growth ends in late fall, the time when the culm harvest usually begins.

Methods for curing bamboo culms are quite varied. Before drying, tropical bamboos are sometimes submerged in water to remove as much starch as possible and reduce the risk of powder post beetle attack, and the culms may be subject to a variety of chemical preservative processes. Such measures are of little concern in most of the continental United States, but may be germane to gardeners and growers in Hawaii and southern Florida.

To assist the drying process, the leaves can be left on the culm until they wither. Experiments have shown that, as the culm dries and cures, it loses 4 to 16 percent in wall thickness and 3 to 12 percent in diameter (Tewari 1992). The culms should be stored so that they are not bent by their own weight.

CHAPTER 4

Propagation

SOME FORM OF VEGETATIVE PROPAGATION is generally the method of choice for establishing and distributing bamboo plant materials. Since most bamboos flower infrequently and unpredictably, one cannot simply buy a packet of seed from the neighborhood nursery. The millions of acres of *Phyllostachys heterocycla* f. *pubescens* forests provide readily available quantities of seed in China, but for practical purposes, in most places and for most bamboos, it is not possible to obtain seed on demand. In fact, many decades may pass before seed for a particular bamboo becomes available. In most instances, ongoing commercial propagation of plant stock from seed is not only impractical, but also impossible. Growing bamboo from seed may be a necessity, however, to replace a grove that is weakened or dying from flowering. This is most prominently a concern for pachymorph bamboos.

Propagating from Seed

Although propagation from seed is a serendipitous method that cannot be relied upon as a predictable source (except for the few bamboos that flower annually or continuously), it nevertheless can be an occasional windfall source of numerous small propagules and can provide the opportunity to obtain interesting variants that would be impossible with the normal means of vegetative propagation. Seed propagation plays a role in developing selections with desirable characteristics for future vegetative propagation. For the gardener, there is something special and magical in growing a plant from seed, whether it is a garden vegetable, a tree, or bamboo. Since bamboo seed is so rare, the opportunity to grow bamboo from seed is all the more special. I find it very satisfying to grow bamboo from seed and am always glad when the opportunity is presented.

In general, bamboos exhibit significant polymorphism, and openly pollinated wild plants often show considerable diversity in the plant material generated from seed. The degree of polymorphism varies, as some species are quite stable, exhibiting little variation in seedling populations, whereas others exhibit significant variation. From the standpoint of survival and evolution, polymorphism helps ensure continuous adaptation in response to changing environments. Apart from variations in gross morphology and readily observable characteristics, molecular markers in DNA, enzymes, and metabolites reveal polymorphic variations that can be correlated with characteristics not readily apparent in seedlings, thus offering the prospect of greater refinement in the selection of desirable propagules—at least in the research and development laboratory, if not for the average gardener.

The flowering of bamboo is not a guarantee that viable seeds will be produced. For example, *Phyllostachys heterocycla* f. *pubescens,* which flowers at intervals of about every 50 to 60 years, has a pollination rate of less than 10 percent. It is wind pollinated, but its flower structure is such that it pollinates only with difficulty. Broadly speaking, Old World pachymorph bamboos ripen about 15 to 30 days after pollination, whereas leptomorph bamboos, such as *P. heterocycla* f. *pubescens,* take longer, from 50 to 70 days (Tewari 1992). When ripe, the seeds fall to the ground.

Reportedly, a few bamboos, such as some *Sasa* and some tropical herbaceous bamboos, may take up to a year to germinate. Seeds from one species of *Fargesia* remained viable after five years in the soil. Some Himalayan bamboos, among others, have a dormant period and may require a period of cold before germinating. *Himalayacalamus hookerianus* seed, for example, needs a dormant period of one to eight months under temperate conditions before germinating, although a period of cold may reduce the dormant period.

The preceding germination behaviors are more exceptions than they are the rule, however. Most bamboo seed has no dormant period and maintains viability less well than common seed grains. Without special measures, some seeds must be afforded the opportunity to germinate in the same year they are produced, otherwise germination may not occur. Generally, bamboo seeds germinate within two to three weeks. *Chusquea coronalis,* a species with very small seeds, can germinate in less than a week. Fresh seed germinates more quickly than seed that has been

stored. Some bamboo seed can be harvested and germinated even if the surrounding bracts are still green and the seed is still tightly affixed, but as a general
rule, seeds are mature and ready for germination when they can be shaken from
the plant.

At maturity, the germination rate of *Phyllostachys heterocycla* f. *pubescens* is about
50 percent, dropping to as low as 10 percent within six months. At eight months,
if the seed is kept at room temperature, the germination rate drops to near 0 percent (Yat et al. 1984). Cold temperatures permit somewhat longer storage with a
higher rate of germination, and special preservation methods can extend viability
to more than three years. Some tropical bamboos, such as species of *Melocanna*,
produce a fleshy fruit rather than a seed grain (caryopsis) typical of most grasses.
The fleshy fruits do not lend themselves to long-term storage, however, so seed
propagation from these species is even more problematic.

In natural conditions, many seed are dispersed in a way that is ill suited to effective germination, and the seeds and new seedlings are subject to attack by all
manner of rodents, insects, birds, slugs, snails, and other beasts of the wild. Greenhouse conditions offer a much higher rate of germination and survival.

Seed propagation requirements vary among species, but as a general practice,
the seed should be planted as soon as possible after maturity. The definition of
maturity, in this context, means viability. Some bamboos, such as *Phyllostachys*,
require the seed to be fully ripened before harvest, particularly if the seed is not
planted immediately. The seed of other bamboos, such as *Sasa, Indocalamus,* and
Pleioblastus, can be successfully harvested and planted even if not fully mature, although the seed will retain viability longer if it is more completely ripened. In
general, seed is ripe when it can be easily removed from the plant by light pressure,
bumping, or wind. Seed can be harvested by hand, or by placing a sheet or tarp beneath the plant and shaking the culms. Chaff can be removed with a hand blower
or fan.

For most bamboos, the soil should be a slightly acidic, loose, moisture-retain-
ing, readily draining mixture. Commercially available potting soils suit the purpose
well, as do many self-mixed soils, such as a composition of half vermiculite and
half peat moss. At planting, the seed should be covered with ⅛ to ¼ in. (0.3 to 0.6
cm) of soil and keep moist. The pots or seed trays can be covered with transparent
plastic or placed in a plastic bag. On a small scale, for even greater reliability and
control, seeds can be layered in moist paper towels and placed in a plastic bag,
then transferred to soil, in small pots, after they sprout. For germination, the seeds
should be kept in a warm, bright environment, but shielded from intense sun-

light or other withering light source. When the seedlings are several inches tall, they should be gradually hardened by increasingly exposing them to more natural conditions. Until they reach maturity, young plants will be more sensitive to extremes of heat and cold and should be shielded accordingly.

Bamboo nurseryman Gib Cooper and his partners were largely responsible for the American reintroduction of *Phyllostachys heterocycla* f. *pubescens* via seed propagation. A brief summary of their propagation efforts illustrates some of the methods and results. Propagation was facilitated by soaking the seeds in warm water for 24 hours prior to planting in a loose, humus-rich soil. At temperatures between 68 and 78°F (20–26°C), the seeds began germinating within a week. The first leaves appeared in 21 days. At about the time the seedlings put out their third leaf, approximately a quarter of the seedlings yellowed and died. It is speculated that this mortality occurs at the transition from dependency on the seed to support from the emerging root system. If the seed was not sufficiently mature or is otherwise deficient, the seed may cease providing critical nutrients before the seedling's root system is fully ready to assume that role.

Seed propagation is sometimes used in afforestation projects in China. After a year, when the seedlings are about 1 to 1½ ft. (30 to 46 cm) tall, they are transplanted. The success rate is high, but a new grove or forest cannot be established nearly as quickly as would be the case if the propagules came from culm and rhizome divisions rather than seedlings. Keeping the seedlings in a nursery until they are 3 to 6 ft. (about 1 to 2 m) tall speeds growth, but also defeats some of the purpose and benefit of seed propagation.

Seedling variations

New plants grown from the seeds of cultivars will generally reflect the characteristics of the type form, rather than the cultivar. Seedlings from cultivars with variegated leaves or differently colored culms, for example, will generally revert to the green culms and leaves of the type form. On the other hand, flowering affords the opportunity of discovering variants with properties different than the type form. Out of many hundreds of seedlings, some may display leaf variegation, unusual culm coloration, exceptional vigor, different growth habit, or any manner of other characteristics. Sometimes these characteristics will appear in a young seedling, only to disappear as the seedling matures. In other instances, these characteristics may not be apparent until the seedling has achieved some maturity.

The seedlings of some species, such as *Otatea acuminata* ssp. *aztecorum*, exhibit very little variation. Others, such as species of *Phyllostachys*, tend to exhibit much more variation, although one may propagate hundreds of seedlings before encountering a variation of significant note, such as leaf variegation or differences in culm color. Sometimes one encounters a much greater frequency of variation—and not always for the better. I once planted a small number of *P. flexuosa* seeds, and well over 10 percent of them were albinos. They were rather striking for a short time, while the seed provided the nutrients for growth, but the absence of chlorophyll ensured a rapid demise.

Desirable variations are a matter of context. Variations may be particularly undesirable in a commercial forest, for example, and in such instances, vegetative propagation assures that new plants will have the same qualities as the mother plant. In China's bamboo reforestation projects, variegated *Phyllostachys heterocycla* f. *pubescens* seedlings are inherently weaker performers and subject to discard, but the better of the variegated plants may be highly desirable ornamentals. The flowering of *Fargesia murielae* in the 1990s gave rise to a number of named variations, including some that were small, slow growing, and weak. Some of the named variations may be of presumptuous merit. On the other hand, a small, weak, slow-growing cultivar might be the ideal plant for a rock garden or similar application.

Seedlings of leptomorph bamboos tend to recapitulate a clumping habit in their early stages of growth. Duration varies. *Sasa tsuboiana,* for example, rapidly displays a running habit, extending leptomorph rhizomes very early in the seedling stage and producing many new culms from lateral buds on the rhizomes. *Sasa kurilensis,* in contrast, initially displays more of a clumping habit with limited lateral expansion.

Hybridization

The lengthy flowering intervals of most bamboos greatly reduce the opportunities for hybridization. The likelihood that two or more species will flower at the same time in the same location is very small and, thus, so is the likelihood of hybridization, either naturally or through conventional breeding programs. Although hybridization from cross-pollination is not easy and is out of the realm of the average gardener, it has been successful. Chinese researchers have produced viable crosses in *Bambusa, Phyllostachys,* and *Dendrocalamus.* Most bamboos flower very infrequently, but China's extensive and widely dispersed groves, with varying flowering cycles, offer an ongoing supply of propagation material. Although flowering usually takes place from February through June, it can occur at any time during the year. Maintaining pollen viability while awaiting flowering of another species is problematic, though more refined storage methods ensure sufficient viability.

Bamboos exhibit few barriers when attempting to cross genera or species. Those that are more similar in their genetics and ecological needs hybridize most successfully, while less similar bamboos are more difficult to successfully cross. In one trial, *Bambusa pervariabilis,* a pachymorph bamboo, was crossed with *P. heterocycla* f. *pubescens,* a leptomorph bamboo. Of 12,000 flowers pollinated, only 34 seedlings were produced, and none was regarded as desirable (Zhang and Chen 1985). Other crosses have produced more promising results. A cross of *Bambusa pervariabilis* and *Dendrocalamus latiflorus,* two similar pachymorph bamboos, produced a high-yielding hybrid with long fibers ideal for papermaking. Once hybrids are selected for further development, they can be propagated vegetatively, thus preserving their genetic mix and desirable characteristics.

Natural and artificial hybridizations of other grasses have played a major role in their evolution and commercial development. Selective breeding programs have produced high-yielding grain crops and increased food production. Hybrids of bamboo and rice displayed widely varying characteristics, but all possessed a strong stalk (Zhang and Ma 1991). Using molecular techniques and genetic mapping, selective breeding of bamboos and rices could one day yield a new and important food crop.

Successful trials have been conducted with *in vitro* induction of flowering in several tropical bamboo species. In this process, bamboo tissue is cultured in a test tube or other vessel, then induced to flower. Although there are limitations, *in vitro* induction of flowering can greatly compress generational cycles, creating the potential for the relatively rapid development of new species and forms.

Hybridizing efforts are generally directed toward developing bamboos with enhanced commercial properties, such as greater productivity, resistance to pests, long fibers for pulping, better taste and enhanced nutritional content of shoots, and so forth. Although variegated forms are appealing from an aesthetic and landscaping standpoint, they are regarded as weaker than the non-variegated forms and are generally eliminated during the selection processes.

Vegetative Propagation

For the farmer, nursery grower, and hobbyist, vegetative propagation is by far the most common method of bamboo propagation. Several methods of vegetative propagation may be employed. Each has its own strengths and shortcomings.

A bamboo plant must have a viable bud to generate a new culm or new rhizome. It is possible to vegetatively propagate a healthy plant that has no viable buds, and is therefore incapable of producing new culms and rhizomes, but a fully successful propagule must be capable of generating them. Although some species of leptomorph bamboos can generate new culms from the basal buds of existing culms, the rhizome is the only permanent source of new culms and rhizomes. A propagule that subsequently generates a new rhizome can be considered fully successful.

If a propagule fails to produce either a new culm or new rhizome for a second year, it is unlikely that it ever will. Although unusual, a propagule may fail to shoot for two years in a row, yet still be viable, as long as new rhizome growth occurs during that time. With care in propagation, creation of fully successful propagules need not be a concern, unless one is forced by circumstances to use marginal material with questionable bud viability.

As with other plants, somatic mutations sometimes occur—that is, occasionally a new bamboo culm may show characteristics that differ from the rest of the plant it came from. If the mutated portion of the plant is propagated, sometimes the mutation is sufficiently stable that it will survive ongoing propagation. Although quite infrequent, constant vigilance may uncover new cultivars with desirable characteristics.

Culm and rhizome divisions

Propagating by division is by far the most common and reliable method for increasing bamboo stock. A culm or culms with associated rhizomes and roots is separated from an existing clump or grove. Because the new propagule is already a complete plant, the success rate of this propagation method is very high, particularly for leptomorph bamboos. Some pachymorph bamboos need a division that includes two or more culms and associated rhizomes to achieve a high success rate.

Failure can occur if the foliage area is greatly out of proportion to the rhizome and roots, as moisture is lost through the leaves. The amount of foliage that can be retained is in direct proportion to the root system and its ability to supply moisture to the leaves. In extreme situations, all leaves may be removed, keeping the plant alive until the root system recovers sufficiently to permit the plant to send out new leaves again. The plant will regulate itself and send out new leaves in proportion to the root system's ability to support the leaves. In such a situation, however, the balance is tenuous, and the plant must be protected from any increased stress. The root system nearly always experiences some damage when plant divisions are taken, but recovery is relatively swift, and the root system will have significant growth in four to six weeks.

Excessive foliage can be reduced by topping the culms, removing some culms from the propagule, pruning branches, or thinning the leaves. Excessive foliage is more likely to be a problem in sunny, hot conditions. The leaves are the plant's primary source of food, however, and the most vigorous growth is realized when the maximum possible foliage is retained. Unbalanced transpiration can also be countered with commercial anti-transpiration sprays. These treatments reduce transpiration, thereby permitting retention of significantly more foliage than would otherwise be possible. Bamboos treated with anti-transpiration sprays should still be kept in partially shaded conditions to prevent leaf browning.

If producing the most new culms possible is the goal, rather than larger if fewer new culms, topping the propagule will encourage more shooting from otherwise latent buds. Partly to ensure a stable propagule, partly to ease mobility, and partly to generate more new shoots, bamboo growers sometimes top propagules to a height of only 3 ft. (1 m) for a 5-gallon (19-liter) container. Practices and preferences vary.

The propagule should be observed for signs of stress. Leaf curl in an adequately watered plant is the most readily apparent stress indicator. Remember, however, that a few bamboos normally curl their leaves in sunlight and uncurl them in the shade, so the propagule's behavior should be compared with the normal behavior of the mother plant. If the propagule experiences only moderate leaf curl during the day and rapidly recovers at night, foliage reduction may not be necessary, unless the plant is expected to experience additional stress, or unless ongoing monitoring is not possible.

If the propagule is stressed and the weather is unusually sunny, hot, or windy, shade and shelter from the wind may be warranted until the root system of the plant has developed enough to more adequately support the foliage. Misting the leaves, moving the plants to a humid greenhouse environment, spraying the leaves with an anti-transpirant, or wetting the leaves and temporarily wrapping the foliage in clear or opaque plastic are additional methods that may be employed. If necessary, topping or partial branch or leaf removal are methods of foliage reduction that can be brought into play to balance the plant.

Although single-culm divisions require slightly more care and caution than multiple-culm divisions, success is routine, and they have the advantage of generating the most new plants from an existing clump or grove. Naturally, if size and vigor of new growth are paramount, a multiple-culm division is preferable. Single-culm divisions usually work well with pachymorph bamboos as well as leptomorph bamboos, though a few pachymorph bamboos, such as *Bambusa textilis,* require a "mother and daughter," two-culm division for best success.

If the rhizome and root system is proportionally large compared to the foliage area, new growth may not be as rapid, but the propagule will be in no danger of failure. Depending on the season, the propagule may attempt to balance itself by sending up new culm shoots—or the tip of a rhizome growing near the surface may turn upward and become a new culm.

Ideally, the propagule's rhizomes should be no more than a few years old and at peak potential for generating new culms and rhizomes. According to bamboo nurseryman Adam Turtle, with a typical *Phyllostachys* rhizome, about 10 percent of the buds in the first 1 to 2 ft. (30 to 60 cm) of rhizome growth from the previous summer and fall will be mature the following spring. In each of the subsequent years, an additional 30 to 40 percent of the buds will mature. By the fifth year, new buds mature only sporadically.

Propagation by division of culm and rhizome is best done just before active bud growth and the initiation of shooting. Division should be avoided during the period of active bud growth and shoot initiation and while the new culms are extending, branching, and leafing. Divisions of leptomorph bamboos can be made successfully during all other times of the year that the bamboo is not suffering undue stress. If divisions are made too near shoot initiation, the new shoots may fail to grow properly and may abort. As a general rule, it is best not to make divisions immediately following the shooting period, as nutrient reserves will be depleted, and division additionally stresses the plant. However, I routinely violate this rule with container-grown plants with no overt negative effect.

A division from a very large plant will not be likely to support similar-sized culms the following year because of its reduced rhizome and root system. The propagule will regulate itself as necessary, and it may produce new culms that are smaller in diameter than the mother plant, or produce culms with compressed internodes and reduced height. Divisions from small to moderately large bamboos, however, will generate new culms that are generally in the size range of the mother plant and produce an attractive and functional propagule.

Macroproliferation of bamboo seedlings is a specialized type of culm and rhizome division. At the seedling stage, both pachymorph and leptomorph bamboos exhibit a clumping habit, forming a cluster of miniature culms, rhizomes, and roots. Divisions can readily be made by separating the cluster into separate portions, permitting additional growth, then separating the clusters once again. With skill and familiarity, success can approach 100 percent, and a geometric increase in the number of propagules can readily be realized. Because the multiplied seedlings are clones, they will tend to flower at the same time as the mother plant. If macro-

Making field divisions of a *Fargesia* species. Although a sharp-edged garden spade can be used to make the divisions, specialized tools make the task easier. Here, a section has been severed from the perimeter of the clump by a tool affectionately known as "The Pink Slammer."

The soil has been removed from this *Fargesia* division, revealing the mass of roots and rhizomes. Examining the division by sight and feel, smaller divisions are identified and severed from the mass.

proliferation is carried out over a number of years with the same clone, the time between division and flowering decreases. Taken to its extreme, a macroproliferated plant could flower before it reached maturity and commercial viability. For practical purposes, this would only become a significant concern if macroproliferation from the same clone were carried out over many years with a species having a relatively short flowering cycle.

Pachymorph bamboos. Creating divisions from pachymorph bamboos, particularly a mature clump of a large species with a caespitose habit, can be difficult. Short rhizomes and tightly packed clumps do not make the job of cutting away sections for propagules easy. The difficulty of breaking apart old clumps is illustrated by the occasional agricultural practice of dynamiting the clumps in lieu of hand labor. The urban or suburban gardener, however, runs the risk of irritating unsympathetic neighbors, and dynamiting cannot be recommended as a general practice. Dynamiting may not be warranted in any case, since the inner culms

This bamboo division has already begun to shoot, and ideally, the divisions should have been made earlier. Propagating now may disturb the plant's delicate balance, possibly causing the shoot to abort and the propagule to fail. Note that this propagule also has a new rhizome that has not yet developed into a shoot. The propagule may also have viable rhizome buds. Even if the elongated shoot aborts, other shoots may develop.

The propagule is placed in a container and the roots are covered with soil.

and rhizomes of an old clump are generally too old to propagate effectively and significant damage is inevitable.

Divisions of pachymorph bamboos are best taken from the periphery of the clump. The culms and rhizomes are generally younger at the periphery, and thus more likely to produce viable propagules. There is also far less congestion of culms and rhizomes inhibiting access and division. When severing a propagule of a pachymorph bamboo from the mother plant, the cut should be made at the narrow rhizome neck. Methods vary, but the propagule's culm or culms are typically reduced to about 6 ft. (2 m) in height.

Dividing large pachymorph bamboos is hardly an easy pleasure. Various methods employ a jackhammer with a blade tip, heavy-duty reciprocating saw, chain saw, and so forth. Sometimes a tractor or a small-scale construction loader and lifter are used to dig a trench around the clump and then push or lift a side of the clump to expose the rhizomes and the culm and rhizome necks. For small clumps or container-grown pachymorph bamboos, the principle is the same but the execution is far easier.

Large pachymorph bamboos with long rhizome necks and a diffuse habit can also be a problem. Although congested clumps are seldom an issue, a viable division comprising a culm, roots, and a rhizome may extend 5 to 20 ft. (1.5 to 6 m) or more, becoming unwieldy at best, and certainly not lending itself to container culture. Most of the more extreme examples are tropical bamboos seldom encountered in the United States.

Leptomorph bamboos. Creating divisions from leptomorph bamboos is relatively easy. The rhizome can be severed anywhere along its length, rather than at the neck, as with pachymorph bamboos. If the culm or culms are near the end of the rhizome, only one cut may be needed. If the culm or culms are removed from mid-length along the rhizome, two cuts to the rhizome will be required. Divisions can be made by plunging a sharp spade or digging tool to a depth of 1 ft. (30 cm) or so around the circumference of the area that will be the new division. The underground path of the rhizome can be ascertained by the placement of the aboveground culms. Culms emerge on alternate sides of the rhizome, and the branching sides of the culms parallel the path of the rhizome. Once the rhizome is identified, the perimeter of the division can be extended to include more of the rhizome and its associated roots. Culms associated with rhizomes that are no more than a few years old ensure propagules with the most vigor and likelihood of producing new culms and rhizomes. Taking divisions from young bamboo on the periphery of a grove ensures that the propagules will include viable and vigorous rhizomes.

The interior of a well-maintained, mature grove will also have many new culms with vigorous and viable rhizomes, but removal will be much more difficult because the rhizomes intertwine to form a dense, barely penetrable mat up to several feet thick. Although the new, viable rhizomes will be closer to the top, separating them from the rest of the rhizome mat is not always easy. In these situations, choose a relatively young culm or culms, then cut through a section of the rhizome mat surrounding it, and lift out the culm or culms with the attached "cake" of rhizomes, roots, and soil. In a thickly matted, mature grove, this task is far from easy, but specialized cutting tools ease the difficulty.

In China, afforestation of *Phyllostachys heterocycla* f. *pubescens* has traditionally been accomplished primarily by culm and rhizome division from existing forests. Healthy, relatively short, two- to three-year-old culms are selected for propagation. Divisions consist of a culm with an attached rhizome about 30 in. (75 cm) in length. Although divisions can be made in fall and winter, spring division is preferable, ideally about one to two months before the start of the shooting period. The divisions are planted at a rate of about 120 to 180 plants per acre (300 to 450 plants per hectare). A "commercially mature" producing forest is achieved in about seven years. With this method, the new plants will be robust and stable, requiring relatively little attention.

Unless one happens to have a Chinese bamboo forest for a backyard, smaller scale growers or gardeners usually have less material available for division, but more time to attend to individual plants. Propagation methods can be modified to reflect these differences by using divisions with shorter rhizomes, and keeping greater leaf area by not topping the divisions, or by topping them less severely. More divisions can be made with shorter rhizome lengths, and greater leaf area will generate faster growth. These plants will be less stable, however, and more attention is required to make sure they remain vigorous. Maintaining an adequate balance between roots, rhizomes, and the leaf area is key to success. Curling leaves are indicators of an out of balance situation that may call for more water or shade or a reduction in leaf area by topping or trimming branches. The most critical periods occur immediately after the divisions are made and during periods of heat and drought.

Rhizomes

Propagation from rhizome sections alone, without any associated culm, is less reliable than culm and rhizome divisions. The rhizome propagules are also initially far less vigorous. Not all species can be successfully propagated from rhizome cuttings. Secondary factors such as soil and time of year are much more critical than in propagation by division of a culm and rhizome unit. To avoid rot, the soil must be well drained and aerated. Taking cuttings too close to shooting interferes with the new growth, but cuttings taken within one or two months prior to shooting help ensure success, since a complete plant is soon formed.

Planting much further ahead of shoot initiation increases the likelihood of rot and failure. Success depends on an adequate store of carbohydrates in the rhizome system. A period of winter cold prior to taking rhizome cuttings causes greater storage of carbohydrates in the rhizomes and improves shoot growth (Adamson et al. 1978). If the rhizomes of leptomorph bamboos are pruned yearly to limit growth, and it is desired to use the rhizomes for propagation material, pruning should be delayed until spring, ideally no more than a month or two prior to the beginning of the shooting period.

Pachymorph bamboos. Rhizomes alone are rarely used to propagate pachymorph bamboos, although it remains an option for some purposes. Observing that small rooted shoots were growing from damaged rhizomes and rhizome fragments that were discarded after making clump divisions of *Bambusa longispiculata*, F. A. McClure constructed a propagation experiment using *Gigantochloa apus* and several species of *Bambusa*. Although the survival rate of the propagules was quite high, the lack of vigor and ability to generate new growth with a robust root system were apparent downsides to the method, as was the threat of rot to the rhizomes (McClure 1966).

In many instances, if one has access to a rooted rhizome suitable for propagation, one also has the option of taking the associated culm as well, topping it, but leaving some foliage, or waiting for the rhizome to develop into a rooted culm, then take the propagule at that time. Both options would offer the likelihood of increased vigor and potential for more rapid growth than would a rhizome alone. However, one might choose to sever the rhizomes to make a compact propagule for ease of transportation and shipping. Also, if rhizomes are severed in the process of creating culm and rhizome divisions, either inadvertently or because they would make the propagule too large, the rhizome pieces offer "extra" propagules. If using a rhizome alone to propagate a pachymorph bamboo, the rhizome should be less than a year old. As with leptomorph rhizomes, pachymorph rhizome propagules must have a developed root system and viable buds.

Leptomorph bamboos. The propagation of leptomorph bamboos via sections of rhizomes is far more viable and common than with pachymorph bamboos.

However, not all species of leptomorph bamboos are amenable to rhizome propagation. Many species of *Phyllostachys* do quite well, but some species of *Sasa, Indocalamus,* and *Arundinaria* propagate poorly from rhizomes (McClure 1966). Leptomorph bamboos with frequent budless rhizome nodes and sparse rhizome roots are less likely to propagate well from rhizome cuttings.

Culm and rhizome division is more reliable and is usually the preferred propagation method. Rhizome cuttings alone can rapidly generate more propagating material, but the propagules will be less well developed. Rhizome cuttings are effective in farming or large-scale nursery operations where covering a large area or generating the most propagules is a prime concern. Rhizome cuttings are com-

A rhizome section from a *Phyllostachys* species. The roots are less developed toward the rhizome tip. A propagule taken from the tip would not be viable. The entire section can be planted in the ground, but if smaller sections are desired, only the portions with developed roots should be used.

A propagule is taken from the larger rhizome section and bent to fit the container. The rhizome will be covered with soil. The normal shooting period for this *Phyllostachys* species begins in about a month. If successful, the propagule will shoot and develop one or more small, bushy culms.

pact and can be readily transported and shipped. Field tests in Alabama indicate that 100 rhizomes, 12 to 15 in. (30 to 38 cm) long, will weigh about 3 to 5 lb. (1.4 to 2.3 kg) each, and under favorable conditions, 50 percent will successfully produce new plants (Sturkie et al. 1968).

For the home grower or landscaper, rhizomes provide an extra source of propagating material. One method for controlling lateral spread of a bamboo grove calls for yearly rhizome pruning. For *Phyllostachys* and other genera of leptomorph bamboos, the new rhizomes on the periphery of a grove lie within the first 6 in. (15 cm) of soil. Lateral spread is controlled by plunging a spade into the soil around the circumference of the desired boundary. Any rhizomes crossing the boundary are severed and pulled from the soil. Those portions that have well-developed roots are suitable for propagating.

For the best success rate, the rhizomes should be no more than a few years old, with vigorous, well-developed roots. The rhizomes, roots, and buds should have a bright, not dark, appearance. Practical and experimental information regarding rhizome length varies, from 6 in. (15 cm) or less to 24 in. (60 cm) or more. Longer rhizomes reduce the number of potential propagules, but with the benefit of a higher success rate and larger and more vigorous new plants. In general, growers of nursery stock may want to use shorter lengths, particularly if the rhizomes are started in pots. Farmers planting in field conditions may tend toward longer lengths.

As much as possible, the rhizomes should be oriented normally in the pot: parallel to the soil surface, with the nodal buds oriented horizontally, covered by 3 to 6 in. (7.5 to 15 cm) of soil, and mulched to protect against cold and moisture loss. If rhizomes are planted too deeply, they may rot before they are able to generate new growth.

For commercial production, rhizomes can be planted end to end in nursery rows, with 3 to 4 ft. (1 to 1.5 m) spacing between the rows. The rhizomes and newly formed culms are divided every one to three years. Some plant material can be left in the nursery beds. The remainder can be transplanted to pots or planted to form a clump or grove. One strategy calls for taking the plants from the original planting rows of rhizomes after the second year, leaving in the ground the culms and rhizomes that were formed between the original rows. The process is then repeated with the newly formed "row" of culms and rhizomes.

Culms or culm segments

McClure (1966) recounts an incident in Jamaica when newly cut culms of *Bambusa vulgaris* were placed in the ground to stake yam vines. The culms subsequently rooted and formed extensive groves. The nodes of many tropical and sub-tropical pachymorph bamboos are capable of forming roots and generating new plants from viable buds. The Jamaican experience is an example of unintentional spread, but culms, culm segments, and even branches can be an effective method of propagation.

Pachymorph bamboos. Most semitropical and tropical bamboos, such as species of *Bambusa*, *Dendrocalamus*, and *Guadua*, can be propagated from culms, culm segments, or branches, though not every species is equally suited to every method. Most, if not all, Old World temperate-climate pachymorph bamboos, including *Fargesia*, *Himalayacalamus*, and *Drepanostachyum*, cannot be propagated by culm or culm segments. Some species of pachymorph bamboos, such as certain species of the New World *Chusquea*, generate new plants in natural environments by layering, a reproductive mechanism that the propagator can replicate and refine.

For whole-culm propagation, a newly cut culm, with or without a portion of its rooty base, is placed into a shallow trench and covered with soil. Ideally, the culm should be fairly large and no more than several years old. One or two leafy branches are left at each node and arranged to project above the soil. After several months, a root system should develop at each node. The soil is then removed from each internode, and the culm is sawed into sections, with the node and new root system roughly at the center of each section. The new propagules are left in the ground for several more months to further develop their root system prior to transplanting.

For propagating with a culm segment, a portion of a culm with one or more nodes is placed in the ground horizontally or at an angle. A small branch, sometimes with and sometimes without leaves, is left to project above the soil. This method is effective for some, but not all, semitropical and tropical species of pachymorph bamboos. *Dendrocalamus strictus*, for example, propagates from culm segments far less reliably than *Bambusa vulgaris*.

Branch cuttings are successful only with certain species that have root primordia or evidence of rhizomatous swellings at the base of the branch. Such bamboos include *Bambusa textilis*, *B. oldhamii*, *B. vulgaris*, *Dendrocalamus asper*, and *Gigantochloa pseudoarundinacea*, among many others. The rhizomatous swellings can sometimes be encouraged by removing new culm shoots generated by the mother plant (Wong 1995b).

For this propagation method, a branch, including its base with prominent root primordia or rhizomatous swelling, is cut from a culm that is no more than a few years old. The branch is trimmed to only a few nodes, and side branches are re-moved. The base is planted in the ground and the twiggy parts with leaves are kept out of the soil. The propagules are kept shaded for ten days. Roots form within two to three weeks.

Sometimes new plants are created spontaneously in nature. The root primordia develop into roots, and new plants are formed at the base of branches. McClure (1966) has suggested that some tropical bamboos that flower rarely, and do not produce viable seed, may be dispersed by a strong wind breaking away the tiny rooted plants and blowing them to a new location.

For some species, layering is a naturally occurring reproductive method. Some *Chusquea,* such as *C. foliosa, C. talamancensis,* and *C. tomentosa,* have rhizomatous swellings at their branch bases and generate roots when brought into contact with the soil. New culms of *C. longifolia* have been observed to develop roots at the nodes that are in contact with the soil. Subsequently, the internodes may decompose, leaving a series of separate plants (Widmer 1997). This naturally occurring reproductive method can be replicated by propagators. Not all chusqueas can be propagated by layering, however.

Propagating by layering is also possible, and more common, for some arborescent tropical bamboos. In this scenario, a one- or two-year-old culm at the edge of a clump is selected in the spring. The culm is cut two-thirds of the way through, just above the ground, and then bent down into a trench. The branches on the lower 20 culm nodes are reduced to their second node and all the side branches are removed. The culm is covered with soil through the length of the 20 nodes. The top of the culm is left out of the soil and is cut off, except for one branch, which is left intact and projecting above the soil with all its side branches and leaves. Roots and new shoots appear within three months. The propagules are removed the following spring.

Air layering bamboo is uncommon and largely untested, but may prove useful in generating new propagules from the branches of standing culms. In this approach, the branch nodes are enveloped in a rooting medium that is kept moist until sufficient roots form to support an independent plant. The propagule is then separated and allowed to grow on its own. Like other propagules, reduction in foliage may be necessary to bring it into balance with the fledgling root system. Although not common for bamboos, air layering is a widespread practice for woody plants, from bonsai to the propagation of fruit trees in China.

Many air-layering variations are possible. Moist sphagnum moss can be placed around the basal node of a branch, and then sealed by wrapping with plastic or foil. The moss must be periodically checked for moisture, which can be replenished with a hypodermic needle or other means. In another variation, an open container is constructed to fit around the culm and branch base, then filled with potting soil or other rooting medium, and watered periodically to keep moist. The container can be a funnel constructed from a waterproof material such as plastic or tarpaper, or it can be a small plastic pot that is slit to fit around the culm and branch base and then resealed. McClure (1966) reports that exploratory air-layering studies with *Bambusa tuldoides* and *Semiarundinaria fastuosa* were not successful. Species that generate aerial roots or abundant root primordia at basal branch nodes, such as *Gigantochloa pseudoarundinacea* and *Bambusa vulgaris,* are the most likely candidates for success.

Leptomorph bamboos. Attempts to propagate leptomorph bamboos from culms or culm segments have not been effective. Leptomorph bamboos are very readily propagated by division or rhizomes, however, so the absence of culms or culm segments as a method is not a great loss.

Container propagation

Container propagation is not a traditional method for bamboo, but it has many applications and is becoming more widespread. Hobbyists and researchers frequently grow bamboo in containers since many different species can be accommodated in a relatively small space, and they can be kept separated from each other far more easily than would be possible by planting them in the ground. Because plants grown in containers require periodic repotting or dividing, container propagation is a natural byproduct. Although rhizome cuttings alone can be taken from plants in containers, container propagation is typically a specialized form of propagation by division of a culm or culms and their associated rhizomes.

Bamboo nurseries that ship over wide distances need a ready supply of small plants that can be easily packed and economically shipped. Container propagation lends itself to this need. By continually dividing the plants, the size is kept small and many new plants are generated. Container propagation should be considered whenever the number of new propagules is more important than their size.

If a large number of plants is desired, the process of dividing and re-dividing can be exaggerated. As the process is repeated, the plants become increasingly smaller, but produce more culms and rhizomes, thus affording the opportunity for further multiplication and size reduction. Leptomorph bamboos grown from seed go through a clumping stage, generating new culms from the base of existing culms. This phase can be extended by continuously breaking apart the plant into smaller sections of culms and roots. The smaller plants are considerably more sensitive to temperature, moisture, and humidity, and they may need increased shelter, attention, and care. A controlled greenhouse environment may be necessary for the smallest divisions or most sensitive plants. A greenhouse and artificial light can greatly extend the growing season, producing divisions for an extended period of time. This exaggerated division process is useful for increasing the number of plants of a rare bamboo. It is also a useful method if a large number of plants is needed to establish a plantation and an adequate number of larger plants is unavailable. In this scenario, a portion of the divided plants would be allowed to grow larger before planting out.

Although not suited to all applications, container propagation has several advantages over field propagation. If the container is not too large, physical labor is far less intensive than taking field-grown culm and rhizome divisions. Container plants can be readily transported to a sheltered work area, out of bright sun, rain, or excess heat or cold. New propagules can easily be moved into a shaded area, or back into bright sun, as required by the plant. For field division and propagation, the spreading root systems are seldom kept entirely intact, and it is frequently necessary to top the culms or otherwise reduce the foliage to balance the propagule and keep it alive and healthy. For container propagation, if a proper regimen is followed, virtually all the roots can be retained, and foliage reduction is seldom necessary.

Plants with impacted root and rhizome systems are much more difficult to divide successfully without damaging the mother plant and propagules. For such plants, the roots and rhizomes cannot be fully disentangled, and division will yield fewer viable propagules. Large container plants are physically more difficult to handle, and impacted root and rhizome systems only compound the difficulty.

Making the divisions. The ease and success of container propagation is dependent on the ability to proportionally divide the culms, rhizomes, and roots so that the roots are not damaged and the components are in balance. A propagule with a large culm and many leaves but few roots will develop slowly and may not survive. Propagules with a small rhizome section will have fewer reserves to withstand stress and decreased ability to issue new growth.

For best success, take the plant out of the container and examine the rhizome, root, and culm arrays. Often it is necessary to remove most of the soil from the plant, particularly if many divisions will be made and the complete structure requires careful examination. The operation should be conducted in a shaded area. The delicate root hairs are easily subject to physical damage and desiccation. It is often helpful to spray the root system with water to keep it moist while exposed.

Select a rhizome section with at least one culm and a proportional comple- ment of roots. Before making divisions, decide how many propagules will be taken and where the divisions should be. An older pair of pruning shears or loppers that can be sacrificed to the grit of the remaining soil are good cutting tools for con- tainer propagation. A medium-toothed saw will also work. Make sure the roots are covered with soil and that there are no pockets devoid of soil. Tap the pot on the ground to settle the soil. A good container soil will settle readily around the roots. A ½ in. (1.25 cm) or more layer of mulch on the top of the soil to help in- sulate and retain moisture is beneficial and recommended, though not essential. Water thoroughly and keep the new propagules shaded until their stability can be determined. Misting the leaves will help them withstand transplanting stresses. In moderate weather, propagules with a good root-to-foliage balance may require no special treatment. Often, however, shading the propagules, then gradually in-

Do not allow plants to become root bound, as has happened here. Not only does it impede healthy growth and subject the plants to a greater risk of cold damage in the winter and rapid desiccation in the summer, but the chances of dividing and propagating the plants successfully are diminished.

Ready to divide, this groundcover bamboo is removed from the container.

Once the bamboo is out from the container, the soil is removed, and the rhizomes are uncoiled to determine where divisions can be made. Any potential propagule must have sufficient roots and one or more rhizome sections with viable buds.

The choices are made, and the three propagules are ready to be potted into new containers.

creasing sun exposure over a several-week period may be appropriate. Observe the propagules for signs of stress so that protective measures can be employed when warranted.

Soils. A loose, well-aerated soil that retains moisture yet drains easily is good for field-grown bamboos, but it is particularly important for container-grown bamboos that will be divided and propagated. It is much easier to work with the plant when the structure is readily presented, rather than trying to pull apart the roots and rhizomes from a packed ball of mud and clay. The soil should be easy to shake from the root and rhizome system so that the roots can be untangled without damaging them. A loose, well-aerated soil also promotes rapid root and rhizome growth.

Many different mixtures are possible. Formulating a mixture depends on the needs of the grower, the plant, and the materials at hand. For container-grown bamboos, texture and moisture retention are more important considerations than available nutrients, since nutrients can be easily supplied through fertilizer applications. A good soil mixture usually consists of several components.

Sand is cheap and promotes aeration, although it is relatively finely textured and holds no water. Sand is heavy, contributing to container stability, but a large container with a high proportion of sand will be too heavy and less manageable. Volcanic cinders, perlite, and vermiculite are lightweight, stable, inorganic components. They hold water in varying degrees, yet promote good drainage and aeration. Compost, bark, and wood chips are organic components that retain moisture, promote aeration, provide some nutrients, and gradually break down. As they decompose, bark and wood chips rob the soil of nitrogen, but since fertilizing is part of the regimen for container-grown plants, augmenting with a slightly higher level of nitrogen is not a problem. Peat holds water very well, but repels moisture when dry. Garden soils provide micronutrients and can be economical. A good garden soil may be satisfactory on its own since, by definition, it already contains textural components that promote soil aeration. An ideal soil for container propagation, however, calls for an even looser, more aerated texture.

Some recommended soils include a mixture of four parts compost and three parts sand for most species, three parts compost and four parts pea gravel for *Fargesia* and other species requiring exceptionally well-drained and well-aerated soil. Examples of other, somewhat more elaborate mixtures are 25 percent sand, 20 percent perlite, 35 percent compost, 20 percent bark chips; or 20 percent sand, 20 percent volcanic cinders, 40 percent bark chips, 20 percent peat; and so on. A wide variety of mixes can be effective as long as basic principles are followed. Bamboo will survive and grow even in very poor soil. Discussions of soils are largely for the purposes of optimizing growth and propagation, rather than a matter of the propagule's survival.

Managing soil for bamboos grown in containers requires more attention than is required for bamboos grown in the ground. The coarse, organic materials that provide necessary aeration tend to break down more quickly in containers, particularly if the bamboo becomes root bound. Inorganic materials such as vermiculite offer advantages in this regard, but their light weight decreases the stability of a bamboo in a container—a potential problem with large, tall bamboos. On the other hand, their light weight makes it easier to move and handle them. More sand can be added as necessary to achieve the desired balance of stability and mobility. Decomposing organic materials reduce the nitrogen in the soil. Organic fertilizers can readily be incorporated when a bamboo is potted, but after potting, inorganic fertilizers are usually more appropriate and practical. Liquid fertilizers, time-release fertilizers, or even lawn fertilizer sprinkled on the surface are all viable choices.

Salt toxicity is usually not a problem if reasonable limits are observed. Bamboo will usually require repotting well before the buildup of fertilizer salts is a concern. Nevertheless, if salt buildup does become a problem, the soil in the container can be flushed by flowing water through it for a period of time.

Container propagation of pachymorph bamboos. As with any form of culm and rhizome division, container propagation is more difficult with pachymorph bamboos than leptomorph bamboos since the root and rhizome system is typically more congested. Balanced divisions are more difficult to create without damaging the mother plant or propagules. On the other hand, container division of a pachymorph bamboo is much easier than field division. For field divisions, the clump sometimes needs to be partially lifted, often with great effort, to gain access to the prospective propagules. For bamboos grown in containers, this is accomplished by simply removing the bamboo from the container. The propagule is usually severed at the narrow neck where the rhizome leaves the base of the parent rhizome.

Container propagation of leptomorph bamboos. Leptomorph bamboos propagate easily. The culms are broadly spaced along the length of a rhizome, and delicate precision is seldom necessary in making the divisions. The rhizomes of leptomorph bamboos will tend to coil around the perimeter of the container. They should be carefully uncoiled so that the distribution of the culms and root system can be better determined. If the plant is two or more years old, the rhizome system may be branched, not simply linear, and division will be somewhat more difficult. With more rhizome area, however, the propagules will be more capable of quickly producing new or larger material than would otherwise be the case.

Toward the tip of the rhizome, the roots may not yet be well developed, and it may be necessary to select a longer section of rhizome so that an adequate proportion of roots can accompany the rhizome, culm, and foliage. Some species generate new roots less rapidly, and so new culms may not yet have an adequate root system to support the foliage. In such cases, propagation will have to be delayed, or larger divisions that include rhizome sections with a more mature root system need to be selected.

If many small propagules are desired, the tip of the rhizome can be twisted so it protrudes upward out of the soil. Often, the rhizome will turn into a culm, thus creating a new potential division. If larger plants are desired, however, the rhizome should be left covered by soil.

Micropropagation

Though hardly a method for the average gardener or grower, micropropagation, or tissue culture, has a number of significant implications for the world of bamboo. In brief, in micropropagation, cells from various parts of the plant are cultured in a specialized medium, *in vitro* (literally, "in glass"). Nutrients and hormones are manipulated so that the test tube grown cultures differentiate into roots and shoots, ultimately forming a complete plant that can be planted in soil.

Micropropagation of bamboo affords the opportunity for large-scale, year-round production of plant material. The role and importance of micropropagation for bamboos is amplified by the absence of a dependable and ongoing source of seed for most bamboos, and by the difficulty in rapidly generating easily transportable propagules on a large scale, particularly with respect to tropical pachymorph species. In addition, through specialized techniques, tissue culture offers the prospect of creating new species and forms.

In plant tissue culture methodologies, cells, tissue, and organs of plants, called explants, are grown *in vitro*, in or on a sterile medium. In general, for the purposes of propagation, a viable methodology must include the ability of the explant to differentiate cell growth and form a small plant, called a plantlet, and a way of weaning the plantlet from the culturing medium to continue growth in ordinary soil.

What was once solely the domain of a few laboratories is now more common-place. According to Stapleton and Rao (1996), more than 70 species of 20 genera have been successfully propagated by tissue culture. Complete plantlets capable of making the transition to soil and full maturity have been achieved in many of these efforts, including for the tropical pachymorph bamboos *Bambusa bambos, Dendrocalamus strictus, Gigantochloa apus, Guadua angustifolia,* and *Thyrsostachys oliveri,* and the temperate-climate leptomorph bamboo *Phyllostachys heterocycla* f. *pubescens.*

A variety of methodologies and approaches are possible, including micropropagation from shoot tips, from seedling tissues, and from mature explants. Each approach has limitations as well as benefits. For culturing from seedling tissues, the most vigorous seedlings can be selected, and a full flowering cycle would likely elapse before the cultured propagules would flower, but as with seeds, seedling tissues are generally available irregularly and at long intervals. When tissues are chosen from mature plants, there is the risk that the propagules will flower when the parent plant flowers. If micropropagation were continued over many years, a point would be reached where there would be little likelihood that the propagule could reach maturity and productivity prior to flowering. The best methodology depends on a number of factors, including the nature of the species to be propagated. *Bambusa vulgaris,* for example, apparently remains indefinitely in a vegetative state. Since there would presumably be no flowering cycle, tissue culture from mature *B. vulgaris* plants would appear to run little risk of a shortened period of viability before flowering. Conversely, because populations of *Dendrocalamus strictus* have different flowering cycles, periods of varying lengths between flowering cycles, and seed that can remain viable for up to three years, seeds and seedling explants are generally available on an ongoing basis. Culturing from *D. strictus* seedling tissues may be the method of choice. Small-scale field trials suggest that micropropagated plantlets of *D. strictus* form clumps and produce culms more quickly than plants grown from seed.

Because many tropical bamboos are more difficult to propagate by other vegetative means, and because they tend to lend themselves more successfully to tissue culture, much of the effort with respect to micropropagation has been directed toward tropical pachymorph bamboos. However, many temperate bamboo species, including species of *Phyllostachys,* have been successfully propagated via tissue culture under laboratory conditions, though success is more tenuous. Reportedly even a slight presence of the chemical herbicide 2,4-D, for example, prevents successful tissue differentiation.

Much of the public knowledge of micropropagation techniques comes from the academic world, and these techniques are most often aimed at academic research rather than mass propagation. A commercial enterprise dedicated to mass propagation must also actively seek reduced cost materials that would be inappropriate in a research environment. For example, a commercial enterprise may use jam jars rather than the expensive glassware of research labs; refined sugar as a source of carbon rather than analytical-grade sucrose; and food-grade agar instead of the highly purified agar of the research world. The commercial enterprises dedicated to mass propagation are understandably less forthcoming with proprietary information, and some methods have been patented. Nevertheless, this once highly experimental propagation method is becoming more commonplace.

Although the seductive glitter of modern technologies often creates a headlong rush to dispense with all that is not "modern," including bamboo, some developing nations are realizing that bamboo's traditional uses still have a role in the day-to-day existence of their peoples and, further, are realizing that bamboo is a significant resource with a role to play in modern culture. Sometimes this realization is late in coming, long after bamboo resources have been decimated. Once pachymorph bamboo has been devastated by overharvesting or elimination of groves by the onslaught of increasing population density and the incursion of modern culture, recovery and reforestation is slow and seldom can keep pace with the decimating onslaught. Micropropagation offers the potential for generating large numbers of readily transportable propagules, and the hope and means for restoring the bamboo resource.

At the Universidad de Caldas in Colombia, *Guadua angustifolia* is propagated by taking microcuttings of the first shoot of a side branch from a bamboo plant exhibiting desirable characteristics. The cuttings are sterilized and planted in a gelatin culture in sealed glass containers. They develop roots, rhizomes, and new shoots, which can then be divided and planted in a soil culture. The small plants continue to generate more shoots, which can be separated into more plants, and so on. The number of propagules increases geometrically and quickly.

While not for the amateur grower or field propagator, tissue culture can play a major role in research, in the reforestation of decimated ecologies, in establishing large commercial groves, and perhaps, in discovering and generating important new food crops.

CHAPTER 5

Landscaping and Maintenance

LONG ASSOCIATED WITH TROPICAL CLIMATES, even the hardy temperate bamboos were once regarded as too delicate for even Great Britain's moderate climate, let alone the European continent or North America's heartland or northern coasts, places where bamboos are now part of the garden environment. In the latter part of the 19th century, the success of 50 species of bamboo at sites in England with some of its harshest winters was clear evidence that bamboos were suited to a much broader climate than was once thought.

Bamboo is native to every continent except Europe and Antarctica. Areas of the southeastern and south-central United States were once covered by great acreages of *Arundinaria gigantea,* but this native "cane" has now been reduced to a vestigial presence. To Americans and Europeans alike, managing, nurturing, using, and enjoying bamboo are foreign. Bamboo's growth habit is quite vigorous and differs from most plants familiar to Americans and Europeans. Vigorous and unfamiliar, it is, thus, threatening.

Understanding bamboo's growth pattern enhances the appreciation of both its beauty and vigor. That something so beautiful and of such great utility can grow so vigorously is a remarkable gift indeed. A newly shooting culm may complete most of its growth in a four-week period, simultaneously branching and leafing-out as it continues its dramatic ascent. A young bamboo plant can display a startlingly rapid increase in presence. Where a bamboo may have been only fence high, it suddenly shields the first story of the house next door. Or where only the

At Hakone Gardens, a simple fence of split bamboo attractively borders a pathway. *Phyllostachys* and *Sasa* species, and another style of bamboo fencing, border the right of the pathway.

Dwarf, shrub, and timber bamboos are an integral part of the Japanese landscaping at Hakone Gardens.

In this suburban landscape in the Pacific Northwest, timber bamboos create a tall screen along the fence line. In the foreground are tomatoes, peppers, eggplants, and herbs.

first-story windows were shielded, the grove suddenly obliterates the looming two-story house, and fills the sky with beautiful culms and shimmering leaves.

The great beauty of arborescent timber bamboos is complemented by smaller-sized arborescent bamboos and by shrub and groundcover bamboos. Widely varying leaf sizes and shapes add texture, and variations in culm coloration and leaf variegation contribute vivid color and striking patterns. As a benefit to its beauty, you can harvest delicious shoots for the table, and culm wood for construction, fencing, or garden stakes. The leaves from the harvested culms are excellent livestock forage, as well as preferred cuisine for any meandering pandas that happen to stop by.

In a variety of ways, bamboos offer a rich and abundant landscape. Once the methods for managing bamboo's growth are understood and applied, trepidation regarding its insistent vigor give way to a profound appreciation of its merit.

Controlling Spread

Mentioning bamboo in a gathering of any size is nearly certain to prompt hysterical cursing from someone who has experienced an attack from the demonic plant that invaded unexpectedly and ceaselessly, and could not be stopped or killed. Such fear and venom is primarily directed at bamboos with a diffuse growth habit. In the United States, this generally equates to temperate-climate leptomorph bamboos—"runners" in the vernacular. Except for a few, usually semitropical or tropical pachymorph bamboos with exceptionally long rhizome necks and a diffuse habit, a pachymorph bamboo behaves much like a "normal" plant, gradually increasing its circumference as it grows. These are "clumpers" in the vernacular.

Leptomorph bamboos with a diffuse habit behave in a manner largely unfamiliar to American and European cultures. Without intervention, a newly planted leptomorph bamboo will send up new culms in a relatively close clump for a year or two, giving the impression of a benign growth habit. Then, suddenly one spring, new culms will emerge (depending on the species and growing conditions) many feet away from the original plant. In subsequent years, the bamboo will make additional leaps, as the now much larger plant further extends itself in proportion to its much larger size and greater vigor. By this time, bamboo is unexpectedly coming up everywhere. The invasion is in full swing, and the battle is forever lost—or so goes the tale of woe.

The spread of leptomorph bamboos can be easily controlled, but to understand the methods of control, it is helpful to first understand bamboo's growth habits. Leptomorph bamboos form a network of rhizomes. If the rhizome network remains unsevered, all the culms, no matter how distant, remain part of the same plant. As we have seen, the rhizomes provide the stores of energy necessary for the brief, intense period of culm growth, and in turn, the rhizomes need the culms and masses of foliage leaves to generate energy reserves for sustenance and storage. Without the culms, and foliage leaves to sustain them, the rhizomes' energy reserves would become exhausted, and the rhizomes would wither and die. If the culms and foliage are removed from the rhizome system, the rhizome system will attempt to generate new culms and foliage to nourish and sustain the system. If the new shoots are removed before they become leaf-bearing culms capable of generating food for the rhizome system, the rhizome system will not be able to sustain itself. No new culms can emerge from a dead rhizome system. As we shall see, understanding this growth habit is key to managing bamboo's growth and spread.

New rhizomes are relatively tender and can easily be severed with a spade. And, lacking an extensive root system, the severed new rhizomes can easily be pulled from the ground. A few species, such as some of the larger *Pleioblastus,* have deeper running rhizomes, but the largest running bamboos, species of *Phyllostachys,* have relatively shallow rhizome systems. In general, the active part of the rhizome system is shallow, not deep. An older grove may have a thick layer of rhizomes, but the lower layers will consist primarily of older rhizomes that are no longer capable of producing new culms or new rhizomes. Unless turned downward by an obstacle, the new rhizomes of most species grow within the first foot (30 cm) or so of soil, and typically within the first 4 to 6 in. (10 to 15 cm) of soil. Like bamboo's aboveground culms, and unlike trees and tree roots, rhizomes do not increase in diameter with the passing years. Bamboo rhizomes are fixed in diameter and shallow running. Unlike tree roots, the shallow-running rhizomes do not invade sewer pipes, nor do they enter cracks in foundations, expanding the cracks and weakening the structure. In this regard, bamboo is far more benign.

The condition and cultivation of the soil at planting is a factor in the ability to control bamboo's spread in future years. Bamboo thrives in loose, loamy, well-drained soil. The top foot (30 cm) of soil should be thoroughly worked to encourage growth, but leaving the soil beneath unworked encourages the rhizomes to remain in the looser soil nearer the surface. A hard-packed, dense layer of soil beneath a shallow layer of loose, loamy soil will make some of the various control methods easier and more effective, particularly for those bamboos that have rhizomes with deeper running tendencies. Control will be more difficult in exceptionally deep, loose, and rich soils if an abundance of water is available to the plant. Soils that are warm at greater depths can also encourage rhizomes to grow more deeply, thus making control more difficult.

The particular species' growth habit and rhizome tendencies will influence the effectiveness of any control method and should be taken into account. The large, temperate-climate species of genus *Phyllostachys* are among the easiest leptomorph bamboos to control due to their relatively shallow rhizomes, whereas bamboos with deeper, rapidly growing, brittle rhizomes, such as some species of *Pleioblastus, Pseudosasa,* and *Sasa,* among others, are more difficult to control. For these bamboos, it is best to make additional allowances when employing any of the control methods. Significant differences also exist among species within the same genus. *Semiarundinaria fastuosa,* for example, spreads relatively moderately, whereas *S. okuboi* is rampant and more problematic, regardless of the control method employed.

Control methods

Interest in controlling the spread of bamboo has long been with us. An old Japanese practice called for digging a trench around the bamboo and filling it with seaweed, or buckwheat husks, or the seeds of Saikachi (*Gleditsia japonica*). Because the growth habits of bamboo differ from other plants in Western culture, its control is often poorly understood. Once understood, however, controlling bamboo's spread and maintaining boundaries is relatively simple. A number of strategies can be employed. Each has its advantages and areas of application.

Rhizome barriers. Although it requires the most initial effort, a rhizome barrier offers a nearly maintenance-free method of control. Where a grove borders an inaccessible area, such as a neighbor's fenced yard, a rhizome barrier is the best method of control. A barrier system is reliable and trouble-free for most bamboos in most climates. However, bamboos with deep-running rhizome systems, in soils that are loosely textured, warm, and moist to a depth of several feet (1 m or so) during the rhizome growth period, could present containment concerns. Consult local bamboo growers with similar bamboos and growing conditions to more specifically assess control concerns and barrier requirements.

In this containment system, a barrier 2½ to 3 ft. (0.8 to 1 m) deep is inserted into the ground around the desired perimeter of the bamboo grove. Approximately 2 in. (5 cm) are left to protrude above ground to allow for a build-up of mulch from leaf fall or added materials and still provide a lip above the soil. Once a year, in late fall or early spring, the barrier should be examined to ensure no rhizome has escaped over the top. In the rare event a rhizome leaps the barrier, it can be cut and pulled from the soil or simply repositioned inside the barrier. Ideally, the barrier should tilt outward slightly at the top so that any rhizomes colliding with the barrier will be directed upward. If a large, vigorous rhizome is redirected downward, it could make its way underneath a marginally deep barrier. A $2\frac{1}{2}$ ft. (0.8 m) barrier is generally safe, but for deep, loose, sandy soils in combination with bamboos having deep and fast-running rhizome systems, one may be better off with a barrier that is 3 ft. (1 m) deep, and even at that, the plants could still cause problems.

Barriers may be made of a variety of materials. Concrete or corrugated metal are traditional barrier materials. Concrete may work well in some situations, but it is heavy, bulky, and difficult to move or remove. Corrugated metal is less attractive, eventually deteriorates, and is not recommended for areas with cold winter climates because the metal conducts heat away from the soil, and so can contribute to plant losses from freezing. Fiberglass is not recommended because it is prone to cracking and breakage. Increasingly, heavy plastic is the material of choice.

High-density polyethylene (HDPE) black plastic barrier material is available from various bamboo nurseries and hardware stores, and can be cut to the length desired. It should be 60 mil thick and, typically, $2\frac{1}{2}$ ft. (0.8 m) wide. It is light, fairly attractive, relatively easy to handle, and is not subject to cracking, corrosion, or decay. Thinner barrier material is sometimes sufficient, but may not be reliable over time, particularly with larger bamboos. My first barrier installations were not ideal. I used plastic barrier material only 30 mil thick. I did not tilt the barrier outward slightly at the top. I installed the barrier with a tight turn, and a portion of the barrier was directly against a jagged concrete fence post. After 10 years, the mass of roots and rhizomes from a very large *Phyllostachys* bamboo forced the barrier into the jagged concrete, splitting the barrier. A sharp rhizome also penetrated the stressed barrier walls at the tight turn. Careful choice of materials and care in installation are key to long-term success, particularly with a large timber bamboo.

When positioning the plastic barrier, the seam should be without gaps and should overlap by a foot or two. Ideally, the seam should be sealed with glue and rivets or small bolts, or some similar sealing and clamping method. As an extra safety precaution, the seam should be situated where any compromise of the seal, and escape of a rhizome, would be readily apparent and manageable. For example, the seam should not be placed on the outer side of the clump or grove, adjacent to the fenced border of a neighbor's property, but on the inner side of the clump or grove, away from the fence.

Phyllostachys bambusoides along a fence line, contained by a black plastic barrier. Approximately 2 in. (5 cm) of the barrier projects above the ground, but the barrier is relatively unobtrusive. As shown in the foreground, the barrier can be hidden with loose, dry leaves, but this is not generally recommended, as an escaping rhizome will be hidden from view, and moist mulch quickly becomes soil, negating the barrier. In any case, the perimeter of the barrier should be inspected in late fall or early spring to ensure no rhizomes have escaped.

Raised beds. A raised bed is really just an aboveground rhizome barrier. A raised bed 2½ to 3 ft. (0.8 to 1 m) high will keep bamboo from spreading, just as it would if the barrier were in the ground. Any rhizomes escaping over the top of a raised bed are even more readily apparent and are less likely to penetrate the soil on the other side of the barrier. Unlike the earth itself that provides supporting structure for a buried barrier, a raised bed that is sufficiently enduring to last many seasons is generally much more complex and expensive to design and build. Incorporated into architectural and landscape design, however, raised beds can offer striking and unique displays of bamboo.

A raised bed of earth with no barrier is another variation on the theme, but supplemental control methods, such as natural barriers, shoot removal, rhizome pruning, and so forth, are usually necessary for complete control.

Rhizome pruning. Rhizome pruning is a relatively easy, seasonal task. It is best used where the clump or grove can be readily accessed on all sides. New rhizomes grow near the surface of the soil and are easily severed. In late fall through early spring, after the rhizomes have completed their yearly period of growth, the rhizomes are pruned by plunging a sharp, flat-bottomed garden spade into the soil around the desired perimeter of the grove. Any of the severed rhizomes that have grown outside the desired perimeter can be easily pulled from the ground.

Another variation of this method calls for digging a narrow trench about 1 ft. (30 cm) deep around the desired perimeter of the grove and filling it with a loose material such as sawdust, cedar bark, wood chips, or other similar materials. Instead of plunging a spade into the soil around the perimeter, a pick or similar tool is dragged through the trench. When rhizomes are encountered, they are severed with pruning shears and pulled out of the ground.

These methods are ideally suited to bamboos of the genus *Phyllostachys,* large bamboos with late-maturing culm and rhizome buds and shallow-running rhizomes that can be easily severed, yet are not too brittle. Bamboos from some other genera, such as the larger species of *Pleioblastus,* have early maturing culm and rhizome buds and brittle, deeper running rhizomes. For these bamboos, depending on growing conditions, it may be necessary to probe more deeply into the soil to sever the rhizomes. The brittle rhizomes are more prone to break, and the earlier maturing buds may mean that any rhizome pieces left behind are much more likely to shoot.

If any of the severed rhizomes or rhizome pieces are overlooked and inadvertently left in the ground, they can still be easily pulled out as they begin to shoot; or all the shoots can be immediately and completely harvested until there are no more new shoots; or the new culms can be cut down before they leaf out. Since the severed rhizomes are no longer connected to the mother plant, they must shoot and produce foliage leaves to sustain themselves. If this is prevented, the weakened, severed rhizomes will perish.

Many garden tillers can readily contend with new, young rhizomes, though a mature rhizome network would stop them. In yet another variation on the rhizome-pruning theme, the perimeter of the grove can be tilled each year, a method that is also conducive to vegetable plots and other annual gardens as one of the sides or perimeter of a grove.

Rhizome pruning is not much more difficult than the task of raking the leaves of deciduous trees in the fall. Nor is it that much more difficult than edging the lawn—another, more familiar grass that requires periodic maintenance to control its spread. Although the task is relatively easy, rhizome pruning is a seasonal task that must be completed each year, without fail, in order to be effective.

The severed rhizomes are easiest to remove in late fall, before any significant root system is formed, but if new plants will be propagated from the severed rhizomes, late winter or early spring pruning and removal are best. Rhizomes propagated at this time will have a much better chance of survival than those propagated in the fall, and they are still quite easy to remove.

Bamboo growers may wish to dig up the severed rhizomes only every other year. The rhizomes and new culms will have generated root systems. They will be somewhat more difficult to remove, but with the benefit of more vigorous and viable material that is ready to pot and sell.

Containers. As we will discuss in more detail later in the chapter, bamboo makes an excellent plant for containers. When grown in this way, the container itself becomes the barrier for controlling spread. The drainage holes, however, are a potential source of escape for the rhizomes. A "saucer" underneath the container, similar to the arrangement for indoor plants, will prevent the rhizomes from escaping into the soil. Alternately, the drainage holes can be covered with a sturdy plastic mesh or something similar.

Even if measures are taken to prevent the escape of rhizomes into the soil outside the container, periodic inspection is still a good idea. In most instances, it is easiest and most convenient to dispense with supplemental control methods for the drainage holes, and simply check the drainage holes in late fall, winter, or early spring. If any rhizomes have escaped, they can either be cut off or repositioned inside the container.

Natural and landscaped barriers. Natural and landscaped barriers have many forms. Usually they work best where precise control is not critical. They may also be employed in conjunction with other control methods.

Hard-packed, unmulched soil is not conducive to either rhizome or culm growth, and so bamboo will not grow in well-used paths and roads. Any new shoots, if not harvested, will be quickly obliterated by foot or wheel. On the other hand, a dirt road that is not hard packed and dust dry during the season of rhizome growth may allow rhizomes to pass under to a more amenable location for shoot and culm growth.

Unless there are existing cracks or fissures, bamboo cannot shoot through solid asphalt roads or solid concrete patios. Shallow asphalt, however, is somewhat friable and subject to incursion, particularly along the perimeter. An asphalt road will easily stop a small suburban plot from spreading, but if the layer of asphalt is shallow, a large grove of timber bamboo could send the rhizomes underneath the road to the other side. A sidewalk may control groundcover bamboos, but not larger bamboos, which can readily send rhizomes to the other side of the sidewalk. Similarly, a wide but shallow concrete patio may not stop a larger grove of bamboo, but it could be an effective barrier for a smaller bamboo grove.

If adequately deep, any manner of unbroken vertical barrier, including rock faces, walls, or building foundations, can stop bamboo from spreading. The hard, pointed rhizome tips may find their way into small openings, but unlike tree roots, bamboo rhizomes remain a fixed diameter and do not expand and break apart what they have penetrated.

Water also stops bamboos from spreading. Streams, ponds, lakes, and irrigation ditches are natural barriers. Because livestock eat new shoots and leaves, a fence with livestock on the other side is also an effective barrier.

Shoot removal. A thick grove of bamboo is very difficult to remove, but removing new shoots before they develop into culms is easy. Most bamboos shoot in spring and early summer. If a new shoot emerges where a culm is not wanted, simply remove the tender shoot by twisting or breaking it off at or slightly below soil level.

Shoot removal is a good method where precise control is not critical. It would not be a good method along a fence line with a neighbor—unless the neighbor is readily willing to participate in the shoot harvest. Shoot removal limits, but does not stop, the spread of rhizomes. The rhizomes of a small clump of bamboo may spread less than 6 ft. (2 m) or so away from the aboveground clump, but the rhizomes of a very large bamboo in amenable soil may eventually generate shoots 50 ft. (15 m) or more from the nearest culm. Even on a smaller scale, in many urban and suburban situations, the incursion of rhizomes into other garden areas may be problematic, and shoot removal may be insufficient for the desired result.

In other situations, where some freedom is permitted, shoot removal is an excellent control method involving relatively little effort. The expanded rhizome and root area provides more energy for the grove, and the harvest of shoots is a welcome boon for the table. If the roaming area for rhizomes happens to be a lawn, lawn mowing is an effective variant of the shoot removal method, though it does not offer a harvest of shoots as a benefit, and bamboo roots will compete fiercely for soil moisture.

Eradication

Bamboo nurseries sometimes offer bamboo removal services. Depending on the type of bamboo, the nursery, and the local market, you may be paid for the bamboo, charged for removal, or the removal may be free. Some nurseries have specialized tools that enable them to cut through a well-established grove's thick cake of rhizomes. These chunks of the grove can then be potted and sold to their customers.

Killing bamboo is not easy, but it can be done. It is essential to remember that a grove is not a group of bamboo plants (unless more than one plant was originally planted to establish the grove), but must be treated as a single plant connected by a network of rhizomes. If only a portion of the grove is to be killed, then that portion must first be separated from the rest of the grove. Such a situation is common when bamboo crosses over from a neighbor's property. Severing all rhizome connections between the property lines is essential. Attempts to kill bamboo on one side of the property line will be unsuccessful as long as the rhizomes remain connected to the bamboo on the other side of the property line.

Unfortunately, unlike the yearly regimen of pruning the tender new rhizomes around the circumference of a grove, cutting through the thick, dense cake of tough, woody rhizomes at the core of an established grove may be very difficult without a specialized tool or reciprocating saw. Lacking such tools, an ax as well as a sharp spade may be necessary.

Several suppliers and bamboo nurseries sell specialized tools for cutting through the cake of old rhizomes. The tool consists of a heavy metal rod with a sharp, heavy cutting blade welded to the bottom of the rod. A long, heavy, metal sleeve fits over the rod. The sleeve is lifted, and dropped or thrust downward, pounding the cutting edge through the cake of rhizomes. The principle is similar in concept to a metal fence post and the sleeve for pounding it into the ground. Reciprocating power saws and power digging tools are other options, though considerably more costly and noisy.

Bamboo can be also eliminated by cutting away all culms and breaking off any new shoots before they leaf out. Because a bamboo plant must have leaves to nourish itself and store energy in the rhizomes, depriving it of this source of food will exhaust the rhizome's energy reserves, causing it to wither and die.

Systemic herbicides alone can often eradicate bamboo, but bamboo is very resistant, and several herbicide applications may be necessary. If herbicide drift is a concern, the tall existing culms can first be cut down or pruned to a height that makes herbicide drift manageable. Although repeated herbicide application may eventually eradicate bamboo, most environmentally tolerable herbicides need a plant to be in foliage for the herbicide to be effective. Bamboo uses the foliage leaves not only to sustain itself, but also to generate energy reserves for its rhizome system. If herbicides are used, they are often best employed in a regimen that, at some point in the process, discontinues herbicide application and calls for removal of new shoots before they leaf out.

Bamboo can be eradicated without the addition of any herbicides or chemical fertilizers, but these can be employed to accelerate the process. There are variations on the theme, but an effective regimen for eradication is as follows: cut the aboveground growth to the ground with a lawnmower, pruning shears, hand saw, chain saw, or other implement, as fits the situation. Water and fertilize to encourage the rhizomes to generate new growth. If necessary, limit the height of the new shoots by pruning. As soon as the new shoots have leafed out, stop all watering, fertilize very heavily with a high-nitrogen fertilizer, and spray with a strong herbicide. Remove the culms and foliage once the herbicide has been fully absorbed. Remove all subsequent shoots before they leaf out. Damaged by the herbicide and stressed and weakened by overfertilization and lack of water, the bamboo's demise is accelerated.

On a larger scale, bamboo can also be removed by cutting down the culms, then ripping up and removing the rhizomes with a tractor or similar machinery.

Controlling Height

In landscaping and garden situations, it is often desirable to have bamboo grow within a specific height range. For example, a bamboo screen may need to grow sufficiently tall to block the view from a neighbor's window, but not so tall as to block the sun. Various strategies can be employed to control height. Selecting bamboo according to its height potential is the most fundamental of these strategies.

Choosing bamboo for height

In selecting bamboo for specific height ranges, one must consider growing conditions, size of the grove, and acceptable time for reaching the desired height. The heights listed in this book represent the maximum height possible for a large, mature grove, under ideal conditions. In most instances, a small grove in a typical landscaping situation will never attain the listed maximum height. It is also well to keep in mind that up to a decade or so is required for a grove to fully mature and for the culms to reach their maximum size. The most rapid gains occur well before the grove matures, and yearly increases diminish as maturity approaches.

If a landscaping need calls for a screen at a height in the range of 15 to 20 ft. (5 to 6 m), for example, *Pseudosasa japonica,* a bamboo with a maximum height of about 18 ft. (5.5 m), would seldom be a good choice. In a small plot, even under ideal growing conditions, the plant would require many years to approximate the desired height range, and even the minimum of the range might never be reached. A much better choice might be *Phyllostachys bissetii, P. aureosulcata,* or even *P. nigra* var. *henonis,* if growing conditions are particularly difficult. Although these species are capable of growing much taller than that desired for the screen —as much as 65 ft. (20 m) in the case of *P. nigra* var. *henonis*—it is much easier to limit the height of a taller bamboo than it is to stretch the growth potential of a smaller one.

Where harsh winters are common, and culms are frequently killed to the ground, a bamboo's maximum attainable height is significantly reduced. Here, the relative hardiness of a species plays a significant role. A hardy bamboo such as *Phyllostachys nuda,* which has a maximum height of about 34 ft. (10 m) under ideal conditions, may actually grow taller than *P. bambusoides,* one of the largest, temperate-climate, timber bamboos, with a maximum height of more than 70 ft. (21 m). When grown in cool temperate climates, semitropical pachymorph bamboos, such as some members of the *Bambusa* genus, may escape winter damage but still not achieve anywhere near their maximum growth potential.

Most bamboos of the sun-loving genus *Phyllostachys* will not grow as tall or spread as fast if they are planted in shadier growing conditions, although *P. nigra* prefers less sun and moister, more temperate conditions than most other members of the genus. It grows much larger in northern California and the Pacific Northwest than in southern California or New England.

Other bamboos seldom achieve anything approximating maximum height, even if the basic climatic factors seem favorable. Among the most notable and notorious is *Phyllostachys heterocycla* f. *pubescens,* the world's largest temperate-climate bamboo, with a maximum height of 90 ft. (27 m). It can, though seldom does, approximate its full growth potential outside of Asia. Although a beautiful and rewarding bamboo, it is somewhat unpredictable and difficult to establish, and it would not be the first choice where a quickly established screen of a reliable height is important.

The experience of other bamboo growers in the same local conditions will provide helpful guidelines in choosing species for height. Although not necessarily in the most ideal ways, the height of a bamboo culm can, at least, always be reduced, but again, you cannot make a bamboo culm taller than it already is. In choosing bamboo for height, it is best to err on the side of too tall, rather than not tall enough.

Limiting height

If landscaping or other needs do not require bamboo within a specific height range, bamboo is best left unlimited. If necessary, however, height can be controlled by modifying growing conditions or through mechanical methods such as pruning.

Water, fertilizer, and sunlight. The general growing conditions for a given area are fixed and should already be part of the criteria when selecting a species for a particular site. Other conditions may be relatively or entirely fixed. The shade provided by a building is usually a fixed condition. Shade provided by tree branches, however, is only a relatively fixed condition, depending on the degree one is willing to prune or let the branches grow.

The amount of water and fertilizer that the plants receive are subject to direct and ongoing modification, and these are key elements that can be manipulated to control height. Particularly in drier growing areas, bamboo can be watered only enough to keep the grove healthy and at the desired height. Little or no fertilizer will also limit growth, particularly in poor soils.

Pruning and other mechanical methods. Pruning is discussed in detail in the following section of this chapter, but cutting the top off a culm at the desired height is a very direct way of limiting height. If much is removed, portions of the upper branches may need to be reduced to restore some of the culm's graceful taper. For a dense hedge effect, the bamboo culms and branches can be topped and pruned in much the same manner as a conventional hedge. Cutting through the rhizomes at periodic intervals within the grove effectively creates smaller plants with less extensive rhizome systems, which may also be effective in reducing the size of the culms and the vigor of the plant.

Removing the culm leaves before the internodes have completed lengthening is another method of limiting height. It also increases branch density. This process requires at least daily attention during the period of most rapid culm growth. A culm can be stopped from growing any further by removing all remaining culm leaves. These practices are more commonly applied to bonsai bamboos, but can be experimentally applied for other purposes as well.

Thinning and Pruning

As with all landscape plants, thinning and pruning contribute significantly to bamboo aesthetics. Thinning and, to some extent, pruning also play a direct role in the health of a bamboo grove. Because their cultural requirements differ from those of other more familiar plants, bamboos are often improperly maintained in Western landscapes and gardens. Bamboo is easily one of the most beautiful landscape plants, yet lack of understanding often conspires against it, and the clumps or groves encountered in landscapes of the Western world are often tattered, unattractive thickets. A thoughtful thinning and pruning regimen will have a major impact on both the aesthetics and ongoing health of your bamboo.

Thinning

Thinning is essential for a healthy and attractive bamboo grove. The need for thinning applies to plantings of all sizes, from a bamboo forest covering many square miles to a small container on the patio. Only groundcover bamboo is not normally thinned, but it benefits from periodic pruning for some of the same reasons.

The heavily shaded interiors of unthinned groves have areas of dead or half-dead branches and leaves. Old and unhealthy culms compete for space and light with new, potentially healthy culms, making the new culms unhealthy and tattered looking as well. Bamboo left unthinned for several years has the appearance of a congested thicket, rather than the striking beauty of a well-tended grove.

A healthy grove must be thinned so that sunlight can penetrate the foliage canopy. If a grove is thickly populated and shady, shoot emergence will be delayed. In addition, densely spaced culms produce correspondingly dense rhizome growth, which in turn produces lower quality shoots for harvesting, and smaller culms. If the culms and branches are too dense, new culms will be unable to properly branch and leaf out, and the new culms may die. Damaged and misshapen culms are the first candidates for thinning. Next are the older culms and under-sized culms. Culms three to five years old have reached their maximum strength and are ready for harvest. Grove density and the importance of strong culm wood versus grove appearance will dictate when the older culms are taken. When shoot production rather than culm wood is the principal interest, vigorous culms may be left unthinned for seven or eight years. Less vigorous culms are harvested earlier.

If bamboo is grown as a hedge, periodic thinning is still warranted, but culm spacing can be much tighter. By definition, a hedge has limited depth, so light can

Looking closely at this grove of *Phyllostachys,* you will note the dark green chairs nestled in the grove. The owner has created a private, tranquil sanctuary by carefully thinning the grove. A narrow pathway leads to this peaceful retreat.

still penetrate relatively well even with close culm spacing. Often bamboo hedges are topped for uniformity or to reduce the height of the hedge. If the bamboo is topped, light can penetrate even more easily than would be the case with an equally dense but taller hedge. An effective screen can provide a partial or total visual obstruction as desired, but sufficient light must nevertheless reach the inner culms and foliage. Conveniently, bamboo lets us know when we have exceeded its density limits—large, new, vigorous, healthy culms will fail to branch, and the culms eventually wither and die. Even in a hedge, culm spacing cannot be overly dense and must allow at least some light to reach the inner leaves some of the time.

In a grove, medium-sized and, especially, timber bamboos look best when spaced so that they appear as individual culms in the grove rather than as an indistinguishable part of a mass planting. This same aesthetic applies in a deciduous forest, as well as with other plants. Space makes the individual culms appear larger and gives stature to the culms as well as the grove. The contrast between massive culms and their delicate foliage is an essence of bamboo's beauty. The substantial stature of the culms emphasizes the delicacy of the foliage, and vice versa. Whether the "grove" is a bamboo forest or a small border plot in suburbia, similar aesthetic considerations apply.

Conveniently, in this regard, the needs of a healthy grove coincide with aesthetics. A rule of thumb for leptomorph bamboos calls for 1 ft. (30 cm) of space between culms for every 10 ft. (3 m) of height. This ratio is merely a rough guideline, however, and should not be adopted as a rigid rule. In practice, the ratio holds better for large groves of tall bamboo, but breaks down for small plots of shorter bamboo. If bamboo is planted in a narrow strip along a border, for example, more light will penetrate than if the grove were larger or wider. If screening is a primary consideration for the border planting, closer culm spacing might be desirable. In a new planting of bamboo, where light has no trouble penetrating the modest "grove," and maximum leaf area is desirable to fuel the engines of growth, culm spacing may be much tighter than the 1 ft. (30 cm) to 10 ft. (3 m) rule, or the interpolated 6 in. (15 cm) to 5 ft. (15 cm) ratio. In a hot, dry climate, it may be desirable to thin less intensely, so that the foliage canopy prevents light from drying out the soil. Conversely, in a cool, wet climate, it may be desirable to thin more, so that the sun can warm the soil and encourage rhizome and shoot growth.

A "walk through" grove of leptomorph bamboo is one of the great aesthetics of the bamboo world, and conveniently again, it generally coincides with commercial interests of pole and shoot production. Additional emphasis is given to thinning out the smallest culms and shoots, letting stand the largest shoots and culms, thereby fostering the production of larger shoots and culms in subsequent seasons. In Japan, it is traditionally said that the optimal spacing in a bamboo forest would allow a person to walk within the forest with an umbrella open. Another guideline indicates that the spacing should allow herbaceous plants to survive on the forest floor, but not grow very thickly.

As the culm size of the grove increases, the spacing between the culms can be increased. Another of the many rules of thumb calls for spacing of at least 2 ft. (0.6 m) for culms 2 in. (5 cm) in diameter, and at least 3 ft. (1 m) for 4 in. (10 cm) culms. As the culms increase in size, the shoots will tend to be fewer in number and more widely spaced, but larger. Caution should be exercised not to space culms too widely. The culms support one another against wind and the weight of snow. If the culms are too widely spaced, some may bend too far in the wind and snow, causing them to break or become lodged against other culms. One strategy calls for spacing the culms more densely at the grove's perimeter, then opening the spacing toward the interior.

Species, foliage density, grove size and shape, the goals of the grower, climate, amount of available light, and other local conditions are all contributing factors in determining optimal culm spacing. Fortunately, great precision is not a requirement, and if it is later decided that a different thinning regimen would be better, new culms will grow within a year, and existing culms can be thinned at any time.

If a grove is used solely for pulp production, it may warrant no thinning. In this scenario, fast-growing varieties are encouraged to grow rapidly and very densely for a few years, and are then harvested. For this purpose, the mass of pulping material is the key element, not shoot size, culm size, or aesthetics.

At the other end of the scale, if the fresh, bright appearance of new culms is paramount, culms can be thinned when they are two to three years old. This is not generally recommended, however, as the harvested culms will be immature and weak, and the grove will never develop its full growth potential.

Although thinning can be done throughout the year, it is typically carried out in the fall or winter, after the culm and rhizome growth periods have been completed, and well before the new season's growth begins. Food reserves are stored in the culms as well as the rhizomes. Pachymorph bamboos are particularly dependent on culms for energy storage. It is best avoid thinning just before or during shooting, as the diminished energy reserves reduce the bamboo's ability to produce new shoots and culms. Moreover, particularly in tropical environments, starches stored in the culms in preparation for the impending shooting period make the harvested culms more vulnerable to insect attack. Sometimes, circumstances force one to thin at the least optimal time, just prior to or during shooting—and as I write this, I am personally seeing the result: far fewer spring shoots from those bamboos that I just recently thinned.

In forests of *Phyllostachys heterocycla* f. *pubescens* in China, it is not permissible to take immature culms, harvest during the growing season, or take culms that bear winter shoots for harvest. In a mature grove of leptomorph bamboo, the number of harvested culms would not exceed the number of newly matured culms. Once a bamboo is established, a portion of new shoots can be harvested for the table. This can be a prospective form of thinning, taking smaller shoots, or shoots from congested areas of the grove, or where new culms are not desired, while letting the shoots grow where new growth is wanted.

Culms should never be thinned with a hatchet or an ax. This method damages the culm that is being harvested, risks damage to nearby culms and rhizomes, and leaves jagged stubs in the grove. Leptomorph bamboo culms should be sawed, flat across, at their base. The culms of subtropical and tropical pachymorph bamboos are vulnerable to rot or rhizome damage and are usually sawed higher, always above a node, at roughly 4 to 8 in. (10 to 20 cm) or more above ground.

Large, old, pachymorph bamboo clumps eventually become impacted at their centers if an ongoing thinning regimen is not followed. One method for revitalizing such a clump calls for cutting a path or section into the center of the clump, thus forming a horseshoe pattern with the remaining culms. This provides access to the center of the clump for additional thinning and management, and it clears away old growth, making way for healthy new growth in the clump's center. This regimen is more effective if it is carried out before the clump becomes too large and too severely impacted.

Pruning

Thinning, in the context of this chapter, is the removal of entire culms. Pruning is the removal of branches or parts of branches and culms. Unlike thinning, pruning is not usually necessary for the health and vigor of a grove. Top pruning, however, is sometimes warranted to prevent wind or snow from breaking new culms. Pruning is not always necessary for aesthetics, but it can significantly enhance the appearance and usefulness of bamboo.

Sometimes limiting the height of a screen is desirable. A strip of bamboo may be planted to shield a sidewalk, roadway, or neighbor's window, but limiting height may be beneficial to allow a distance view or to prevent excess shading.

Planting bamboo that grows only to the desired height is one way to achieve the goal, but a new planting may require many seasons to attain its maximum height—and then one is betting that the theoretical maximum height can be achieved in one's local conditions. Another method calls for planting bamboo that is readily capable of achieving more than the desired maximum height, then limiting water and fertilizer when the desired height is achieved. Simply topping the bamboo at the desired height is another, more precise, though less natural, option. Depending on the degree of topping, the upper branches may need pruning so the plant will have a more natural taper. The culms should be topped just above a node.

This bamboo hedge consists of several *Phyllostachys* species. The roof of the home is visible from the roadway, but the living room windows are shielded from view. The homeowner maintains the hedge at a height that screens the view from the street, but still permits a distance view and allows ample sunlight to enter the garden. On the left and right areas of the hedge, the season's unbranched new culms project far above the pruned height of the screen. The new culms will be topped and the branches pruned to integrate the new growth with the old and maintain the same relative height of the hedge.

From the interior, looking toward the roadway, this photo was taken one year later than the preceding one. The new growth from the previous year has been integrated into the hedge. The hedge was thinned in the fall to make way for the new growth. This year's new spring growth, illuminated by the setting sun, has begun to branch. As with the previous year's new growth, the culms will be topped and the branches pruned to integrate the new growth with the old and maintain the hedge's height.

If a more severe hedge effect is desired and culm spacing is sufficiently dense, the side branches can be pruned in much the same manner as a conventional hedge. If the side branches are left unpruned, or only slightly pruned, the hedge will have a more informal, natural appearance. For the same screening effect, however, this type of hedge requires more lateral space than a bamboo hedge that is pruned more severely. Depending on the landscaping need, one hedge-pruning regimen may be preferable to the other. Both are attractive.

Pruning allows bamboo to be used in many more ways in the garden and land-scape, and it allows specific bamboo to be used in ways that would otherwise be unsuitable. For example, some bamboos, like *Phyllostachys bambusoides,* have a strongly upright habit, but others, like *P. nigra,* have an arching habit. With its black culms and branches, gracefully arching stature, and delicate foliage, *P. nigra* is among the most beautiful and graceful bamboos. Its arching habit, however, can be a problem in some settings if the arching culms block pathways or shade other plants. The culms arch more as the foliage fills out. Rain or snow will make the culms arch considerably more. Topping the culms and pruning the upper branches reduces the arching tendency and may permit *P. nigra* to be planted where it might otherwise not be suitable. And although some might regard pruning *P. nigra* into a hedge as heresy, the black culms and branches and the delicate foliage make a strikingly beautiful hedge.

As suggested in the section on thinning, the contrast between sturdy culms and delicate foliage is an important aspect of bamboo's appeal and beauty. Just as a tree has more stature when its trunk is not covered to ground level by branches and foliage, so too, medium-sized and timber bamboos have more stature when the bases of their culms are not covered by foliage, but are exposed so that the masses of delicate foliage contrast and emphasize the stature and strength of the supporting culms. In some species, the lower branch nodes remain dormant. Other species immediately branch at the lower nodes. Removing the lowermost branches to expose the lower part of the culms can enhance the beauty of a grove. In a larger, more mature grove, the lower nodes are more likely to remain bare. An immature grove, or a smaller grove or plot typical of landscape situations, is more likely to have branches on the lowermost nodes that can be removed to enhance aesthetics.

A variety of special effects are possible with pruning. Each season, existing branches ramify, producing more branches and more foliage. Shortening the branches the first year, and continuing to prune back the longer new branches, produces very dense foliage close to the culm. Most shoots can be removed so that the specially pruned bamboo can stand apart as a specimen plant. One culm, a small group, or many culms can be pruned in this way. In another, more unusual technique, culms are encouraged to grow very close together in a tight clump and the lower branches are removed. The dense clump of culms has the composite effect of a "trunk" supporting the foliage. A well-developed root and rhizome system is required to support tall growth of this density. The root and rhizome system is encouraged to grow outside of the tight clump, but shoots emerging outside of the clump's perimeter are removed. These examples illustrate two of the many special effects that are possible with pruning.

Culms and branches should be pruned just above a node. Smaller branches, and bamboo that is pruned into a hedge, can be pruned more casually along the internode, though pruning just above the node is always preferable. A long, open section of internode is aesthetically undesirable, and it can trap water or harbor undesirable organisms. If a culm is topped, it should be topped just above the node, and the upper branches should be pruned to restore the natural taper of the foliage canopy.

First-year culms and branches are easily pruned with pruning shears or loppers. If the culm is an inch (2.5 cm) or more in diameter, sawing with a fine- to medium-toothed saw is preferable. As the culms get older and harder, a saw becomes the tool of choice. When entire branches are removed at the culm node, different methods may apply, depending on the species. *Pseudosasa japonica* branches, for example, can usually be removed by snapping them downward. The branches of most bamboos can usually be removed satisfactorily with pruning shears or loppers. Sawing the branches instead of severing them with pruners or loppers typically yields a cut more flush with the node. To cleanly remove a branch from *Phyllostachys* bamboo, saw the underside of the branch about a third of the way through at its base, where it joins with the culm, then snap the branch downward. The branch should break away cleanly and evenly at the node.

Small bamboos benefit from periodic trimming to renew their bright fresh appearance. Most variegated forms lose some of their bright variegation by the end of summer. Cold winters also take their toll, browning parts of the leaves and giving the plant a tattered look. Trimming the outer foliage renews its appealing freshness. New branches and leaves will grow to cover the exterior of the plant. Early spring is the best time to trim the plants, just before the new shoots, branches, and leaves emerge. Hedge trimming shears work well for most dwarf bamboos. A large area of dwarf groundcover bamboo can be cut with a lawnmower. Every few years, in late winter or early spring, groundcover bamboo can be more thoroughly freshened and revitalized by completely cutting it to the ground. The spring's new shoots and leaves will completely restore the groundcover. This procedure should not be applied, however, unless the groundcover bamboo is well established and healthy.

The *Pleioblastus fortunei* in the foreground suffered heavy winter damage. In the background, *Sasaella masamuneana* 'Albostriata' is not heavily winter damaged, but the variegation has diminished. Both can benefit from heavy pruning.

The *Sasaella* and *Pleioblastus* plants from the previous photo, as well as *Pleioblastus pygmaeus* var. *distichus* (bottom), have been heavily pruned in early spring.

After the heavy pruning in early spring, the lush, fresh foliage is restored by early summer.

Container Bamboos

Bamboos make excellent container plants, although their vigor often demands relatively frequent repotting. Because most bamboo culms and branches are hollow, a container of bamboo weighs much less than a container of most other plants of similar size. A large potted bamboo remains relatively mobile, limited more by the weight of the soil than the weight of the bamboo itself.

In urban and suburban settings, a strategically placed container along the perimeter can immediately create a much needed privacy screen. Container bamboo can also play a transitional role in the landscape or garden, providing a temporary screen until a more permanent screen, such as a tree or shrub or a new desirable bamboo, grows to size, or as a supplemental screen in the winter months when deciduous trees lose their leaves and screening ability. In the summer months, the same bamboos can be moved to a deck or porch to provide a secluded and welcoming environment for summer's outdoor activities. The scenarios and possibilities are open-ended.

Container bamboos are also a boon to hobbyists and researchers, as many different bamboo varieties can be grown and observed without a major commitment of space and other resources. Small plants that exhibit desirable characteristics can be moved to larger pots or planted in the ground. Bamboo nurseries, particularly those that specialize in shipping small plants, find container growing and propagating ideally suited to their needs.

Growing leptomorph bamboos, and pachymorph bamboos with a diffuse habit, in containers automatically controls their spread. If containers of these bamboos are placed on the ground, they should be examined at least once a year, and any rhizomes that poke through the drainage holes should be cut off or repositioned back into the container.

Although pachymorph bamboos with a caespitose habit do not need the benefit of a rhizome barrier to limit their spread, they also grow well in containers. Many of these bamboos are not hardy. Container growing allows the plants to be moved to more protected areas, as necessary, according to climate and season—or they can be grown indoors.

Container-grown bamboos are more subject to various stresses. Soil dries out more quickly, particularly if the rhizome and roots fill the container solidly. If winter temperatures drop to freezing and below, an unprotected container will freeze much more quickly than the ground. Even if the cold would not otherwise harm a plant, if the root system remains frozen for an extended time, unreplenished moisture loss from the leaves may eventually kill it. Drying winds and sun exacerbate the problem. Smaller containers are more prone to freezing than larger containers. In marginal climates, wood chips, sawdust, leaves, or other forms of mulch can be mounded up around the containers. Where practical, containers can be clustered together, with the less hardy plants in the center, then mounded with mulch. The larger mass of the cluster better resists freezing, and the dense foliage of the clustered plants also helps insulate the plants and containers. In more severe climates, where winter damage and survival is a concern even for field-grown bamboos, container bamboos may need to be buried, container deep, in the ground, or moved to a sheltered greenhouse area.

A soil mixture for containers must drain quickly yet retain moisture—seemingly conflicting requirements. In general, coarser material promotes drainage and aeration, but moisture requirements can be met if at least some of the coarsely textured material is capable of retaining moisture. Moisture retention is more of an issue with container-grown plants, and all the more so for plants with an extensive leaf canopy and extensive root and rhizome systems. A top layer of mulch helps retain moisture.

Fertilizer requirements for container bamboos are similar to that for field-grown bamboos (discussed in the "Cultural Requirements" section of chapter 3), but a few other considerations apply. Some soil mixes, particularly those specifically chosen for seed propagation, may contain little or no organic matter. For those soil types, a weak application of fertilizer should be given at each watering. The soil mixtures with little or no organic materials, clay, or loam will benefit from fertilizers containing micronutrients, particularly if the plants are expected to remain in container for any length of time. Mixtures with wood chips need a fertilizer with slightly higher nitrogen to compensate for the nitrogen loss as the wood chips decompose.

If a bamboo remains in container and is fertilized regularly, harmful salts may gradually build up. Indoor plants are more susceptible to salt buildup, and they benefit from leaching every few years. Taking the container outdoors and running water through it flushes the salts from the soil. This treatment can be applied to plants grown outdoors in containers as well. Climates with seasonally heavy rainfalls will automatically accomplish the task without additional help from the grower.

Most plants grown in containers eventually become root bound and require repotting, dividing, or root pruning to revitalize them and make room for healthy growth. Bamboos are no different, except that they are very vigorous and become root bound more quickly than many other plants. Because several factors are involved, declaring a simple rule of thumb on repotting is problematic. In general, plants in containers should be checked every two years to see if repotting, dividing, or root pruning is needed. Large, vigorous bamboos may require examination every year.

A root-bound plant is far more susceptible to winter freezing and summer desiccation. A soilless, root-filled container saps vigor, inhibits healthy growth, and diminishes the likelihood that healthy vigorous propagules can be made by dividing the plant. I have thoroughly watered a root-bound bamboo only to find that the center of the soil and root mass remained completely dry. Root-bound bamboos may shoot weakly, if at all, and new rhizome growth may be limited or nearly absent. Bamboos are excellent container plants, but one must remember to repot, divide, or root prune them with some frequency.

Sizes, Shapes, and Colors

Bamboos in cultivation range in height from a few inches to 100 ft. (30 m). Diameters range from less than one-sixteenth of an inch (about 2 mm) to a full foot (30 cm). Leaves range from delicate and tiny to leathery and 2 ft. (0.6 m) long and 4 in. (10 cm) wide, with colorations that include deep green, lime green, yellow, white, and a variety of striping combinations. Culms come in varying shades of green, black, yellow, brick red, and green-blue, and they can be variously spotted and striped.

Landscaping considerations call for choosing bamboo first according to size requirements, then selecting suitable shapes, textures, and colors. As with any landscaping plant, contrasting sizes, textures, and colors help individual differences stand out and more readily engage the eye and spirit. A towering timber bamboo, for example, is nicely set off by an understory of variegated dwarf bamboo. The timber bamboo can also help create the partially shaded environment that many of the dwarfs need. Both of these may be enhanced by a nearby large-leaved bamboo "bush." Bamboos with yellow culms and bamboos with black culms are all the more striking when planted next to each other. The possibilities are endless.

Like most things, especially living things, bamboo does not lend itself to simple categorization. *Pleioblastus chino* var. *vaginatus* f. *variegatus* is commonly grown as a groundcover, but it can reach a height of 10 ft. (3 m). *Hibanobambusa tranquillans* 'Shiroshima' is sometimes grown as a bush, but it can reach a height of 16

Clumps of *Bambusa textilis* are an attractive backdrop for the pond at Quail Botanical Gardens.

ft. (5 m). Bamboos of the genus *Phyllostachys* have a treelike shape and can reach a height of 90 ft. (27 m), but they can also be pruned and trained to form a hedge.

Most bamboos only reach their maximum size under ideal conditions in large, free-running groves that are 10 or more years old. For typical landscaping situations, anticipate a size of less than the listed maximum. As discussed elsewhere in this book, it is easier and better to limit the size of a bamboo than it is to wait for the bamboo to attain a size that it may never achieve.

Dwarf bamboos

Dwarf bamboos include species that typically reach a maximum height of less than 6 ft. (1.8 m), though most in this category have a maximum height of no more than 4 ft. (1.2 m). In a typical landscape or garden setting, they are usually less than 2 ft. (0.6 m) tall, employed as bamboo lawns, groundcovers, or low-growing understory plants. Dwarf bamboos are almost exclusively associated with small, woody, leptomorph bamboos. Most dwarf bamboos are bushy plants with leptomorph rhizomes, having culms no more than a ¼ in. (6 mm) in diameter. Many herbaceous species of bamboo also fit the dwarf category. They can be quite attractive, but the tropical requirements of most herbaceous bamboos limit their usefulness in North America.

Typically, the culms of dwarf bamboos are nearly obscured by the foliage. Many of the dwarfs, particularly those of the genus *Pleioblastus,* are excellent groundcovers. In areas at risk from soil erosion, a groundcover of dwarf bamboo is highly effective at knitting the soil together and preventing erosion. Dwarf bamboos also make attractive container plants for an outdoor deck or the confines of a condominium balcony.

Height is controlled and leaves are freshened by trimming or mowing in early spring. Many species of the genus *Pleioblastus,* as well as other genera in the dwarf category such as *Sasaella* and *Shibataea,* can grow taller to form a bush or low hedge.

The dwarf bamboos include many with variegated leaves. Leaf size, striping patterns, and coloration vary considerably, offering a wide choice for the landscape. Variegation is usually strongest in the spring, fading as the season progresses. Some species hold their variegation better than others. *Pleioblastus fortunei,* for example, retains its variegation exceptionally well, whereas *P. viridistriatus,* though striking in the spring, fades more quickly as the season progresses, particularly if exposed to direct sun. Some varieties react to other conditions. In *Sasaella masamuneana* 'Albostriata', for example, the first leaves to appear are the most reliably and strikingly variegated, the later leaves less so.

Although the variegated forms are among the most appealing dwarf bamboos, the green-leaved forms are varied and attractive as well. *Pleioblastus pygmaeus,* often mislabeled *Sasa pygmaea,* is among the most widely available dwarfs, although the name has become a misused generic for any small bamboo. *Pleioblastus pygmaeus* var. *distichus* is very short, with small leaves densely distributed along the culm. It is an attractive groundcover that can even be mowed like a lawn. *Shibataea kumasaca* has short wide leaves, an unusual shape for bamboo, offering an alternate look and texture.

Shrub bamboos

Although more commonly grown as groundcover plants, several of the dwarf bamboos, such as *Pleioblastus chino* var. *vaginatus* f. *variegatus* and *Sasaella masamuneana* 'Albostriata', are capable of growing to a larger shrub size. Shrub bamboos typically have a maximum height of less than 10 ft. (3 m). Culm diameter can reach ¾ in. (2 cm), but ½ in. (1.25 cm) is a more typical maximum.

This category includes a number of very large-leaved species with a tropical appearance, such as *Sasa palmata* and *Indocalamus tessellatus.* The latter has the largest bamboo leaves in cultivation, up to 2 ft. (0.6 m) long and 4 in. (10 cm) wide.

Pleioblastus pygmaeus var. *distichus* with fern and rock wall.

On the left, a *Sasa* species forms a shrubby border at Hakone Gardens.

These and many others in the shrub category are also aggressive runners. Their growth must be effectively controlled or limited, or they will become very large shrubs indeed. Branching, culm size, and leaf habit vary among species in this group, providing several different effects. The substantial culms and semi-erect leaf habit of *S. palmata* convey the look of a woody shrub, with the culms and branches readily visible. The large, drooping leaves of *I. tessellatus,* however, obscure the culm and stems, creating a more rounded, bushy effect.

The larger culms and leaves exclude most shrub bamboos from use as groundcovers in the landscape, though many are groundcovers on a larger scale, as ubiquitous understory plants in native forests. In typical landscaping settings, shrub bamboos are often at their best when their circumference is limited to form shrublike shapes, or as hedges, or as accent plants along a stream or contour. Many make excellent container plants and can be used as a low screen on a deck or balcony.

Small-sized bamboos

Small-sized bamboos range in maximum height from 10 ft. (3 m) up to 20 ft. (6 m), with culm diameters of up to 2 in. (5 cm) or more. In many ways, this size category encompasses the greatest diversity of bamboo types. In the United States, *Pseudosasa japonica* is among the most commonly available bamboo in this size range. The small-sized bamboos also encompass most of the Old World's pachymorph "mountain" bamboos, such as those from the genus *Fargesia,* with their small, delicate leaves and gracefully arching culms. Also in this category are many of the New World's *Chusquea,* as well as *Arundinaria gigantea* at its typical height, the American native that once sprawled across vast areas of the Southeast. A few of the smallest species in the larger running and clumping genera begin to show up in this size category, such as *Phyllostachys humilis* and some of the *Bambusa multiplex* cultivars.

Very few pachymorph bamboos are hardy, but most of those that are hardy are found in this size category. Unlike most tropical pachymorph bamboos, which, as a group, have relatively large leaves, most of the hardy pachymorph bamboos have small, delicate leaves. *Fargesia nitida,* a montane pachymorph bamboo, is among the hardiest of all bamboos.

Some erect running bamboos, such as *Phyllostachys humilis,* make excellent hedges or screens along a property line. Many of the small pachymorph bamboos, such as most *Fargesia,* arch too strongly and grow too slowly to make an effective hedge or screen along a perimeter, unless the space available is generous, but they

In the foreground, *Himalayacalamus asper.*

are beautiful specimen plants and attractive "spot screens," such as one might want for blocking the view from a neighbor's window.

Medium-sized bamboos

Medium-sized bamboos range in maximum height from 20 ft. (6 m) up to 50 ft. (15 m), with culm diameters of up to 3 in. (7.5 cm) or more. This size category includes the majority of species in *Phyllostachys*, the genus of the classic hardy "tree" bamboos. Other hardy genera represented here include *Arundinaria, Semiarundinaria,* and *Sinobambusa.* Hardy pachymorph bamboos are virtually absent from this category, but semitropical and tropical pachymorph bamboos are well represented, including species of *Gigantochloa* and many species and forms of *Bambusa*. Bamboos in this category tend to be more uniformly upright rather than weeping, but significant variation exists, even within the same genus. *Phyllostachys nigra* often exhibits a pronounced arching tendency, as contrasted with others of the genus, such as *P. bissetii* and *P. atrovaginata,* which are more stiffly upright.

Medium-sized bamboos are among the most useful for creating screens. Although they would seldom reach their maximum height in a narrow strip or small grove typical of a screen planting in a garden, they nevertheless rapidly reach a significant portion of their maximum height. Medium-sized bamboos make excellent one-story-high screens and, depending on conditions, can make excellent two-story-high screens as well. Although they are capable of substantial height, medium-sized bamboos can also be pruned to form a hedge of 10 ft. (3 m) or less. Since medium-sized running bamboos spread rapidly, they are useful in quickly establishing a screen along a perimeter. These plants readily meet diverse landscaping needs.

A mature clump or grove of medium-sized bamboo establishes a substantial presence that lends itself well to a specimen planting. Enhancing this prospect, many bamboos in this size category have strikingly colored culms, such as the green culms and yellow-striped sulcus of *Phyllostachys aureosulcata*, the yellow culms and green-striped sulcus of *P. bambusoides* f. *castillonis,* the multiple stripes of *Bambusa multiplex* 'Alphonse Karr,' or the striking black culms of *P. nigra* and *Gigantochloa atroviolacea.*

Although some smaller bamboos produce good-quality edible shoots, their smaller size makes them less desirable for shoot harvest. Many medium-sized bamboos are prolific producers of relatively large, choice tasting shoots, including *Phyllostachys praecox, P. dulcis, P. rubromarginata,* and *P. iridescens.* Once the plant is established in the landscape, only a few shoots are needed for culm replacement. The "extra" shoots are a boon for the table.

Shown at Hakone Gardens in the fall, *Semiarundinaria fastuosa,* on the right, contrasts with the large culms of the timber bamboo *Phyllostachys vivax,* to the left.

Timber bamboos

Timber bamboos have a maximum height of up to 100 ft. (30 m) or more, with culms up to 12 in. (30 cm) in diameter. These giant grasses are the classic tree bamboos. In their native environments, they form not just groves, but true forests that dominate the landscape.

Within this size category, large-leaved semitropical and tropical pachymorph bamboos are predominant in both size and numbers. Some authorities assert that a clumping growth habit, large leaves, and large-sized culms are among the indicators of more primitive forms. For humankind, however, the largest bamboos are the most useful. For many cultures, these towering grasses are the fiber of life. Once shunned as irrelevant to modern, technology-based economies, these enduring grasses are gaining new acceptance as potentially major players in our modern world. Among the species of pachymorph timber bamboos are *Bambusa bambos, B. tulda, Gigantochloa pseudoarundinacea, Guadua angustifolia,* and *Dendrocalamus giganteus.* This last species is probably the world's largest bamboo, reaching a height of 100 ft. (30 m) or more and a culm diameter of 12 in. (30 cm). Its leaves can be up to 20 in. (50 cm) long and 4 in. (10 cm) wide.

Of the hardy, leptomorph bamboos, only *Phyllostachys* can hold claim to membership in the timber bamboo category. The smaller timber bamboos in the genus include *P. nigra* var. *henonis, P. makinoi,* and *P. rubromarginata.* The larger ones include *P. bambusoides, P. vivax,* and the world's largest hardy timber bamboo, *P. heterocycla* f. *pubescens,* which reaches a height of 90 ft. (27 m) and a diameter of 7 in. (18 cm).

Timber bamboos are the bamboos of choice for tall screens, whether for two-story houses or towering apartment buildings. Leptomorph bamboos can rapidly fill a large area and can form a walk-through forest given the time and space. Pachymorph varieties with a caespitose habit less readily fill an area, but they are more self-contained, and the clumps form an impressive fountain of large culms. Climate generally dictates whether pachymorph or leptomorph varieties can be planted, but in some climates, such as in the more southerly coastal parts of the United States, selected species of both types may thrive, offering additional interest in the landscape as the often larger leaved pachymorph bamboos contrast with the smaller leaved leptomorph species.

Typically, timber bamboos in cultivation will not achieve the towering height of a native forest habitat, but they can achieve a formidable height and presence nonetheless. *Phyllostachys heterocycla* f. *pubescens,* however, is particularly difficult to establish and is likely to be outgrown, especially in the early years, by many species of the same genus with a smaller size potential. Even after a half dozen years or more, the prospects may seem doubtful. Although the potential is there, *P. heterocycla* f. *pubescens* may ultimately gain no more stature than that of a medium-sized bamboo—although a highly attractive and desirable one. A much safer bet is *P. vivax*, a very hardy, fast-growing giant with good tasting shoots. Weak culm wood is its only major drawback, but this is less important in a landscaping situation. *Phyllostachys bambusoides* is somewhere in the middle: reliable, but much slower to develop than *P. vivax*. In some ways *P. bambusoides* is the inverse of *P. vivax*, in that its culm wood is exceptionally strong, but its shoots are somewhat bitter.

Not unexpectedly, timber bamboos are not the best choices for hedges, but height can be controlled by limiting water and fertilizer. Top pruning is another op-

In the bamboo garden at Hakone Gardens, a variety of sizes and shapes comprise a richly textured landscape, highlighted by the large grove of *Phyllostachys heterocycla* f. *pubescens* in the background.

tion and can usually be accomplished without significantly detracting from the aesthetics of the bamboo. With top pruning, it is possible to limit height, yet preserve the striking contrast between the delicate leaves (especially in species of *Phyllostachys*) and large culm diameter.

Climbing bamboos

The other size categories have been defined primarily by maximum height. With respect to climbing bamboos, this criterion alone would be quite deceptive. *Chusquea valdiviensis,* for example, clambers to a height of 30 ft. (9 m), but its characteristics are far different from medium-sized bamboos of a similar or even lesser height. Other climbing bamboos include *C. uliginosa* and *Rhipidocladum racemiflorum.* These bamboos attain their height by clambering up trees or other tall supports. They are not treelike themselves, in the manner of the medium-sized and timber bamboo "tree grasses," but rather, they depend on trees for their height and support.

Most climbing bamboos do not have a true vining habit, with culms twining around a support, but the Old World tropical genus *Dinochloa* offers an exception. Many climbing bamboos begin growth with a semi-erect, arching habit, but soon droop under their own weight to the nearest support. Much like other plants of this nature, they may be variously regarded as obnoxious weeds or highly decorative plants. Climbing bamboos have been cultivated only recently in the United States, but they offer yet another application for bamboo in the garden and landscape. Some are quite beautiful, but many require a tropical or warm subtropical climate, and thus are unsuited to most of the U.S.

Creating Screens and Hedges

In the preface to this book I described how I first became interested in bamboo when what was a greenbelt of large trees, natural vegetation, and wildlife, which was the extension of my backyard, precipitously became a treeless wasteland sprouting two-story homes. My privacy devastated, I desperately went looking for a tall, rapidly growing, evergreen screen. I found a large, costly, non-evergreen maple with an expansive habit that was wholly unsuited to the fence line in my narrow backyard. I bought it anyway and had it delivered. I also purchased an attractive ornamental spruce that was equally unsuited to the space. It did not help that the spruce was also a slow grower, nor did it help that it was very heavy for its modest size, and that I injured my back planting it, and that I was not able to sit upright in a chair for many days afterward.

On a whim, I visited a bamboo nursery, saw stunningly beautiful arborescent bamboos, and listened to the scarcely believable growth claims made by the nursery assistant. I bought bamboo.

Over the next several years, I kept careful growth records. Under my enthusiastic but amateur care, the most vigorous species did not quite achieve the yearly doubling of height that was suggested by the nursery assistant—but the growth rate was not too far from the mark. I had purchased vigorous plants in 5-gallon (19-liter) containers. The following year, the bamboo was tall enough to screen me from the first-story windows of the new suburban homes. The next year, the second-story windows were partially screened. By the third year after planting, the second-story windows were completely screened. The fourth year, I started topping the bamboo, limiting its height, but still benefiting from the impressive look of the large-diameter culms.

Although bamboo is considered the world's fastest growing plant (not counting giant oceanic kelp, which is not very effective as a residential hedge or screen), we must remember that maximum growth rate is a function of climate and matching species to the climate. A bamboo grower in New England would not likely experience the same rapid growth that I did in my Pacific Northwest environment, whereas a grower in parts of the southern United States can find species that will create a screening hedge even more rapidly and taller in their climate. In the coldest and snowiest parts of the country, one may need to make do with bamboo screens that are less tall and perhaps only seasonal, if the leaves and culms die back each winter, or if they are weighted down by the snow in winter. Nonetheless, even in the most difficult climates, bamboo is a remarkable landscape plant.

Because my backyard is narrow, I do not have the luxury of creating a bamboo grove. The bamboo runs along my fence line, and I have purposely limited its width. In some places, the culms emerge in an area less than 1 ft. (30 cm) wide. In other areas, the width is up to 3 ft. (1 m). Bamboo branches readily take to pruning, so their expanse can also be limited to a narrow width if desired. Consider this: depending on climate and species, if the total planting area is sufficiently large, as it generally would be running along the perimeter of a residential lot, in only a few years' time, you can have a highly attractive, two- or even three-story, evergreen screen in a space only 2 ft. (0.6 m) wide.

As discussed under "Controlling Spread" earlier in the chapter, if one is growing leptomorph bamboos (or pachymorph bamboos with a diffuse habit) along a fence line, a barrier is essential. A barrier offers additional advantages in some instances: since bamboo's expansive and hungry root system is confined along with the rhizomes, it is possible to grow a wider variety of ornamentals or garden vegetables at the foot of the bamboo.

For tall, narrow hedges, select bamboos that have an erect growth habit. For shorter hedges, it is sometimes possible to use bamboos that are inherently less erect. If culms are topped, they have far less of a tendency to lean, and when allowed to grow closely together for a hedge, the intertwined branches further support the culms. Treated in this manner, bamboos with a normally leaning habit can form stiffly erect hedges.

Large arborescent bamboos are usually devoid of branches on the lower portion of their culms, although this varies among species. Indeed, it is partly this growth habit that creates their treelike appearance. The growth habit usually works quite well if a solid fence blocks the lower view, but can be less than optimal if there is no solid fence, or if a more complete barrier is required. In this instance, bamboos with ample branching on their lower nodes may be the bamboos of choice, such as *Phyllostachys aurea,* with its compressed lower internodes and corresponding dense branching at the lower nodes. One can have a visual barrier to ground level, yet maintain the arborescent look by allowing the culms on the outside of the screen to branch closely to the ground, while pruning the branches from the lower nodes on the culms in the foreground view. If sufficiently vigorous, the arborescent habit of some of the large timber bamboos may outgrow their ability to provide effective screening at lower heights. If a large timber bamboo ceases to develop branches at the lower nodes, such that the first branches and leaves are well above the fence line, it may be necessary to interplant a smaller species to provide the screen near the top of the fence. Alternatively, severing the rhizomes near some of the culms will cause the newly created smaller plants to put forth smaller culms with more branching at the lower nodes.

Interplanting different species can be a useful practice for other reasons as well. If a hedge composed of a single species flowers, part or all of the foliage may be lost, as will be the bamboo's ability to provide an effective screen, and the entire hedge will be severely weakened or may die altogether. If at least two species are interplanted, the species that is not in flower can continue to provide foliage and an effective screen while the flowering species recovers or is replaced. The species can be similar, such as *Phyllostachys nuda* and *P. bissetii,* so that it is scarcely noticeable to the casual viewer that the hedge consists of more than one species, or the species can be dissimilar, with contrasting foliage variegation or culm coloration, such as the black culms of *P. nigra* intermingled with *P. aureosulcata* f. *spectabilis* with its yellow culms and green sulcus, offering a striking appearance.

In some instances, it may be desirable to stake bamboo or tie it to a support to prevent a culm from drooping excessively. Or, a culm can be tied to a fence post or other support, pulling it to one side or another to better position it for screening. Caution is in order, however, if the bamboo will be subject to strong winds or snow. Staking or tying a culm effectively limits its ability to bend under stress. A bamboo that would otherwise bend to the ground under heavy snow, and then return erect with the snowmelt, may snap and break if denied its full range of compliant bending.

View from the rooftop. From the living quarters, all windows of the adjacent home are screened. The bamboos are along a fence line, contained by black plastic barriers. On the far left, *Phyllostachys vivax* has been topped to limit its height. *Phyllostachys viridis* 'Robert Young', to the right, grows more slowly in the cool Pacific Northwest, but its continued development will be encouraged so that more of the adjacent home will be screened. *Phyllostachys bambusoides* is next to the right. It has roughly the same size potential as *P. vivax*, but it develops more slowly. Next to the right, *P. nigra* has been topped to permit a distance view and reduce its arching habit, which would intrude into the sunlight for the garden. At the far right, container bamboos provide additional privacy screening as desired.

Hedges are effective barriers against strong winds, shielding the home and protecting the more delicate parts of the garden. Ironically, the most effective barrier for most purposes is one that allows some air passage. Solid barriers, such as walls, create air turbulence on the leeward side, potentially causing havoc and damage in affected areas. A bamboo hedge will block some air passage and diffuse the air that does filter through, avoiding the turbulence problems of a solid barrier.

Shrub or groundcover bamboos that are not clipped, but allowed to grow taller, also make excellent hedges when a low screen is required, or when one wants to deter the path of people or animals. More closely clipped groundcover bamboos make excellent borders, attractively delimiting an area, or deflecting the paths of small animals.

Bamboos in containers offer additional options for creating portable screens. Bamboo is very light for its size and grows well in containers. If a new planting of bamboo, or existing or recently removed vegetation, is not providing the desired screen, a container of bamboo be can be strategically moved into place to fill the need.

A heavy snowfall once snapped the young culms of part of the bamboo screen along my fence line. I moved container bamboos in place to temporarily replace the broken screen while awaiting the shooting season and growth of the new culms that would replace those that had snapped. Container bamboos, as mobile screens, can come into play in a wide range of scenarios. A less hardy bamboo can be grown in a container to provide a supplemental screen or shade for the patio in the summer, then moved to a more protected area for the winter. A deciduous tree or shrub may provide the desired screen when in full leaf, but can be supplemented with container bamboo in the winter months—perhaps a container bamboo that had been providing shade or additional screening for the patio in the summer months. A container of bamboo can provide an excellent screen for the deck or lanai of the apartment or condominium dweller, bringing a welcome touch of the garden in the process. These are but a few examples of ways that container bamboos can be used as portable screens. Both in the ground and in container, bamboo is a superb evergreen screen.

CHAPTER 6

Bamboo Uses

THE SUBJECT OF BAMBOO USES can readily fill several volumes. Though it is not the focus of this book, I would be remiss if I did not touch on the subject at least briefly.

From an economic standpoint, bamboo is popularly associated with Asian cultures and economies. The enhancement of bamboo resources for traditional uses remains an important means of improving the general well being of many peoples, and it will likely remain so for a good long time. Runaway population growth, and the absence of adequate management of bamboo resources, increasingly threaten bamboo and jeopardize the populations that depend on it.

While it is important not to ignore the continuing role of bamboo in traditional economies, it is equally important not to assume that bamboo has little place in our modern economies. The first commercial light bulbs were made from bamboo fibers, then the only material found suitable for the task. Today, bamboo fibers offer advantages over synthetic fibers and other organic fibers in the manufacture of sophisticated structural composites.

Bamboo in Traditional Economies

In *The Bamboo Garden*, published in 1896, A. B. Freeman-Mitford describes some of bamboo's traditional uses in China and Japan. An excerpt from his lengthy description illustrates bamboo's pervasive importance in the culture and economy of those countries.

The Bamboo is of supreme value; indeed, it may be said that there is not a necessity, a luxury, or a pleasure of his daily life to which it does not minister. It furnishes the framework of his house and thatches the roof over his head, while it supplies paper for his windows, awnings for his sheds, and blinds for his verandah. His beds, his tables, his chairs, his cupboards, his thousand and one small articles of furniture are made of it. Shavings and shreds of Bamboos are used to stuff his pillows and his mattresses. The retail dealer's measures, the carpenter's rule, the farmer's water-wheel and irrigating pipes, cages for birds, crickets, and other pets, vessels of all kinds, from the richly lacquered flower-stands of the well-to-do gentleman down to the humblest utensils, the wretchedest duds of the very poor, all come from the same source. The boatman's raft, and the tool with which he punts it along; his ropes, his mat-sails, and the ribs to which they are fastened; the palanquin in which the stately mandarin is borne to his office, the bride to her wedding, the coffin to the grave; the cruel instruments of the executioner, the lazy painted beauty's fan and parasol, the soldier's spear, quiver, and arrows, the scribe's pen, the student's book, the artist's brush, and the favorite study for his sketch; the musician's flute, mouth-organ, plectrum, and a dozen various instruments of strange shapes and still stranger sounds—in the making of all these the Bamboo.

In China's Henan Province, excavated ruins dating from the Yin Dynasty, in the 16th to 11th century B.C., revealed bamboo winnowing implements, *ji,* and arrow containers, *fu,* in the writings on bones and tortoise shells. A collection of poems from the early years of the Western Zhou Dynasty that dated from the 11th to 5th century B.C. include references to eating bamboo shoots. In China's Zhejiang Province, the excavation of 5000-year-old ruins revealed baskets, mats, and other articles woven from bamboo. At least as early as the spring and autumn period (770 to 476 B.C.) of the Western Zhou Dynasty, historical and cultural events were carved on bamboo splits, *zhu-jian.* Bamboo papermaking began during the Western Jin Dynasty in the 3rd century. By the 17th century A.D., some 960 characters contained bamboo radicals, a testimony to the importance of bamboo and its integral role in culture and daily life (Chen and Chia 1988; Wu and Ma 1985).

In the 11th century A.D., Su Dongpo, a famous Chinese poet of the Sung Dynasty, proclaimed:

There are bamboo tiles for shelter, bamboo hats for shading, bamboo paper for writing, bamboo rafts for carrying, bamboo skin for clothing, bamboo shoes for wearing, bamboo shoots for eating and bamboo fuel for fires. Indeed, we cannot live without bamboos for a single day (Wu and Ma 1985).

In the Western world, to the extent that we think of it at all, we tend to view China's extensive bamboo forests as a natural phenomenon, but many of China's great forests are the result of human intervention and conscious management. China's active reforestation projects began more than 500 years ago, when some of the dynastic emperors undertook massive bamboo reforestation programs. As much as a thousand years ago, many of China's natural tree forests had been clear-cut or severely decimated. The emperors saw bamboo as a way to reclaim the once-forested lands.

Even in the New World, humankind's association with bamboo has a lengthy history. The earliest evidence, so far, dating to roughly 3500 B.C., are fragments of walls, in Valdivia, Ecuador, made from *Guadua* and mud. Like the Proto-Malays of what is now Indonesia, who are believed to have actively and systematically cultivated bamboo thousands of years ago, ancestral indigenous peoples of the western Amazon basin are believed to have cultivated bamboo, resulting in some of the bamboo-dominated areas currently found in the region (Judziewicz et al. 1999).

Bamboo in Modern Economies

A relatively early meeting of bamboo and technology occurred in the development of the light bulb. In the latter half of the 19th century, Thomas Edison conducted some 400 experiments to find a material suitable for a light bulb filament, without success. Discovery of a suitable material came unexpectedly in 1878, when Edison and a group of scientists gathered at a site in Wyoming to observe the eclipse of the sun. While camping, a bamboo fishing pole was accidentally knocked into the campfire. Observing that the bamboo did not disintegrate, Edison began experimenting with bamboos upon return to his New Jersey laboratory (Shor et al. 1996). After extensively evaluating bamboos from throughout the world, Edison selected a variety from Japan. In 1882, he established a company to produce incandescent lamps using bamboo filaments. The world's first commercial light bulbs used filaments made from carbonized bamboo. Although eventually replaced by tungsten, literally millions of bamboo filament bulbs were produced, illuminating the night with this defining technology.

As the population density on this finite planet increases with headlong rapidity, the world's forests are diminishing at a similar pace. The forests that remain are often overstressed and overused. The wood forests of Europe and North America have suffered a long decline that has accelerated in recent years. In some regions of the United States, the forest-products industries and local economies, as well as the forests themselves, are at risk. Alternative wood and fiber sources are needed to supplement or replace the wood-forest resource. In the future, and out of necessity, fiber composites will increasingly replace wood boards in construction. Facial tissues, boxes, and writing paper will increasingly come from nonwood fiber sources. Bamboo is among the more promising sources of fiber.

Unfortunately, just as the world's wood forests have been decimated by the demands of expanding populations, so too have the world's bamboo forests. Unlike the wood forests, bamboo's rapid regenerative ability lends itself to intensive, ongoing harvest and use—at least as long as good management practices are observed. Bamboo can also be planted and harvested as an agricultural crop. It often thrives in marginal use areas unsuitable for other crops. Aside from the elimination of bamboo lands to make room for more people, bamboo resources are frequently at risk today because bamboo has simply been taken, without regard to maintaining it as an ongoing resource. In 1952, over 70 percent of India's paper production came from bamboo; by 1980, only 30 percent came from bamboo. Although the percentage decrease was partly attributable to increased paper consumption, a shortage of bamboo and the failure to restore and maintain decimated plantations and natural stands played a significant role in the decline.

Once associated solely with traditional cultures and undeveloped economies, the value of bamboo transcends all cultures and all economies. In developing economies, it is a bridge between the traditional and modern. While some economic policies have been quick to abandon bamboo as representative of the past, other more enlightened policies have initiated intensive research and development programs. China has long recognized the importance of bamboo in a modern economy. Even as the nation's economy becomes more mechanized and industrialized, bamboo remains an emphasis. As in many areas of the world, some of China's bamboo lands and forests have diminished under population pressures. The plains along the Chang River Valley, for example, were once densely covered with bamboo and other forests, but these have been reduced to small areas around homesteads. At the same time, China's active development practices increased the acreage of *Phyllostachys heterocycla* f. *pubescens,* a commercially highly valuable bamboo for both food and fiber, from approximately 3.5 million acres (1.4 million hectares) in 1950 to more than 7 million acres (2.8 million hectares) by 1987. Today, *P. heterocycla* f. *pubescens* accounts for more than two-thirds of China's immense bamboo acreage.

As important as bamboo has been to both the traditional and modern economies of Asia, India, and other regions where bamboo is a prominent native plant, its commercial capabilities have never exported well. In Europe and the United States, bamboo has found hospitable growing climates, yet it rarely plays a role other than as a garden ornamental. The frustrations of bamboo's early advocates are evident in the commentary of A. B. Freeman-Mitford in *The Bamboo Garden* (1896):

> It is to be regretted that, however well we may succeed in the cultiva-
> tion of Bamboos for pleasure and ornament, the plant which is so rich
> in economic value in its own country is not likely to prove useful here.
> I consulted a leading London umbrella and stick maker on the subject,
> and he told me that in his trade they were obliged even to eschew the
> canes of the South of France as insufficiently ripened, and conse-
> quently liable to split. It would seem, then, that we must be contented
> with the beauty of our plants and ask no more of them than they can
> give; but it is hard to think that out of so much wealth we cannot even
> achieve the humble triumph of an umbrella stick.

Efforts in America have suffered similar frustration. After nearly three-quarters of a century, the United States Department of Agriculture ceased large-scale bamboo research in 1965, then in 1975, stopped its program of importation and introduction of new bamboo plant materials from foreign sources. Bamboo is unlike any other of the West's familiar agricultural plants, and its acceptance has been hard in coming.

Pulp and wood

In the United States, the first comparative yield assessments of bamboo and the more traditional sources of pulp were made in 1966. Loblolly pine, *Pinus taeda,* and the bamboo *Phyllostachys bambusoides* were chosen for the comparison study. The species were planted in adjacent plots in 1959. For the test, strips were cut from the test plots, the bark was removed from the loblolly pine, and the leaves removed from the bamboo. The wood was oven dried, then weighed. The bamboo yielded nearly twice the weight of the loblolly pine. In addition, and unlike loblolly pine, bamboo has the capacity for rapid regeneration from its rhizome system. In separate tests, other bamboo species produced yields of more than double those of *P. bambusoides,* compounding the potential advantage of bamboo. The study report further indicated that bamboo fiber has a much greater length-to-width ratio than pine, allowing the final product to be more pliable, softer, and smoother—a benefit in such items as facial tissue and writing paper.

The comparative yield study with loblolly pine demonstrated the superiority of bamboo in key aspects of fiber production. Regrettably, further studies were ceased for want of funding. Before bamboo can be fully compared to other competing wood and fiber sources, more studies are needed to determine optimal growing and harvesting regimens, cultivation and harvest methods suitable to mechanized economies with high labor costs, expected ongoing yields for established groves, and other related concerns. The extensive research in China and other countries must be supplemented with additional research germane to Western economies.

In China, bamboo is harvested and sorted according to size and quality. Among the best quality culms, the larger ones are used for flooring, the smaller for weaving. Bent culms and tops of culms are used for chipboard, a bamboo product that is similar to plywood. Lesser quality bamboo goes into pulp production.

The best quality culms command the highest prices, but maximizing the yield of the highest quality culms and selectively harvesting and processing them is a labor-intensive process. What makes economic sense in less mechanized economies with a lower wage scale may not work as effectively in a highly mechanized economy with a much higher wage scale. In economies such as that of the United States, producing quality culm wood competitively in the world market might be a difficult proposition, but the production of pulp, chips, and chipboard much more readily lends itself to the efficiencies of technology and mechanization. In general, as economies become more modernized and mechanized, the use of whole culms declines, and the use of processed bamboo increases.

In America and much of Europe, trees are broadly regarded as the sole source of fiber for pulp and paper. Much of the rest of the world has never had access to vast forests of inexpensive trees and has always relied on other sources of fiber. Now that the Western world is increasingly coming hard against the limitations of forests that are rather less vast and increasingly overstressed, the prospect that there are other effective fiber sources comes as something of a surprise.

Nonwood sources of fiber can be broken into four broad categories: seed hull fibers, such as cotton; leaf fibers, such as sisal, abaca, and palm; bast fibers, such as flax, hemp, and jute; and culm fibers, such as cereals, grasses, reeds, and bamboos. Most nonwood fiber crops grow in semitropical or tropical environments, but some are adapted to the temperate climates of the United States and Europe. The American West and Mediterranean Europe, however, also incur the additional limitation of minimal precipitation or of precipitation that comes predominantly at times other than the growing season.

Flax is an example of an alternate fiber source that produces high-quality fiber but relatively low yields per acre. In the United States, flax finds its way into paper as a harvest byproduct. After oil seed flax is combined, the "waste straw" is baled and shipped to paper mills. Hemp, *Cannabis sativa,* produces high yields of high-quality fiber. In 1989, the European Economic Community established subsidies for industrial hemp that is certified low in THC (the psychoactive substance in marijuana). It remains illegal to grow any kind of hemp in the United States. Kenaf (*Hibiscus cannabinus*) produces high-quality fiber but requires warm growing conditions and ample moisture to achieve high yields. It is best suited to regions approximating semitropical conditions with high summer rainfall or ample irrigation. Waste straw from grain production is a low-cost fiber source, but high silica content and the tendency to retain water is detrimental to milling processes. Hybrid poplar (*Populus trichocarpa* × *P. deltoides*) is a conventional wood fiber source that can be managed unconventionally and treated more like an agricultural crop. The Pacific Northwest has had extensive test acreage planted since the 1960s. Hybrid poplar propagates easily from cuttings and has an 8- to 10-year harvest rotation. It is shallow rooted, however, and requires intensive management and weed suppression if its yield potential is to be realized.

The preceding examples are only a very few of the world's possible fiber sources, but they illustrate a range of options that pulp and fiber industries situated in temperate climates may consider when confronted with the need to supplement or replace traditional wood fiber resources.

Another alternate fiber source is bamboo.

Bamboo is a high-yielding perennial that produces very high quality fiber, can be harvested on a needs basis rather that at a narrowly defined harvest period, and can regenerate rapidly. Approximately 4 tons (3600 kg) of fresh culms are required to produce one ton (900 kg) of unbleached pulp. It is a highly productive, advantageous source of fiber, but it has a few disadvantages as well. Like other grasses, bamboo's high silica content is a disadvantage in pulp and paper manufacturing. High silica content causes problems with chemical recycling and impedes the papermaking process. Wood, bast fibers (such as flax, hemp, and kenaf), as well as some other fiber sources, have little or no silica. Maximum fiber content is reached by the time a bamboo culm is one year old, but lignin and silica, undesirable elements for pulp and paper, continue to increase. For these reasons, younger culms are preferable for pulp and paper (Fu and Banik 1996).

Both China and India extensively use bamboo as a fiber source for paper manufacturing. Bamboo was first used in India as a source of paper pulp on an experimental basis in 1923. Now, nearly two-thirds of India's annual bamboo production is consumed by the papermaking industry. Since bamboo harvesting is not necessarily confined to a narrow season, many Asian mills use bamboo when other seasonal fiber sources are unavailable. Traditional papermaking on a small scale is still practiced in the Chinese countryside, but modern paper mills geared to pulp supplied by bamboo have also been established in China.

The relevance and importance of bamboos to modern technologies remains largely unrecognized. The role of bamboos in structural composites illustrates a facet of bamboo's potential. Bamboo poles, strips, and fibers offer potential strength, weight, and cost advantages over the synthetic reinforcing fibers used in structural composites. An extrusion incorporating bamboo culms and recycled plastics (including recycled garbage bags, milk jugs, disposable diapers, and the like) can produce telephone poles that are stronger, lighter, and less costly than conventional wood poles—and they do not further tax declining harvestable timber resources.

In more sophisticated applications, bamboo fiber and plastic resins can be used to produce dimensional lumber that can replace wood in housing construction. In other applications, because of bamboo's cost advantages over synthetic fibers, composites made with bamboo may become cost-competitive with concrete for highway bridges and other similar uses, while offering structural benefits superior to conventional concrete construction. Development has been slow and long in coming, but bamboo holds great potential for structural composites and other technological applications.

Forage

Bamboo leaves can provide excellent animal forage. Although the giant panda's penchant for bamboo is well known, it is not common knowledge that bamboos are a desirable forage for many animals. The consumption of bamboo leaves by animals other than pandas, and as livestock forage, is often overlooked—though not by the animals. Some Himalayan bamboos almost never achieve full height in their native environments because indigenous animals browse them so heavily.

In Oregon, bamboo grower Garold Nelson noted his cattle's enthusiasm for bamboo leaves when he began feeding them prunings from his bamboos. This observation prompted additional experimentation, funding from regional chapters of the American Bamboo Society, and the involvement of Oregon State University. The tests showed that although bamboo leaf samples had a significantly lower percentage of dry matter digestibility than alfalfa, it was generally similar to other common hay crops. This suggests that, although bamboo leaves may not be an ideal feed for dairy cattle, they would be quite suitable for beef cattle, horses, sheep, and goats. The protein content of bamboo leaf forage also was found to increase toward winter, a time when other common forages decrease in protein content. Included in the testing were species of *Hibanobambusa, Phyllostachys, Pleioblastus, Sasa,* and *Semiarundinaria.* Of more than 10 species evaluated, all tested well (Nelson 1997).

One can readily envision a scenario for seasonal utilization of a temperate-climate bamboo grove. Fresh shoots are harvested in the spring. During fall and winter, the normal harvest season for mature culms, the leaves from the harvested culms are also used, as a high-protein winter forage.

Food

In Thailand, China, Japan, and Taiwan, more than a million tons of bamboo shoots are harvested every year. In China alone, more than 100 kinds of bamboo shoots are harvested for food. The Chinese bamboos most often cultivated for shoots include *Phyllostachys heterocycla* f. *pubescens, P. praecox, P. dulcis,* and *P. iridescens. Phyllostachys heterocycla* f. *pubescens* and *P. praecox* are exceptionally productive, yielding between 8 and 12 tons of fresh shoots per acre (20 to 30 tons per hectare). A 1931 Japanese text on the culture of *P. heterocycla* f. *pubescens* in Japan describes a similar yield, citing a shoot harvest ranging from 3 to 12 tons per acre (7 to 30 tons per hectare), with 8 tons per acre (20 tons per hectare) being the typical yield. An unmanaged stand is likely to produce far less, perhaps under 1 ton per acre ($2\frac{1}{2}$ tons per hectare).

In Asia, both commercial shoot production as well as the market for fresh shoots (and canned and dried shoots) are large and well established. In the United States, despite some notable exceptions and tentative success stories, the absence of an established market for fresh shoots for the grocery trade, or for processors to can, freeze, or dry, is a disincentive for establishing, maintaining, and harvesting a shoot-producing grove. At the same time, the lack of shoot producers means that fresh shoots will be unavailable and that no market can be established. Each one needs the other in order to exist. Both the producers and the markets are destined to be small, marginal, and erratic until and unless a critical mass is reached. Not unexpectedly, areas of the country with significant Asian populations are the best prospects for establishing a market for fresh shoots.

Eating Bamboo

Shoots

In Asia, bamboo shoots are harvested and consumed in great proportions. In the New World's bamboo-growing regions, shoots play far less of a role as a food item. Some of the prominent New World tropical bamboos, such as *Guadua angustifolia,* are very bitter and unsavory. In one region of Colombia, however, the shoots of a *Guadua* species are sweetened with brown sugar and consumed as a dessert. At least some New World bamboo shoots can be very good without amelioration. I have eaten *Chusquea* shoots that were excellent, arguably superior in character to the shoots of most *Phyllostachys* species.

The shoots of some tropical and semitropical clumping bamboos have notable concentrations of cyanogens prior to parboiling. Examples include species of *Bambusa, Dendrocalamus, Gigantochloa,* and *Guadua,* among others (Guala 1993). Not all the species contain cyanogens. *Dendrocalamus giganteus,* for example, is said to be safe even when eaten raw (Liese 1991). As a precaution, however, all semitropical and tropical bamboo shoots should be parboiled before eating, a process that eliminates the cyanogens. Parboiling is not a culinary handicap, as the crunchy texture remains, and the parboiling enhances the flavor of the shoots. Once boiled, some of the same species that have significant cyanogens in the raw state are also among those regarded as choice eating, and they are cultivated for their shoots. These include *Dendrocalamus latiflorus, Bambusa beecheyana, Gigantochloa levis,* and *Schizostachyum brachycladum,* among many (Hsiung, 1991).

To reiterate the general rule and precaution, the shoots of tropical and semitropical species should never be eaten raw, unless one has certain knowledge that a specific and accurately identified bamboo is entirely safe.

Among the temperate bamboos, *Phyllostachys* is the predominant source for shoots. All species are suitable for the table, though some are better than others. *Phyllostachys nuda, P. platyglossa, P. nidularia, P. dulcis,* and *P. vivax* are among those with excellent tasting shoots. The shoots of *P. bambusoides* are rather bitter, but can be tamed by boiling.

Species of other temperate genera, such as *Semiarundinaria fastuosa,* also produce fine tasting shoots. Some, like *Qiongzhuea tumidissinoda,* are considered exceptional. The quality of the shoots can vary widely within the same genus. *Pleioblastus amarus,* for example, is considered very bitter and inedible, whereas *P. hindsii* produces choice tasting shoots. Many temperate bamboo species produce shoots that taste good but are too small to bother harvesting.

Bamboo shoots are at their best when harvested young. They taste better and are nutritionally superior. According to a Chinese study, bamboo shoots have a higher protein content than any other vegetable. Using *Phyllostachys heterocycla* f. *pubescens,* the study found that protein content was highest in shoots that had not emerged from the ground, and subsequently decreased with time out of the ground, when measured at 5 and 10 days.

There are many ways of preparing the shoots to eat. As a first step, the culm leaves can be peeled away from the edible part of the shoot. A quicker and easier method that I prefer calls for cutting the shoots in half along their length. With the cut face of one of the halves facing you, start to push the tip of the shoot (which will be the culm leaf material) down and away with one hand, while pressing upward from underneath in the middle or upper part of the shoot with the other hand. The tender shoot will separate from the culm leaves and can then be readily removed. The white or lightly colored bases of the culm leaves near the tip of the shoot will stay behind. These are also tasty to eat and can be ripped away from the less tender portions of the leaf material. The entire operation is quick, requires little skill or practice, and is much easier to do than to describe.

At this point, the shoots can be parboiled and used in a variety of recipes. Some shoots are completely free of bitterness and, in the case of temperate-climate bamboos, can be eaten raw (remember the precaution for tropical and semitropical bamboos mentioned earlier). The raw, crisp texture may be desirable for some culinary uses, such as in a salad, but bamboo generally improves in flavor after parboiling.

A freshly harvested *Phyllostachys vivax* shoot is ready to prepare for the table.

Five minutes is sufficient for shoots that are not bitter. Bitter shoots can be boiled up to 20 minutes or more. Exceptionally bitter shoots should be boiled in one or more changes of water. The shoots can be left whole or in large sections, but if bitter, they should be cut into smaller chunks or slices to allow better contact with the water.

Bamboo shoots retain a pleasant crunchy texture even after they have been parboiled for some time. After parboiling, the shoots are ready for soups, a light lacing of soy sauce, grilling on the barbecue, or any of a wide variety of preparations. They integrate well with many dishes and readily take on the flavors of herbs, spices, and foods cooked with them. Bamboo shoots can also be salt-pickled, in the manner of Japanese vegetables, and eaten after a day or two or for up to a month, depending on the flavor desired.

Tastes for astringency vary. Some people prefer shoots with a degree of bitter-

The shoot is cut in half along its length. The segmented structure of nodes and internodes is clearly revealed. The internodes are just beginning their extension.

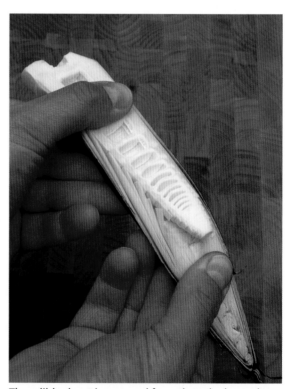

The edible shoot is removed from the culm leaves by pushing the tip of the shoot (which is all leaf material) down and away with one hand, while the other hand presses upward from underneath at the middle or upper part of the shoot. This frees the edible shoot from the leaf material.

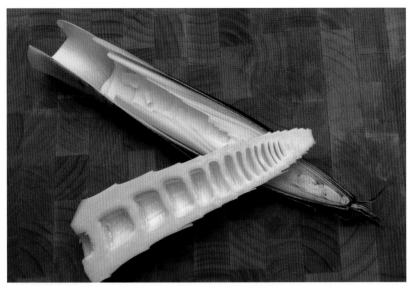

The edible shoot resting on the remaining leaf material.

The lowermost portions of the undeveloped culm leaves, toward the tip of the remaining leaf material, are tender and edible, much like the leaves of an artichoke. If desired, the tender parts can be pulled away and saved for eating.

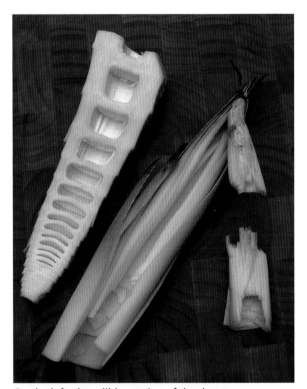

On the left, the edible portion of the shoot after removal from the leaf material. On the right, the edible portions of the undeveloped culm leaves from the upper area of the leaf material. In the center, the remaining, inedible leaf material.

ness for pungently flavored stir-fries or other recipes. The astringently bitter shoots of *Bambusa vulgaris* are highly regarded in some cultures. Although the absence of bitterness is almost always preferred, astringency can be regulated by the choice of species and length of boiling time.

A variety of commercially dried shoots is available. Chinese or other Asian grocery stores are excellent sources. *Qiongzhuea tumidissinoda* is regarded as a choice shoot for drying, though I cannot say whether or not I have ever had it. I have never found dried or canned shoots that were identified as to the species, though one can sometimes make educated guesses by size, general appearance, and country of origin.

Sliced shoots can be thoroughly dried to the point of hardness, or salted and dried to the point that they are still soft and pliable. The ones that I have encountered that had been dried to the point of hardness require extensive soaking and subsequent steaming, boiling, or cooking in liquid before they can be eaten. Although sometimes very fragrant, they can be problematic to reconstitute satisfactorily. Nevertheless, hard-dried shoots can add an excellent flavor to many dishes. I have greatly enjoyed many of the more pliable salted shoots, though quality can vary widely. I have had some that were bitter, with an unsavory taste and mushy texture. Most, however, are very good, and some are excellent, highly fragrant, and have outstanding flavor.

For a simple and delicious way to explore the salted, pliable, dried shoots, soak them in water until mostly tender, then put them in a mixture of sliced beef or pork, minced ginger, green onion, leek, or shallot, sliced mushrooms, sugar, soy sauce, and sesame oil. Place in an open bowl and steam for 20 minutes or so, until the meat is cooked. Serve with steamed rice.

As with most vegetables, canned shoots are inferior to fresh—but they are far better than none at all. The quality of canned shoots is generally consistent, with a good if somewhat bland character, but I have encountered some that were mushy with little taste. Canned shoots that have been pickled or combined with other flavorings can be very good. The species of shoot is rarely, if ever, found on the can. Although shoot-producing countries may process a number of species, one species usually predominates. China's canned shoots are mostly *Phyllostachys heterocycla* f. *pubescens*. Thailand processes primarily *Dendrocalamus asper*. In general, shoots from Thailand tend to be quite good, particularly those that have been salt pickled with additional ingredients.

I have not included a listing of recipes, as many Asian cookbooks already include recipes with bamboo shoots. In recipes, fresh shoots can be "substituted" for canned shoots (which are, of course, substitutes for fresh shoots). For a quick way to sample your harvested shoots, sauté the parboiled shoots with garlic and ginger, adding soy sauce with a bit of sugar to taste. A few drops of sesame oil is also a nice addition. Or, Western style, sauté in olive oil or butter, with some chopped garlic if desired, and salt to taste.

Other bamboo foods

In addition to the shoots, bamboo plants offer other, less common food possibilities. When topped at a height of roughly 3 ft. (about 1 m), the growing shoots of *Oxytenanthera braunii* continue to exude sap for many weeks. In Tanzania, the sap is collected and fermented into a wine-like drink called *ulanzi*.

Bamboo leaves are seldom eaten, but in rural mountainous areas of Japan where *Sasa* is plentiful, new *Sasa* leaves are harvested while they are still tightly rolled and light green in color, and are then sautéed. It is a seasonal delicacy served in the local hotels and inns.

Bamboo seed is edible like other food grains. It can be consumed in a variety of ways: cooked like rice, or ground into a flour to make dumplings, noodles, or gruel. It can be fermented to make an alcoholic beverage, or roasted to eat as a snack, or included in pancakes, muffins, or other baked goods. A few bamboos produce fleshy fruits. The indigenous peoples of Peru eat the fruits of *Guadua sarcocarpa*, both cooked and raw. The fruits of *Olmeca* species are also edible, if not particularly good.

Although not a food, per se, large-leaved bamboos are used for wrapping food, the bamboo leaves containing a natural preservative that helps prevent deterioration. Carrying this theme further, a filling of meat and condiments is placed inside a ball of rice, wrapped in bamboo leaves, and then steamed. The bamboo leaves impart a subtle flavor to the mixture. Rice is also sometimes boiled in the joints of the tropical bamboo *Cephalostachyum pergracile*, imparting a distinctive flavor and providing a convenient carrying vessel when traveling.

CHAPTER 7

Bamboo in America

AMERICA'S NATIVE CANE *Arundinaria gigantea* once spanned thousands of acres from Virginia and Florida across to Texas, north to Missouri, and up the Ohio River Valley. Buffalo migrated through these cane meadows into Kentucky and Tennessee to feed during winter. The canebrakes offered prime hunting ground for local Native Americans and provided pasture and winter shelter for the livestock of the European settlers. Prior to the Civil War, the canebrakes helped hide slaves escaping to freedom in the North.

In spite of its widespread presence in the early days of the United States, bamboo was never really assimilated into American culture in any major or lasting way. Bamboo was something that was used as long as it was around, but it was never absorbed into life's fabric, to be cherished, nurtured, and restored. The canebrakes were regarded as indicative of fertile soil, and were thus targeted by the early settlers. Land clearing, fires, flowering cycles, and overgrazing all contributed to the decimation of the once-great expanses of the native cane. Once gone, either intentionally or inadvertently, it was never replaced.

For many people throughout the world, bamboo is an intrinsic part of their lives and their landscape. Its presence, its beauty, and its utility are part of the living fabric of the land and the human spirit. But bamboo is virtually absent from European and American culture and tradition. It plays little or no role in the United States as building material, food, forage, ornamental plant, or anything of significance, except, perhaps, for the occasional garden stake.

Utility and beauty are the warp and weft of bamboo culture. One calls for the other, gives form to the other, sustains the other. For bamboo, if one is after beauty, one also encounters utility. If one is after utility, one also encounters beauty. Societies that have assimilated bamboo into the human spirit know its full fabric. In the European world and in America, the beauty in the landscape may be a seductive gateway that leads us to consider and explore its utility.

The first foreign species were introduced into the United States when *Arundinaria gigantea* ssp. *gigantea* and *A. gigantea* ssp. *tecta,* the native American cane, still covered large expanses of land. The very first introduction may have been *Bambusa vulgaris,* which was cultivated by Spanish colonists in southern Florida in the 1840s. Other sources cite an earlier introduction of *Phyllostachys aurea* by a Mr. G. H. Todd of Montgomery, Alabama, in 1822. Documentation of subsequent introductions is incomplete, but some that are known include *Pseudosasa japonica* in 1860; *Pleioblastus simonii* to Wallingford, Pennsylvania, in 1876; *Phyllostachys aurea* in 1882 (possibly a subsequent introduction); *Sasa palmata* in 1891; and a grove of *P. nigra* var. *henonis* was established near Shreveport, Louisiana, around 1894.

American Researchers and Proponents

In 1896, while on a trip to Sumatra, an American plant pathologist, David Fairchild, and his friend and benefactor, Barbour Lathrop, were struck by bamboo's great beauty and utility. In 1897, Fairchild and Lathrop entered into an informal partnership to study and seek out plants useful to humankind and introduce them to America. This informal partnership lasted until Lathrop's death in 1927, and it has been attributed to the introduction of a large portion of the bamboos in the United States today.

Under the United States Department of Agriculture (USDA), Fairchild helped organize the Section of Foreign Seed and Plant Introduction and established a formalized method for recording new plant introductions. Beginning in 1898, new bamboos were assigned plant introduction numbers and cataloged in the USDA journal, *Plant Inventory.* Subsequently, Fairchild held the position of Agricultural Plant Explorer, enabling him to introduce many new bamboos. He was responsible for establishing a network of plant introduction stations where plant explorers could send new introductions. The stations included sites in Florida, Georgia, Louisiana, Maryland, California, and Puerto Rico. The Maryland site played a major role in the introduction of bamboos into the northeastern United States.

The plant introduction station near Savannah, Georgia, has a story of its own. Its origins grew out of a decision by a local resident to plant three bamboo plants next to a well on her property. Planted in 1890, these three bamboo plants were later determined to be the large timber bamboo *Phyllostachys bambusoides*. By 1915, the bamboo covered approximately an acre (0.4 hectares) and literally surrounded the property's two-story farmhouse. Fairchild learned of the 46 acre (19 hectare) farm and, it is said, half jokingly wrote to his friend, Barbour Lathrop, asking him if he wanted to own a bamboo grove on the Ogeechee River. Lathrop immediately agreed, authorized the purchase of the farm, and presented it as a gift to the USDA Office of Plant Introduction. The station was to play a major role in the introduction of bamboo in the South and to botanical gardens across America. After Lathrop's death, the station was named "The Barbour Lathrop Plant Introduction Garden." For three-quarters of a century, the site has been informally known as the "Bamboo Farm." Closed by the USDA in 1980, the Bamboo Farm was kept in caretaker status until 1983, when it was given to the University of Georgia. Throughout its history, the Bamboo Farm has been involved in widely varied research, as well as in applications for private industry and government. Some of these include the use of bamboo as a source of pulp for papermaking by the Champion and Scott paper companies, bamboo shoots and water chestnuts for the Campbell Soup Company, and bamboo for training purposes during the Vietnam War.

In 1905, Fairchild hired Frank Meyer as an Agricultural Explorer. Although Meyer initiated the introduction of many Chinese bamboos, mishaps and bad luck prevented the successful introduction of all but a few. One, *Phyllostachys meyeri*, was subsequently named for him. In another unfortunate turn, Meyer made an extensive search for a new bamboo introduction station, finally settling on a site at Brooksville, Florida. He believed that the site's clay subsoil was necessary to support tall bamboos. Unfortunately, the clay greatly impeded growth, and heavy rains often turned the area into a swamp. Meyer drowned in China's Chang River in May of 1918. The Bamboo Farm in Georgia became the replacement site for Brooksville, and in the early 1930s, Meyer's struggling collection of introductions at Brooksville was moved to the Bamboo Farm.

Other American bamboo researchers and growers who made notable contributions in the first half of the 20th century include Robert A. Young and E. A. McIlhenny. Young, through his work at the USDA plant introduction stations, contributed significantly to the bamboo research and literature. A striking and attractive cultivar of *Phyllostachys viridis*, 'Robert Young', is named after him. McIlhenny, of Tabasco sauce and Avery Island fame, was an ardent bamboo grower and advocate. His skills and devotion to bamboo were responsible for the survival of more than one of the new introductions. He wrote popular articles promoting the merits of bamboo.

Perhaps the greatest bamboo researcher of all, American or otherwise, was F. A. McClure. Born on a farm in Ohio, McClure attended Ohio State University with the intention of returning to the family farm. Upon graduation in 1919, he unexpectedly received an offer to become an instructor in horticulture at Lingnan University in Canton, China. A youth in search of adventure, he accepted the offer and, except for two furloughs, remained in China until 1932. During that time, he became fluent in Cantonese and led numerous plant exploration trips, in part for the USDA. McClure was made curator of the herbarium at Lingnan, and he initiated a bamboo garden there.

In 1936, after earning his doctoral degree, McClure returned to China, where he remained until 1941, when the war forced his return. Subsequently, he visited nearly every Latin American country, researching and collecting bamboo. McClure probably saw and studied more species of bamboo in their native habitats than anyone before or since. During his time in China, McClure shipped hundreds of plants to the United States and was directly responsible for the introduction of 56 new species and cultivars of bamboo, more than any other plant explorer. In the U.S., McClure was actively involved in researching commercial bamboo applications. Many decades later, McClure's research and writings still form a sound basis and foundation for bamboo inquiry. For a plant that is still relatively unknown, and about which much of what is "known" is still in flux, and much new has been discovered, the continuing importance and validity of McClure's research and writings speak eloquently of the substance of McClure and his work.

McClure's successor, Thomas R. Soderstrom, conducted extensive research on New World bamboos. His efforts, and those of his colleagues, especially Cleo Calderón, helped to bring to light, classify, and define the more than 120 species of herbaceous, neotropical bamboos and bamboo allies.

More recent carriers of the torch include Emmet J. Judziewicz, with his extensive research and writings on New World bamboos and grasses, Margaret J. Stern for her work on bamboo ecology, and Lynn G. Clark. The studies conducted by Clark and her colleagues have been landmarks in bamboo research, uncovering the origins of bamboos and, in the process, redefining both bamboos and the basal grasses. Clark's extensive research and writings on New World bamboos have helped fill a once-great gap in bamboo literature. Of particular interest to the bamboo gardener are Clark's contributions to our understanding of *Chusquea*. Clark is currently the leading authority on *Chusquea,* the world's largest and most diverse bamboo genus.

These leading researchers have largely focused on the bamboos of the New World, a relatively overlooked but important area of study. In their study of New World bamboos, they join their colleagues from other parts of the Americas, including Ximena Londoño in Columbia, the current authority on *Guadua,* Gilberto Cortés in Mexico, Tatiana Sendulsky in Brazil, and Fernando Zuloaga from Argentina.

End of an Era

From 1898 to 1975, through the efforts of its plant explorers and researchers, the U.S. Department of Agriculture introduced hundreds of different bamboos from around the world, under the assumption and hope that bamboo would become a widely planted and commercially viable crop in the United States. The expectation was never realized. The efforts of the USDA, dedicated researchers, and other proponents of bamboo were brought to an abrupt close in the 1960s, just as the viability of large-scale commercial production was about to be tested.

Two important experiments were initiated with the active cooperation of the New Crops Branch of the USDA around 1960. The first, a study of *Phyllostachys bambusoides* and the loblolly pine (*Pinus taeda*) to compare yields for pulp production, was launched in 1959, and the following year some 100 acres (40 hectares) of five *Phyllostachys* species were planted at Auburn University's main Agricultural Experiment Station in Alabama in order to study the problems of production, harvesting, and utilization.

On July 1, 1965, the United States Department of Agriculture discontinued co-operation in these programs, ostensibly as an economy measure. As a result, harvest research was drastically curtailed, and utilization research was abandoned. It is speculated that large commercial interests with extensive holdings of loblolly pine were a force in the cessation of research efforts. At about the time that large-scale research on bamboo ceased, the Southeast began intensively cropping loblolly pine for pulp production.

Bamboo research was killed just as preliminary results of the experiments were becoming known. The cessation of virtually all support and funding halted further assessments. Still, the preliminary results were compelling to anyone with a mind not tainted by competing economic interests. (See the preceding chapter for a further discussion of the comparison study of bamboo and loblolly pine.)

Overcoming an Archaic Law

In 1918, under the authority of law enacted by Congress on August 20, 1912, the Secretary of Agriculture issued a directive that prohibited the importation of bamboo seeds, plants, or cuttings capable of propagation. The object of the order was to prevent the introduction and spread of bamboo smut (*Ustiliago shiraiana*) and "other dangerous plant diseases." At the time of the quarantine, the United States was embroiled in World War I, and there was a critical dependence on the cereal crops of the Midwest. Grain smuts were seen as a considerable threat, and there was concern that bamboo smut and other bamboo diseases could affect the cereal crops. At least one search of USDA archives indicates that the threat may have been more hypothetical than real, however, and that there may never have been a substantive basis for the quarantine (Cooper 1995). Neither bamboo smut nor any of the other "dangerous diseases" have posed a threat or problem, yet the ruling remains.

It has been suggested that the same business interests that were a factor in the Department of Agriculture's cessation of bamboo research in the 1960s also helped keep the quarantine regulation in force. These two developments had a major and lasting impact on bamboo in the United States. Through the decades, the USDA staff had included some of the world's greatest and most committed bamboo researchers, explorers, and proponents, and the cessation of large-scale bamboo research by the USDA in 1965 brought an end to a significant and active contributor to the field. The subsequent cessation of new USDA bamboo introductions in 1975 seemed to spike the final blow. The elimination of this important force in new bamboo introductions, combined with an archaic law and a regulation derived from it, threatened to thwart any and all future introductions of "foreign" bamboo seeds and plants. The future of bamboo in America appeared bleak.

Richard Haubrich, founding president of the American Bamboo Society, succeeded in obtaining a limited permit to import bamboo under an exception that allows importation for "experimental or scientific purposes by the Department of Agriculture." Under this provision, up to six plants of a given type can be brought into a USDA-approved quarantine facility. As of this writing, there are no more than half a dozen permit holders and quarantine facilities in the United States. Because of their rarity and limited number, the first plants released for sale typically bring exceptionally high prices, which progressively drop to normal levels as propagation stocks increase and the bamboos become more readily available.

The American Bamboo Society

For anyone interested in bamboo, membership in the American Bamboo Society (ABS) is essential. The society embraces a broad range of interests and is inclusive of all that is related to bamboo. Far more than most societies devoted to a single plant type, the American Bamboo Society has played a critical role in the preservation and resurgence of bamboo in America.

Interest in bamboo as a premier landscaping plant is dovetailing with a renewed awareness of bamboo as an important source of food and fiber. In part because of the dedication of the American Bamboo Society's founders and members, bamboo may yet fulfill and exceed the promise of a century ago, when American plant explorers were captivated by a plant whose exceptional beauty was only equaled by its utility, and who dedicated themselves to bringing its bounty to America.

The cessation of large-scale bamboo research in 1965 and the cessation of new plant introductions by the Department of Agriculture in 1975 marked the end of an exciting era for bamboo proponents and enthusiasts. Filling this void, the American Bamboo Society was formed on October 20, 1979, in Encinitas, California. Founding president Richard Haubrich had become intrigued by the beauty of the bamboo in the garden of the house he was renting. He watered and fertilized the bamboo to encourage its growth. The bamboo, *Phyllostachys aurea,* predictably spread into his lawn. Later, at a home of his own, he began growing a variety of bamboos. Kenneth Brennecke, a colleague of Haubrich's, also liked bamboo. Both of them knew Gilbert Voss, who was then the curator at Quail Botanical Gardens in Encinitas. In 1979, while riding in a car together to attend a meeting at Huntington Gardens, they decided to establish an organization dedicated to bamboo. That October, the American Bamboo Society was formed, consisting of all of seven members.

In February of 1980, Haubrich traveled to the former USDA introduction station near Savannah, Georgia, to obtain bamboo plants. While there, he also obtained a special permit to import bamboos "for experimental or scientific purposes" and made arrangements at Quail Botanical Gardens for the necessary quarantine facilities. Haubrich arranged for plants to be sent from Europe and Asia. He and society member Bill Teague made a collecting trip to Costa Rica, and Voss went to Mexico. Gib Cooper obtained *Phyllostachys heterocycla* f. *pubescens* seeds through a partner in China, and arrangements were made with Quail Botanical

Gardens to sell the seedlings to help finance the quarantine greenhouse. In subsequent years, other members made collecting trips to South America and China.
Gerald Bol dedicated extensive time and effort to bring back many New World
Chusquea bamboos, his name becoming virtually synonymous with their American
horticultural introduction.

An article in the *Los Angeles Times* generated a growth spurt to 50 members.
Critical mass achieved, the ABS continued to grow. The Northern California Chapter was formed in 1982, the Pacific Northwest and Caribbean Chapters in 1983,
the Northeast Chapter in 1989, the Southern California Chapter in 1989, the
Southeast Chapter in 1990, the Texas Chapter in 1992, and so on. New chapters
continue to form, and the American Bamboo Society's individual chapters now
cover most of the United States and beyond, from Puerto Rico and Florida, to New
England, to the Southwest, to Alaska, and to Hawaii.

Among its stated objectives, the American Bamboo Society provides a source
of information on bamboo identification, propagation, and utilization; stores and
disseminates this information through a journal and other publications; preserves
existing bamboo species; and increases the number of bamboo species in the
United States by maintaining quarantine facilities for importation of bamboos
from foreign sources. Although still relatively modest in size, and run and managed by volunteers, including its board of directors and officers, the American
Bamboo Society has grown tremendously since its inception. Continuing to fulfill
its original objectives, the society imports new bamboos through several quarantine greenhouses; reprints out-of-print bamboo books; publishes a newsletter,
journal, species and source list, and an Internet web site; and funds bamboo research and publications.

Sales of plants and other bamboo-related items are a major source of funding
for the ABS. At periodic sales, the American Bamboo Society and its regional chapters offer a wide selection of reasonably priced bamboos, expensive rare bamboos,
and a variety of bamboo items. The annual auction, conducted at the society's national meeting, is one of the ABS's largest fundraising events. The annual meeting
rotates around the country among hosting chapters, offering a broader opportunity for society members and interested public to attend.

Publications

The American Bamboo Society publishes *Bamboo: The Magazine of the American
Bamboo Society, The Journal of the American Bamboo Society,* and the *American Bamboo*

Society Bamboo Species Source List. All are free to society members, and all are excellent sources of information. During his long tenure as editor of the *American Bamboo Society Newsletter,* Michael Bartholomew played a pivotal role in expanding the newsletter into a highly informative, bimonthly publication containing technical information, news of events, and information on new publications, conferences, meetings, and all manner of topics related to bamboo. For the first two decades of the society's existence, founding member and author of the society's bylaws, Kenneth Brennecke, edited *The Journal of the American Bamboo Society,* an excellent reference source for both practical and technical research articles on bamboo. Richard Haubrich, the founding president, compiled and produced the annual *American Bamboo Society Bamboo Species Source List* for 16 years, from 1981 through 1996, creating a standard format for comparatively listing bamboos. The role of editor was subsequently passed to former-president George Shor. The source list is a comprehensive listing of all bamboos in cultivation in the United States. It includes a concise description of the bamboos, and the addresses, phone numbers, and requirements of the nurseries that offer the plants for sale. The source list also includes chapter addresses, common bamboo synonyms, and sources for a variety of bamboo products, including books, crafts, fences, hardwood flooring, musical instruments, poles, and rhizome barriers. These publications, and membership in the American Bamboo Society, are essentials for anyone interested in bamboo.

The American Bamboo Society's web site (http://www.bamboo.org/abs/), developed and maintained by Barry and Peter Abrahamsen, is available to anyone with an Internet connection and is a rich source of bamboo information, as well as links to other bamboo web sites.

Membership

As of this writing, joint membership in the American Bamboo Society and one of its regional chapters is $35.00 per year. You can apply for membership through a regional chapter or through the society's national address:

> American Bamboo Society
> 750 Krumkill Road
> Albany, NY 12203

Additional information, regional chapter contacts, and the most current membership requirements can be obtained from the American Bamboo Society's web site, at http://www.bamboo.org/abs.

Related organizations

Although most bamboo organizations throughout the world operate with minimal funding and no paid staff, the sense of community and common purpose is strong. The Internet, through web sites and e-mail discussion groups, has fostered an even greater level of sharing and communication. The societies with Western cultural roots, including the American Bamboo Society, European Bamboo Society (an umbrella organization composed of bamboo societies throughout Europe), and Bamboo Society of Australia, all have a natural affinity in that they are made up by bamboo enthusiasts and advocates from countries and cultures without strong historical ties to bamboo. To a large degree, these societies share a common focus and mission, spreading knowledge, understanding, and acceptance of this remarkable plant, exploring its role in the modern economy and culture, and fostering a bamboo culture where there had been none. The societies from countries with existing bamboo cultures tend to have a slightly different focus, more directed at the immediate and future economic implications of bamboo for their peoples, but the purposes of all the bamboo societies and organizations dovetail quite well, forming a loose but cohesive global community.

The idea for some sort of formal international bamboo association emerged from discussions during the Second International Bamboo Congress, in Prafrance, Anduze, France, in 1988. In 1992, M. Watanabe of Japan, Karl Bareis of the United States, Dr. Adkoli of India, and Yves Crouzet of the European Bamboo Society prepared a working document for an international association of bamboo societies. The association began to take formal shape later that same year at the Third International Bamboo Congress in Minamata, Japan. By mid-1993, the International Bamboo Association (IBA) had formally emerged, building on earlier cooperative efforts. By the time of the Fourth International Bamboo Congress, in 1995 in Bali, the world gathering drew nearly 3000 participants.

The International Bamboo Association is composed of member organizations from around the world. Focus varies among the participating groups, but the furtherance of bamboo binds the groups together. The American Bamboo Society is one of the member organizations. Others include such diverse groups as the Forest Research Institute of Bangladesh, various European bamboo societies, the India Bamboo Society, China's Bamboo Information Center and Nanjing Forestry University, the Japan Bamboo Society, the Zaire Bamboo Workshop, and others.

Other international bamboo organizations include the International Network for Bamboo and Rattan (INBAR), an intergovernmental organization established by treaty in November 1997, dedicated to improving social, economic, and environmental conditions through bamboo and rattan. Previously headquartered in India and now with primary headquarters in China, INBAR connects a global network of participants from the government, private, and nonprofit sectors in more than 50 countries. Its stated mission is to define and implement a global agenda for sustainable development through bamboo and rattan.

Because addresses change with some frequency for these largely volunteer organizations, the Internet is the best source for current information on them. Most bamboo web sites contain links to others, so once started on one web site, you can readily explore the rest. The American Bamboo Society's web site is a good beginning point. Failing that, the numerous Internet search engines will quickly ferret out the various bamboo web sites and bamboo resources.

The Future

There has been a resurgent interest in incorporating bamboo in landscape design. As with most plants, interest waxes and wanes as plants go in and out of style. The resurgent interest in bamboo in the United States, however, has emerged in conjunction with a broad base of committed and knowledgeable laypeople with an understanding of bamboo's great utility, as well as its great beauty and its profound cultural importance for many of the world's peoples throughout the history of humankind. It was the hope and vision of David Fairchild, Barbour Lathrop, Frank Meyer, Robert Young, E. A. McIlhenny, Floyd McClure, and other American bamboo pioneers that the utility and beauty of bamboo would be recognized in this country. All these pioneers were dedicated to the belief that bamboo could and should be a widely planted commercial crop in the United States. This commercial-agricultural connection was seen as the gateway for the development of a genuine bamboo culture in America. Although gardening and landscaping will help bring bamboo's beauty and enchantment to the U.S. and other parts of the world where bamboo is not a prominent native plant, the emergence of an enduring bamboo culture most likely will still be partially dependent on an agricultural connection—food and fiber, to nourish and sustain, in both a physical and cultural sense.

Through the efforts of the bamboo pioneers, by the 1960s, bamboo came very close to establishing a commercial-agricultural connection in the southeastern United States. Because it did not then achieve the goal, and because governmental funding was all but eliminated, bamboo in America was threatened with a return to the Dark Ages—a fate from which it was rescued, thanks largely to the founders of American Bamboo Society.

Primarily through the initiatives and projects of ABS members, a renewed effort to reestablish the commercial-agricultural connections began in the 1990s. An example of one such effort is the series of Pacific Northwest Bamboo Agro-Forestry Workshops, initiated by Gib Cooper, a bamboo nurseryman and long-time member of the American Bamboo Society. The decline in the Pacific Northwest's timber industry helped create a receptive environment for alternative approaches that are applicable not only within the region, but throughout the world. Workshop participants have come from throughout the United States, Canada, Europe, South America, the Caribbean, China, and other Asia-Pacific countries. Although any major results from the conferences are likely to be a long time in coming, the conferences offer the prospect of the adoption of bamboo by large-scale, conventional, mainstream business interests and cultures, as well as the fostering of smaller scale, non-conventional agricultural interests, under the auspices and legitimizing umbrellas of university extension services and chambers of commerce. This workshop model is now being extended to other regions of the United States.

The bamboo center of the United States began in the Southeast, with the indigenous presence of the country's only native bamboo species, *Arundinaria gigantea*. For about three-quarters of a century, spurred by the USDA's active plant-introduction and research efforts, the active bamboo center remained in the Southeast. Other historical centers emerged in Hawaii and on the West Coast, often in association with Asian immigrants who brought with them an appreciation and understanding of bamboo culture.

With the cessation of USDA involvement and support, the center of bamboo activity shifted to California and the West Coast, which offered both an excellent range of climates suitable to bamboo, and an ardent group of supporters who founded the American Bamboo Society. In the ensuing years, the American Bamboo Society helped fan the fires of interest and provided a geographically diverse center for bamboo, as new chapters were established throughout the United States. Bamboo is now grown in the Northeast and Northwest, the Southeast and Southwest, the Midwest, and all along the West Coast from the Mexican border to the Canadian border and beyond, including Hawaii and Alaska. Although the focus differs—from the hardy bamboos in the Northeast to the tropical species in southern Florida and Hawaii—the interest in bamboo is no less ardent. Today, perhaps as it should be, America's bamboo center is everywhere.

CHAPTER 8

Taxonomy

ESTIMATES VARY, BUT AT LEAST 90 genera and 1200 species of bamboos exist worldwide (Judziewicz et al. 1999). At various times, bamboos have been classified as a separate plant family, Bambusaceae, as a subfamily, Bambusoideae, or as a tribe, Bambuseae (McClure 1966). Taxonomists now generally agree that bamboo is properly classified as Bambusoideae, a subfamily of the grass family, Poaceae. Controversy continues, however, regarding the major taxonomic divisions within the subfamily. Various systems cluster tribes, supertribes, subtribes, and genera differently. Bamboos are the only woody grasses, but the existence of herbaceous as well as woody bamboos has further complicated classification. It is now generally accepted, however, that bamboos, the subfamily Bambusoideae, consist of two tribes: the tribe of herbaceous bamboos, Olyreae, and the tribe of woody bamboos, Bambuseae.

A significant portion of bamboo nomenclature can only be regarded as provisional. It is not uncommon for a bamboo to come into flower, only to be reclassified and renamed. The analysis of cryptic characteristics of leaf anatomy and biochemical methodologies have given rise to taxonomic realignments. Within the last 20 years or so, refined molecular techniques have been a revelatory new tool. In conjunction with other morphological information, molecular techniques have helped researchers uncover the evolutionary origins of grasses, resolve taxonomic inconsistencies, and more accurately assign taxonomic membership. The flowering of an infrequently flowering bamboo, new taxonomic methodologies, and revised thinking among taxonomists can give rise to proposals for new genera or membership in a different tribe or subfamily—or a return to a prior grouping.

Although complex taxonomic issues are as interesting to the dedicated researcher as they are seemingly unstable, most of these issues need not greatly trouble the average gardener, grower, or landscaper. With a few exceptions, notably the Himalayan mountain bamboos, species assignment is generally stable. Uncertainty and confusion have entered more often at the genus, subtribe, tribe, and subfamily levels—and at the other end of the naming scale, with the accepted names for varieties, forms, and cultivars. Most of the apparent instability is manifest among closely related genera, as opinions vary on how inclusive or narrow the definition of a given genus should be. For the most part, for practical purposes, the confusion and disputes can generally be "resolved" by memorizing a few synonyms.

One can look at bamboo taxonomy as having two missions. One mission is the delineation and definition of bamboo within the world of grasses, including all its groupings and subgroupings, in accord with natural evolutionary lines, including genera and the member species and forms belonging to the genera. This mission is best addressed by research scientists armed with the tools of their trade, which may include such methodologies as the analysis of lodicule morphology, photosynthetic pathway variations at the biochemical level, molecular markers in DNA extracts, and so forth.

A second mission of taxonomy may be regarded as one that meets the needs of the average gardener, grower, and landscaper, by providing a means for readily identifying bamboo in the field without resorting to cryptic characteristics or arcane methodologies. This mission addresses such questions as, "Is this the bamboo I want to dig, to plant, to buy, to sell, to harvest for shoots, to harvest for culms, to use to create a tall screen, and so forth?" and, "Is it a *Semiarundinaria* or *Phyllostachys*; a *P. bambusoides* or *P. vivax*?" and so on.

The average gardener, grower, or landscaper has a more basic taxonomic need that cannot be met by the more precise mechanisms of research taxonomy. Taxonomic classifications based on the characteristics of leaf anatomy, for example, are "derived from the leaf blade as viewed in transverse section and from the abaxial epidermis," and woody bamboos are characterized by "arm and fusoid cells, complex vascular system of the midrib imbedded in sclerome tissue, and vertically oriented silica bodies" (Ellis 1986). Molecular DNA markers, the current taxonomic tools of choice, are even further removed from lay application—clearly, one is not likely to draw these sorts of distinctions during a walk through the garden or while identifying the bamboo in a neighbor's grove. And further, in the words of C. M. A Stapleton (1997), in *The Morphology of Woody Bamboos,* "Even if technology provides a hand-held DNA extractor and sequencer and access to vast data banks of known sequences for identification of plants, someone is still going to ask, 'What do they look like?'"

The flowering parts of grasses have traditionally played a prominent role in bamboo taxonomy. Since most bamboos flower with great infrequency, dependence on the inflorescences for field identification is far from a viable option. Fortunately, among the grasses, bamboos have relatively distinctive vegetative features, and field identification of bamboos is almost entirely dependent on these characteristics. Vegetative keys for field identification, while somewhat problematic, are nonetheless generally viable, working best in a geographic area or other venues where the range of species to be distinguished is limited and known.

Overt characteristics are not sufficient to render taxonomic assignments, but once the assignments have been made, vegetative keys are useful tools for field taxonomy. In his book, *The Bamboos,* McClure (1966) states the case, though from a different angle:

> While it is possible to recognize and identify individual species of bamboos, once they are thoroughly known, by an adequate array of vegetative characters, it is not always possible, given the present state of our knowledge, to determine the generic affinities of an unknown bamboo with certainty, by means of vegetative structures alone.

Once a bamboo is thoroughly known, its vegetative characteristics can provide a relatively reliable means of identification and an excellent field tool for the gardener, grower, and landscaper. The culm leaf is one of the most distinctive vegetative features, and it provides a ready method for field identification—at least during the bamboo's shooting period. Culm leaves and branching patterns are two prominent characteristics employed in field classification methodologies.

Evolution of Bamboo Taxonomy

Since 1789, when the first bamboo genus was identified, approximately 150 genera and well more than 1000 species names have been assigned, many later to fall from use because they were either illegitimate or synonymous with existing classifications. The first recorded attempts to rationally classify bamboo date to as early as China's Jin Dynasty, around 317 to 420 A.D. The Bamboo Chart, compiled by Dai Kaizhi, identified 61 different bamboo types. Of the original 61 identified types, 34 remain today as distinctive species or varieties (Li 1997).

In 1623, Caspar Bauhin used the name *Arundo* to describe reed grasses, and he further classified the plant that he called *Arundo arbor* as a woody, treelike reed. He subsequently referred to a type of *Arundo* by the Indian term *Bambus*. His grouping included plants other than bamboo, but the classification had been narrowed, and the root terminology, *Arundo* and *Bambus*, is carried forward, in modified form, to today's taxonomy.

Thomas R. Soderstrom summarized some of the history of bamboo taxonomy in his 1985 paper "Bamboo Systematics: Yesterday, today, and tomorrow." In 1753, in the seminal work *Species Plantarum*, Linnaeus included all bamboos under *Arundo bambos*. In the ensuing decades, it became clear that the grouping *Arundo* actually encompassed many genera. In 1789, two botanists, Retzius in Sweden and Schreber in Germany, decided that what had been called *Arundo bambos* was actually a distinct genus, Bambos, or in its Latin form, *Bambusa*. Identification of new genera and species proceeded at a rapid rate. In 1815, the German botanist Kunth classified grasses into ten groups of genera, one of which was Gramina Bambusacea. This scheme was a precursor to the system of subfamilies in use today and to the bamboo subfamily of grasses, now known as Bambusoideae. In 1835, in his study of Brazilian bamboos, Nees von Esenbeck recognized three groups of bamboo: Bambuseae and Arundinariae, both encompassing woody bamboos, and Streptochaeteae, which encompassed herbaceous bamboos. As early as 1835, then, researchers recognized the possibility, or necessity, of including herbaceous species in bamboo taxonomy.

Since the time of Linnaeus in the mid-18th century, until relatively recently, the taxonomy of all angiosperms has been based primarily on reproductive structures. Traditionally, grass taxonomy has been based largely on the overt characteristics of the plant's flowering parts. Extensive analysis of spikelet structure evolved into a complex cataloging system for taxonomic assignment. For most grasses, dependence on the flowering parts of the plant for classification seemed to work well, but most bamboos flower very infrequently, sometimes for periods that may span more than a century. At least one bamboo, *Bambusa vulgaris*, has never had a recorded period of full inflorescence. The sometimes absence of fruit, even when flowering does finally occur, and the practical lack of rigorous, controlled field observation under the infrequent flowering conditions made bamboo classification all the more problematic.

More than a century ago, it became apparent that dependence on the overt characteristics of inflorescence was problematic for all grasses, leading to artificial groupings that did not reflect a common ancestry. Parallel or convergent evolution could and did lead to artificial groupings when plants from separate evolutionary lines grew to resemble one another, tempting classification groupings that did not reflect their dissimilar evolutionary origins. For example, fleshy fruit was once the basis for placing bamboo in the tribe Bacciferae, but fleshy fruit is an evolutionary path taken more than once in widely separated evolutionary groups in both the New World and Old World. The apparent development of leptomorph rhizomes from pachymorph rhizomes is another common parallel development among separate evolutionary lines.

In the 1930s, cell structure and other less obvious aspects of plant physiology were correlated with the structure of the flowering parts to resolve some of the problems with the earlier classification systems. Grass tribes could then be separated into broad natural groups. Yet, these elements were themselves subject to some, though fewer, of the traps of parallel evolution, and they were sometimes self-contradictory, or too obtuse and indefinite to be practical.

Until the late 1950s, most classification systems recognized two subfamilies of Poaceae: Panicoideae and Festucoideae. These systems reduced bamboo to tribal status (Bambuseae) and included only woody plants in the tribe. With only two subfamilies, these systems were unable to account for several tribes that did not fit in either subfamily, and it became increasingly apparent that these systems were, at least in part, arbitrary and artificial.

In 1961, Lorenzo Parodi established a system of classifying the grasses of his native country. Under the grass subfamily Bambusoideae, Parodi described four tribes found in Argentina—all the woody bamboos in the tribe Bambuseae, and three tribes of herbaceous bamboos, Olyreae, Phareae, and Streptochaeteae.

Although the great bamboo researcher F. A. McClure did not include herbaceous species in his writings on bamboo, Soderstrom (1985) cites discussions with McClure during the late 1960s and just prior to McClure's death in 1971, where McClure expressed his conclusion that the herbaceous species as well as the woody species should be included in the subfamily Bambusoideae.

In 1959, during the IX International Botanical Congress in Montreal, Canada, the symposium on the Natural Classification of the Gramineae emphasized the synthesis of traditional morphological characteristics of the flowering parts of grasses with non-morphological, covert attributes. This approach gained increasing acceptance, and the analysis of leaf anatomy, in particular, was employed in classifying bamboos and other grasses. The epidermis of ligules and the type and arrangement of cell tissues in the culm walls are examples of other cryptic features that were of value in tracing the evolution of bamboos and establishing their taxonomy (Ellis 1986).

Leaf anatomy, in conjunction with other indices, proved productive in delineating evolutionary groups of grasses, in general, and bamboos, in particular. Studies of leaf anatomy have shown the similarity in basic structure among woody and herbaceous bamboos, as well as suggested distinctions at tribal and subtribal classification levels. Attempts to employ leaf anatomy to draw distinctions at the generic level were not particularly successful. Even at the subfamily and tribal level, inconsistencies remained, leaving the subfamily Bambusoideae, and thus "bamboo," with uncertain membership, and the origins and evolution of bamboos and grasses fundamentally unresolved. The rightful inclusion of the herbaceous species in the Bambusoideae subfamily resolved some taxonomic issues, but many more remained.

Molecular Techniques and Cladistics

Before the advent of cladistic analysis and the assistance of molecular techniques, which offer a greater array of discrete, identifiable characteristics, traditional methods of taxonomy relied on differences among a relatively small number of characteristics. Deciding which characteristics were taxonomically significant, and yielded the most meaningful distinctions, was a task fraught with pitfalls, with results that were inevitably incomplete and arbitrary. All such taxonomic systems, at least with plants as taxonomically difficult as bamboos, ultimately break down.

In some nebulous way, it has been hoped that if a plant is like another plant in certain ways then the plants should be grouped together and would bear some relationship to their evolution and ancestry. But plants with very different lineages may evolve along parallel lines and have identical characteristics. *Guadua,* a South American bamboo once thought to be of the *Bambusa* genus of India and Asia, for example, is now known to be a distinct genus with a separate evolutionary path. The similarities between *Guadua* and *Bambusa* are the result of parallel evolution.

Plants can be grouped together in a variety of ways for a variety of purposes. They can, for example, be grouped by how they look, how they function, or by their evolutionary relationships. In taxonomy, these grouping methods have often been muddled together, and the methodology has sometimes become confused with the purpose. A plant's structure offers information that can help us to draw conclusions about a plant's ancestry, evolution, and evolutionary relationships, and thus its taxonomy, but in and of itself, a plant's structure is not, or should not be, the reason or basis for taxonomic assignment. Only within the last 20 years or so have the tools of molecular data and analysis been available to focus on the purpose and separate it from the method. Fundamentally and authentically, taxonomy is not about a set of arbitrary similarities, but is a response to the questions, What plants is this plant related to? What is its lineage? What are its ancestors? These are questions of evolution and evolutionary relationships.

In cladistic analysis, plants are classified into groups according to "recency of common descent," basing the groupings on shared derived characteristics. Plants are grouped together if they share one or more characteristics that are derived from a common ancestor and are not present in any ancestral group. Given sufficient, informative data, this methodology can reconstruct evolutionary relationships and give rise to an authentic and meaningful taxonomy. The problem with this approach lies in gathering accurate data on characteristics that are capable of revealing discrete differences and descent. Molecular data, particularly molecular data from DNA sequences, in conjunction with morphological data, help fill that need.

Molecular techniques offer a large number of readily measurable characteristics. DNA sequences that change very little can reveal the evolutionary changes at the higher levels of taxonomy, such as subfamily and tribe. More rapidly changing sequences can show relationships between genera or species. DNA markers are in every part of the plant and are not dependent upon a given state. Even dry leaves from herbarium collections can be used.

Unfortunately, molecular studies are not cheap; the techniques are only in their early stages of development; and effective analysis is best accomplished in conjunction with other taxonomic tools and indicators. Nevertheless, molecular techniques and cladistic analysis have emerged as powerful taxonomic tools—so powerful that these analytical tools are redefining their task and may one day call into question the conceptual tools (the binomial system and traditional taxonomy) they are meant to serve.

Fundamentally, the purpose of taxonomic methodologies is not to classify all living entities into genera and species, but rather to understand the evolution and relationships of living things. As we learn more, the concepts of genera and species, and the binomial system itself, may one day prove to be artificial constructs that need to be set aside (Stapleton 1997a) in favor of different conceptual constructs that do a better job of revealing the world and helping us grasp it. In the end, with respect to the adequacy of our analytical and conceptual tools, the world itself is the final arbiter.

Bamboo Redefined

Early studies using molecular data were not very successful, leading to weak or erroneous conclusions. In these early studies, a limited sampling of woody bamboos and rice seemed to indicate, rather inconclusively, that bamboos were the oldest grasses and that rice might be a bamboo.

In a landmark study, published in 1995, Lynn G. Clark of Iowa State University, and others, conducted a survey of virtually every tribe of grasses that had been included in the subfamily Bambusoideae (bamboos) in any classification system, as well as samples from all the major tribes of grasses. The study revealed that characteristics that had previously been associated with Bambusoideae were actually shared ancestral characteristics of the grass family. These characteristics had been retained in bamboos, but they were not defining characteristics of Bambusoideae. The study also showed that some (but not all) of the herbaceous grasses, specifically Anomochloeae, Streptochaeteae, and Phareae, that had been classified as tribes of Bambusoideae could no longer be regarded as such and, thus, were not bamboos. In conjunction with fossil evidence, the study results suggested that grasses likely evolved during the late Cretaceous period in Gondwanaland (Clark et al. 1995), some 65 million years ago, possibly coexisting with the dinosaurs. Bamboos (Bambusoideae) likely evolved later, probably in the Oligocene or Miocene epochs, some 30 to 40 million years ago (Lynn Clark, personal communication).

Although an exceptionally powerful tool, molecular techniques, even in conjunction with other analytical tools, have not yet resolved many of the larger issues of bamboo and grass taxonomy or of bamboo evolution. So far, molecular data support two major clades (evolutionary groupings) of woody bamboos (Bambuseae): "temperate" bamboos from both Asia and the New World, and "tropical" bamboos from both Asia and the New World. The "tropical" clade includes taxa that have adapted to the southern temperate zone and the equatorial highlands, including species of *Chusquea, Aulonemia,* and *Neurolepis*. Molecular data additionally support subdivision of the tropical woody bamboos into New World and Old World clades (Clark 1997a). To illustrate the implications, molecular data confirm that the *Bambusa* genus of the Old World tropics and the *Guadua* genus of South America, although very similar, evolved separately.

In contrast with the open habitats of their ancestors and most other grasses, the early bamboos, including both the woody tribe Bambuseae and the herbaceous tribe Olyreae, were adapted to forest environments. The once-held concept that bamboos are the most ancient grasses has proven untenable. In the words of Lynn G. Clark in her article "Bamboos: The centrepiece of the grass family" (1997a), "the true bamboos must be seen as a more recently evolved group of grasses adapted to the forest habitat, and although they retain some ancestral features, particularly the inflorescences and flowers, true bamboos are anything but primitive grasses."

Identification and Naming

The taxonomy is relatively stable for most bamboo groups at the species level, but for many bamboos, genus assignment is tenuous, as are the accepted names and designations of variety, form, and cultivar. All of this is subject to ongoing inquiry, debate, and revision. The estimated number of bamboo genera in the world has been variously placed at 49, by Clayton and Renvoize in 1986; 59, by Soderstrom and Ellis in 1986; 77, by Dransfield and Widjaja in 1995; and at least 90, by Judziewicz et al in 1999. Because bamboo is an under-studied and taxonomically difficult group, it is perhaps no surprise that succeeding studies and assessments uncover additional genera and species. Within the last decade, for example, new studies have revealed that 23 out of 56 species in Sumatra had not previously been described, and that 11 out of 42 species in Nepal and Bhutan were newly identified taxa. In her 1992 book, *The Bamboos of Sabah,* Soejatmi Dransfield points out that it is a mistake to generalize that bamboos are widely distributed, suggesting that only a few species are widely distributed in nature. For this reason, even studies that are focused on a relatively narrow geographical area are likely to miss bamboo taxa. Many more bamboos are awaiting identification and description, even as some become obliterated forever by the onslaught of irresponsible land clearing and other ecological travesties.

Classification of some genera, for example *Phyllostachys,* is quite stable. The overt vegetative characteristics are distinct and uniform among its members, and few other genera even approximate its appearance. It is relatively easy, even for the lay observer, to identify a bamboo as a *Phyllostachys.* For other genera, such as *Arundinaria* and *Sasa* and the genera that have been separated from them, the overt characteristics are less distinct and uniform, and their taxonomic assignments are more provisional. Many *Arundinaria,* for example, differ considerably from other members of the genus, but the lines of natural groupings and the determination of which groupings legitimately require a separate genus is problematic, at least at the current stage of research.

New research has uncovered new genera and species and has given rise to the realignment or redesignation of the genera of some species. Following the literature over the course of more than a century, one may see a given species change its genus several times. And generic changes are not uncommon today, as new research continues to modify our understanding of bamboo. From the mid-1970s to mid-1980s, Chinese researchers defined four new genera and more than 250 new species and forms. It should be noted, however, that Chinese researchers, as researchers everywhere, do not subscribe to a single point of view, and they differ on various taxonomic issues, including the appropriateness of some of the new species and generic designations.

New genera are often created as breakouts of existing genera. For example, from *Sasa* come *Sasaella* and *Sasamorpha*; from *Chimonobambusa* comes *Qiongzhuea*; and from *Arundinaria* come *Bashania, Pleioblastus,* and *Pseudosasa.* Controversy persists on how many of the new genera are legitimate. Soderstrom and Ellis (1986) included these and related bamboos in the subtribe Arundinariinae, a group of bamboos that they regarded as taxonomically problematic. In their words, Arundinariinae is "a complex subtribe in which the generic limits are far from adequately resolved, particularly in the type genus itself and obviously closely related genera such as *Fargesia.* Numerous genera have been described, but many seem to have been erected on minor and insignificant characters." *Sasaella* and *Sasamorpha* will very likely be eliminated as distinct genera one day and placed, once again, with *Sasa.*

Some genera, such as *Phyllostachys,* and the entire genera of some subtribes described by Soderstrom and Ellis, such as the subtribe Arthrostylidiinae, are far more stable. A stable and accurate assignment of bamboo genera is one of the current challenges in bamboo taxonomy. Again, in the words of Soderstrom and Ellis (1986), "In some subtribes, such as the Arthrostylidiinae, many of the genera are clear-cut, but in other subtribes, such as the Arundinariinae, they are not. A neat definition of all the genera of bamboos is still far off." With cladistics, and the assistance of the molecular tools that are now available, a more authentic delineation should emerge as research progresses.

The inherent difficulties of bamboo taxonomy are further compounded by a system of taxonomy that is sometimes at odds with what we now know as a result of molecular analysis and other modern scientific techniques. The need to better ground our taxonomy on evolutionary relationships, and the far better understanding of these relationships that modern scientific methods afford, will inevitably bring about changes in taxonomy.

In 1753, with the publication of *Species Plantarum,* Linnaeus promulgated the fundamental unit of naming, which remains in use to this day, a binomial name consisting of the genus and the specific member of the genus. For example, the binomial *Phyllostachys aurea* consists of the genus, *Phyllostachys,* and a modifier that designates the specific member of the genus, *aurea.* The species name is the binomial, *Phyllostachys aurea.* The naming of plants of wild origin is now under the sanction of the International Code of Botanical Nomenclature (ICBN). Identifying and naming additional variations within the species is permitted and can be employed as warranted. In descending order of significance are subspecies (abbreviated ssp.), variety (var.), and form (f.). Examples are *Chusquea mimosa* ssp. *australis, Thamnocalamus spathiflorus* var. *crassinodus,* and *Pleioblastus chino* f. *elegantissimus.* Combinations are possible. For example, a variety may have more than one form, and thus require further distinction. An example of such is *Pleioblastus chino* var. *vaginatus* f. *variegatus.* Plants of cultivated origin are under the sanction of the International Code of Nomenclature for Cultivated Plants (ICNCP). Cultivars may be propagated vegetatively or from seed. A cultivar may consist of plants that either are or are not genetically identical, but they must nonetheless have characteristics that distinguish them from other cultivars (Griffiths 1994). The cultivar designation follows the species name. In earlier literature, one may see a cultivar designated by the abbreviation "cv.," as in *Phyllostachys aurea* cv. Koi. However, the 1995 International Code for Cultivated Plants specifies that a cultivar is indicated by using single quotation marks, as in *Phyllostachys aurea* 'Koi'.

The two sanctioning groups have different but somewhat overlapping responsibilities, and the lines of distinction are not always clear. Bamboos with new and distinctive features can arise either vegetatively or from seedlings, in both cultivated and indigenous plants. Certain features, such as yellow culms with green striping, may arise from cultivated plants and may then be perpetuated through cultivation, yet these features may also reoccur spontaneously and repeatedly in nature. Some bamboo plants have long been known in cultivation, and their origins in the wild, if such exist, are unknown. On the other hand, some cultivated bamboos rapidly become feral and are found in the wild. The origins are not always clear. Also, many Malaysian bamboos, for example, that are "in the wild" may actually have been selected and propagated over the course of thousands of years by the ancient ancestors of modern-day Malaysians. The distinctions between wild and cultivated plant forms become blurred. And further, because the criteria for nomenclature under ICBN are considerably more restrictive than those for the ICNCP, some taxa are designated as cultivars even though they more properly should be treated as varieties or forms.

CHAPTER 9

Bamboo Genera, Species, and Cultivars

SOME BAMBOO characteristics lend themselves to numeric summary or broadly grouped categorization. Among these are maximum height, maximum diameter, minimum temperature, and light requirements. This chapter's listing of bamboo species and varieties presents this summary information in a format similar to the *American Bamboo Society Bamboo Species Source List*. I wish to acknowledge the source list's creator, Richard Haubrich, for creating, designing, and for many years, maintaining what has become a standard format and reference for listing and describing bamboo for the gardener, grower, landscaper, and aficionado.

Descriptive Limitations

The information cited for sunlight requirements, maximum height, maximum diameter, and minimum temperature is intended only as rough, relative guides, not as absolutes. Minimum temperatures, in particular, are subject to wide variation and, in many cases, are untested best estimates. Bamboo is a highly responsive plant. Many bamboos can adapt and survive in widely varied growing conditions,

but will only achieve maximum growth when cultural conditions are optimal. The numeric information offers a quick, relative comparison among species, but actual performance will depend on specific growing conditions. The characteristics of the species will also play a role in performance. For example, a bamboo that tolerates alkaline soils may demonstrate more vigorous growth in a site with alkaline soil than a species that is intolerant of alkaline soil, even if the alkaline-intolerant species would otherwise be more vigorous.

Height and diameter

In some instances, information from new sources or different growing sites may differ greatly from previous information. For example, Chinese sources generally indicate a height of around 20 ft. (6 m) for *Phyllostachys rubromarginata*, yet it grows much larger in many parts of the United States. A harvested culm of *P. rubromarginata* growing near Bloomingdale, Georgia, measured 60 ft. (18 m) long (Turtle 1995b). On the other hand, *P. heterocycla* f. *pubescens* may readily grow to 90 ft. (27 m) or more in China, with a culm diameter of 7 in. (18 cm) or more, but it is a difficult spe-

233

cies to establish, and achieves its maximum potential only within a relatively narrow range of growing conditions. Under growing conditions that are far from the mark, *P. heterocycla* f. *pubescens* may not even achieve the more modest height expectations of some of the smaller species of the genus.

It is also important to note that the figures cited for maximum height and diameter are only achievable with ideal climate, soil, nutrients, and moisture, in a large grove, clump, or forest that has been established for perhaps a decade or more. Although it is startling to see the impressive size that can quickly be achieved in a small garden plot, or even a container, such plants will nevertheless be considerably smaller than the cited maximums.

Temperatures significantly colder or warmer than the ideal will also limit size. Many *Phyllostachys* bamboos, for example, grow much smaller in southern Florida or the northeastern United States than they do in either Georgia or Oregon. *Phyllostachys makinoi,* a species of *Phyllostachys* that prefers more warmth, will grow much larger in Texas than it will in Washington state. Conversely, *P. nigra,* a species that does well in cooler sites and prefers less intense sunlight, may grow larger in Washington than it would in Texas.

Minimum temperature

Wind, humidity, sun, duration of low temperatures, soil moisture, presence or absence of protective snow cover, and so on, all play a role in determining whether or not a bamboo will be damaged by low temperatures. By convention, minimum temperatures cited in this book refer to the point at which leaf damage begins to occur. The temperatures at which culm and rhizome death occur is generally far lower. The minimums cited assume short term rather than protracted exposure to the minimum temperature. If cold temperatures are persistent rather than brief, the damage will be more severe. A semitropical bamboo may be able to tolerate a brief frost for an evening or two, but not a full winter of that same temperature. In general, if continuing low temperatures at or near the minimum are expected, choosing a more cold hardy bamboo may be warranted. See chapter 3 for more information on cold hardiness and on growing bamboo at temperatures colder than the normal minimum.

Minimum temperatures are only approximations. Often, particularly with more recent introductions, insufficient data are available, and the cited minimums reflect only the best estimates of performance. The minimum temperatures cited are merely rough, relative estimates and are not intended to be definitive or absolute.

Sunlight

In the descriptions that follow, sunlight requirements are listed as full shade, partial shade, mostly sunny, and full sun. The requirements are only an approximation. Most bamboos will grow, if not necessarily flourish, in a wide range of light conditions.

A bamboo's light requirements and tolerances are partially determined by environmental conditions. For example, a *Phyllostachys* that generally thrives in full sun may need some sheltering in the nearly cloudless, arid American Southwest. A *Fargesia* that generally requires cool summers and partial shade may thrive in "full sun" in some of the cloudier parts of the coastal Pacific Northwest. Refer to the "Heat and Light" section of chapter 3 for additional examples and information.

The Bamboos

Because some botanical names change with relative frequency, any listing of bamboo species, varieties, forms, and cultivars is, of necessity, subject to ongoing revision. The species listing in this book is not intended as a definitive proclamation regarding naming conventions. Indeed, such matters are the proper domain of research botanists and taxonomists and are considerably beyond my own knowledge and abilities. In some instances, research by accepted experts may offer a compelling basis for changing a long-established name. In other instances, expert opinion may vary widely, and there may be little agreement on the correct name for a taxon. In some instances, I have incorporated name changes when the information available to me seemed to warrant a change. In other instances, some long-standing names are clearly in need of revision, but the correct new name is unclear, and I have elected to continue with the existing naming convention, rather than further muddying the waters with new names that may not be appropriate. These are all judgment calls. Six months from now, or even a month from now, it is likely that I would make some of the judgment calls differently.

The index of this book includes name cross-references. The American Bamboo Society's *Bamboo Species Source List,* updated yearly, is another source of information for alternate or new names. If it is any concession to us, it is the plant itself that has meaning. The names are only tools to refer to the thing itself. Perhaps, one day, our bamboo names will be better, more reliable tools. The situation is not too onerous, however. For the most part, we can readily make our way among the muddle by simply learning a few synonyms.

While the unusual and exotic have considerable appeal for the collector, even the most common bamboos have much to offer the gardener, grower, and landscaper—as well as the collector. Often, the intrinsic beauty or usefulness of certain bamboos caused them to become popular in the first place, and thus more common—but only in number, not character.

Although some of the plants listed here may be rare or difficult to find, all are currently cultivated in the United States.

Acidosasa

Native to China's southeastern provinces, *Acidosasa* consists of medium-sized, arborescent bamboos with leptomorph rhizome systems. The genus comprises some 22 species. The leaf sheaths are deciduous. Three to five principal branches are produced per node. The tessellated foliage leaves are generally large, suggesting sasa bamboos, hence the derivation of the latter part of the genus name. The other part of the genus name arises from the purported sour, or acid, nature of its shoots, many of which are regarded as choice and are pickled by local peoples.

Acidosasa edulis

Maximum height: 40 ft. (12 m)
Maximum diameter: 2¼ in. (6 cm)
Minimum temperature: 15°F (−9°C) estimated
Light: full sun

Native to China's Fujian and Jiangxi Provinces, and cultivated in Zhejiang Province, *Acidosasa edulis* is regarded as an excellent species for commercial shoot production for late spring and early summer shoots. The shoots are regarded as choice.

Acidosasa gigantea

Common synonym: *Sinobambusa gigantea*
Maximum height: 55 ft. (17 m)
Maximum diameter: 4 in. (10 cm)
Minimum temperature: 15°F (−9°C) estimated
Light: full sun

An attractive ornamental, this species also has straight culms that are useful as bamboo timber. Introduced into Europe in the mid-1990s, it is native to Zhejiang, Fujian, and Guangxi in China.

Ampelocalamus

This genus consists of subtropical and temperate bamboos with pachymorph rhizomes. Some species reach a height of 40 ft. (12 m). The branches are distinctively arranged in vertical groups that curve outward from the culm.

The upper portions of the culms are heavily pendulous, nodding deeply. *Ampelocalamus* species are semi-scandent bamboos. In the Himalayas, this genus is generally found in wetter subtropical forests than *Himalayacalamus* and *Drepanostachyum*. *Ampelocalamus* bamboos are tender to somewhat frost hardy. *Ampelocalamus* is native to China, India, Burma (Myanmar), Nepal, and Vietnam. There are 11 known species.

Ampelocalamus scandens

Maximum height: 34 ft. (10 m)
Maximum diameter: ⅓ in. (0.8 cm)
Minimum temperature: 32°F (0°C) estimated
Light: mostly sunny

Ampelocalamus scandens can be found growing in steep rocks at elevations up to approximately 1000 ft. (300 m) in China's Guizhou Province.

Arundinaria

In the 19th century, nearly all Asian temperate and subalpine bamboos (except *Phyllostachys*) were heaped into the genus *Arundinaria*. Today, *Arundinaria* remains something of a catchall genus, even as classification efforts define new genera within the group. Recognition of the new genera and the proper demarcations for those genera is a matter of ongoing debate. In China and Japan, in the 20th century and particularly the 1980s, many new genera were separated out from *Arundinaria* and newly defined. The new genera were not always cogently defined, however, and not always widely accepted outside their country of origin—or even within their country of origin. Adding to the fracas, some of the new genera were found to be identical to previously described genera, and therefore unnecessary. More recently, with increased sharing and availability of research information, more of the new genera from the *Arundinaria* heap are becoming increasingly accepted.

For most bamboos assigned to the genus *Arundinaria*, the placement may be regarded as provisional. Only *A. gigantea*, the type species for the genus, is secure. It is native only to North America, and is North America's only native species.

As currently constituted, *Arundinaria* comprises shrublike or treelike bamboos with three to numerous principal branches and leptomorph rhizomes. *Arundinaria* species are generally hardy, but typically less cold tolerant than *Phyllostachys*, although the hardier of the *A. gigantea* clones may equal or better any *Phyllostachys* in cold tolerance. Although usually smaller than those of *Phyllostachys*, the rhizomes of some *Arundinaria* species run more deeply and are more brittle, making management of lateral spread more difficult. The leaves at the tip of a new shoot are closely arrayed in a fanlike cluster. In some species, the culm leaves are deciduous, but in others, the culm leaves persist and may convey a less pristine, more unkempt look in the landscape.

Arundinaria funghomii

Maximum height: 30 ft. (9 m)
Maximum diameter: 1⅛ in. (3 cm)
Minimum temperature: 0°F (−18°C)
Light: mostly sunny

An attractive bamboo that may grow only 4 ft. (1.2 m) tall in cooler climates, *Arundinaria funghomii* shoots in late spring or summer. The new culms are densely covered with a gray bloom, handsomely setting off the dark green foliage.

Arundinaria gigantea ssp. gigantea

Common names: cane, giant cane, river cane, canebrake bamboo
Maximum height: 33 ft. (10 m)
Maximum diameter: 1½ in. (4 cm)
Minimum temperature: −10°F (−23°C)
Light: full sun

Morphologically varied, and divided into two subspecies, *Arundinaria gigantea* is the only bamboo species native to the United States. Its natural habitat includes moist woodlands and areas along streams and backwaters, typically at elevations below 650 ft. (200 m). The predominant distribution of the two subspecies differs. *Arundinaria gigantea* ssp. *gigantea* is more widely distributed in inland habitats and to the west; *A. gigantea* ssp. *tecta* is more common along the southeastern coastal plain (Judziewicz et al. 1999). *Arundinaria gigantea* ssp. *macrosperma* had previously been described as another subspecies, with characteristics that combine elements of *A. gigantea* ssp. *gigantea* and *A. gigantea* ssp. *tecta,* but it is not generally recognized as a valid name.

At one time, thousands of acres of cane, the name given to *Arundinaria gigantea,* spanned a range from Maryland, Virginia, and Florida, across to Texas, north to Missouri, and up the Ohio River Valley. The cane meadows provided food sources for herds of migrating buffalo, as well as for cattle and other domesticated animals. In some stands, the vegetation density was remarkable, reaching up to 65,000 culms per acre (160,000 culms per hectare). The canebrakes offered a unique habitat for nesting birds and other wildlife. The decimation or demise of Bachman's warbler, the passenger pigeon, and the Carolina parakeet has been attributed to the loss of the canebrakes (Billings and Houf 1995; Judziewicz et al. 1999).

Although the species still extends over much of its former range, the acreage it covers is greatly diminished. Land clearing and overgrazing by livestock has decimated the oncegreat expanses of the native cane. It has been suggested that hogs rooting and feeding on rhizomes were the principal cause of the rapid disappearance of cane in Missouri. Early settlers regarded canebrakes as indicators of fertile soil, and as a consequence, the canebrakes were subjected to intensive clearing for farmland.

Arundinaria gigantea ssp. *gigantea* exhibits considerable variation, culm coloration and cold hardiness among the notable differences.

According to one report, after a winter low temperature of −4°F (−20°C), some forms exhibited little or no damage, while other forms grown in the same area lost all their leaves. The 'Macon' variant from northern Tennessee and central Kentucky has a strongly upright growth habit and is reportedly evergreen down to −22°F (−30°C) (Turtle 1995a).

In the 1788 book *Flora Caroliniana,* the "large cane" of the southern United States was termed *Arundo gigantea.* In 1803, Michaux elevated *Arundo gigantea* to the genus *Arundinaria,* thus separating it from the genus *Bambusa,* and making the bamboo of the southern United States the first species of the genus to be described. It is the only New World member of the genus, and some authorities have sug-

The gray bloom on a new *Arundinaria funghomii* culm.

gested that it is the sole legitimate member of the genus. Nearly all New World bamboos have pachymorph rhizome systems, and *A. gigantea* is rare in the New World for its leptomorph rhizome system.

A matter of speculation, *Arundinaria gigantea* may have migrated from Asia, across the Bering Bridge, during a time of ample warmth and moisture in the early to middle Miocene epoch, somewhere between 10 and 20 million years ago. If so, *A. gigantea* may be the only New World bamboo of Asian origin.

Arundinaria gigantea ssp. *tecta*
Common name: cane, switch cane
Maximum height: 6 ft. (1.8 m)
Maximum diameter: ½ in. (1.25 cm)
Minimum temperature: –10°F (–23°C)
Light: full sun

This subspecies of *Arundinaria gigantea* has at times been regarded as a separate species. *Arundinaria gigantea* ssp. *tecta* is a generally smaller variant with persistent culm leaves and air canals in the rhizome system. Although neither subspecies is among the more attractive landscaping bamboos, *A. gigantea* ssp. *tecta* has a scruffier and less desirable appearance. Both *A. gigantea* ssp. *gigantea* and *A. gigantea* ssp. *tecta* are polymorphic, exhibiting significant morphological differences. Although most bamboos will suffer leaf mortality and drop their leaves if conditions are too cold, then grow leaves again in the spring (if the branches and culms have not died), some variants of *A. gigantea* ssp. *tecta* are naturally deciduous in their native habitats, routinely dropping their leaves each winter.

Bambusa
A large genus comprising some 139 known species, *Bambusa* is endemic to the semitropical and tropical regions of the Old World. Some of its species, notably *B. vulgaris,* have been distributed and cultivated for so long throughout the tropics, including the New World, that it is

often assumed that the genus is native to those areas as well. Most members of the genus are large timber bamboos. All have pachymorph rhizome systems. Some species have a very tight caespitose growth habit, but others have longer rhizome necks and form open clumps with more widely dispersed culms. *Bambusa* has a multiple branching habit with a principal branch that is generally significantly larger than the others. In a few species, thorny spines replace some of the branchlets. The culm leaf blades are erect and triangular. Culms are typically thick walled.

Several species of *Bambusa* have considerably greater cold tolerance than species of other semitropical and tropical genera, and they can be successfully grown in temperate climates with mild winters, expanding the geographic reach of arborescent bamboo with a clumping habit—and giving the gardener, grower, and landscaper additional options. As the outer limits of cold tolerance are approached, however, the size and rate of growth is considerably reduced. In most American growing regions, shoot initiation naturally occurs in late summer to fall, presenting difficulties in marginal climates if the cold of winter arrives before the culms have finished shooting and hardening sufficiently, or before branching and leafing has been completed. As with other bamboo, if normal shooting and growth is disrupted, *Bambusa* will often initiate new shoots outside of its normal shooting interval. Because *Bambusa* does not require a period of cold dormancy, the plants can successfully be grown indoors as houseplants if light and humidity are sufficient. The smaller ornamental species of *Bambusa* are particularly suited to this purpose.

The International Network for Bamboo and Rattan (INBAR), in cooperation with the International Plant Genetic Resources Institute, developed a list of priority bamboos that they regarded as meriting focused research and wider use. Although the listing and choices are

Bambusa bambos. Quail Botanical Gardens.

somewhat controversial, it is nonetheless interesting to note that the original list of 19 species included 6 *Bambusa: B. bambos, B. blumeana, B. polymorpha, B. textilis, B. tulda,* and *B. vulgaris.* In suitable climates, many *Bambusa* also rank highly as garden and landscape ornamentals, providing attractive tall screens along perimeters and striking specimen plants in open areas.

Bambusa albostriata

Common synonym: *Bambusa textilis* var. *albostriata*
Maximum height: 40 ft. (12 m)
Maximum diameter: 2 in. (5 cm)
Minimum temperature: 32°F (0°C) estimated
Light: full sun

This bamboo was originally classified as *Bambusa textilis* var. *albostriata,* but has been given its own species ranking. Native to China's Guangdong Province, it is differentiated by attractive white striping on the lower culm internodes and culm leaves.

Bambusa arnhemica

Maximum height: 26 ft. (8 m)
Maximum diameter: 4 in. (10 cm)
Minimum temperature: 32°F (0°C)
Light: full sun

Indigenous to the moist tropical areas of Australia's Northern Territory, this species is named for Arnhem Land, a region of northern Australia west of the Gulf of Carpentaria, and home of the country's largest aboriginal reservation. *Bambusa arnhemica* is found along water sources, becoming partially deciduous during dry periods. The species is polymorphic, exhibiting different characteristics in different areas. An attractive bamboo with thick culms, it is suited to only the warmest growing regions of the United States.

Bambusa bambos

Common synonyms: *Bambusa arundinacea,*
    B. spinosa

Common names: giant thorny bamboo, Indian thorny bamboo
Maximum height: 100 ft. (30 m)
Maximum diameter: 7 in. (18 cm)
Minimum temperature: 27°F (–3°C)
Light: full sun

Bambusa bambos is one of the most important bamboos in its native India. It is distributed throughout almost all of India and can be found at elevations up to nearly 4000 ft. (1200 m). In the Indian state of Maharashtra alone, *B. bambos* covers nearly 4900 square miles (12,750 sq. km) (Tewari 1992). This very vigorous tropical species is a tender bamboo, and is suited to only a few areas in North America. It grows well at the Quail Botanical Gardens in southern California, and thrives in southern Florida, generally shooting in the fall, but delaying branching until the following spring.

At the lower nodes, the branchlets are modified into sharp thorns, making an established clump nearly impenetrable by large animals. At the upper nodes, the branchlets become less thorny and more normally leaf bearing. The shoots are edible, but bitter, and require parboiling in at least two changes of water before they are ready for the table. Some sources regard them as excellent after parboiling. Because of its vigor and availability, *Bambusa bambos* has been used extensively in India for paper pulp production, but it is not the best quality for this purpose. Similarly, although its large, thick-walled culms are used in construction, the wood is less dense and lower quality than that of other bamboos.

Bambusa beecheyana

Common synonym: *Sinocalamus beecheyanus*
Common name: Beechey bamboo
Maximum height: 50 ft. (15 m)
Maximum diameter: 5 in. (13 cm)
Minimum temperature: 15°F (–9°C)
Light: full sun

Although fairly tolerant of cold, *Bambusa beecheyana* thrives and grows vigorously in

Bambusa beecheyana. Quail Botanical Gardens.

warm climates. New culms are covered by a white powder. The culms are elliptical in cross section and rapidly tapering. In southern China, *B. beecheyana* is a prime source of summer bamboo shoots. To prevent bitterness in the shoots, the soil is mounded around the base of the clump to keep the new shoots in darkness until they are dug. The clump forms a fountain of arching culms. It is an attractive ornamental, but requires space, particularly in warm climates, where it grows large quickly. It was named for Captain F. W. Beechey, when a naturalist on his ship collected the species in Macao, in 1827.

Bambusa blumeana

Maximum height: 82 ft. (25 m)
Maximum diameter: 8 in. (20 cm)
Minimum temperature: 28°F (−2°C)
Light: full sun

This native of India and Indonesia has branches with short, crooked thorns. Air roots sometimes develop at the base of the nodes. *Bambusa blumeana* is used in a variety of ways, including hedges, windbreaks, furniture, farm implements, baskets, and edible shoots. Reportedly, it is in such demand in the Philippines for furniture making that it is being imported from Vietnam.

Bambusa burmanica

Maximum height: 60 ft. (18 m)
Maximum diameter: 4 in. (10 cm)
Minimum temperature: 32°F (0°C)
Light: full sun

Indigenous to Burma and northern Thailand, *Bambusa burmanica* inhabits dry hillsides in evergreen and deciduous forests, and in open forests of pine and grasslands. It grows at elevations of up to 4300 ft. (1300 m). Used for construction, fences, and weaving, the culms are strong and nearly solid. The large leaves may be up to 12 in. (30 cm) long and 2 in. (5 cm) wide.

Bambusa dissimulator

Maximum height: 50 ft. (15 m)
Maximum diameter: 3 in. (7.5 cm)
Minimum temperature: 22°F (−6°C)
Light: full sun

The branches of *Bambusa dissimulator* are somewhat thorny, but not as pronounced as those of other thorny species of *Bambusa*. The thick-walled culms are strong and can be used for scaffolding and other supports. The species is native to Guangdong Province and Guangxi in China.

Bambusa dissimulator var. albinodia

Maximum height: 50 ft. (15 m)
Maximum diameter: 3 in. (7.5 cm)
Minimum temperature: 22°F (−6°C)
Light: full sun

Bambusa dissimulator var. *albinodia* is similar to the principal form, but the culm base nodes have white circular stripes. It is native to Guangdong Province and is cultivated in Hong Kong.

Bambusa dolichoclada 'Stripe'

Maximum height: 64 ft. (20 m)
Maximum diameter: 4 in. (10 cm)
Minimum temperature: 20°F (−7°C)
Light: full sun

An attractive ornamental cultivated in Taiwan and southern Japan, *Bambusa dolichoclada* 'Stripe' has culms that are waxy yellow with dark green stripes.

Bambusa dolichomerithalla

Common name: blowpipe bamboo
Maximum height: 35 ft. (11 m)
Maximum diameter: 2 in. (5 cm)
Minimum temperature: 15°F (−9°C)
Light: full sun

Native to Taiwan and cultivated in Japan, *Bambusa dolichomerithalla* was introduced into America in 1980. Its common name, blowpipe bamboo, is derived from its long internodes and its traditional use as a blowpipe for cooking. It is found along streams and waterways at lower elevations.

Bambusa dolichomerithalla 'Green Stripestem'

Maximum height: 35 ft. (11 m)
Maximum diameter: 2 in. (5 cm)
Minimum temperature: 15°F (–9°C)
Light: full sun

Similar to the principal form, but the culms are yellow-green to orange-yellow, with dark green stripes on the internodes.

Bambusa dolichomerithalla 'Silverstripe'

Maximum height: 35 ft. (11 m)
Maximum diameter: 2 in. (5 cm)
Minimum temperature: 15°F (–9°C)
Light: full sun

Similar to the principal form, but the culms are dark green, with silver-white striping on the internodes.

Bambusa eutuldoides

Maximum height: 45 ft. (14 m)
Maximum diameter: 2 in. (5 cm)
Minimum temperature: 22°F (–6°C)
Light: full sun

This species is widely cultivated in southern China, where the thick-walled culms are used in constructing farm buildings and farm implements. Unusually, the culm leaf auricles differ greatly in size. One of the pair is five times as large as the other.

Bambusa lako

Common synonyms: *Gigantochloa atroviolacea* 'Timor Black', *Gigantochloa* sp. 'Timor Black'

Bambusa dolichoclada 'Stripe'. Quail Botanical Gardens.

Bambusa dolichomerithalla 'Silverstripe'. Quail Botanical Gardens.

Common name: Timor black
Maximum height: 70 ft. (21 m)
Maximum diameter: 4 in. (10 cm)
Minimum temperature: 25°F (–4°C)
Light: full sun

A choice ornamental bamboo, until recently *Bambusa lako* was known as *Gigantochloa* sp. 'Timor Black'. Its common name derives from its indigenous habitat on the island of Timor. The culms are initially green, turning brown-black to black with age, but retaining light green stripes. It is often mistaken for *Gigantochloa atroviolacea*, which it closely resembles. The culms of *B. lako* have a shiny surface, while those of *G. atroviolacea* have more of a matt finish. The shoots are edible.

Bambusa lako. Quail Botanical Gardens.

Bambusa longispiculata
Maximum height: 50 ft. (15 m)
Maximum diameter: 4 in. (10 cm)
Minimum temperature: 28°F (–2°C)
Light: full sun

In the early 1930s, *Bambusa longispiculata* was introduced into Puerto Rico from India. It now grows in many New World regions. In China, *B. longispiculata* is used on farms for building simple utilitarian constructions. Its appearance is similar to that of *B. tulda*. An attractive ornamental, it forms open clumps and has the added bonus of good tasting shoots.

Bambusa malingensis
Maximum height: 35 ft. (11 m)
Maximum diameter: 2½ in. (6.3 cm)
Minimum temperature: 20°F (–7°C)
Light: full sun

A native of China's Hainan Island, the strong culms of this species are used to make farm implements and frames for farmhouses. The lower branches may develop into soft or hard thorns. It forms tight erect clumps. At Quail Botanical Gardens in southern California, it reportedly tolerates salty sea breezes without damage.

Bambusa membranacea
Common synonym: *Dendrocalamus membranaceus*
Maximum height: 80 ft. (24 m)
Maximum diameter: 4 in. (10 cm)
Minimum temperature: 25°F (–4°C)
Light: full sun

Until the late 1990s, *Bambusa membranacea* was classified as *Dendrocalamus membranaceus*. It is distributed in Burma, India, Laos, Thailand, and China. The culms, slender for their height, grow in loose clumps. Used for construction and tools, *B. membranacea* reportedly is also considered a promising species for paper pulp. The young shoots are choice.

Bambusa membranacea. Quail Botanical Gardens.

Bambusa multiplex

Common synonym: *Bambusa glaucescens*
Common name: hedge bamboo
Maximum height: 35 ft. (11 m)
Maximum diameter: 1½ in. (4 cm)
Minimum temperature: 12°F (−11°C)
Light: full sun

One of the hardiest of the semitropical pachymorph bamboos, *Bambusa multiplex* is widely cultivated throughout the world as a windbreak and privacy hedge. In China, it has been used in weaving and papermaking, but because its culms are relatively slender, and the culm walls rather thin, *B. multiplex* is not one of the most desirable species for wood or pulp production. The shoots are not amenable to the table, being quite bitter. This species does, however, excel as an attractive, clumping, hedge bamboo suited to a broad range of climate conditions, from the tropics to northern California and coastal climates even farther north.

Indigenous to China, *Bambusa multiplex* is known as Chinese bamboo in India, where it was introduced in 1794. The species has long been cultivated in many areas, and a number of distinctive ornamental cultivars have developed over time. The species had already made its way to Europe prior to 1800, and a presumed variant, *B. nana,* was referenced as early as 1812. The culms of the principal type naturally arch, forming a rather broad hedge, but they take well to pruning and shaping, permitting a reasonably upright shape. Contributing to its appeal as a hedge, the culms emerge in a tight clump, and bushy branches grow on the lower nodes of the culms.

Bambusa multiplex 'Alphonse Karr'

Common name: Alphonse Karr
Maximum height: 35 ft. (11 m)
Maximum diameter: 1½ in. (4 cm)
Minimum temperature: 12°F (−11°C)
Light: full sun

General characteristics of this cultivar are the same as *Bambusa multiplex,* but the culms are yellow with irregular green striping. The new culms often have a reddish blush, particularly when exposed to strong sunlight. 'Alphonse Karr' is a choice ornamental in the landscape, and an excellent container plant for the home. It prefers full sun in the areas of North America where it can be grown, yet in the tropics, it needs shade to reach its maximum height—an example of the relativity of light requirements. It is very widely cultivated, and additional variants have emerged, includ-

Bambusa membranacea, new shoots in the fall. Quail Botanical Gardens.

ing some with light green culms and dark green stripes.

Bambusa multiplex 'Fernleaf'

Common name: fernleaf bamboo
Maximum height: 20 ft. (6 m)
Maximum diameter: ½ in. (1.25 cm)
Minimum temperature: 12°F (−11°C)
Light: full sun

An unstable cultivar, *Bambusa multiplex* 'Fernleaf' is characterized by small, tightly spaced, closely two-ranked leaves. Long distributed in the nursery trade, it generally keeps its notable characteristics in infertile, drier conditions when its height is kept to no more than 10 ft. (3 m) or so. When offered better soil and moisture, 'Fernleaf' tends to grow taller and

Bambusa multiplex 'Alphonse Karr'. Bamboo Sourcery.

lose its fernlike characteristics. It has hollow culms, unlike the solid-culmed *B. multiplex* var. *riviereorum*, which it otherwise resembles.

Bambusa multiplex 'Golden Goddess'

Common name: golden goddess bamboo
Maximum height: 10 ft. (3 m)
Maximum diameter: ½ in. (1.25 cm)
Minimum temperature: 12°F (−11°C)
Light: full sun

A cultivar perhaps developed in the San Diego area of southern California, 'Golden Goddess' is similar to *Bambusa multiplex* 'Fernleaf,' but the plant is smaller and the leaves are generally larger. The culms have a yellowish cast.

Bambusa multiplex 'Goldstripe'

Maximum height: 35 ft. (11 m)
Maximum diameter: ½ in. (1.25 cm)
Minimum temperature: 12°F (−11°C)
Light: full sun
Similar to the typical form, but the culms have a gold stripe that bleeds into the green.

Bambusa multiplex var. riviereorum

Common name: Chinese goddess bamboo
Maximum height: 6 ft. (1.8 m)
Maximum diameter: ¼ in. (0.6 cm)
Minimum temperature: 12°F (−11°C)
Light: full sun

Unlike the cultivar *Bambusa multiplex* 'Fernleaf', which it generally resembles, *B. multiplex* var. *riviereorum* is a stable form, maintaining its low height and delicate fernlike foliage. Its solid culms are a way to distinguish it from a small *B. multiplex* 'Fernleaf' plant. In the landscape, a slight breeze readily animates its lacy foliage, and it is also an excellent houseplant, given sufficient sun.

Bambusa multiplex 'Silverstripe'

Maximum height: 45 ft. (14 m)
Maximum diameter: 1½ in. (4 cm)
Minimum temperature: 12°F (−11°C)
Light: full sun

Bambusa multiplex 'Stripestem Fernleaf'. Quail Botanical Gardens.

The most vigorous cultivar of the species, *Bambusa multiplex* 'Silverstripe' requires a warm climate and ample moisture to achieve its size potential, but like the other cultivars, it tolerates a wide range of conditions, from cool summers and winters to the conditions of a home interior. Many of the leaves are variegated with white striping. The culms also bear occasional threadlike white striping.

Bambusa multiplex 'Stripestem Fernleaf'

Maximum height: 20 ft. (6 m)
Maximum diameter: ½ in. (1.25 cm)
Minimum temperature: 12°F (–11°C)
Light: full sun

Similar to *Bambusa multiplex* 'Fernleaf' except the culms are yellowish to reddish, striped with green.

Bambusa multiplex 'Tiny Fern'

Common name: tiny fern bamboo
Maximum height: 3 ft. (1 m)
Maximum diameter: ⅛ in. (0.3 cm)
Minimum temperature: 12°F (–11°C)
Light: full sun

This cultivar is a dwarf form of *Bambusa multiplex* var. *riviereorum*. Its leaves are often less than 1 in. (2.5 cm) long. Small and delicate, 'Tiny Fern' is an excellent container plant.

Bambusa multiplex 'Willowy'

Common name: willowy hedge bamboo
Maximum height: 20 ft. (6 m)
Maximum diameter: ¾ in. (2 cm)
Minimum temperature: 12°F (–11°C)
Light: full sun

The culms, branches, and twigs are exceptionally slender, and the leaves narrow. The culms have a very pronounced arching and drooping habit. Although 'Willowy' is not a new cultivar, its characteristics are not in much demand, and it is not widely distributed in the nursery trade.

Bambusa mutabilis

Maximum height: 23 ft. (7 m)
Maximum diameter: 2 in. (5 cm)
Minimum temperature: 22°F (–6°C)
Light: full sun

Native to China's Hainan Island, *Bambusa mutabilis* is an attractive bamboo, somewhat resembling *B. textilis* in clump habit and leaf shape. The culms are thin walled. New culms have a light covering of waxy powder, and a ring of white waxy powder below the node.

Bambusa nana

Maximum height: 20 ft. (6 m)
Maximum diameter: 2 in. (5 cm)
Minimum temperature: 15°F (–9°C)
Light: full sun

Bambusa nana was referenced as early as 1812, as an herbarium specimen from northeastern India. Commercially cultivated in Thailand, *B. nana* is an old synonym for *B. multiplex*. However, the *B. nana* of Thailand appears to be a different species than *B. multiplex*.

Although its authentic identity may be in question, *Bambusa nana* is nevertheless a very worthy bamboo. An appealing ornamental, it forms a tight clump with erect culms that are devoid of leaves on the lower nodes. The culms arch outward near the top to complete an attractive silhouette. The straight culms are also very strong and are highly desirable for construction when smaller diameter culms are required.

Bambusa nutans

Maximum height: 40 ft. (12 m)
Maximum diameter: 3 in. (7.5 cm)
Minimum temperature: 25°F (–4°C)
Light: full sun

Widely cultivated in northwest India, Orissa, West Bengal, and Bangladesh, *Bambusa nutans* is an attractive ornamental, but also possesses good commercial attributes. The culm wood is straight and strong. It is one of the six species commonly used in the Indian paper industry.

Bambusa nutans is also cultivated commercially in Thailand. In China, it is used for farm implements and building material.

Bambusa odashimae

Common synonym: *Bambusa edulis*
Maximum height: 65 ft. (20 m)
Maximum diameter: 3 in. (7.5 cm)
Minimum temperature: 20°F (–7°C)
Light: full sun

Widely known by the name *Bambusa edulis*, *B. odashimae* is cultivated in the northern part of Taiwan. It either is native to the island or, more likely, was naturalized long ago. The culms can be used for construction and paper production, but it is primarily grown for its shoots.

Bambusa oldhamii

Common synonym: *Sinocalamus oldhamii*
Common names: giant timber bamboo, Oldham's bamboo
Maximum height: 65 ft. (20 m)
Maximum diameter: 4 in. (10 cm)
Minimum temperature: 20°F (–7°C)
Light: full sun

Bambusa oldhamii is an attractive timber bamboo, and the most commonly grown tropical clumper in America. It thrives in southern California and Florida, where it reaches a height of 55 ft. (17 m). In warmer areas, such as Central America and its native China, it can grow even taller. Although the plant is relatively cold hardy, its maximum size is considerably smaller as warmth decreases, reaching less

Bambusa nana. Quail Botanical Gardens.

Bambusa oldhamii. Quail Botanical Gardens.

than 10 ft. (3 m) tall at the cooler limits of its growing range. In North America, it was once misidentified as *Dendrocalamus latiflorus*.

This species has an erect habit, relatively short branches, and large, long leaves. Native to southern China, *Bambusa oldhamii* was introduced into Taiwan long ago, where it is now widely cultivated for its excellent tasting shoots. The culm wood is only marginally suitable for building construction, but it is attractive and is a good choice for furniture making.

Bambusa oldhamii takes well to pruning and makes a spectacular, tall hedge. For the scale of many of today's landscaping needs, however, other shorter and more compact bamboos, such as *B. textilis*, have been suggested as a substitute, but when space permits, and where strong, dry winds are not a threat to its large leaves, the towering presence of *B. oldhamii* is impressive in the landscape.

Bambusa oliveriana
Maximum height: 45 ft. (14 m)
Maximum diameter: 2 in. (5 cm)
Minimum temperature: 32°F (0°C)
Light: full sun

Native to India and Burma, *Bambusa oliveriana* is named for J. W. Oliver, who collected it in flower in the 1890s. The culms are glossy green and thick walled. It reportedly has good tasting shoots.

Bambusa pachinensis
Maximum height: 33 ft. (10 m)
Maximum diameter: 2½ in. (6.3 cm)
Minimum temperature: 20°F (–7°C)
Light: full sun

This species is indigenous to Taiwan and the mainland Chinese province of Fujian. *Bambusa pachinensis* was once classified as a variant of *B. textilis*. It is commonly employed as a windbreak in its native environment.

Bambusa polymorpha
Maximum height: 80 ft. (24 m)

Maximum diameter: 6 in. (15 cm)
Minimum temperature: 27°F (–3°C)
Light: full sun

Bambusa polymorpha is one of India's most important bamboo species. It is widely distributed in the Old World tropics, and among its growing regions are China, Thailand, Bangladesh, Burma, and Indonesia. *Bambusa polymorpha* excels in almost all respects. It is an attractive, graceful, ornamental, timber bamboo with superior wood quality. It is excellent for pulp and paper, building construction, and fiberboard. Some reports indicate that the shoots are distinctively sweet, even in the raw state. Other reports indicate that they are edible, but somewhat bitter. As with all semitropical and tropical bamboos, unless you truly know what you are doing, the shoots should first be parboiled as a precaution to purge any possible cyanogens—the volatile poisons are readily eliminated by parboiling.

Although introduced into the United States in 1924, *Bambusa polymorpha* remains relatively rare in this country. In mature clumps, the lower nodes are free of branches. The branches and twigs themselves are long and slender, and the leaves are among the more slender and delicate of the arborescent tropical bamboos. Its cold sensitivity, however, significantly restricts its domain.

Bambusa rigida
Maximum height: 40 ft. (12 m)
Maximum diameter: 2¼ in. (6 cm)
Minimum temperature: 32°F (0°C) estimated
Light: full sun

Bambusa rigida is indigenous to southern and southeast coastal China, where the culms are used variously for paper, tools, and construction of sheds and other utility buildings. The shoots are bitter and are not harvested for food.

Bambusa rutila
Maximum height: 40 ft. (12 m)
Maximum diameter: 2¼ in. (6 cm)

Bambusa pachinensis. Quail Botanical Gardens.

Minimum temperature: 32°F (0°C) estimated
Light: full sun

Distributed in Guangdong Province in China's southern coastal region, and cultivated in Hong Kong, *Bambusa rutila* is weakly thorny on the lower culm nodes. The thick-walled culms are strong, but not straight, relegating them to utilitarian construction.

Bambusa sinospinosa

Common names: Chinese thorny bamboo, spiny bamboo
Maximum height: 70 ft. (21 m)
Maximum diameter: 5 in. (13 cm)
Minimum temperature: 20°F (−7°C)
Light: full sun

Bambusa sinospinosa is native to China. Many of its branchlets are hardened into thorny spines, making an effective barrier or natural fence. The thick-walled culms are used to make rafts, water pipes, the buckets of waterwheels, and other construction. The shoots are edible and often pickled.

Bambusa textilis

Common name: weaver's bamboo
Maximum height: 40 ft. (12 m)
Maximum diameter: 2 in. (5 cm)
Minimum temperature: 13°F (−11°C)
Light: full sun

Native to China, *Bambusa textilis* has long internodes and strong but pliable fiber, making this a choice bamboo for weaving all manner of materials, from delicate baskets to strong rope. The absence of branches and branch scars, and the absence of prominent culm nodes, contributes to its desirability as a source of weaving material. The thin-walled, but strong, whole culms are used in craftwork and some furniture making. Silicic acid, known as tabasheer, is collected from the internodes for use in Chinese medicines. *Bambusa textilis* is also resistant to the dreaded powder post beetle, a pest of great concern in tropical environments.

The culms grow strongly upright before nodding gracefully at their tips. The lower nodes are free of branches to a greater degree than most of the genus, up to as much as three-quarters of the culm height in mature specimens, adding to its arborescent stature and ornamental appeal. The delicate foliage is ttractive, matching the gracefulness of the rest of the plant. *Bambusa textilis* is justly regarded as an attractive ornamental. *Bambusa oldhamii* has long been a landscaping standard in America's warmest regions, but for today's landscaping needs, the shorter and more compact *B. textilis* may be a better choice. Its smaller leaves are also less subject to damage from strong, drying winds.

Bambusa textilis var. gracilis

Common name: slender weaver's bamboo
Maximum height: 26 ft. (8 m)
Maximum diameter: 1⅛ in. (3 cm)
Minimum temperature: 15°F (−9°C)
Light: full sun

This ornamental variety of *Bambusa textilis* has culms that are much more slender than the type form, and have nodding tops.

Bambusa tulda

Common names: Bengal bamboo, spineless Indian bamboo, Calcutta cane
Maximum height: 70 ft. (21 m)
Maximum diameter: 4 in. (10 cm)
Minimum temperature: 27°F (−3°C)
Light: full sun

A tender, giant timber bamboo native to India, *Bambusa tulda* was introduced into the United States in 1907. Its areas of distribution include Bangladesh, Burma, Thailand, and China. The lower branches on large culms are leafless and nearly thornlike. The culms are thick walled, and the culm wood is dense and fairly strong. Although the fibers are only moderately long, this species is suitable for papermaking. The culms are used in heavy construction and scaffolding, as well as craftwork. In northern Thailand, *B. tulda* is report-

Bambusa textilis. Quail Botanical Gardens.

edly one of the two most important species for shoot production, although the shoots are said to be somewhat bitter. The culms are imported into the United Kingdom as "Calcutta cane" for the construction of split-bamboo fishing rods.

Bambusa tuldoides

Common name: punting pole bamboo
Maximum height: 55 ft. (17 m)
Maximum diameter: 2¼ in. (6 cm)
Minimum temperature: 15°F (−9°C)
Light: full sun

Similar in appearance to *Bambusa tulda*, *B. tuldoides* is a native of China's Guangdong

Bambusa tuldoides. Quail Botanical Gardens.

Province. It produces numerous culms, growing in a tight clump. The culm wood is strong, and useful for weaving and building sheds and other utility constructions. Traditionally the culms are used as punting poles to propel watercraft, hence its common name, punting pole bamboo. The shoots are edible. Shavings from the culm cortex are used in Chinese medicines. The Portuguese first introduced *B. tuldoides* to the New World, in Brazil, around the 1840s.

Bambusa tuldoides 'Ventricosa'

Common synonym: *Bambusa ventricosa*
Common name: Buddha's belly bamboo
Maximum height: 55 ft. (17 m)
Maximum diameter: 2¼ in. (6 cm)
Minimum temperature: 15°F (−9°C)
Light: full sun

A native of southern China, *Bambusa tuldoides* 'Ventricosa' exhibits a conventional growth habit when planted in the ground and given ample water and nutrients. Although useful as a tall hedge in this context, it is most known for its appearance when potted, pruned, and stressed by withholding water. Under these conditions, the plant readily becomes dwarfed and develops shortened, swollen internodes, hence its common name, Buddha's belly bamboo. It is generally grown as an ornamental potted plant or as bonsai. The shoots reportedly taste excellent. Long known as *B. ventricosa*, this cultivar is now regarded by authorities as a selection of *B. tuldoides*.

Bambusa tuldoides 'Ventricosa Kimmei'

Maximum height: 55 ft. (17 m)
Maximum diameter: 2¼ in. (6 cm)
Minimum temperature: 15°F (−9°C)
Light: full sun

This cultivar is similar to *Bambusa tuldoides* 'Ventricosa', but the culms are yellow with a few green stripes, and the foliage leaf blades have a few white stripes.

Bambusa vulgaris

Common name: common bamboo
Maximum height: 70 ft. (21 m)
Maximum diameter: 4½ in. (11 cm)
Minimum temperature: 27°F (−3°C)
Light: full sun

An Old World bamboo, *Bambusa vulgaris* propagates easily and is one of the most widely distributed tropical bamboos in both the Old and New World. It was cultivated by Spanish colonists in southern Florida in the 1840s, and it may have been the first foreign species introduced into America. *Bambusa vulgaris* was also among the first bamboos introduced into Europe, and was well established as a hothouse plant by the late 1700s. The actual origins of the species is uncertain.

Its rhizomes may extend up to 2½ ft. before turning upward, creating open, relatively fast spreading clumps. *Bambusa vulgaris* is an attractive ornamental timber bamboo. Its shoots are edible, though bitter. Although the starchy culm wood is vulnerable to powder post beetle attack and is relatively soft, the culms are often used for scaffolding and basic construction. Long culm fibers, rapid growth, and ease of propagation recommend *B. vulgaris* as a choice source of pulp for paper production. Although there are reports of sporadic flowering, *B. vulgaris* has never had a period of gregarious flowering that periodically decimates most other bamboos. Because of this, *B. vulgaris* is all the more valuable as a reliable and predictable commercial resource.

Bambusa vulgaris 'Vittata'

Common name: painted bamboo
Maximum height: 50 ft. (15 m)
Maximum diameter: 4 in. (10 cm)
Minimum temperature: 27°F (−3°C)
Light: full sun

A variegated form of *Bambusa vulgaris*, 'Vittata' is a highly attractive, large ornamental bamboo. Its culms are golden-yellow, with green vertical striping of varying widths. The new culm leaf sheaths are green with yellow striping.

Bambusa vulgaris 'Wamin'

Maximum height: 16 ft. (5 m)
Maximum diameter: 3 in. (7.5 cm)
Minimum temperature: 27°F (−3°C)
Light: full sun

Depending on one's taste, 'Wamin' is a somewhat bizarre looking cultivar of *Bambusa vulgaris*. The lower internodes are swollen and very short, dwarfing the plant. Grown as an ornamental, it requires pruning to look its best. Some selections show additional variations, such as light green culms with darker green stripes.

Bambusa vulgaris 'Vittata'. Quail Botanical Gardens.

Bashania

A relatively new genus consisting of six known species, *Bashania* was previously included in *Arundinaria*. Rugged and hardy, *Bashania* bamboos are endemic to the mountainous regions of central China, where they share forest habitats with broad-leaved trees and conifers. They are also sometimes found in pure stands. The bamboos are medium sized and have leptomorph rhizomes.

Bashania faberi

Common synonyms: *Arundinaria fangiana,*
    Bashania fangiana, Gelidocalamus fangianus
Maximum height: 10 ft. (3 m)
Maximum diameter: ¼ in. (0.6 cm)
Minimum temperature: 10°F (−12°C)
Light: mostly sunny

Bashania faberi is a shrub bamboo with many branches in clustered tufts at each node. It is distributed in the Chinese provinces of Sichuan, Shaanxi, Gansu, and Ningxia, and can be found at elevations of more than 12,000 ft. (3700 m). The species is more commonly known by variations of the name "fangiana," including *Arundinaria fangiana, B. fangiana,* and *Gelidocalamus fangianus.*

Bashania fargesii

Common synonyms: *Arundinaria fargesii*
Maximum height: 30 ft. (9 m)
Maximum diameter: 2 in. (5 cm)
Minimum temperature: 0°F (−18°C)
Light: mostly sunny

Distributed in the Shaanxi, Hubei, and Gansu Provinces of China, *Bashania fargesii* is a rugged plant with thick culm walls and tough, robust leaves. The culm and branch leaf sheaths are persistent or late in shedding. Initially, there are three branches at each node, later becoming many.

Sixty-four species of bamboo were evaluated in winter hardiness trials designed to select the best bamboos for the Beijing area in China, a region with hard winters and no in-digenous bamboos. Of the 20 hardiest selections, 17 were *Phyllostachys. Bashania fargesii* was one of the three that were not *Phyllostachys,* but still ranked in the top 20 for hardiness (Qui and Ma 1992).

Borinda

A recently described genus of attractive, Old World, montane bamboos, *Borinda* is composed of 18 species that had previously been assigned primarily to *Fargesia,* as well as to *Arundinaria, Thamnocalamus,* and *Yushania.* Placement of these bamboos has been problematic. In China, two schools of thought sought to place these species either in *Yushania,* based primarily on the structure of the flowering parts, or in *Fargesia,* based primarily on rhizome form and other vegetative characteristics. Both approaches proved problematic, and ultimately untenable. The research of C. M. A. Stapleton (1998b) of the Royal Botanic Gardens, Kew, led to the establishment of a new genus, *Borinda.*

Nearly all *Borinda* species have fine longitudinal ridges on either the culm internodes or the branch internodes—or both, distinguishing them from *Fargesia* and most other genera. *Borinda* generally resembles *Thamnocalamus,* but it differs by having up to seven branches in the first year, including two that extend behind the culm. *Thamnocalamus* has fewer first year branches, none extending behind the culm. *Borinda* culm internodes are long and usually finely ridged. Those of *Thamnocalamus* are shorter and smoother. *Borinda* has a pachymorph rhizome system with short rhizome necks, and forms clumps with culms less than 12 in. (30 cm) apart, distinguishing it from *Yushania,* with its typical, long-necked rhizomes.

Borinda foliage leaves are tessellated, and the bamboos have some frost hardiness, though less than the more frost hardy species of *Fargesia, Thamnocalamus,* and *Yushania.* The foliage leaf blades of *Borinda* are thin, soft, and

Borinda boliana. Bamboo Sourcery.

pliable, with a matt finish. The high altitude species of *Borinda* are deciduous in the winter. *Yushania* bamboos have tougher glossy leaves, and typically remain evergreen. New *Borinda* shoots often have a tuft of long, generally erect, leaf blades at the apex.

Borinda are distributed along a continuous chain of mountain ranges, at elevations ranging from 6000 to 11,800 ft. (1800 to 3600 m), or possibly even as high as 13,800 ft. (4200 m), from Annapurna in western Nepal and Tibet, across to China's Yunnan Province, and down to within 150 mi. (240 km) of Ho Chi Minh City (Saigon) in southern Vietnam.

Some highly attractive evergreen species just coming into cultivation in the Western world include *Borinda fansipanensis*, *B. grossa*, *B. hygrophila*, *B. macclureana*, *B. papyrifera*, and *B. perlonga*. Borinda can be separated into two groups, larger evergreen species, and smaller deciduous species found at higher elevations. Although additional species may become known, the deciduous group presently consists of only three species, *B. emeryi*, *B. frigidorum*, and an additional species from Sichuan. (Stapleton 1998b; personal communication).

Borinda boliana

Common synonyms: *Himalayacalamus intermedius* (hort.), *Yushania boliana*
Maximum height: 50 ft. (15 m)
Maximum diameter: 2 in. (5 cm)
Minimum temperature: 10°F (−12°C)
Light: partial shade

Borinda boliana is a large, robust, highly attractive montane bamboo. The new culms are bright pale blue-green, sometimes turning reddish purple with age. The true identity of this bamboo remains something of a mystery. It was reportedly collected in the mountains of Sichuan, China, and brought to Japan in the late 1980s. From Japan, Gerald Bol, former president of the American Bamboo Society, introduced it to the West under the provisional name *Himalayacalamus intermedius*. It was sub-

sequently renamed *Yushania boliana* in honor of Gerald Bol. However, neither *Himalayacalamus* nor *Yushania* are appropriate genera for the plant.

Molecular evidence and morphological features such as branching structure indicate that it belongs in the same clade as *Fargesia*, *Yushania*, and *Borinda* (Chris Stapleton, personal communication). At the moment *Borinda* is the best match, but its genus could change yet again, possibly to a completely new genus of its own. Regardless of the difficulties in nomenclature, it is a very desirable ornamental.

Borinda fungosa

Common synonym: *Fargesia fungosa*
Maximum height: 20 ft. (6 m)
Maximum diameter: 1 in. (2.5 cm)
Minimum temperature: 15°F (−9°C)
Light: partial shade

Formerly classified as a *Fargesia*, which it generally resembles in form, *Borinda fungosa* has somewhat larger leaves than many Old World montane bamboos, up to 6¼ in. (16 cm) long and ⅔ in. (1.7 cm) wide. An attractive ornamental, it is more cold sensitive than the *Fargesia* bamboos in cultivation, but more heat tolerant. Though small, the shoots are reportedly good tasting. The culms are used in weaving. Native to China's Yunnan and Sichuan Provinces, it is distributed at an elevation range of 6000 to 8900 ft. (1800 to 2700 m). A gregarious flowering in the early 1990s resulted in wide distribution of the seedlings in America, Europe, and elsewhere.

Brachystachyum

A genus comprised of one species and an additional variety, *Brachystachyum* is a shrublike leptomorph genus native to China. The culms are round, with a slight compression on the branching side of the internode. Each node has three principal branches. *Brachystachyum* generally resembles *Semiarundinaria*, but its floral parts are much shorter.

Borinda fungosa. Author's garden.

Brachystachyum densiflorum

Maximum height: 10 ft. (3 m)
Maximum diameter: ½ in. (1.25 cm)
Minimum temperature: 0°F (−18°C)
Light: partial shade

Brachystachyum densiflorum is similar in appearance to a smaller scale *Semiarundinaria.* The culm leaves shed promptly. The foliage leaves are up to 7 in. (18 cm) long and 1 in. (2.5 cm) wide.

Brachystachyum densiflorum var. *villosum*

Maximum height: 10 ft. (3 m)
Maximum diameter: ½ in. (1.25 cm)
Minimum temperature: 0°F (−18°C)
Light: partial shade

Similar to the principal type, *Brachystachyum densiflorum* var. *villosum* differs by having a mass of yellowish brown hairs at the base of the culm leaf sheath.

Cephalostachyum

Cephalostachyum includes tropical bamboos with pachymorph rhizome systems that range in appearance from shrublike, to climbing, to tall and treelike. The culms are generally slender and thin walled. The genus consists of some 16 known species.

Cephalostachyum pergracile

Common synonym: *Schizostachyum pergracile*
Maximum height: 40 ft. (12 m)
Maximum diameter: 2¾ in. (7 cm)
Minimum temperature: 32°F (0°C)
Light: mostly sunny

A tender, tropical bamboo, *Cephalostachyum pergracile* is known for both its beauty and utility. Native to India and Burma, and widely cultivated in China's Yunnan Province, it is a very attractive arborescent bamboo with tufted foliage and nodding culm tips. The culm leaf sheaths are shiny, leathery, and chestnut brown, covering about a third of the inter-node. It is a striking specimen in the landscape.

Cephalostachyum pergracile is used for construction, paper pulp, and basket, mat, and crate weaving. Split culms are used to make fishing rods. Locally, rice is boiled in the culm joints, flavoring the rice and making a convenient carrying vessel for travel.

Chimonobambusa

Chimonobambusa bamboos typically spread aggressively, and they range in size from shrublike to medium-sized and treelike. Unusual for bamboos with leptomorph rhizomes, they typically shoot in fall or winter. Although well adapted to its native environments, *Chimonobambusa* does not always fit perfectly in other climates. Some species are moderately winter hardy, but the tender shoots that come in fall and winter are readily susceptible to cold damage, disrupting the plant's growing cycle and threatening its health. If fall and winter shoots are damaged or destroyed, *Chimonobambusa* often compensates by shooting again in the spring and summer. These out-of-cycle shooting periods may permit the plant to survive and grow, but without the vigor a normal growth cycle would provide.

Bamboo shooting generally occurs earlier in warmer areas than in cooler areas, but *Chimonobambusa* behaves in an opposite manner, shooting earlier in cooler areas and later in warmer areas. In its native environment, one species of *Chimonobambusa* yields three times as many pounds of shoots per acre in higher, cooler areas than it yields in lower, warmer areas (Wen 1994).

In China, *Chimonobambusa* is found at elevations of 300 to 6600 ft. (90 to 2000 m). These are short-day, understory plants that thrive when the forest canopy reduces sunlight by about 60 percent.

Chimonobambusa plants typically bear three principal branches at each node. The nodes are prominent, and the lower nodes of some species have aerial roots or spines. This latter feature helps to distinguish this genus from the genus *Qiongzhuea*, which lacks aerial roots or spines.

Qiongzhuea is very closely related to *Chimonobambusa*, and some taxonomists regard *Qiongzhuea* as a section within *Chimonobambusa*. In this book, *Qiongzhuea* is treated as a separate genus. Evidence supports both treatments, and thus does not definitively validate either. In addition to the controversy regarding the status of *Qiongzhuea* as a separate genus, there are also differences of opinion regarding the assignment of individual species (Clark 1995).

Chimonobambusa marmorea

Common name: marbled bamboo
Maximum height: 8 ft. (2.4 m)
Maximum diameter: ¾ in. (2 cm)
Minimum temperature: 15°F (−9°C)
Light: partial shade

Although *Chimonobambusa marmorea* likely originated in the Honshu district of Japan, other authorities place its origins in the Guangxi region of China. It was introduced into Europe in 1889. Its name derives from the marbled appearance of the new shoots and culm leaf sheaths. New shoots include purple and cream colorations. The new shoots are initially without branches, branching out near the top of the culm the following summer, then branching further down the culm in subsequent years. The culm leaves are longer than the internodes, and tardy to shed. Although small, the shoots reportedly have exceptionally good flavor. The culms are very thick walled. This species is an attractive but aggressive runner.

Once highly valued as whips, the rhizomes of *Chimonobambusa marmorea* were at one time restricted for use only by the Shogun. Rhizomes with tightly spaced nodes were preferred. In his 1899 work, *The Cultivation of Bamboos in Japan*, Sir Ernest Satow relates:

According to tradition, the proper measurement was from the nipple of the right breast to the end of the middle finger of the outstretched left hand, of which the handle took up six sun, and the remainder must have thirty-three nodes. Such were called yurushi muchi (the right to use them being reserved to riders who had special permission from their ridingmasters) and they were highly valued by teachers of equitation, but the whips with thirty-three knots were very rare.

Chimonobambusa marmorea f. *variegata*

Maximum height: 8 ft. (2.4 m)
Maximum diameter: ¾ in. (2 cm)
Minimum temperature: 15°F (−9°C)
Light: partial shade

Similar to the principal form, except that the leaves have narrow white stripes.

Chimonobambusa quadrangularis

Common name: square bamboo
Maximum height: 25 ft. (7.5 m)
Maximum diameter: 1½ in. (4 cm)
Minimum temperature: 15°F (−9°C)
Light: mostly sunny

Native to southeast China, *Chimonobambusa quadrangularis* is an attractive ornamental bamboo with distinctive squarish culms, a trait that is most pronounced in established groves with mature culms. The lower nodes have small, spinelike root primordia. The culm walls are thick, but not very strong. They are used as walking sticks and for craft items, but are unsuitable for construction or weaving. There are no records of this species flowering. The shoots, coming in the fall, are regarded as choice edibles.

Chimonobambusa quadrangularis 'Suow'

Maximum height: 25 ft. (7.5 m)
Maximum diameter: 1½ in. (4 cm)

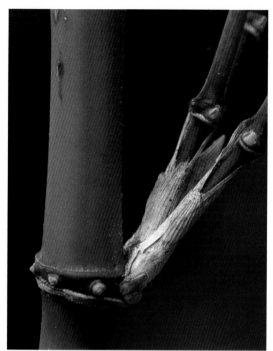

Chimonobambusa quadrangularis, showing the aerial roots or spines on the nodes characteristic of some *Chimonobambusa* species. Author's Garden.

Minimum temperature: 15°F (–9°C)
Light: mostly sunny

Similar to the type form, but the culms are yellow with a few green stripes of varying width. The foliage leaves may have occasional variegation.

Chusquea

A New World counterpart to the Old World's "mountain bamboos," the genus *Chusquea* is associated with the Andes, just as many of the Old World's mountain bamboos are associated with the Himalayas. There is even somewhat of a corollary between China's giant panda and the speckled bear of the central Andean cloud forests. Like the giant panda, the highly reclusive speckled bear is believed to feed on bamboo—although, in the case of the speckled bear, not as an exclusive food. New *Chusquea* shoots are reportedly part of the speckled bear's dining habit (Judziewicz et al. 1999).

Chusquea is closely related to *Neurolepis*. Lynn G. Clark, the authority on *Chusquea*, suggests that the genus probably originated in what is now Brazil, subsequently radiating to the Andes and Central America (Clark 1997b). Central American, Andean, and high-altitude species appear to be more recently evolved. Despite the considerable diversity, morphological and molecular analyses show that the genus is monophyletic—that is, all *Chusquea* species are descendant from a common ancestor.

The natural habitat for *Chusquea* ranges from northwestern Mexico to the West Indies to southern Chile and Argentina, at altitudes ranging from sea level to more than 14,000 ft. (4300 m), from tropical lowlands to high-altitude grasslands and pine forests (Judziewicz and Clark 1991). Many chusqueas inhabit open, high-elevation grasslands called *páramos* and the slightly lower elevation *subpáramos*, habitats that are windy, humid, and rainy. Daily temperature fluctuations typically exceed seasonal fluctuations. The nights are cool, dipping to near freezing or below, followed by daytime temperatures sometimes reaching to the upper 60s (about 20°C) (Judziewicz et al. 1999). At their southernmost extension, chusqueas are ubiquitous in the beech forests of the cool temperate zone of southern Chile. Although most chusqueas inhabit higher elevations and montane environments, such as the montane cloud-shrouded regions of the Andes, where precipitation is primarily received in the form of fog and mist, some species, including the earliest evolving of the chusqueas, are native to the hot, sunny lowlands. More than a third of the named *Chusquea* species, and the majority of the undescribed species, are indigenous to the Andes, where all major groupings of *Chusquea* are represented (Clark 1997b). Some species have a wide geographic distribution, while others are known to exist in only a single population. From both a latitude and altitude standpoint, *Chusquea* has a broader distribution than any other bamboo genus.

Although a few chusqueas are quite cold hardy, most are relatively tender, which would seem to limit them to the warmest parts of the United States. However, most chusqueas are not heat tolerant either. Warm nights and warm soil temperatures are particularly problematic for many of the species, especially the hardier ones. A few species do match up quite well with some American growing climates, however. Many of the chusqueas introduced into the U.S., for example, thrive in the fog-shrouded environment of California's San Francisco Bay area. It is regrettable that a broader spectrum of the genus is not well suited to more American growing climates. Many chusqueas are quite beautiful ornamentals, and it is worth the effort to explore them.

The genus *Chusquea* was first recognized in 1822. Its name is derived from *chusque,* the name given to the bamboo by the indigenous peoples of Colombia and Ecuador (Judziewicz et al. 1999). Among the native uses for *Chusquea* are construction, forage, fencing, and craft, including tools, furniture, decorative ornamental baskets, and sturdy baskets for transporting fruit and produce.

Of an estimated 200 *Chusquea* species, only about two-thirds have yet been named and taxonomically described. A few species exist only as herbarium specimens, having become extinct in the 20th century. For *Chusquea,* the culm leaf and bud complement are sufficient to determine species in nearly all cases (Clark 1989). The research by Lynn G. Clark has greatly expanded our knowledge of this unusual genus.

Solid culms are a distinctive characteristic of *Chusquea,* although the pith in older culms of some species may break down, forming hollows in the culm, and among the more recently evolved chusqueas, at least two known species have hollow culms—an evolutionary reversal. In the main, however, solid culms remain a typifying characteristic. Most *Chusquea* species have pachymorph rhizomes, but two,

C. fendleri, and *C. scandens,* have amphimorph rhizomes (Judziewicz et al. 1999). As more species are investigated, the possibility remains that chusqueas with strictly leptomorph rhizome systems will be found.

Chusquea is one of only two bamboo genera that truly have multiple branch buds at the culm node—although at least one species, *C. smithii,* generally develops only a single branch at each node (Clark 1997b). In some *Chusquea* species, the bud complement is quite complex, with sometimes numerous buds, of up to three sizes, arranged in various configurations. Except for *C. culeou, C. juergensii,* and a few species in subgenus *Swallenochloa,* there is a pronounced size difference between the large central bud and the smaller subsidiary buds (Judziewicz et al. 1999). Typically, the subsidiary buds are arrayed around or below the central bud in a crescent shape, but in some species, such as *C. pittieri,* they may be arranged in a whorl around the circumference of the node. In some species, the subsidiary buds can number as many as 80 or more (Clark 1989). These branching patterns are fascinating to observe, particularly as the new buds begin to emerge from the culm.

A common feature in many bamboos, fimbriae, or fringelike hairs, are entirely lacking on *Chusquea* culm leaf sheaths. Similarly, auricles are never present (Judziewicz et al. 1999).

Flowering cycles vary widely in the genus, from as short as 2 to 3 years, to as long as 60 to 70 years in the case of *C. pittieri.* The species in *Chusquea* subgenus *Swallenochloa* tend to flower at shorter intervals (Judziewicz et al. 1999).

The genus *Chusquea* is subdivided into three subgenera: *Rettbergia, Chusquea,* and *Swallenochloa,* in order of their evolutionary emergence. Each subgenus is presumed to be monophyletic—all members of each subgenus are derived from the same common ancestor. So far, the evidence for this is strongest for *Rettbergia.* Some species have not yet been assigned a subgenus, and some subgenera contain additional informal groups within them. Further study is likely to yield additional evolutionary groupings within *Chusquea* (Judziewicz et al. 1999).

Chusquea subgenus *Rettbergia*

The earliest *Chusquea* forms, identified with subgenus *Rettbergia*, have characteristics associated with a clambering habit, including sharply bending branches, particularly at the lower nodes, infravaginal branching, and a horizontally emerging central branch bud that may be adaptive for scrambling support. The culms typically hang or trail as they scramble opportunistically over and through any convenient supports. The culm leaves have a rough, gripping texture that also assists the clambering habit.

The branching habit is distinctive. Referred to as starburst or arachnoid (spiderlike), the branches are bent sharply at one of the lower nodes such that they radiate away from the culm and one another in a starburst pattern that also resembles the bent legs of a spider (Judziewicz et al. 1999).

Culm diameters range from $\frac{1}{16}$ in. (2 mm) to $\frac{3}{4}$ in. (2 cm), culm lengths from 5 ft. (1.5 m) to 50 ft. (15 m). The internodes are round or, rarely, slightly flattened just above the branch complement, sometimes glaucous, but never waxy. A few species have fine hairs just below the node. Culm leaves are persistent. At mid-culm, the nodes have a single, usually circular branch bud, surrounded by 4 to 30 smaller branch buds of equal size. The foliage leaves are untessellated and generally pliable.

Many species of this subgenus inhabit hot, sunny lowlands and have an unsavory reputation for weedy, aggressive growth that threatens more desirable vegetation (Judziewicz et al. 1999). A few are far less aggressive, and quite delicate and attractive. The members of the subgenus are quite tender, however, and only potentially suited to the outdoors in a very few of the warmest climates in the United

States. None are currently in cultivation. The subgenus consists primarily of Brazilian species. Examples of this subgenus include *Chusquea bahiana, C. bambusoides, C. capitata, C. capituliflora, C. oxylepis, C. sellowii,* and *C. urelytra* (Clark 1997b).

Chusquea subgenus *Chusquea*

Culm diameters in subgenus *Chusquea* range from $\frac{1}{4}$ in. (0.6 cm) to $2\frac{1}{4}$ in. (6 cm), culm lengths from 5 ft. (1.5 m) to 82 ft. (25 m). Culms are erect at the base, becoming arching or clambering, hanging, or sometimes trailing off supports. Internode characteristics vary among the species from round to flattened or shallowly or deeply grooved above the branch complement. The solid internodes may become hollow with age. The internodes vary in surface coating and texture, but are usually not waxy. The culm leaves are not rapidly shedding, and they may be persistent. At mid-culm, the nodes have a single, usually triangular but sometimes circular, branch bud surrounded by two to numerous smaller buds of sometimes two sizes, with thorny root primordia present in some species. Branching is either infravaginal or extravaginal. The subsidiary branches sometimes rebranch. Foliage leaves are untessellated, or only weakly tessellated, and are generally pliable.

The *Chusquea* subgenus is largely Andean and Central American. Some bamboos within the subgenus are aggressive colonizers. When disruption occurs in their mountain forest habitats, their aggressive nature can have a major ecological impact. The type species for the subgenus is *C. scandens*, but the bamboos in this subgenus show considerable diversity, and groupings that are already known within the subgenus suggest that additional subgenera may be indicated. Additional species in subgenus *Chusquea* include *C. circinata, C. coronalis, C. cumingii, C. fendleri, C. liebmannii, C. macrostachya, C. pittieri, C. quila, C. simpliciflora, C. uliginosa,* and *C. valdiviensis* (Judziewicz et al. 1999).

Chusquea subgenus *Swallenochloa*

Short, waxy internodes and a shrubby habit typify subgenus *Swallenochloa*. Culm diameters range from ⅟₁₆ in. (2 mm) to 2¼ in. (6 cm), culm lengths from 10 ft. (3 m) to 60 ft. (18 m). The culms are usually erect, sometimes arching toward the tip. The short internodes are round to slightly flattened or grooved above the branch complement. Young culms are solid, but may become less so with age, and are usually covered with a thin waxy coat. Primarily because of the tendency toward hollow culms, *Swallenochloa* was once regarded as a separate genus.

Branching is more linear than clustered, and the branches are usually erect. Deciduous in a few species, the culm leaves are usually persistent but eventually disintegrate and shed. At mid-culm, the nodes typically have a single, usually triangular branch bud, surrounded or flanked by one to numerous smaller buds of sometimes two sizes. Branching is intravaginal or extravaginal. Subsidiary branches usually rebranch. Foliage leaves are often stiff and sometimes tessellated (Judziewicz et al. 1999).

Most of the species in subgenus *Swallenochloa* can tolerate a light frost, and some are far hardier. Most are native to high-altitude grasslands, but a few may occur in a range of forest environments. The forest species are generally more rugged and have longer internodes and arching culms (Clark 1997b). Examples of this subgenus include the various forms of *Chusquea andina*, *C. culeou*, *C. heterophylla*, *C. montana*, and *C. nudiramea* (Judziewicz et al. 1999).

Chusquea circinata

Maximum height: 22 ft. (7 m)
Maximum diameter: 1 in. (2.5 cm)
Minimum temperature: 26°F (−3°C)
Light: mostly sunny

This species somewhat resembles *Chusquea coronalis*, but is not as ornamentally impressive. The subsidiary branches of *C. circinata* are coarser and more erect, and the foliage leaves are narrower. Like those of *C. coronalis*, *C. pittieri*, and *C. liebmannii*, the branches of *C. circinata* grow in a whorl around the circumference of the culm, and spiny root primordia form at the nodes.

Chusquea coronalis

Maximum height: 23 ft. (7 m)
Maximum diameter: ¾ in. (2 cm)
Minimum temperature: 26°F (−3°C)
Light: partial shade

A highly desirable but somewhat temperamental ornamental, *Chusquea coronalis* is native to warm lowlands and cloud forests from Mexico to Costa Rica. As with other members of section *Verticillatae* of subgenus *Chusquea*, this species produces branches in a whorl around the circumference of the culm.

Chusquea coronalis is a delicate bamboo, with a profusion of subsidiary branches and foliage leaves arrayed more or less horizontally. One of the more widely cultivated bamboos of the genus, it prefers a moist habitat and moderate sun. In cultivation in the United States, this species typically experiences a significant leaf drop in winter, leafing out again and regaining its delicate attraction with the changing seasons. Dry, indoor conditions, particularly in winter, will cause it to suffer.

Chusquea culeou

Common synonym: *Chusquea breviglumis*
Maximum height: 25 ft. (7.5 m)
Maximum diameter: 1½ in. (4 cm)
Minimum temperature: 0°F (−18°C)
Light: mostly sunny

Among the most widely cultivated species of all the chusqueas, finding its way to both American and European gardens, *Chusquea culeou* is one of the hardiest of the genus. It is among the few chusqueas in which there is no pronounced difference in branching size between the central branch bud and the subsidiary buds, the multiple branches all appearing generally equal.

Chusquea circinata. Quail Botanical Gardens.

Chusquea coronalis. Quail Botanical Gardens.

A polymorphic species responsive to environmental conditions, *Chusquea culeou* exhibits significant variation in form. The culms are erect to leaning. The leaf size of some forms is up to three times larger than that of other forms. Under strong sun, *C. culeou* has a more compact, shrubby form, with smaller branches. In more shaded conditions, it is taller with longer branches and a more open habit.

Chusquea culeou is a dominant understory plant in the southern Andean beech forests of its native Argentina and Chile. It forms dense stands where the overstory has been disturbed or eliminated, such as by fire or logging. Culms of this species have been estimated to live up to 33 years. The flowering cycle is said to be approximately 45 years (Judziewicz et al. 1999).

Chusquea breviglumis is synonymous with *C. culeou*. However, one of the bamboos in the garden trade that is sold under the name *C. breviglumis* is a different taxon, provisionally identified as *C.* aff. *culeou*.

Chusquea culeou 'Caña Prieta'

Maximum height: 10 ft. (3 m)
Maximum diameter: ½ in. (1.25 cm)
Minimum temperature: 0°F (−18°C)
Light: mostly sunny

It is curious that some of bamboo's worst taxonomic muddles seem to reside with the Old World montane bamboos of the Himalayas and the New World montane bamboos of the Andes. *Chusquea culeou* 'Caña Prieta' is one such bamboo. It is in widespread cultivation in the United States under the name *C. nigricans*. The accepted botanical name for *C. nigricans* is *C. montana*. However, the bamboo widely cultivated in the U.S. as *C. nigricans* is not *C. montana*, but a dwarf form of *C. culeou* that was collected near a bog in Chile.

Regardless of its taxonomy, it is an attractive landscape plant, with relatively small, deep green leaves (see frontispiece photo). Its culms turn a very dark red-brown that is sometimes almost black. The cultivar name, *Chusquea culeou* 'Caña Prieta', is derived from the Spanish words meaning blackish or very dark cane. The culm leaves may persist, looking slightly disheveled, but they eventually disintegrate and diminish. 'Caña Prieta' prefers acidic soil to thrive and look its best, but will do well in soils that are only moderately acidic.

As an experiment while propagating the plant, I placed one of the divisions in 100 percent peat moss. As with my other container plants, I occasionally added fertilizer, but provided no special treatment. After a year, the plant showed no signs of suffering and, if anything, displayed more vigor with more vivid leaf color than the other propagules.

Chusquea aff. *culeou*

Common synonym: *Chusquea gigantea*
Maximum height: 60 ft. (18 m)
Maximum diameter: 2¼ in. (6 cm)
Minimum temperature: 0°F (−18°C)
Light: full sun

Chusquea aff. *culeou* is one of two bamboos in the garden trade sold under the name *C. breviglumis*. True *C. breviglumis* is synonymous with *C. culeou*. *Chusquea* aff. *culeou*, however, may be a different taxon. Its true botanical name is uncertain, hence the provisional nomenclature.

Believed to be a close relative of *Chusquea culeou*, it differs distinctively from that species by having one to three branch buds that are much larger than the other subsidiary buds, rather than the uniform array typical of *C. culeou*. In an individual culm's second year, an additional one to three new large buds appear and generate even larger primary branches. In my relatively small clump, a central branch on one 14 ft. (4.2 m) tall culm measured nearly 5 ft. (1.5 m) in length. In field studies in Chile, Lynn G. Clark observed that *C. culeou* and *C.* aff. *culeou* appear to intergrade (Lynn Clark, personal communication), making demarcation of the taxa even more problematic.

Reportedly based on a cultivated garden specimen in France, the plant has been de-

Chusquea culeou. Bamboo Sourcery.

Chusquea aff. *culeou*. Author's garden.

scribed and published with the name *Chusquea gigantea*. However, since field studies have shown that intermediate forms exist in different populations, and have revealed the apparent intergrading of *C. culeou* and *C.* aff. *culeou*, publication of *C. gigantea* as a new species may be premature. Its status awaits further study.

Some reports indicate that *Chusquea* aff. *culeou* is slightly less hardy than *C. culeou*, in part because its new shoots are damaged by frost. My *C.* aff. *culeou* produces shoots in the fall as well as in the spring, and the fall shoots are inevitably killed all or in part by the winter cold. Although the *C. culeou* growing in my garden is admittedly less well established than the *C.* aff. *culeou*, it seems to be slightly more abused by winter conditions than the *C.* aff. *culeou*, which, except for tender shoots, appears entirely unfazed.

As with most chusqueas, *Chusquea* aff. *culeou* performs far better in the ground than in a container. It is an exceptionally vigorous plant, and its pachymorph rhizomes have rather long necks, creating an open, relatively rapidly spreading clump. The culms quickly increase in size from year to year. The partially red-brown culms can be striking, though they are often partially covered with tattered culm leaves, giving a slightly unkempt appearance. Stripping the culm leaves enhances the plant's appearance, as does pruning back the large dominant branches if they get out of hand.

The long rhizome necks and the irregular association of roots with individual portions of the plant make propagation of larger specimens rather challenging. One inevitably ends up with sections of the plant that are unsuited for propagation. As a side benefit, however, the new shoots and rhizomes from these sections are fair game for the table. The rhizomes taste excellent. The more mature shoots are somewhat bitter, but can be tamed by parboiling.

Chusquea cumingii

Maximum height: 12 ft. (4 m)
Maximum diameter: ¾ in. (2 cm)
Minimum temperature: 10°F (−12°C) estimated
Light: full sun

Native to semiarid regions of central Chile, *Chusquea cumingii* has distinctive, small, stiff, sharply pointed leaves with a blue-green colorcast. The leaf characteristics are most prominent when grown in full sun. This species reportedly prefers somewhat alkaline soil, as would be expected given its semiarid native habitat. *Chusquea cumingii* is distinctive, and attractive, at least on a small scale. It may be hardier than the current estimate indicates.

Chusquea cumingii. Author's garden.

Chusquea foliosa

Maximum height: 65 ft. (20 m)
Maximum diameter: 2 in. (5 cm)
Minimum temperature: 24°F (–4°C)
Light: mostly sunny

Indigenous to Chiapas, Mexico, and the montane, oak, cloud forests of Costa Rica, at elevations of 7200 to 8500 ft. (2200 to 2600 m), *Chusquea foliosa* grows in gaps in the tree canopy. It is common on the slopes of Costa Rican volcanoes. The culms are erect at the base, then begin an arching habit. This species has unusual infravaginal branching that is shared by several other chusqueas. The branches emerge by popping out at the base of the culm leaf sheath without rupturing it. The foliage leaf blades are long and narrow with a smooth undersurface. It is a very desirable ornamental.

Chusquea galeottiana

Maximum height: 50 ft. (15 m)
Maximum diameter: ⅝ in. (1.5 cm)
Minimum temperature: 26°F (–3°C) estimated
Light: mostly sunny

Chusquea galeottiana is a member of section *Verticillatae* of subgenus *Chusquea*. Like the other members of the section, *C. galeottiana* has branches that grow in a whorl around the circumference of the culm. Within the section, only *C. galeottiana* and *C. pittieri* routinely grow at elevations higher than 6500 ft. (2000 m). The culms are erect at the base, then arch broadly, befitting its clambering, climbing habit. It is indigenous to Oaxaca and Guerrero, Mexico (Clark 1989).

Chusquea liebmannii

Maximum height: 33 ft. (10 m)
Maximum diameter: 1 in. (2.5 cm)
Minimum temperature: 32°F (0°C)
Light: mostly sunny

Unlike most chusqueas currently in cultivation, *Chusquea liebmannii* tolerates periods of dryness. Among its native habitats are pine and oak forests from Mexico to Costa Rica. Of all the chusqueas, this species grows in the driest habitats and tolerates the driest conditions. Like those of *C. pittieri* and *C. circinata,* its branches grow in a whorl around the circumference of the culm, and it has spiny root primordia at the nodes.

Somewhat uncommon for the genus, the culm leaves are rapidly deciduous, exposing a clear view of the culm. And somewhat unusually for bamboos in general, when stressed, the leaf blades fold together along their length rather than rolling up.

Chusquea macrostachya

Maximum height: 20 ft. (6 m)
Maximum diameter: 1½ in. (4 cm)
Minimum temperature: 0°F (–18°C)
Light: mostly sunny

Along with *Chusquea culeou* and *C. montana, C. macrostachya* thrives as an understory plant in its native environment in the beech forests of Argentina and Chile. Among the hardiest of the chusqueas, it is also a choice ornamental, with delicate leaves and arching culms and branches. As with some other bamboos, if the culm is damaged, a primary branch can elongate and effectively take the place of the culm.

Many of the plants cultivated in the United States as *Chusquea macrostachya* are misidentified and are actually *C. culeou*. The two species can be readily distinguished, however. *Chusquea culeou* branches are all approximately the same size, and the leaf blades are relatively stiff. *Chusquea macrostachya* has a dominant branch per node, which is subtended by a number of smaller subsidiary branches. Its leaf blades are relatively soft compared to those of *C. culeou* (Lynn Clark, personal communication).

Chusquea mimosa ssp. australis

Maximum height: 16 ft. (5 m) estimated
Maximum diameter: ½ in. (1.25 cm) estimated
Minimum temperature: 22°F (–6°C) estimated
Light: mostly sunny

Native to southeastern Brazil, *Chusquea mimosa* ssp. *australis* is an attractive ornamental with small leaves on deep red culms. An un-

Chusquea foliosa. Quail Botanical Gardens.

common feature for chusqueas, the leaf sheaths drop away to expose the branches.

Chusquea montana

Common synonym: *Chusquea nigricans*
Maximum height: 10 ft. (3 m) estimated
Maximum diameter: ½ in. (1.25 cm) estimated
Minimum temperature: 0°F (–18°C) estimated
Light: mostly sunny

Chusquea montana is the accepted name for *C. nigricans*. The plant cultivated in the United States under the name *C. nigricans*, however, is a dwarf form of *C. culeou*, and not *C. montana* (see *C. culeou* 'Caña Prieta'). *Chusquea montana* is uncommon in cultivation.

Chusquea montana is part of the understory in the beech forests of Argentina and Chile. Capable of thriving in subalpine conditions, it is somewhat smaller and more delicate than many of the other hardy chusqueas. Its swollen nodes are a distinguishing feature.

Chusquea muelleri

Maximum height: 6 ft. (1.8 m)
Maximum diameter: ¼ in. (0.6 cm)
Minimum temperature: 32°F (0°C)
Light: mostly sunny

From eastern Mexico, *Chusquea muelleri* is one of 26 named species of *Chusquea* that do not "fit" any of the three established subgenera. It is a small, delicate plant with trailing culms and up to six branches per node.

Chusquea pittieri

Maximum height: 65 ft. (20 m)
Maximum diameter: 2 in. (5 cm)
Minimum temperature: 26°F (–3°C)
Light: mostly sunny

Chusquea pittieri is one of the largest and most robust species of the genus. It is native to Central America and Mexico. In Costa Rica it forms dense stands on canyon walls, covering them with cascading foliage. When canyon walls are not at hand, the plant threads its way into trees, or arches and hangs on other convenient supports. In its native habitat, it is also capable of achieving considerable heights without exhibiting any type of climbing behavior, though its culms are heavily arching (Lynn Clark, personal communication).

Like *Chusquea liebmannii* and *C. circinata*, this species has spiny root primordia at the nodes. It has the longest flowering cycle of any *Chusquea*, an interval of some 60 to 70 years. Unlike typical *Chusquea*, in which branches are arrayed in a crescent shape around or below a larger central branch, the branches of *C. pittieri* grow in a whorl around the circumference of the culm, like other members of section *Verticillatae* of subgenus *Chusquea*. Within the section, only *C. galeottiana* and *C. pittieri* routinely grow at elevations higher than 6500 ft. (2000 m).

The branching is extravaginal, with branches bursting through the culm leaf sheath, but the culm leaves then generally fall away as the branches develop, exposing the culm. *Chusquea pittieri* is attractive on a smaller scale as well as a larger scale, surviving nicely and handsomely as a house plant. It is quite tolerant of dim winter light and dry conditions, as long as one can accommodate considerable winter leaf fall and the plant's abandonment of the smaller culms.

Chusquea quila

Maximum height: 15 ft. (4.5 m) estimated
Maximum diameter: 1 in. (2.5 cm) estimated
Minimum temperature: 26°F (–3°C) estimated
Light: mostly sunny

Chusquea quila is an aggressive colonizer in disturbed forest areas. It is similar to *C. valdiviensis*, though smaller. In the past, *C. valdiviensis* has been sold as *C. quila*.

Chusquea simpliciflora

Maximum height: 82 ft. (25 m)
Maximum diameter: ⅜ in. (1 cm)
Minimum temperature: 32°F (0°C)
Light: mostly sunny

Native to tropical and lower montane forests of Central America and the northern regions of South America, *Chusquea simpliciflora* is a tender species with very slender culms. It

Chusquea uliginosa. Bamboo Sourcery.

vines, climbs, and hangs in surrounding vegetation. The subsidiary branches extend at least halfway around the culm. It is believed to flower approximately every 30 years.

Chusquea subtilis

Maximum height: undetermined
Maximum diameter: undetermined
Minimum temperature: 26°F (–3°C) estimated
Light: mostly sunny

Indigenous to the Talamanca Range of Costa Rica, *Chusquea subtilis* has numerous branches per node and long, narrow foliage leaf blades. Its populations are denser in more humid areas and along streams in montane forests.

Chusquea sulcata

Maximum height: 15 ft. (4.5 m)
Maximum diameter: ½ in. (1.25 cm)
Minimum temperature: 28°F (–2°C)
Light: mostly sunny

Chusquea valdiviensis. Bamboo Sourcery.

From southern Mexico, *Chusquea sulcata* grows at middle elevations and exhibits an open clumping habit. The culms turn golden yellow with age, and they arch to form an attractive umbrella-shaped profile.

Chusquea tomentosa

Maximum height: undetermined
Maximum diameter: undetermined
Minimum temperature: 26°F (–3°C) estimated
Light: mostly sunny

Indigenous to the montane oak forests of Costa Rica, *Chusquea tomentosa* prefers slightly drier conditions than some of the other chusqueas of the area, including *C. foliosa* and *C. subtilis.* It grows under the tree canopy, as well as in exposed gaps in the canopy, at elevations of 8200 to 9800 ft. (2500 to 3000 m). The culms are erect at the base, then begin to arch.

Chusquea tomentosa has an unusual, infravaginal branching habit that is shared by several other chusqueas. The branches emerge by popping out at the base of the culm leaf sheath without rupturing it. The foliage leaf blades are long and narrow with a velvety undersurface. It is an attractive bamboo, with tufts of branches and foliage along the culm.

Chusquea uliginosa

Maximum height: 30 ft. (9 m)
Maximum diameter: 1 in. (2.5 cm)
Minimum temperature: 10°F (–12°C)
Light: mostly sunny

In its native habitat in southern Chile, *Chusquea uliginosa* grows along the perimeter of seasonal wetlands. It can clamber up to 30 ft. (9 m) high or more into trees. In the landscape, it can be pruned to an attractive, strongly arching habit.

Chusquea valdiviensis

Maximum height: 30 ft. (9 m)
Maximum diameter: 1½ in. (4 cm)
Minimum temperature: 20°F (–7°C)
Light: mostly sunny

Native to southern Chile, *Chusquea valdiviensis* clambers to a height of 30 ft. (9 m). It is an aggressive colonizer in disturbed forested areas, often readily overwhelming other foliage. It is less appealing as an ornamental than many other chusqueas.

Dendrocalamus

Dendrocalamus is a genus of arborescent Old World tropical bamboos with pachymorph rhizomes. Comprising 52 known species, *Dendrocalamus* includes the world's largest bamboos, several reaching heights of 100 ft. (30 m) or more. Culms may be up to 1 ft. (30 cm) in diameter. The large leaves are up to 20 in. (50 cm) long and 4 in. (10 cm) wide in some species. *Dendrocalamus* generally resembles *Bambusa,* but unlike in *Bambusa,* the culm leaf auricles are either absent or not prominent, and *Dendrocalamus* does not include species with spiny branches. Some species of *Bambusa* are moderately cold tolerant, whereas *Dendrocala-mus* requires a semitropical or tropical environment. Most *Dendrocalamus* species are associated with areas of high rainfall or montane habitats, but *D. strictus* is a prominent exception, inhabiting lowlands and drier regions.

Dendrocalamus is an economically important genus for both traditional and modern economies. On the list developed by the International Network for Bamboo and Rattan, in cooperation with the International Plant Genetic Resources Institute, which delineated priority bamboos meriting focused research and wider use, four *Dendrocalamus* were included among the original 19 species: *D. asper, D. giganteus, D. latiflorus,* and *D. strictus.*

Dendrocalamus asper

Maximum height: 100 ft. (30 m)
Maximum diameter: 8 in. (20 cm)
Minimum temperature: 23°F (−5°C)
Light: full sun

    Dendrocalamus asper is an attractive orna-

Dendrocalamus asper. Quail Botanical Gardens.

mental, and it is more cold tolerant than most of the genus. It is native to Southeast Asia and widely cultivated throughout tropical Asia. Its culms are used for paper pulp and construction. It is also cultivated for its large and excellent tasting shoots. A single *D. asper* shoot can weigh up to 16 lb. (7.2 kg) or more (Cusack 1997).

Dendrocalamus brandisii

Maximum height: 100 ft. (30 m)
Maximum diameter: 8 in. (20 cm)
Minimum temperature: 28°F (−2°C)
Light: full sun

Native to India and Southeast Asia, *Dendrocalamus brandisii* is among the world's largest bamboos. The lower nodes are branchless, but may have pronounced aerial roots. The thick-walled culms are used in construction, and the new shoots are harvested for the table.

Dendrocalamus giganteus

Common synonym: *Sinocalamus giganteus*
Maximum height: 100 ft. (30 m)
Maximum diameter: 12 in. (30 cm)
Minimum temperature: 25°F (−4°C)
Light: full sun

The name of this species is an apt descriptor of the plant. *Dendrocalamus giganteus,* in close competition with *D. sinicus,* is the world's largest bamboo. Indigenous to India, Burma, and Thailand, it is also cultivated in China's Yunnan Province and in Taiwan, where it was introduced in 1966. It may not perform as well as the other giants of the genus if grown in a cooler climate. Lower nodes may be branchless for 40 ft. (12 m) or more. The leaves can be up to 20 in. (50 cm) long and 4 in. (10 cm) wide. Its culms are used for building construction, boat masts, furniture, buckets, water pitchers, vases, and other crafts. The young shoots are suitable for the table. Comparative experiments with *D. strictus* indicate that *D. giganteus* is a preferable raw material for papermaking.

Dendrocalamus hamiltonii

Maximum height: 80 ft. (24 m)
Maximum diameter: 7 in. (18 cm)
Minimum temperature: 27°F (−3°C)
Light: full sun

The culms of *Dendrocalamus hamiltonii* are sometimes erect, but often grow in a curved or arching fashion. Lower nodes are bare of branches. Upper nodes branch thickly. The quality of the culm wood is not as high as some of the other *Dendrocalamus* species, but it is nonetheless used for construction, vessels for water and milk, floats for rafts, fuel, paper pulp, and basket making. The young shoots are suitable for the table.

Dendrocalamus jianshuiensis

Maximum height: 60 ft. (18 m)
Maximum diameter: 4¾ in. (12 cm)
Minimum temperature: 28°F (−2°C) estimated
Light: full sun

Dendrocalamus jianshuiensis is native to China's Yunnan Province, at an elevation range of 2600 to 5000 ft. (800 to 1500 m). The young culms are covered with waxy powder and needlelike hairs. In the clump, the culms nod toward the tip. Cured culms are used in construction.

Dendrocalamus latiflorus

Common synonym: *Sinocalamus latiflorus*
Maximum height: 80 ft. (24 m)
Maximum diameter: 10 in. (25 cm)
Minimum temperature: 25°F (−4°C)
Light: full sun

Dendrocalamus latiflorus is native to China. The culms have excellent buoyancy and are used for floats and making rafts, as well as for the typical uses of construction, crafts, and paper pulp. The young shoots are considered delicious. *Dendrocalamus latiflorus* is one of the more important bamboos for shoot production. In southern China and Taiwan, shoots average 9 lb. (4 kg) each.

Dendrocalamus giganteus, at an entrance to the bamboo groves at Quail Botanical Gardens.

Dendrocalamus latiflorus 'Mei-nung'
Maximum height: 80 ft. (24 m)
Maximum diameter: 10 in. (25 cm)
Minimum temperature: 25°F (−4°C)
Light: full sun

Introduced from Taiwan in the 1980s, *Dendrocalamus latiflorus* 'Mei-nung' is similar to the principal form, but the culms and branches are light green, striped with dark green. The large leaves have occasional yellow stripes.

Dendrocalamus minor
Maximum height: 26 ft. (8 m)
Maximum diameter: 2¼ in. (6 cm)

Dendrocalamus latiflorus 'Mei-nung'.
Quail Botanical Gardens.

Minimum temperature: 28°F (−2°C) estimated
Light: full sun

One of the smaller species of the genus, *Dendrocalamus minor* is native to China's Guangdong, Guangxi, and Guizhou Provinces. Its culms are used for weaving and for farm tools and utility construction.

Dendrocalamus strictus
Common name: male bamboo
Maximum height: 60 ft. (18 m)
Maximum diameter: 5 in. (13 cm)
Minimum temperature: 30°F (−1°C)
Light: full sun

Dendrocalamus strictus possesses neither great beauty nor exemplary physical properties, yet it is perhaps the Old World's most important tropical bamboo. It tolerates drought and low humidity, growing well in areas marginally suitable for other bamboos. The lower portion of the thick-walled culms is sometimes nearly solid, particularly in dry environments.

Dendrocalamus strictus is used by local populations for construction, furniture, mats, and baskets. In India, it is extensively cultivated for paper pulp. Although other bamboos have superior pulping characteristics, the abundance and rugged nature of the plant has made *D. strictus* the foundation and mainstay of India's paper industry.

Dendrocalamus yunnanicus
Maximum height: 82 ft. (25 m)
Maximum diameter: 7 in. (18 cm)
Minimum temperature: 28°F (−2°C) estimated
Light: full sun

Distributed in northern Vietnam and the adjacent Chinese regions of Yunnan and Guangxi, *Dendrocalamus yunnanicus* has erect culms with nodding tops. The culms of this large bamboo are used for construction, water pipes, and rafts. The shoots are reportedly delicious.

Dendrocalamus minor. Quail Botanical Gardens.

Dinochloa

A tropical genus of some 27 species (or perhaps closer to 20, according to some authorities), *Dinochloa* bamboos have a pachymorph rhizome system, large leaves, and a climbing habit. More than any other climbing bamboos, they exhibit a true vining habit, presumably in adaptation to their rainforest environment. To facilitate the climbing habit, the internodes zigzag, helping the culms twine around tree trunks and limbs, and the culm leaf sheaths are rough at the base, helping to grip tree bark or other climbing surfaces. The primary branch bud is capable of taking the place of the culm in the event the culm is damaged. The genus is native to China, Southeast Asia, and the Pacific Islands.

Dinochloa malayana

Maximum height: 30 ft. (9 m)
Maximum diameter: ½ in. (1.25 cm)
Minimum temperature: 28°F (−2°C)
Light: partial shade

A vining bamboo from Thailand and Malaysia, distributed along forest margins, from near sea level to 1600 ft. (500 m).

Dinochloa scandens

Maximum height: 30 ft. (9 m)
Maximum diameter: ½ in. (1.25 cm)
Minimum temperature: 28°F (−2°C)
Light: partial shade

A tropical climbing bamboo with black culms and large leaves, *Dinochloa scandens* can be grown as a decorative indoor plant. Reportedly, the plants under this species name in the United States are actually *D. malayana*.

Drepanostachyum

Drepanostachyum is a genus of somewhat tender, montane bamboos that grow up to 16 ft. (5 m) tall and have pachymorph rhizome systems. It is found primarily at elevations of 3300 to 7200 ft. (1000 to 2200 m) in the dry semitropical forests of the Himalayas. In its native habitats, *Drepanostachyum* does not survive below about 1600 ft. (500 m), where maximum temperatures can reach 104°F (40°C). Above 6100 ft. (1850 m), *Himalayacalamus*, another genus of Himalayan montane bamboos that resemble *Drepanostachyum*, become increasingly prominent. Cold temperatures and the greater levels of UV light cause increasing leaf damage at higher elevations. Unlike those of truly hardy bamboos, the foliage leaf blades of *Drepanostachyum* are not tessellated. On a mature plant, in the first year of culm growth, each node has around 25 branches. In subsequent years, a node may have as many as 70 branches. The branches are similarly sized, and they wrap around much of the circumference of the culm (Stapleton 1994d, 1994c).

The new shoots of *Drepanostachyum* are very bitter and are not suited for the table. The genus is useful as forage or pasture for animals and, despite the somewhat swollen nodes, as weaving material. In the main, however, most species are not widely cultivated or harvested. Where available, other genera are more often favored. In their natural environment, *Drepanostachyum* bamboos are often heavily browsed by animals, and often do not reach their full height.

Significant polymorphism is found among the known species, and additional species will likely be identified beyond the 11 currently named. Considerable confusion surrounds the identity and classification of many of the pachymorph montane bamboos. *Drepanostachyum* can be distinguished from *Thamnocalamus* by the absence of leaf tessellation and by branch buds, which, unlike in *Thamnocalamus*, are wider than they are tall. The identity problem is most acute between *Drepanostachyum* and *Himalayacalamus*. Not only are the genera frequently confused, but some of the species have long been interchangeably labeled in the nursery trade as well, exacerbating and perpetuating the problem. Several features distinguish the two genera. On the inside, upper part of the culm leaf sheath, adjacent to the ligule,

Drepanostachyum khasianum. Quail Botanical Gardens.

Drepanostachyum sheaths are rough, whereas *Himalayacalamus* sheaths are smooth. *Himalayacalamus* branches differ from *Drepanostachyum* in that they vary in size, grow more erect, and are not arrayed as broadly around the circumference of the culm. *Drepanostachyum* is less cold tolerant than *Himalayacalamus,* but more tolerant of drought (Stapleton 1994d).

Drepanostachyum falcatum

Common synonym: *Sinarundinaria falcatum*
Maximum height: 12 ft. (4 m)
Maximum diameter: ½ in. (1.25 cm)
Minimum temperature: 26°F (–3°C)
Light: partial shade

Heavily browsed, *Drepanostachyum falcatum* is seldom found in an unpillaged state in its natural habitats. Although the culms are not very straight and have somewhat swollen nodes, they are often used for basket weaving.

Drepanostachyum khasianum

Maximum height: 16 ft. (5 m)
Maximum diameter: ½ in. (1.25 cm)
Minimum temperature: 22°F (–6°C)
Light: partial shade

In its natural environment, *Drepanostachyum khasianum* is heavily browsed and is most often encountered as a scruffy scrub plant less than 10 ft. (3 m) tall. Protected, it is an attractive, somewhat tender, mountain bamboo. Although the name has been misapplied to other species, the plants in general circulation in the United States appear to be correctly named. The American variants, however, have larger leaves and are apparently less hardy than examples of the species observed elsewhere.

Drepanostachyum sengteeanum

Maximum height: 16 ft. (5 m)
Maximum diameter: ½ in. (1.25 cm)
Minimum temperature: 20°F (–7°C)
Light: partial shade

This bamboo is in distribution in the United States as *Himalayacalamus falconeri* or *Arundinaria falconeri,* but it is a different species and has been given the name *Drepanostachyum sengteeanum.* It flowered gregariously in the 1990s, disclosing its identity as a *Drepanostachyum.* Analysis of the material sent by bamboo nurseryman Gib Cooper to C. M. A. Stapleton at the Royal Botanic Gardens, Kew, led to identification of a new species, *D. sengteeanum* (Chris Stapleton, personal communication). It is an attractive, tightly clumping bamboo with relatively small foliage leaves for a *Drepanostachyum.* It is somewhat hardier than *D. khasianum* in marginal winter climates.

Fargesia

Most pachymorph bamboos are semitropical or tropical, with little cold tolerance, but some species of *Fargesia,* a genus of pachymorph bamboos, are among the most cold hardy of all bamboos. Both *F. nitida* and *F. murielae,* for example, reportedly can withstand temperature drops to –20°F (–29°C) without leaf damage. These species have been growing successfully in Norway for more than 30 years, and *F. nitida* has survived winters as far north as Tromsø, Norway, at nearly 70°N latitude, well into the Arctic Circle (Flatabø 1995). It should be noted that the concept of cold tolerance is relative. Although foliage damage has become a standard indicator of winter hardiness, some bamboos in their native environments are naturally deciduous in winter, putting on a flush growth of foliage in the spring.

The genus *Fargesia* was once thought to be a small one, comprising perhaps three species, but Chinese research has brought the total to approximately 80 species. However, some of those recently identified are now known to belong in the newly identified genus *Borinda.* The towering mountains and terrain of central China create isolated pockets and unique environments, such that the entire population of some species may exist on a single mountain, or even on a single mountain slope.

Fargesias range in size from small plants about 5 ft. (1.5 m) tall, to much larger plants up to 27 ft. (8 m) tall and 2 in. (5 cm) in diameter. In general, particularly with respect to the species cultivated in the West, the plants exhibit a typical montane bamboo form, with numerous branches and delicate leaves on slender arching culms—more bushlike than arborescent. Befitting their hardiness, the leaves are prominently tessellated.

Although many species are exceptionally cold tolerant, most fargesias, like other Old World montane bamboos, do not thrive in strong sunlight, high temperatures, warm soils, or drought conditions. In a landscape or other controlled environment, shade and water can be provided, but ensuring moderate summer temperatures is more of a problem. Most fargesias are not the best choice in climates where the severe cold temperatures of winter are matched by the intense heat of summer. As usual, there are exceptions. Some clones of *F. nitida* are reportedly more heat tolerant.

Fargesia adpressa

Maximum height: 18 ft. (5.5 m)
Maximum diameter: 1¼ in. (3.2 cm)
Minimum temperature: 0°F (−18°C)
Light: partial shade

The culm leaf of *Fargesia adpressa* is shorter than the internode and not readily deciduous. In its native China, this species does not shoot until midsummer. In the United States, at least some the material in circulation as *F. adpressa* is probably misidentified, and is likely *F. murielae* or another *Fargesia* species.

Fargesia angustissima

Maximum height: 23 ft. (7 m)
Maximum diameter: ¾ in. (2 cm)
Minimum temperature: 15°F (−9°C)
Light: partial shade

Native to the evergreen, broad-leaved forests of Sichuan, *Fargesia angustissima* is used for weaving and provides food for the giant panda.

New shoots are purple to purple-green. The young culms are heavily covered with white powder.

Some species that were formerly placed in *Fargesia* have been moved to the new genus *Borinda*. *Fargesia angustissima* is probably a species of *Borinda*, although as of this writing, a change has not yet been made.

Fargesia dracocephala

Common name: dragon's head bamboo
Maximum height: 16 ft. (5 m)
Maximum diameter: ¾ in. (2 cm)
Minimum temperature: −10°F (−23°C)
Light: partial shade

Fargesia dracocephala is one of the bamboos that provide food for the giant panda in its native China, and it is also a highly attractive ornamental. When exposed to the sun, the culms may turn red or reddish black. The dense, dark green foliage leaves do not curl in the sun and heat like many others of the genus. This species appears to be less vigorous, however, and slower to develop significant size. Many of the plants in circulation have been propagated from seedlings grown in the late 1980s or early 1990s. The numerous seedlings have resulted in plants with slightly different culm coloration and growth habit.

Fargesia murielae

Common synonyms: *Sinarundinaria murielae,*
    Thamnocalamus spathaceus
Common name: umbrella bamboo
Maximum height: 15 ft. (4.5 m)
Maximum diameter: ½ in. (1.25 cm)
Minimum temperature: −20°F (−29°C)
Light: full shade

Fargesia murielae is one of the world's most winter hardy bamboos. Its green culms bear masses of delicate pea-green leaves. In a clump, the upper portion of the culms arch in a manner reminiscent of an umbrella's shape, thus its common name, umbrella bamboo. A choice ornamental, *F. murielae* needs some shade, and a wide space to display its airy, arching mass of foliage. It grows at elevations of up to 10,000 ft. (3000 m) in China and is a food source for the giant panda. Collected in China's Hubei Province in 1907 by the famous British plant collector Ernest H. Wilson, the bamboo is named after Wilson's daughter, Muriel.

Fargesia nitida

Common synonyms: *Fargesia spathacea, Sinarundinaria nitida*
Common name: blue fountain bamboo
Maximum height: 12 ft. (4 m)
Maximum diameter: ½ in. (1.25 cm)
Minimum temperature: −20°F (−29°C)
Light: full shade

Along with *Fargesia murielae, F. nitida* is one of the world's most winter hardy bamboos, and a choice ornamental. The dark red-purple or dark brown-purple of the culms becomes more pronounced with some sun exposure, setting off the masses of delicate dark green leaves. Young culms are coated with a blue-white waxy powder. New shoots are branchless in the first season, branching in the second year. The culms are more upright than those of *F. murielae,* giving the clump more of a fountain shape than an umbrella shape. The shape and the blue-white coating on the new culms give rise to the plant's common name, blue fountain bamboo. *Fargesia nitida* has a number of cultivars that differ more or less distinctly according to growing conditions. In China, this species is one of the food plants for the giant panda.

Fargesia nitida 'Anceps'

Maximum height: 12 ft. (4 m)
Maximum diameter: ½ in. (1.25 cm)
Minimum temperature: −20°F (−29°C)
Light: full shade

Longer leaves, less pronounced culm coloration, and a more open growth habit are characteristics of the *Fargesia nitida* cultivar 'Anceps'.

Although its leaves curl more readily in the sun, it is reportedly more heat tolerant than other *F. nitida* clones. It may be slightly less cold tolerant.

Fargesia nitida 'De Belder'

Maximum height: 10 ft. (3 m)
Maximum diameter: ½ in. (1.25 cm)
Minimum temperature: −20°F (−29°C)
Light: full shade

Possessing the dark red-purple or dark brown-purple culm coloration of the type form, this cultivar of *Fargesia nitida* is reportedly shorter, but more rapidly spreading, with culms that bend outward at their base before becoming vertical. *Fargesia nitida* 'De Belder' forms a foliage canopy of short, dark green leaves, which curl less in the sun than those of the principal form.

Fargesia nitida 'Eisenach'

Maximum height: 14 ft. (4.2 m)
Maximum diameter: ½ in. (1.25 cm)
Minimum temperature: −20°F (−29°C)
Light: full shade

Fargesia nitida 'Eisenach' has the dark red-purple or dark brown-purple culm coloration of the type form, but it has smaller dark green leaves, a more arching habit, and culms that tend to bifurcate at their base. In parts of Europe, this cultivar grows taller than the type form. In parts of the eastern United States, it grows significantly less tall, possibly suggesting a greater sensitivity to growing conditions.

Fargesia nitida 'Ems River'

Maximum height: 14 ft. (4.2 m)
Maximum diameter: ½ in. (1.25 cm)
Minimum temperature: −20°F (−29°C)
Light: full shade

Fargesia nitida 'Ems River' is reportedly among the more upright of the numerous cultivars. The bamboos in circulation under this name may in fact be multiple cultivars, rather than plants of the same cultivar. Reported

Fargesia nitida. Author's garden.

characteristics are inconsistent. The leaves, for example, are reportedly both smaller and larger than the type form.

Fargesia nitida 'McClure'
Maximum height: 18 ft. (5.5 m)
Maximum diameter: ½ in. (1.25 cm)
Minimum temperature: –20°F (–29°C)
Light: full shade

This bamboo once grew in the private garden of the renowned bamboo researcher F. A. McClure, after whom the cultivar is named. It is the largest of the *F. nitida* cultivars, has longer leaves and branches than the type form, and develops a weeping habit. Because of its size, vigor, and growth habit, 'McClure' requires more space than other cultivars, and it can sometimes look a bit unkempt in comparison.

Fargesia nitida 'Nymphenburg'
Maximum height: 12 ft. (4 m)
Maximum diameter: ½ in. (1.25 cm)
Minimum temperature: –20°F (–29°C)
Light: full shade

Because of its long narrow leaves, *Fargesia nitida* 'Nymphenburg' is reminiscent of some of the delicate Himalayan mountain bamboos, but it is far hardier. It lacks the hairs on the culm leaf sheaths that are typical of the type form and the other cultivars. Regarded as an outstanding specimen plant, 'Nymphenburg', along with 'Anceps', looks and grows best in somewhat shadier locations.

Fargesia robusta
Maximum height: 20 ft. (6 m)
Maximum diameter: 1 in. (2.5 cm)
Minimum temperature: 0°F (–18°C)
Light: partial shade

Among the larger and more vigorous of the genus, *Fargesia robusta* is used for weaving and walking sticks in its native China, and the shoots are harvested for the table. It is also a major food source for the giant panda.

Fargesia utilis
Maximum height: 15 ft. (4.5 m)
Maximum diameter: ¾ in. (2 cm)
Minimum temperature: 0°F (–18°C)
Light: mostly sunny

An excellent ornamental, *Fargesia utilis* grows in a tight clump, with small, delicate leaves supported by culms and branches that turn burgundy red in the sun. Leaf tessellation is relatively indistinct. In China, shooting occurs in August. The shoots are edible.

Gigantochloa
Native to Asia and the Pacific Islands, *Gigantochloa* is a genus of giant, clumping, tropical bamboos that generally resemble *Bambusa*. Unlike many other tropical bamboos, *Gigantochloa* is generally not monocarpic, but may partially flower on an irregular basis, creating more frequent opportunity for hybridization. On the other hand, only six *Gigantochloa* species are known to have produced viable seed, and many of today's *Gigantochloa* may be sterile hybrids.

It has been suggested that many of the *Gigantochloa* forms in cultivation in Indonesia today are the result of selection, cultivation, and vegetative propagation of elite hybrid forms dating back to the Proto-Malays thousands of years ago. Over many millennia, the selection process may have excluded bamboo strains with gregarious flowering cycles that would threaten the demise of the stand, or perhaps, it may have excluded bamboos with flowering of any kind.

Gigantochloa apus and *G. levis* have not readily hybridized, but other species, such as *G. atroviolacea* and, particularly, *G. atter,* have multiple hybrid forms. There are some 37 known species, but it has been estimated that there may be as many as 200 *Gigantochloa* forms. Further investigations of these forms likely will show that some should be accorded species status (Muller 1996a).

Some of the cultivated *Gigantochloa* are

reportedly less starchy than *Bambusa,* and thus are far more resistant to attack by beetles and fungus. *Gigantochloa* propagates easily by division or from single-node culm cuttings. The International Network for Bamboo and Rattan (INBAR), in cooperation with the International Plant Genetic Resources Institute, developed a list of priority bamboos that merited focused research and wider use. Although the listing and choices are somewhat controversial, it is nonetheless notable that the original list of 19 species included 3 *Gigantochloa: G. apus, G. levis,* and *G. pseudoarundinacea.*

Gigantochloa albociliata

Common synonym: *Pseudoxytenanthera albociliata*

Maximum height: 30 ft. (9 m)
Maximum diameter: 1 in. (2.5 cm)
Minimum temperature: 30°F (–1°C)
Light: full sun

Gigantochloa albociliata flowers weakly almost every year, but does not produce viable seed. The green culms are covered with white, stiff hairs and are bending, not strongly upright. The shoots are edible, and the species is cultivated commercially in Thailand. Some authorities place this species in the genus *Pseudoxytenanthera.*

Gigantochloa apus

Maximum height: 65 ft. (20 m)
Maximum diameter: 4 in. (10 cm)
Minimum temperature: 27°F (–3°C)
Light: full sun

Native to Java, *Gigantochloa apus* is an exceptionally strong bamboo, both as a whole culm and split for woven work. The strong culms taper very little and are used for roof rafters. The bitter shoots are buried in the mud for several days before being cooked and eaten. The leaves are up to 15 in. (38 cm) long and 2½ in. (6.3 cm) wide. *Gigantochloa apus* was introduced into the United States in about 1932,

and subsequently established in other New World locations, including Puerto Rico and Nicaragua.

Gigantochloa atroviolacea

Maximum height: 55 ft. (17 m)
Maximum diameter: 4 in. (10 cm)
Minimum temperature: 28°F (–2°C)
Light: full sun

Gigantochloa atroviolacea is a highly attractive ornamental bamboo from Java and Sumatra. The young culms are initially dark green, turning rapidly to deep brown-black or deep purple-black. The deciduous culm leaves ensure that the attractive culms are visually unencumbered. Lower nodes may have aerial roots. The cured culms retain their black color and

Gigantochloa atroviolacea. Quail Botanical Gardens.

are used for building and furniture construction, musical instruments, and other craft items. The shoots are edible. This species is often mistaken for *Bambusa lako,* which it closely resembles. The culms of *B. lako* have a shiny surface, however, whereas those of *G. atroviolacea* have more of a matt finish.

Gigantochloa atter
Maximum height: 72 ft. (22 m)
Maximum diameter: 6 in. (15 cm)
Minimum temperature: 28°F (−2°C)
Light: full sun

Long cultivated in Indonesia by indigenous peoples, *Gigantochloa atter* has many related forms that may one day be accorded species status. Known only in cultivation, the species has no recorded flowering. It is speculated that selection by indigenous peoples over the millennia has resulted in forms that exist only in a vegetative state, and thus do not threaten the demise of the resource with gregarious flowering cycles. The productive clumps of *G. atter* yield many exceptional tasting shoots. The culms are straight and strong, and the wood is used in construction and for musical instruments and other handicraft.

Gigantochloa hasskarliana
Maximum height: 30 ft. (9 m)
Maximum diameter: 2½ in. (6.3 cm)
Minimum temperature: 28°F (−2°C)
Light: full sun

Native to Java, *Gigantochloa hasskarliana* is planted as a hedge and is used for weaving and basket making. It is fast growing and vigorous, rapidly forming a dense clump.

Gigantochloa pseudoarundinacea
Common synonym: *Gigantochloa verticillata*
Maximum height: 100 ft. (30 m)
Maximum diameter: 5 in. (13 cm)
Minimum temperature: 28°F (−2°C)
Light: full sun

This bamboo was introduced into the United States and other parts of the New World as *Gigantochloa verticillata.* Many different species in the genus have been erroneously included under that name. *Gigantochloa pseudoarundinacea* is one that is now separated from the cluster and given its own identity. It has likely been in cultivation for thousands of years, and reportedly there are a number of cultivars with distinct characteristics. All have striped culms. Although potentially among the tallest timber bamboos, *G. pseudoarundinacea* seldom approaches its maximum height.

This giant bamboo is of significant economic importance. Its culms are strong, straight, and easily worked, its large shoots reportedly taste excellent, and the species is regarded as an outstanding candidate for the production of paper pulp. In addition to its utility, *Gigantochloa pseudoarundinacea* is a very attractive ornamental.

Gigantochloa pseudoarundinacea.
Quail Botanical Gardens.

Gigantochloa wrayi

Maximum height: 34 ft. (10 m)
Maximum diameter: 3 in. (7.5 cm)
Minimum temperature: 30°F (–1°C)
Light: full sun

Distributed in peninsular Malaysia and peninsular Thailand, *Gigantochloa wrayi* is an attractive bamboo with long internodes. The split culms are used for making baskets.

Guadua

Most New World bamboos are relatively small, but some species of *Guadua* rival the largest of the Old World bamboos. A New World tropical bamboo, *Guadua* was once classified as a subgenus of *Bambusa,* but is now recognized as a distinct genus. *Guadua* consists of approximately 24 described species and a few more undescribed species, ranging from various vining types to the giant *Guadua,* for which the genus is noted. Unlike some *Bambusa, Guadua* bamboos are intolerant of any cold. *Guadua* generally has thorny basal branches. The internodes may contain water, suggesting that the water may be stored and reused during dry periods. The culm leaves are deciduous (Judziewicz et al. 1999).

The natural habitat of *Guadua* ranges from sea level to 7200 ft. (2200 m), from Mexico through Uruguay and Argentina, excluding Chile. The name *Guadua* is a Latinized version of the name given to these bamboos by the indigenous peoples of Ecuador and Colombia. The genus comprises the most extensive bamboo forests of any New World bamboo, covering vast areas of up to 47,000 square miles (122,000 square kilometers) in the Brazilian Amazon and Peru alone (Londoño 1996). Much more is now known about the genus as a result of the work of Ximena Londoño, the current authority on the genus.

The rhizome structure and growth habit of *Guadua* reveals the limitations and occasional inadequacy of common terminology. Bamboos with pachymorph rhizome systems are commonly termed "clumping bamboos" because of their generally clumping habit, but some species of *Guadua* are hardly clumping. The long-necked rhizomes of certain species may extend some 20 ft. (6 m) or more before turning upward into a new culm, easily outdistancing many "running" bamboos with leptomorph rhizome systems. Rather than "clumping" bamboo, *Guadua* bamboos are more properly characterized as having a pachymorph rhizome system and a diffuse habit—though even this rather understates the matter.

Guadua amplexifolia

Maximum height: 60 ft. (18 m)
Maximum diameter: 4 in. (10 cm)
Minimum temperature: 30°F (–1°C)
Light: full sun

Guadua amplexifolia has a more pronounced arching habit than other large *Guadua* species. Typically thorny, it may be thornless in the more northerly reaches of its range. The lower culm leaves are persistent, but upper culm leaves are rapidly deciduous.

Guadua angustifolia

Maximum height: 100 ft. (30 m)
Maximum diameter: 9 in. (22 cm)
Minimum temperature: 30°F (–1°C)
Light: full sun

The type species of the genus, *Guadua angustifolia* is the largest of all the New World bamboos. Native to northeastern South America, it is prominent in Colombia and Ecuador, where it is known, respectively, as *guadua* and *caña brava.* China has its remarkable moso forests; South America has its guaduales, expanses of land dominated by species of *Guadua,* prominent among them *G. angustifolia.* The species thrives in a fairly broad elevation range, from sea level to 5900 ft. (1800 m). It grows best within a temperature range of 63 to 75°F (17 to 24°C)—clearly not a bamboo that thrives on frosty conditions. Nor is it a bamboo for dry conditions, thriving in natural habitats with an annual precipitation ranging from 80 to 240 in. (2000 to 6000 mm) a year (Judziewicz et al. 1999).

Guadua angustifolia has outstanding mechanical properties. Very strong and easily workable, it is used in construction of modest homes by indigenous peoples, as well as in multimillion-dollar architectural masterpieces. Most tropical bamboos are chronically subject to insect attack and rot, but *G. angustifolia,* even when untreated, is highly resistant. Documented accounts have demonstrated that its longevity is greater than that of hardwoods used alongside it (McClure 1966).

The list of priority bamboos compiled by the International Network for Bamboo and Rattan, in cooperation with the International Plant Genetic Resources Institute, included *Guadua an-*

Guadua angustifolia. Quail Botanical Gardens.

gustifolia, the only New World bamboo on the original list of 19 species. The list and criteria are somewhat controversial, and the paucity of New World species on the list suggests a lack of familiarity with the breadth and depth of New World bamboos.

Guadua angustifolia var. *bicolor*
Maximum height: 100 ft. (30 m)
Maximum diameter: 8 in. (20 cm)
Minimum temperature: 30°F (–1°C)
Light: full sun
Similar to the principal form, but the culms have yellow and green striping.

Guadua angustifolia 'Less Thorny'
Maximum height: 100 ft. (30 m)
Maximum diameter: 8 in. (20 cm)
Minimum temperature: 30°F (–1°C)
Light: full sun
Similar to the type form, but the culms have fewer and smaller thorns.

Guadua chacoensis
Maximum height: 60 ft. (18 m)
Maximum diameter: 6 in. (15 cm)
Minimum temperature: 30°F (–1°C)
Light: full sun
Sometimes mistaken for *Guadua angustifolia,* the thorny *G. chacoensis* is native to northern Argentina and southern Paraguay. Its culms are used in construction.

Guadua velutina
Maximum height: 60 ft. (18 m)
Maximum diameter: 4 in. (10 cm)
Minimum temperature: 28°F (–2°C)
Light: full sun
Guadua velutina has the northernmost distribution of the genus, extending into Mexico, from Tamaulipas to Oaxaca. The culms are thick walled and are used in construction. The species epithet references the velvety pubescence on the spikelets (Lynn Clark, personal communication).

Hibanobambusa

The name *Hibanobambusa* means bamboo growing on Mt. Hiba. This single-species genus reportedly originated in the wild from a crossing of *Sasa veitchii* f. *tyugokensis* and *Phyllostachys nigra* var. *henonis* sometime around the end of the 19th century or beginning of the 20th century. *Hibanobambusa* has a leptomorph rhizome system and characteristics that suggest its alleged parents. The culm leaves are deciduous, as with *Phyllostachys*, but each node generally bears only one branch (or occasionally two or three branches after the first year). *Hibanobambusa* flowered in the early 1970s, but apparently few seeds were produced and none proved viable. The flowers are reportedly similar to those of *Phyllostachys*, but they usually have six stamens, as in *Sasa*. Doubt remains as to whether the genus is the hybrid that has been suggested. Studies using molecular techniques could help reveal more about the origins of the genus (Lynn Clark, personal communication).

Hibanobambusa tranquillans

Maximum height: 16 ft. (5 m)
Maximum diameter: 1¼ in. (3.2 cm)
Minimum temperature: 0°F (−18°C)
Light: mostly sunny

Sharing some of the overt characteristics of its alleged parents, *Hibanobambusa tranquillans* has the larger leaves of a *Sasa*, up to 10 in. (25 cm) long and 1¼ in. (3.2 cm) wide, and the deciduous culm leaves characteristic of *Phyllostachys*.

Hibanobambusa tranquillans 'Shiroshima'

Maximum height: 16 ft. (5 m)
Maximum diameter: 1¼ in. (3.2 cm)
Minimum temperature: 0°F (−18°C)
Light: mostly sunny

A very attractive ornamental, *Hibanobambusa tranquillans* 'Shiroshima' is similar to the type form, but with strongly variegated, white-striped leaves. When grown in strong sun, some of the leaves may have purple tones in the variegation.

Himalayacalamus

Himalayacalamus is a genus of marginally hardy, pachymorph, montane bamboos that grow up to 26 ft. (8 m) tall. Species are found at elevations of 6100 to 9200 ft. (1850 to 2800 m) in the cool, broad-leaved forests of the Himalayas. Slender culms, profuse with fine branches and delicate leaves, are the hallmark of these attractive bamboos. Two additional species from Nepal are just now coming into cultivation, *H. porcatus* and *H. cupreus*.

Unlike in truly hardy bamboos, the leaf veins are not prominently tessellated in *Hima-*

Hibanobambusa tranquillans 'Shiroshima'.
Author's garden.

layacalamus. This genus can be distinguished from the similar-looking *Thamnocalamus* by the absence of prominent leaf tessellation. In the first year of culm growth, each node has about 15 branches. In subsequent years, a node may have up to 40 branches. *Himalayacalamus* plants are useful as forage, pasture for animals, and as weaving material. The new shoots of many species are excellent for the table (Stapleton 1994d).

Considerable confusion surrounds the identity and classification of many of the pachymorph montane bamboos. As early as 1896, in *The Bamboo Garden*, A. B. Freeman-Mitford refers to a history of confusion and widespread misidentification. The identity problem is most acute between *Himalayacalamus* and *Drepanostachyum*. Not only are the genera frequently confused, but also some of the species have been mistakenly interchangeably labeled in the nursery trade, exacerbating and perpetuating the problem. In the case of *H. falconeri* and *D. falcatum*, the source of confusion rests as much with the similarity of the names as with the similarity between the species.

Several features distinguish the two genera. On the inside of the culm leaf sheaths, near the top, *Himalayacalamus* is smooth. *Drepanostachyum* is rough. *Himalayacalamus* branches differ from *Drepanostachyum* in that they vary in size, grow more erect, and are not arrayed as broadly around the circumference of the culm. In its natural environment, *Himalayacalamus* is generally found at higher elevations than *Drepanostachyum*, and it is more cold tolerant. *Drepanostachyum*, however, is more tolerant of drought. The culms of some *Himalayacalamus* species are slightly larger, reaching 1⅜ in. (3.5 cm), versus a maximum of 1 in. (2.5 cm) for *Drepanostachyum* (Stapleton 1994d).

Unlike many bamboos, at least some *Himalayacalamus* species require a period of dormancy before their seed will germinate. At a temperature of 68 to 77°F (20 to 25°C), *H. hookerianus* reportedly requires one to eight months before germination occurs.

Himalayacalamus asper

Maximum height: 20 ft. (6 m)
Maximum diameter: ¾ in. (2 cm)
Minimum temperature: 15°F (−9°C)
Light: partial shade

Indigenous to Nepal, at elevations ranging from 6000 to 7500 ft. (1800 to 2300 m), *Himalayacalamus asper* is generally similar to *H. falconeri*, but the surface of *H. asper* culm leaf sheaths is rough or slightly hairy. The culms have a drooping habit. Flexible, they are often used for weaving, although when available, other *Himalayacalamus* species with longer internodes are used in preference. In the United States, the bamboos in the garden trade that were grown under the name of *Neomicrocalamus microphyllus* are actually *H. asper* (Stapleton 1994c, 1994e, personal communication).

Himalayacalamus falconeri

Maximum height: 25 ft. (7.5 m)
Maximum diameter: 1⅜ in. (3.5 cm)
Minimum temperature: 15°F (−9°C)
Light: partial shade

In its native environment, *Himalayacalamus falconeri* is found at relatively high elevations, ranging from 6600 to 8200 ft. (2000 to 2500 m). The shoots are edible and can be found for sale in the markets of Katmandu. The relatively large, flexible culms make excellent weaving material. Cultivated plants came to the United States from northwest India in the 19th century. Unfortunately, some or all of the plants in distribution under the names *H. falconeri* and *Arundinaria falconeri* in the United States, and perhaps elsewhere, are a different species, the newly named *Drepanostachyum sengteeanum* (Chris Stapleton, personal communication).

Himalayacalamus falconeri 'Damarapa'

Common synonym: *Drepanostachyum hookerianum*
Maximum height: 25 ft. (7.5 m)
Maximum diameter: 1⅜ in. (3.5 cm)

Himalayacalamus asper. Bamboo Sourcery.

Minimum temperature: 15°F (−9°C)
Light: partial shade

Often found in the trade under the name *Drepanostachyum hookerianum*, *Himalayacalamus falconeri* 'Damarapa' is a striking plant, displaying culms with green and yellow stripes that change to lavender, red, and pink tones, depending on exposure to the sun and cool air.

Himalayacalamus hookerianus

Common synonyms: *Arundinaria hookeriana*,
    Sinarundinaria hookeriana
Maximum height: 23 ft. (7 m)
Maximum diameter: 1¼ in. (3.2 cm)
Minimum temperature: 15°F (−9°C)
Light: partial shade

This species is an exceptionally attractive bamboo. The new culms are a striking blue color, complemented by a profusion of small, delicate leaves. In subsequent years, the culm coloration ranges from yellow-green to purple-red. The lower nodes are free of branches, and the internodes are long, contributing to the desirability of the culms for weaving. In its natural environment, *Himalayacalamus hookerianus* is an understory plant. Sheltered by the forest canopy that mitigates the harshness of wind and cold, it can prosper in spite of its marginal hardiness.

Named after Sir Joseph Hooker, who found the bamboo in flower in 1848 on an approach to a mountain pass in Sikkim, *Himalayacalamus hookerianus* has probably suffered more nomenclature abuse than any other bamboo. Besides the species being incorrectly associated with several other genera, at least two other bamboos are commonly labeled and traded with variants of the name *"hookerianus,"* including *Drepanostachyum hookerianum*, which, in itself, is a striking bamboo, now thought to be a cultivar of *H. falconeri* (Stapleton 1994f).

Indocalamus

Somewhat similar to *Sasa*, *Indocalamus* is a genus of broad-leaved bamboos with a single main branch per node (except near the top of the culm where nodes may have up to three branches). Unlike *Sasa*, the supranodal ridges are unswollen, and the leaves typically have a greater length to width ratio—a length of over four or more times their width in *Indocalamus*, but frequently less than four times their width in *Sasa*. Also unlike *Sasa*, *Indocalamus* suffers little from withering of the leaf tips or margins, thus sometimes offering a brighter, fresher look. *Indocalamus* culm leaf sheaths are persistent and usually shorter than the internodes. The diameter of the branches is nearly the same as the diameter of the culm. The approximately 35 known species of *Indocalamus* have leptomorph rhizome systems and a strongly running habit. Most prefer some shade and are cold hardy.

Indocalamus latifolius

Maximum height: 10 ft. (3 m)
Maximum diameter: ⅜ in. (1 cm)
Minimum temperature: 0°F (−18°C)
Light: full shade

Native to central and eastern China, *Indocalamus latifolius* culms are used for making chopsticks, brushes, and pens. The leaves are up to 15 in. (38 cm) long and 3 in. (7.5 cm) wide, and are used to make mats, the lining of hats, or for wrapping food. In the landscape, it makes a large attractive bush.

Indocalamus longiauritus

Maximum height: 10 ft. (3 m)
Maximum diameter: ⅜ in. (1 cm)
Minimum temperature: 0°F (−18°C)
Light: partial shade

Native to China, this species is attractive and more tolerant of sun than others of the genus. The large leaves of *Indocalamus longiauritus* are used to make mats, the lining of hats, or for wrapping food. The culms are used for making chopsticks, brushes, and pens.

Indocalamus tessellatus

Maximum height: 7 ft. (2.1 m)
Maximum diameter: ⅜ in. (1 cm)

Indocalamus tessellatus. RKR Bamboo Plantation.

Minimum temperature: −5°F (−21°C)
Light: full shade

Indocalamus tessellatus leaves are up to 2 ft. (0.6 m) long and 4 in. (10 cm) wide, the largest leaves of any temperate-climate bamboo. The large drooping leaves obscure the culms and branches, giving the plant more of a mounded bush appearance than some of the other members of the genus. Despite the tropical look of its foliage, this species is very hardy, and it grows well in containers. Its large leaves are used for making mats and for wrapping food.

Lithachne

A member of the Olyreae, a tribe of tropical, herbaceous, forest bamboos, *Lithachne* is somewhat more tolerant of occasional dryness and cool growing conditions than most other tropical, herbaceous genera. Consisting of four species, *Lithachne* is distributed from Mexico and the Caribbean to Paraguay and northern Argentina (Judziewicz et al. 1999).

The base of *Lithachne* leaves are distinctively truncated and asymmetrically attached to the pseudopetiole. *Lithachne* foliage leaves fold downward at night, beginning at sunset, progressing over a four-hour period, then reversing the process at dawn. The plants flower throughout the year. Some species are considered weedy in their native habitats.

Lithachne humilis

Maximum height: ½ ft. (15 cm)
Maximum diameter: ¹⁄₁₆ in. (0.2 cm)
Minimum temperature: 32°F (0°C)
Light: partial shade

Lithachne humilis flowers regularly throughout the year and produces viable seed without threatening the plant's vigor. Its distinctive foliage leaves fold down at night. *Lithachne humilis* is more tolerant of cool, dry growing conditions than most herbaceous species. It is only moderately attractive, but its distinctive flowers are appealing and add interest, as does the folding of its leaves at night.

Neomicrocalamus

Neomicrocalamus is a genus of pachymorph bamboos from Bhutan, northeastern India, China, and Vietnam. It is generally found in wetter subtropical forests than *Himalayacalamus* and *Drepanostachyum*. As suggested by its untessellated leaf blades, *Neomicrocalamus* is not frost hardy. The culm internodes are long and shiny. Each node may bear up to 18 principal branches of similar size, or there may be dominant branches. The culm leaf blades are erect and needlelike. The plants often exhibit a scrambling, clambering habit, spreading and draping over small trees for support. The flexible culms are choice material for weaving.

In the United States, the plants in the garden trade that were identified and marketed as *Neomicrocalamus microphyllus* are actually *Himalayacalamus asper* (Chris Stapleton, personal communication).

Neomicrocalamus andropogonifolius

Maximum height: 40 ft. (12 m)
Maximum diameter: 1 in. (2.5 cm)
Minimum temperature: 26°F (−3°C)
Light: partial shade

Distributed in Bhutan, southeastern Tibet, and northeastern India, *Neomicrocalamus andropogonifolius* is a pachymorph bamboo, with rhizomes up to 6 ft. (1.8 m) long, forming very open clumps. It is an attractive clambering bamboo, with elegant curtains of shiny foliage cascading from its supports.

Olmeca

Indigenous to southern Mexico, *Olmeca* is named after the Olmecs, an ancient civilization predating the Mayas. The genus consists of two species, *O. recta* and *O. reflexa*. These bamboos are prime examples of the breakdown in the terminology "clumping bamboo" when referring to any bamboo with a pachymorph rhizome system. While synonymizing the terms may work moderately well for many bamboos grown in the garden, it certainly does not work

Olmeca recta. Quail Botanical Gardens.

well for all bamboos. *Olmeca,* for example, is characterized by exceptionally long rhizome necks that may extend up to 26 ft. (8 m) before turning upward to form a culm—hardly a clumping habit.

The branching habit is also somewhat unusual. A single branch may form at each node, but then branch no further. Also relatively uncommon for bamboos, *Olmeca* produces fleshy fruits when it flowers.

Olmeca recta

Maximum height: 45 ft. (14 m)
Maximum diameter: 2 in. (5 cm)
Minimum temperature: 32°F (0°C)
Light: mostly sunny

Olmeca recta is indigenous to the wet lowland forests of southern Mexico, at elevations from sea level to 2600 ft (800 m). The culms are hollow and thin walled, covered by hard, persistent culm leaves. Branching begins at about 10 ft (3 m) above the ground, and the foliage leaves have very short pseudopetioles, giving a palmlike appearance. In its native environment, *O. recta* forms dense stands known locally as *jimbales.*

Otatea

A New World genus of subtropical or tropical pachymorph bamboos, *Otatea* consists of two known species (Judziewicz et al. 1999). It is more drought resistant than most New World bamboos, and its habitat includes seasonally dry areas along the Pacific Coast of Mexico and Central America, where the bamboos share their territory with cacti and agaves. Given the limestone soils typical of their habitat, otateas prefer less acidic soils than most bamboos. The genus name is a derivative of "otate," the name used by the Nahuatl Indians of central Mexico.

Otatea acuminata ssp. *acuminata*

Common synonym: *Otatea acuminata*
Maximum height: 15 ft. (4.5 m)

Maximum diameter: ¾ in. (2 cm)
Minimum temperature: 28°F (−2°C)
Light: full sun

Otatea acuminata ssp. *acuminata* is noted for its slender arching culms covered with delicate, feathery masses of leaves. Native to the hot lowlands of Mexico, and among the earliest cultivated New World bamboos, this species is used to make baskets, corrals, furniture, and toys. It is also incorporated into the walls, doors, and ceilings of buildings. *Otatea acuminata* ssp. *acuminata* is particularly desirable as roofing material, since it is more resistant than other bamboos to rot, fungi, and insects.

Otatea acuminata ssp. *aztecorum*

Common name: Mexican weeping
Maximum height: 20 ft. (6 m)
Maximum diameter: 1½ in. (4 cm)
Minimum temperature: 22°F (−6°C)
Light: mostly sunny

Otatea acuminata ssp. *aztecorum* is larger than *O. acuminata* ssp. *acuminata,* and its masses of leaves nearly obscure the culms. It is a pachymorph bamboo, but its rhizome necks are long, and the culms are spaced up to 2 ft. (0.6 m) apart.

Otatea fimbriata

Maximum height: 14 ft. (4.2 m)
Maximum diameter: ¾ in. (2 cm)
Minimum temperature: 24°F (−4°C)
Light: mostly sunny

Otatea fimbriata has larger leaves than the other members of the genus, measuring up to 12 in. (30 cm) long and ¾ in. (2 cm) wide.

Oxytenanthera

Oxytenanthera is a genus of tropical bamboos with pachymorph rhizome systems. The scope of the genus is currently a matter of discussion, ranging in inclusion from a monotypic genus exclusive to tropical Africa, to a wider ranging genus including species from the Asia-Pacific. The more narrow delineation of the genus

Otatea acuminata ssp. *aztecorum,* in flower and setting seed. Quail Botanical Gardens.

Oxytenanthera braunii. Quail Botanical Gardens.

places previously included species in *Dendro-calamus, Gigantochloa,* and *Pseudoxytenanthera.*

Oxytenanthera abyssinica

Maximum height: 30 ft. (9 m)
Maximum diameter: 4 in. (10 cm)
Minimum temperature: 30°F (−1°C)
Light: full sun

   Oxytenanthera abyssinica is distributed throughout tropical Africa at elevations rang-ing from near sea level to 6600 ft. (2000 m), in savannas and on hillsides. It prefers moist con-ditions along waterways, but it is also drought resistant, though it may become deciduous in hot, dry conditions. The new shoots are blue-green, with cream-yellow leaf blades. *Oxy-tenanthera abyssinica* has been introduced into India as a source of pulp for paper, and it re-portedly produces high yields of somewhat in-ferior pulp.

Oxytenanthera braunii

Common name: wine bamboo
Maximum height: 30 ft. (9 m)
Maximum diameter: 4 in. (10 cm)
Minimum temperature: 30°F (−1°C)
Light: full sun

   Some authorities regard *Oxytenanthera brau-nii* and *O. abyssinica* as synonymous, but at least some examples of *O. braunii* in cultivation, and from some indigenous regions, are distinctively different. This, of course, raises the issue of whether they are correctly identified or are some other species altogether. For the mo-ment, *O. braunii* is treated as a distinct species of *Oxytenanthera.*

   The growing shoots of *Oxytenanthera braunii* exude sap for many weeks after being topped. In Tanzania, they are topped at a height of roughly 3 ft. (about 1 m), and the sap is col-lected and fermented into a wine-like beverage called *ulanzi,* hence the common name wine bamboo. A single culm yields about 2¾ gallons (10 liters) of sap. Reports of the drink's merit range from tasty to quite foul.

Phyllostachys

Phyllostachys is a large genus of approximately 75 species and more than 200 varieties and forms. The species are widely distributed in the wild, in the temperate and semitropical areas of eastern Asia, from sea level up to 12,000 ft. (3700 m). *Phyllostachys* is the most northerly of all the giant arborescent bamboos. Eastern China appears to be the center of distribution. As with many species that have long been cul-tivated, the original, natural pattern of distrib-ution of *Phyllostachys* is unclear, and some dis-tribution is likely to have occurred via human migration in very early times. Nearly all *Phyllo-stachys* species can be found in China, though *P. humilis* is an exception. Cultivated in Japan, *P. humilis* is assumed to have originated in China, but has not yet been recorded there.

   An impressive genus, *Phyllostachys* com-prises many of the world's most beautiful, and economically important, hardy bamboos. In China and Japan, it is the principal source of edible bamboo shoots, paper pulp, craftwork, and timber. In established forests, some species can reach a height of more than 90 ft. (27 m) and a diameter of 7 in. (18 cm). Although some *Phyllostachys* are huge plants with rapidly spreading leptomorph rhizomes, new rhizomes grow very close to the soil surface. As a result, the plant's spread can be readily controlled with barriers or rhizome pruning more easily than other genera of leptomorph bamboos that may be much smaller, but have more rampant and deeper running rhizomes.

   Siebold and Zuccarini first described the genus in 1843, separating it from *Bambusa.* They included only one species, *Phyllostachys bambusoides,* but suggested that *"Bambusa nigra"* might also belong in *Phyllostachys.* Bam-boos of the genus *Phyllostachys* are readily iden-tifiable by a pronounced sulcus (groove) that runs the length of the internode on the branching side. The branch buds, already prominent, are pressed against the emerging internode by the tightly wrapped culm leaf sheaths, creating the sulcus as the internode elongates. On a *Phyllostachys* culm, only the lowermost internodes that emerge from branchless nodes are absent a sulcus. Some other bamboo genera, such as *Semiarundinaria*, have a partial sulcus, but a pronounced sulcus running the full length of the internode is unique to *Phyllostachys*. It is, perhaps, the most readily identifiable bamboo genus. In some forms and cultivars, the sulcus is a different color than the rest of the culm, typically yellow on a green culm or green on a yellow culm.

Except for the lower nodes of older culms where the branch buds may remain dormant, branch development and emergence begins concurrently with the growth of the culm. The lowest nodes on the culm may have solitary

As seen on this new culm of *Phyllostachys vivax*, and characteristic of the genus, the culm leaves are rapidly deciduous, clinging only briefly at the edge of the sheath base.

branches, but the typical branching pattern is two major, but unequally sized branches at each node. Occasionally, a third, much smaller branch may develop between the two principal branches. The culms and branches encompass a broad range of colors and surface finishes, including lime green, sulfur green, sulfur yellow, bluish green, chocolate, olive, straw yellow, green and yellow striped, shiny and waxy, velvety, matt finished, or white powdered.

The coloration and patterns of *Phyllostachys* culm leaf sheaths are highly distinctive, and they are often an excellent means of readily identifying the species in the field. The culm and branch leaves are immediately deciduous, dropping from the lower nodes, even as the upper internodes continue their extension. The immediately deciduous nature of *Phyllostachys* culm and branch leaves enhances their appeal in the landscape—not only is a scruffy look avoided, but the visual appeal is enhanced by immediate exposure of the bright fresh look of new culms and branches.

Although, like virtually all bamboos, *Phyllostachys* is evergreen, it replaces its leaves gradually. The replacement is inconspicuous except for the carpet of fallen leaves beneath the plant, which adds to the desirable layer of mulch. The principal leaf fall occurs in the spring. New leaves appear on new twigs, generated from lower buds on the existing twigs.

The leaves of *Phyllostachys* are lanceolate and distinctly tessellated. The lower leaves on a twig are somewhat shorter and broader, the upper leaves somewhat longer and narrower. A very young plant often has larger, sometimes much larger, leaves than an older plant of the same species. Older plants, with "normal," smaller leaves and larger culms, begin to assume more of the arborescent stature and beauty for which this genus of giant, hardy, tree grasses is known.

Shoot initiation varies according to local conditions, but generally begins in March or April for early shooting species, through June

A portion of the leaves of this *Phyllostachys* plant are withering and falling away, making way for new branchlets.

for late-shooting species. Some species, such as *Phyllostachys aurea*, exhibit a propensity for continued sporadic shooting throughout the growing season. *Phyllostachys bissetii, P. heterocycla* f. *pubescens, P. nuda,* and *P. violascens* are examples of early shooting species. *Phyllostachys bambusoides* and *P. viridis* are examples of late-shooting species.

It is not uncommon for the culms of the earliest shooting species to have completed their vertical growth and be fully branched out before the latest species have even begun shooting. The difference in the time of shooting extends the length of bamboo's most dramatic and interesting period, and it extends the season for harvesting shoots for the table.

In 1913, using growth habit and inflorescence as criteria, Camus was the first to attempt a description of identifiable groups within the genus. Subsequent investigations employing morphological, biochemical, and molecular data have tended to support two sections within the genus, section *Phyllostachys* and section *Heteroclada*. Wang et al. (1980) proposed these two sections, based on morphological characteristics.

Except for differences in the sectional assignment of a few species, the sections and their membership are supported by subsequent morphological information and by the DNA sequencing investigations of Renvoize and Hodkinson (1997). Wang et al. (1980) placed *Phyllostachys aureosulcata, P. nigra,* and *P. heterocycla* in section *Phyllostachys*. Renvoize and Hodkinson place the three in section *Heteroclada*, based on their interpretation of morphological information (DNA sequencing data were not available for these three species). Additional studies will likely produce adjustments in species membership in the two sections, and perhaps reveal additional sections of *Phyllostachys*, as the current two are not monophyletic.

Phyllostachys section Heteroclada

Characteristic of this section are culm leaf blades at the tip of young shoots, forming a tight, erect bunch, and congested or glomerate (rounded, tightly clustered mass) inflorescences. Some members of this section, and perhaps all, depending on the methods employed to determine section assignment, have rhizomes with air canals. The air canals are regarded as an adaptation to water-saturated soils. The type species for this section, *Phyllostachys heteroclada*, is commonly called water bamboo. Species in this section include *P. atrovaginata, P. bissetii, P. heteroclada, P. humilis, P. incarnata, P. mannii, P. nidularia, P. parvifolia,* and *P. stimulosa*.

Phyllostachys section Phyllostachys

Characteristic of this section are culm leaf blades at the tip of young shoots forming a loose bunch, and lax (loose and open, not tightly clustered) inflorescences. Species in this section include *Phyllostachys acuta, P. angusta, P. arcana, P. aurea, P. bambusoides, P. dulcis, P. flexuosa, P. glauca, P. iridescens, P. makinoi, P. meyeri, P. nuda, P. platyglossa, P. praecox, P. propinqua, P. rubromarginata, P. viridiglaucescens, P. viridis,* and *P. vivax*.

Phyllostachys acuta

Maximum height: 28 ft. (8.5 m)
Maximum diameter: 2½ in. (6.3 cm)
Minimum temperature: 0°F (−18°C)
Light: full sun
This species was introduced into the United States from China's Zhejiang Province in 1984. The young culms are dark green with purple nodes. With age, the culms turn lighter, to yellow-green. The shoots are harvested in China and are reportedly good tasting.

Phyllostachys angusta

Common name: stone bamboo (see text)
Maximum height: 25 ft. (7.5 m)
Maximum diameter: 1½ in. (4 cm)
Minimum temperature: 0°F (−18°C)
Light: full sun

Introduced from Zhejiang Province into the United States in 1917 by plant explorer Frank Meyer, this bamboo has also been called by what was purportedly its Chinese name, *Sah Chu,* or stone bamboo. Chao (1989) indicates that Meyer's field notes were in error, and that *Sah Chu* was actually a name ascribed to *Phyllostachys nuda.* The name "angusta" means narrow, referring to the culm leaf's narrow sheath apex, ligule, and blade. The culms are straight with a narrow crown. In China, they are used for weaving, craftwork, and making fishing rods. The midseason shoots of this species are free of bitterness.

Phyllostachys arcana

Maximum height: 27 ft. (8 m)
Maximum diameter: 1½ in. (4 cm)
Minimum temperature: 0°F (−18°C)
Light: full sun

The name *Phyllostachys arcana* has been variously attributed to the initial difficulty in establishing its distinguishing characteristics or, alternatively, to the supranodal ridge's partial coverage of the dormant branch buds at the lower culm nodes. The internodes may develop an irregular pattern of black spots with age and exposure to sunlight. The nodes are rather prominent, and the size of the two main branches is more closely equal than is the case in most other species of *Phyllostachys.* In China, the culms of *P. arcana* are used for weaving and for handles on farm implements. The early season shoots are harvested for the table.

Phyllostachys arcana f. luteosulcata

Maximum height: 27 ft. (8 m)
Maximum diameter: 1½ in. (4 cm)
Minimum temperature: 0°F (−18°C)
Light: full sun

Same as type form, but with yellow sulcus.

Phyllostachys atrovaginata

Common synonym: *Phyllostachys congesta*
Common name: incense bamboo

Maximum height: 30 ft. (9 m)
Maximum diameter: 2¾ in. (7 cm)
Minimum temperature: −5°F (−21°C)
Light: full sun

In the United States, this bamboo was long known by the name *Phyllostachys congesta,* but is now thought to be properly termed *P. atrovaginata.* The culms taper rapidly, giving it a relatively large diameter in relation to its height. *Phyllostachys atrovaginata* is very useful in landscape settings where the substantial look of relatively large bamboo is desired, but not the height that typically accompanies the girth.

The shoots of this species resemble those of *Phyllostachys heteroclada* and its forms, but can be distinguished by the absence of auricles and fimbriae from the culm leaf. Like *P. heteroclada,* it has air canals in the rhizomes and roots, an adaptation for growing in wet or boggy soils. The shoots are good tasting, and nearly free from bitterness even when raw. *Phyllostachys atrovaginata* is sometimes called incense bamboo because the surface of the culm has a scent that is said to resemble sandalwood. Rubbing your thumb and index finger along the internode of a young culm exposed to the sun releases the subtle but distinct fragrance.

Phyllostachys aurea

Common names: golden bamboo, fish-pole bamboo, hoteichiku
Maximum height: 27 ft. (8 m)
Maximum diameter: 1¾ in. (4.4 cm)
Minimum temperature: 0°F (−18°C)
Light: full sun

Also known as golden bamboo, *Phyllostachys aurea* is the most commonly cultivated bamboo in the United States. The new culms are green, not golden as the name suggests. Older culms that have been exposed to the sun take on more of a golden yellow color, providing the source of inspiration for the name. This was likely the first species of *Phyllostachys* in America. Some reports place its introduction in the year 1882, in Alabama. Other reports cite an even earlier introduction date of 1822, also in Alabama. *Phyllostachys aurea* is distinguished by its frequently compressed internodes on the lower portions of the culms. The compressed internodes provide a ready-made gripping area, and the bamboo is used for walking sticks and umbrella handles in Asia. In the American South, the use of the culms as fishing poles has given it the name fish-pole bamboo.

When a dense screen close to the ground is needed, *Phyllostachys aurea* can be more effective than other *Phyllostachys,* since the density of nodes on the lower portion of the culms also means a greater density of branches. The branches can also be pruned away to expose

Phyllostachys aurea, showing the characteristic compressed internodes on the lower portion of the culm. The branches are newly formed.
Carol Giberson's Garden.

the ornamental aspects of the compressed internodes. The culms are straight, stiffly erect, and do not strongly bend toward the light, as is the case with many other bamboos. The mid-season shoots are relatively free from bitterness, even when raw. Depending on growing conditions, this species has a tendency for additional, sporadic shooting throughout the growing season.

Phyllostachys aurea is heat, cold, and drought tolerant, and it does well in a container and as a hedge. Most *Phyllostachys* species grow poorly in subtropical and tropical environments, but *P. aurea* is more tolerant than most, and it is even grown commercially in Costa Rica for furniture construction. Its reputation for spreading rapidly may be partially attributable to its ubiquity, and to the fact that most westerners are unfamiliar with managing bamboo's growth habits. An excellent ornamental, *P. aurea* is sometimes ignored by collectors because it is so prevalent.

Phyllostachys aurea f. *albo-variegata*
Maximum height: 27 ft. (8 m)
Maximum diameter: 1¾ in. (4.4 cm)
Minimum temperature: 0°F (−18°C)
Light: full sun

The general characteristics are the same as *Phyllostachys aurea.* This is one of the few *Phyllostachys* with variegated leaves, and the white stripes give *P. aurea* f. *albo-variegata* a more delicate look. Like all *Phyllostachys* bamboos, it is a sun lover, but in hot, sunny climates some shading benefits the plant and the look of its leaves. Although it is an excellent ornamental, it receives less interest and attention than it would if it were of a less common species. *Phyllostachys aurea* f. *albo-variegata* flowered gregariously in the United States in the late 1990s, placing it in jeopardy for many growers. As is usual for most variegated bamboo forms and cultivars, most seedlings lack variegation and merely show the characteristics of the principal form.

Phyllostachys aurea f. *flavescens-inversa*

Maximum height: 27 ft. (8 m)
Maximum diameter: 1¾ in. (4.4 cm)
Minimum temperature: 0°F (−18°C)
Light: full sun

The general characteristics are the same as *Phyllostachys aurea,* but the culms have a yellow sulcus. The compressed lower internodes on some of the culms, combined with the yellow sulcus that alternates from side to side along the internodes, offer a pleasing display of color and texture.

Phyllostachys aurea f. *holochrysa*

Maximum height: 27 ft. (8 m)
Maximum diameter: 1¾ in. (4.4 cm)
Minimum temperature: 0°F (−18°C)
Light: full sun

This form of golden bamboo actually reflects the species's common name. The new culms are pale green, turning progressively to a golden yellow or orange-gold. It is otherwise similar to the type form.

Phyllostachys aurea 'Koi'

Maximum height: 27 ft. (8 m)
Maximum diameter: 1¾ in. (4.4 cm)
Minimum temperature: 0°F (−18°C)
Light: full sun

The inverse of *Phyllostachys aurea* f. *flavescens-inversa,* the culms of *P. aurea* 'Koi' turn yellow, but the sulcus remains green. The leaves may have an occasional white stripe. Richard Haubrich discovered the bamboo at a booth at the county fair in San Diego, California. He named it 'Koi', a Latinization of the first name of the plant's owner, Ko Tsushima. The general characteristics are the same as *P. aurea.*

Phyllostachys aurea f. *takemurai*

Maximum height: 32 ft. (9.6 m)
Maximum diameter: 2½ in. (6.3 cm)
Minimum temperature: 0°F (−18°C)
Light: full sun

Phyllostachys aurea f. *takemurai* lacks the compressed internodes of the type form, and it grows somewhat larger.

Phyllostachys aureosulcata

Common synonym: *Phyllostachys nevinni*
Common name: yellow groove bamboo
Maximum height: 45 ft. (14 m)
Maximum diameter: 2¼ in. (6 cm)
Minimum temperature: −15°F (−26°C)
Light: full sun

Known as yellow groove bamboo, *Phyllostachys aureosulcata* is an excellent, cold hardy ornamental with dark green culms and a yellow sulcus. It is further distinguished by the sharp bending and zigzagging of the lower part of some of the culms. As they are growing, they look at times as if someone had bent or broken them—when I first saw this, I thought that someone had vandalized my precious new shoots. The culms regain their vertical direction, however, and the grove has an upright habit. The early midseason shoots are attractive and free of bitterness even when raw. The new culms have a matt finish and are rough to the touch. The crooked lower culms enhance the ornamental appeal, though the bends limit the usefulness of the culm wood, which is, in any case, not of the highest quality.

Phyllostachys aureosulcata is one of the more widely planted ornamental bamboos in China and the United States. First introduced into America in 1907 from Zhejiang Province, it was widely distributed by the USDA in the 1920s, when it was identified as *P. nevinni.* The species establishes rapidly and is an excellent choice for climates with cold winters, such as in the American Northeast and Midwest—and in Beijing, where Chinese studies have recommended it as a hardy, winter survivor. Although it will not achieve its largest size in cold climates, *P. aureosulcata* is nevertheless an excellent ornamental and screen for cold climate conditions. It is a vigorous grower and runner in warm climates with favorable conditions.

Phyllostachys aureosulcata f. *alata*
Common synonym: *Phyllostachys aureosulcata*
    f. *pekinensis*
Maximum height: 48 ft. (15 m)
Maximum diameter: 2¼ in. (6 cm)
Minimum temperature: –15°F (–26°C)
Light: full sun

The general characteristics are the same as *Phyllostachys aureosulcata,* except the sulcus is green, not yellow. Under similar growing conditions, it reportedly grows larger.

Phyllostachys aureosulcata f. *aureocaulis*
Maximum height: 32 ft. (9.6 m)
Maximum diameter: 1¾ in. (4.4 cm)
Minimum temperature: –15°F (–26°C)
Light: full sun

Phyllostachys aureosulcata f. *aureocaulis* is a very attractive ornamental. The culms are entirely yellow, except for occasional green striping on the lowest internodes. Like in the other variants of this species (as well as many other bamboos with yellow culms), the culms and branches often take on rose-red to purple-red tints with exposure to the sun. This characteristic seems to be most evident on young culms and when there is nighttime cooling. It is otherwise similar to the type form.

Phyllostachys aureosulcata 'Harbin'
Maximum height: 32 ft. (9.6 m)
Maximum diameter: 1¾ in. (4.4 cm)
Minimum temperature: –15°F (–26°C)
Light: full sun

Another attractive variation of *Phyllostachys aureosulcata,* 'Harbin' has yellow culms with multiple, thin, green stripes and ribbing that run the length of the internodes. In 1990, New England bamboo nurseryman Chris DeRosa discovered it growing at the USDA Plant Quarantine Station in Glendale, Maryland. It was subsequently introduced into Europe in 1991.

Phyllostachys aureosulcata f. *spectabilis*
Maximum height: 32 ft. (9.6 m)
Maximum diameter: 1¾ in. (4.4 cm)
Minimum temperature: –15°F (–26°C)
Light: full sun

A choice ornamental, *Phyllostachys aureosulcata* f. *spectabilis* is similar to the principal form in general characteristics, but the coloring is much different. The culms are yellow with a green sulcus. The culms and branches often take on rose-red to purple-red tints with exposure to the sun. Some leaves have light, variegated striping, though this is not a prominent feature. During shooting, and as the new culm elongates, the attractive culm leaves are further set off by the emerging yellow internodes.

Phyllostachys bambusoides
Common synonyms: *Phyllostachys quilioi, P. reticulata*
Common names: Japanese timber bamboo, madake
Maximum height: 72 ft. (22 m)
Maximum diameter: 6 in. (15 cm)
Minimum temperature: 5°F (–15°C)
Light: full sun

Phyllostachys bambusoides originated in China, but has long been cultivated in Japan, where it is the most widely grown timber bamboo. Introduced into Europe in 1866 by the French admiral Du Quilio, the species was once named *P. quilioi.* It first came to America around 1890.

One of the latest shooting species of the genus, *Phyllostachys bambusoides* sometimes does not initiate shoots until early summer. The young culms are glossy green, not pruinose. Young plants have long, prominent lower branches. Mature plants are free of branches on the lower nodes. An emerging culm in a mature grove has been recorded at a growth rate of 47.6 in. (121 cm) in a single day (Austin et al. 1970). Individual culms are among the longest lived, producing new leafy

Phyllostachys aureosulcata f. *spectabilis,* showing the characteristic bending of the lower portions of some culms. Author's garden.

twigs each year for two decades or more. The culms of many other woody bamboos may live for only 5 to 10 years.

Phyllostachys bambusoides is one of the true giant tree grasses. Of the temperate timber bamboos, only *P. heterocycla* f. *pubescens* is potentially larger. It must be said, however, that *P. bambusoides* seldom achieves its maximum stated diameter. In the long-established forests of Japan, the culms reportedly average closer to 3½ in. (9 cm) in diameter (Haubrich 1996). In the United States, even in established groves, the diameter rarely exceeds 3 in. (7.5 cm). In Japan, *P. bambusoides* and *P. heterocycla* f. *pubescens* are primarily distributed in the warmer regions. Japan's third major timber bamboo, *P. nigra* var. *henonis,* is generally distributed in cooler or more mountainous areas.

The culm wood of *Phyllostachys bambusoides* is ideal for construction—thick, straight, and strong—among the best of the *Phyllostachys,* and far superior to *P. vivax,* which it somewhat resembles. Relative to *P. vivax,* the culms of *P. bambusoides* are straighter and the branches more upright and are produced at lower culm nodes. *Phyllostachys bambusoides* is one of the latest shooting of the genus; *P. vivax* shoots relatively early. Unlike *P. vivax,* the shoots of *P. bambusoides* are somewhat bitter, though they are acceptable for the table after parboiling. *Phyllostachys bambusoides* establishes and attains size much more slowly than *P. vivax,* and it is not as cold hardy. Because *P. bambusoides* takes longer to establish, it is not ideal when a tall screen is quickly needed, but rewards those who can afford the extra wait. From a landscaping perspective, *P. bambusoides* and *P. vivax* are similar in appearance. From a commercial or utilization perspective, they are quite different.

Reportedly, *Phyllostachys bambusoides* flowers every 120 years, but this must be regarded as somewhat speculative. After the Second World War, approximately three-fourths of the *P. bambusoides* in Japan flowered and died back. In America, in the 1970s, it flowered extensively, and many plants died or were severely weakened.

A decade or so before I became interested in bamboo, a beautiful plant emerged in my greenbelt area. It had apparently migrated from my neighbor's yard. I first noticed it in the winter, after the foliage from the deciduous trees had fallen away, and the first snowfall graced the bamboo's delicate leaves. I think I dimly realized at the time that it was a bamboo, but I thought little else about it. As I was clearing back some of the greenbelt growth the following year, I saved a culm. After that, no more bamboo appeared, and I wondered why.

Phyllostachys bambusoides. The culm leaf is beginning to drop away as the new branches emerge. Author's garden.

Phyllostachys bambusoides. Author's garden.

Some twenty years later, and by then rabidly interested in bamboo, I came across the culm I had saved. A tiny branchlet had remnants of flowering. It was *Phyllostachys bambusoides.*

Phyllostachys bambusoides 'Allgold'

Maximum height: 38 ft. (12 m)
Maximum diameter: 2½ in. (6.3 cm)
Minimum temperature: 5°F (−15°C)
Light: full sun

'Allgold' is much smaller than the typical form. The new culms are yellow, turning golden with age. The culms are "all gold," without striping, except for an occasional thin green stripe on a lower internode. The coloration of

Phyllostachys bambusoides f. *castillonis.*
Author's garden.

the young culms is quite striking, sometimes appearing translucent in the sunlight. The leaves have occasional cream striping.

Phyllostachys bambusoides f. *castillonis*

Common synonym: *Phyllostachys bambusoides* 'Castillon'
Common name: Castillon bamboo
Maximum height: 38 ft. (12 m)
Maximum diameter: 2½ in. (6.3 cm)
Minimum temperature: 5°F (−15°C)
Light: full sun

Much smaller than the principal form, *Phyllostachys bambusoides* f. *castillonis* is nonetheless a substantial arborescent bamboo, and a choice ornamental. The new culms are bright straw yellow, with broad, dark green striping in the sulcus. The culms and branches may sometimes take on rosy tints. Some of the leaves have occasional cream pinstripes. The shoots are reportedly less acrid in the raw state than those of the type form of the species. This form has been in Europe since 1886, and in the United States since the early 1900s, but a period of flowering in the late 1960s and early 1970s severely diminished its distribution. It is once again becoming more widely available.

Phyllostachys bambusoides f. *castillonis-inversa*

Common synonym: *Phyllostachys bambusoides* 'Castillon Inversa'
Maximum height: 38 ft. (12 m)
Maximum diameter: 2½ in. (6.3 cm)
Minimum temperature: 5°F (−15°C)
Light: full sun

The "inverse" of *Phyllostachys bambusoides* f. *castillonis,* with green culms and a yellow sulcus.

Phyllostachys bambusoides f. *kawadana*

Common synonym: *Phyllostachys bambusoides* 'Kawadana'
Maximum height: 38 ft. (12 m)

Maximum diameter: 2½ in. (6.3 cm)
Minimum temperature: 5°F (–15°C)
Light: full sun

The culms of this form have fine gold pin-striping, and the leaves are lightly striped with gold as well. It has arisen on various occasions, at least once as a sport from a flowering *Phyllostachys bambusoides*. The plants currently in circulation in the United States originated in England, as a sport from a recovering *P. bambusoides* f. *castillonis* that had flowered.

Phyllostachys bambusoides f. marliacea

Common synonym: *Phyllostachys bambusoides* 'Marliac'
Common name: Marliac bamboo
Maximum height: 20 ft. (6 m)
Maximum diameter: 1¾ in. (4.4 cm)
Minimum temperature: 5°F (–15°C)
Light: full sun

Introduced into Europe in the 1800s, and named after Latour-Marliac, *Phyllostachys bambusoides* f. *marliacea* has wrinkled culms formed by many small longitudinal grooves around the circumference of the culm, running the length of each internode. An unusual ornamental, it is also used in craftwork.

Phyllostachys bambusoides f. subvariegata

Maximum height: 32 ft. (9.6 m)
Maximum diameter: 2¼ in. (6 cm)
Minimum temperature: 5°F (–15°C)
Light: full sun

The culms are lighter in color than those of the principal form. Its leaves are smaller, with light green stripes on a darker green background. The variegation is most pronounced in the spring, then fades and softens.

Phyllostachys bambusoides 'Slender Crookstem'

Common synonyms: *Phyllostachys bambusoides* f. *geniculata, P. reticulata* f. *geniculata*
Common name: slender crookstem
Maximum height: 48 ft. (15 m)
Maximum diameter: 2¾ in. (7 cm)
Minimum temperature: 5°F (–15°C)
Light: full sun

Much smaller than the principal form of the species, but larger than most of the other variants, 'Slender Crookstem' was introduced into America in 1925 by F. A. McClure. In a high percentage of its culms, within the first several feet (1 m) of growth, the culm curves back and forth, deviating an inch or more from center, but returning to center and the original direction of growth. Unlike in *Phyllostachys aureosulcata*, the deviations are not abrupt. The curves may be simple, involving only two or three internodes, or complex, involving many.

Phyllostachys bambusoides 'White Crookstem'

Common name: white crookstem
Maximum height: 48 ft. (15 m)
Maximum diameter: 2¾ in. (7 cm)
Minimum temperature: 5°F (–15°C)
Light: full sun

Similar to *Phyllostachys bambusoides* 'Slender Crookstem', but the culms develop a deposit of white powder that persists and, in older culms, virtually obscures their green color.

Phyllostachys bissetii

Maximum height: 40 ft. (12 m)
Maximum diameter: 2 in. (5 cm)
Minimum temperature: –20°F (–29°C)
Light: full sun

Named after David Bisset, longtime manager of the bamboo introduction station at Savannah, Georgia, *Phyllostachys bissetii* is vigorous and establishes rapidly. It is a good choice for a hedge. The maximum height and diameter is generally listed as smaller than indicated here. In addition to size differences attributable to growing climate, it appears that there may be at least two distinct clones of the species.

The culms, as well as the foliage leaves, are

dark green, and the culm leaves are also predominantly green, offering an attractive backdrop for other bamboos and other plants. *Phyllostachys bissetii* is exceptionally cold hardy. Its rhizomes are reputedly even more resistant to cold than those of *P. aureosulcata* or *P. nuda*. After hard winters, it is among the best of the *Phyllostachys* for retaining a fresh, unbattered look. The early season shoots can be harvested for the table. It has been in America since 1941.

Phyllostachys decora

Common names: meizhu, beautiful bamboo
Maximum height: 30 ft. (9 m)
Maximum diameter: 2 in. (5 cm)
Minimum temperature: –5°F (–21°C)
Light: full sun

In a variety of climates, *Phyllostachys decora* has shown itself to be one of the more aggressive runners of the genus *Phyllostachys*. It is also reportedly among the more tolerant *Phyllostachys* species with respect to drought, temperature extremes, high pH soils, and sandy soils.

Shooting occurs in early to late midseason. The strikingly attractive culm leaves are dark purple to pale green or white striped with purple and green accents. The culm leaf blade is unusually broad for a phyllostachys. A Chinese name for *Phyllostachys decora* is meizhu—beautiful bamboo. With exposure to sun, the light green culms may sometimes turn a yellow-orange. F. A. McClure introduced it to the United States from China in 1938. It is likely that *P. decora* and *P. mannii* are conspecific.

Phyllostachys bissetii. Author's garden.

Phyllostachys decora. The showy culm leaf is more distinctive on mature specimens. Author's garden.

Phyllostachys dulcis

Common name: sweetshoot bamboo
Maximum height: 40 ft. (12 m)
Maximum diameter: 2¾ in. (7 cm)
Minimum temperature: 0°F (−18°C)
Light: full sun

Called sweetshoot bamboo because of its mild-tasting shoots, *Phyllostachys dulcis* establishes rapidly, and quickly yields large shoots. As it grows, it bends more toward the sunlight than many *Phyllostachys* plants do. It is also less steadfastly upright than many of the genus, its culms twisting and arching somewhat as they wander their way vertically, rapidly tapering toward the tip. It is not the best bamboo for narrow areas. The culm wood is not particularly good, but the early season shoots are choice. It is attractive, but less stately than others of the genus.

Phyllostachys elegans

Maximum height: 32 ft. (9.6 m)
Maximum diameter: 2¼ in. (6 cm)
Minimum temperature: 0°F (−18°C)
Light: full sun

More erect and evenly tapering than *Phyllostachys dulcis*, *P. elegans* is also noted for its excellent shoots but relatively poor culm wood. It has a very early shooting period. In appearance, *P. elegans* is most similar to *P. viridiglaucescens*, with which it is sometimes confused. Very unusual for the genus, at least one clone of *P. elegans* has flowered sporadically, every year, for more than a decade, while continuing to grow with moderate vigor.

Phyllostachys flexuosa

Maximum height: 32 ft. (9.6 m)
Maximum diameter: 2¾ in. (7 cm)
Minimum temperature: 0°F (−18°C)
Light: full sun

Phyllostachys flexuosa is a cold-hardy bamboo that tolerates difficult growing conditions, including wind, and soils that are saline, sandy, or alkaline. The shoots initiate in early midseason and are considered choice. Some culms show pronounced zigzags. The foliage and branching is somewhat more open than average. It was introduced into Europe in 1864 by the French Société d'Acclimatation and came to America from France in 1921.

Phyllostachys flexuosa 'Kimmei'

Maximum height: 32 ft. (9.6 m)
Maximum diameter: 2¾ in. (7 cm)
Minimum temperature: 0°F (−18°C)
Light: full sun

A cultivar grown from seed in 1992 by bamboo nurseryman Gib Cooper, *Phyllostachys flexuosa* 'Kimmei' has yellow culms with a green sulcus. New foliage leaves are white tipped, gradually becoming more variegated with green.

Phyllostachys glauca

Maximum height: 46 ft. (14 m)
Maximum diameter: 3½ in. (9 cm)
Minimum temperature: 0°F (−18°C)
Light: full sun

The young culms of *Phyllostachys glauca* have an evenly distributed white waxy powder on their surface that gives them a very attractive blue-green appearance. This look gradually dissipates throughout the growing season. Not stiffly erect, the culm tops are somewhat arching. This species is reportedly tolerant of difficult growing conditions, such as poor or alkaline soils and some drought. In China, it grows on flood lands, plains, and hillsides. F. A. McClure introduced *P. glauca* into the United States in 1926. The attractive shoots are good tasting, and they initiate in early midseason. The culms are used for fishing rods and woven articles.

Phyllostachys glauca f. *yunzhu*

Maximum height: 46 ft. (14 m)
Maximum diameter: 3½ in. (9 cm)
Minimum temperature: 0°F (−18°C)
Light: full sun

Similar to the type form, but with irregular, brownish purple spots on the culm.

Phyllostachys heteroclada

Common synonym: *Phyllostachys purpurata*
    'Straightstem'
Common name: water bamboo
Maximum height: 33 ft. (10 m)
Maximum diameter: 1½ in. (4 cm)
Minimum temperature: −5°F (−21°C)
Light: full sun

In part because of its relatively frequent flowering, as well as its wide dispersal in its native China, this species has varying forms that have complicated identification and classification. In the United States, it has gone by the name *Phyllostachys purpurata* and its variants, *P. purpurata* 'Solidstem' and *P. purpurata* 'Straightstem'. Consistent with the writings of Chinese botanists, *P. heteroclada* is treated here as the principal (and larger) form, synonymous with *P. purpurata* 'Straightstem'. Unlike other forms of the species, the type form of *P. heteroclada* has a stiffly erect growth habit.

Phyllostachys heteroclada is the type species for the *Heteroclada* section of *Phyllostachys*. Characteristic of many, and perhaps all, members of section *Heteroclada,* air channels in the rhizomes enable these bamboos to grow in wet and highly saturated soils. The roots of *P. heteroclada* may have also been modified in adaptation to wet conditions. For these reasons, this species is sometimes called water bamboo.

Phyllostachys heteroclada f. purpurata

Common synonym: *Phyllostachys purpurata*
Maximum height: 18 ft. (5.5 m)
Maximum diameter: ¾ in. (2 cm)
Minimum temperature: 0°F (−18°C)
Light: full sun

Apart from size and growth habit, *Phyllostachys heteroclada* f. *purpurata* differs from *P. heteroclada* and *P. heteroclada* f. *solida* in the coloration of the culm leaf blade, which is distinctly purple throughout, rather than primarily green as in the other forms. The slender culms have long internodes, a zigzag growth habit, and an arching profile. Wind, rain, and the weight of the foliage can readily bend the culms to the ground. The nodes are large with subhorizontal branches.

Phyllostachys glauca, displaying the distinctive coloration of new culms. Author's garden.

Phyllostachys heteroclada f. solida

Common synonyms: *Phyllostachys heteroclada*
    'Solidstem', *P. purpurata* 'Solidstem'
Maximum height: 18 ft. (5.5 m)
Maximum diameter: ¾ in. (2 cm)
Minimum temperature: 0°F (−18°C)
Light: full sun

Phyllostachys heteroclada f. *solida* is also known as *P. purpurata* 'Solidstem'. The internodes on the lower half to two-thirds of the culm are solid rather than hollow. Its growth habit is otherwise similar to *P. heteroclada* f. *purpurata*.

Phyllostachys heterocycla

Common synonym: *Phyllostachys edulis* f. *heterocycla*

Common name: tortoise shell bamboo

Maximum height: 40 ft. (12 m)

Maximum diameter: 5 in. (13 cm)

Minimum temperature: 0°F (−18°C)

Light: full sun

A unique and famous ornamental bamboo, *Phyllostachys heterocycla* is a mutation of *P. heterocycla* f. *pubescens*. Called tortoise shell bamboo because its appearance replicates the pattern of a tortoise shell, this species has internodes that are bulged on one side, but nearly nonexistent on the other side, never extending from the node. This pattern alternates from side to side along the length of the culm, creating an unusual and distinctive appearance. This species is a highly valued ornamental in Japan and China, and its cured culms are also highly prized. An unstable form, a plant may produce normal culms as well as the convoluted form. *Phyllostachys heterocycla* occasionally arises spontaneously in natural stands of *P. heterocycla* f. *pubescens*.

Phyllostachys heterocycla. Hakone Gardens.

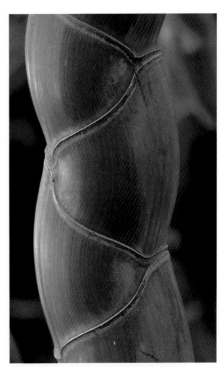

Phyllostachys heterocycla, showing its unique, bizarre, and highly ornamental culms, with unextended internodes on alternating sides. Hakone Gardens.

Phyllostachys heterocycla f. *pubescens*

Common synonyms: *Phyllostachys edulis,*
   P. pubescens
Common names: moso, mao zhu
Maximum height: 90 ft. (27 m)
Maximum diameter: 7 in. (18 cm)
Minimum temperature: 0°F (−18°C)
Light: full sun

Phyllostachys heterocycla f. *pubescens* is the world's largest hardy bamboo. Only a few tropical bamboos grow larger. A single day's growth of a new culm has been measured at 46.8 in. (117 cm) (Austin et al. 1970). The plant's botanical name is rather awkward, and it is commonly referred to by its Japanese name, moso. The moso forests of China and Japan are one of nature's great beauties. In

China, *P. heterocycla* f. *pubescens* forests cover more than 7 million acres (2.8 million hectares) (Hsiung 1991). More than two-thirds of China's immense bamboo acreage is forested by *P. heterocycla* f. *pubescens* (Zhu et al. 1994b).

The leaves, among the smallest of all *Phyllostachys*, contrast with the massive, towering culms. Its pendulous tops, nodding with masses of tiny shimmering leaves, are said to resemble giant green ostrich plumes. The internodes are relatively short, particularly near the base. The matt finish and the velvety coat of hairs on new culms reflect the name *pubescens*.

The culm wood is thick, but softer and less resistant to cracking than that of other timber bamboos, such as *Phyllostachys bambusoides* and *P. nigra* var. *henonis*. *Phyllostachys heterocycla* f.

Phyllostachys heterocycla f. *pubescens,* showing the culm leaf beginning to separate from a new culm. Author's garden.

A close-up of a new *Phyllostachys heterocycla* f. *pubescens* culm, showing the source of its name— the fine velvety hairs, or pubescence, on the surface of the culm.

Phyllostachys heterocycla f. *pubescens* along a pathway at Hakone Gardens.

pubescens is nevertheless widely used as timber, as well as pulpwood, and in a wide variety of craftworks. When polished, the thick-walled culms take on a characteristic decorative luster.

More *Phyllostachys heterocycla* f. *pubescens* shoots are harvested for food than any other bamboo species. It initiates shoots from fall through spring. Shoots initiated in fall and winter remain underground. Called winter shoots, they are highly regarded for their quality and are harvested as part of the seasonal cuisine. Spring shoots are also harvested for food, but they have some bitterness and, though very good, are less highly esteemed.

Sometimes special methods are employed to encourage harvestable winter shoots. Traditional methods call for warming the soil with heat-generating composting material. Sometimes a trench is dug adjacent to a shoot-producing rhizome, or topsoil is removed so that the heat-generating compost can be placed near the rhizome. A soil temperature of 60°F (16°C) will produce harvestable shoots in 30 days. In this way, prized winter shoots can be had in December and throughout the winter.

Although *Phyllostachys heterocycla* f. *pubescens* is the world's largest temperate bamboo, it is also one of the most difficult in the genus to establish. New plantings are not prone to failure, but they are often slow to develop the size and dramatic beauty of their native environments. *Phyllostachys heterocycla* f. *pubescens* is perhaps more particular about its growing environment than any other *Phyllostachys*. It benefits from ample moisture, warmth, and manure. It is intolerant of alkaline soils, but develops chlorosis if the soil is too acidic. In Japan, *P. heterocycla* f. *pubescens* attains greater size in the warmer south. Toward the north, less of it is grown, and its culm size is progressively smaller.

Phyllostachys heterocycla f. *pubescens* first came to Europe in 1880. Ten years later, it arrived on America's West Coast. Some have said that this bamboo cannot be grown fully successfully outside of its native environment, but evidence shows otherwise. Japan's impressive moso forests have led to the common assumption that *P. heterocycla* f. *pubescens* is native to Japan as well as China, but this is not true. Though it is now well established in that country, the plant was introduced into Japan from China long ago. Details of its introduction vary, but one account indicates that it was introduced from China to the Kagoshima Prefecture, Kyushu, in southern Japan, in 1746 by the Shimazu clan.

Success of nonnative groves is not confined to Asia. The renowned and long-established Bambouseraie in Prafrance, France, demonstrates that impressive stands of giant-sized *Phyllostachys heterocycla* f. *pubescens* are indeed possible outside of Asia, if growing conditions are amenable. In the United States, the Southeast, among other regions, also has stands of large-sized culms.

Other temperate-climate timber bamboos, such as *Phyllostachys vivax*, *P. bambusoides*, and *P. nigra* var. *henonis*, establish much more rapidly and reliably than *P. heterocycla* f. *pubescens*, attaining a larger size in the first years of growth. *Phyllostachys heterocycla* f. *pubescens* is highly desirable for the collector and hobbyist, but it cannot be universally recommended for the landscape when rapid spread and attainment of height is essential. On the other hand, in situations where slower growth and a range of possible maximum heights is acceptable, this is a highly desirable bamboo for the landscape.

A commercial grower will want to ensure that growing conditions are ideally suited to *Phyllostachys heterocycla* f. *pubescens* before committing a large planting to this species. The commercial grower should also be mindful of the longer development time for a *P. heterocycla* f. *pubescens* grove. Even in some regions in the plant's native China, the largest culms in a 12-year-old grove may only achieve a height of 20 ft. (6 m) and a diameter of 2 in. (5 cm). Still, when the development time can be accommodated and growing conditions are optimal, *P.*

heterocycla f. *pubescens* is perhaps the world's premier commercial bamboo for temperate climates. It is arguably the world's most commercially important bamboo, as well as the most beautiful timber bamboo. While its beauty can only be fully appreciated in a mature forest, among the towering culms and masses of tiny shimmering leaves, many of its distinctive features can nevertheless be appreciated on a smaller scale in the landscape or garden.

Phyllostachys heterocycla f. pubescens 'Goldstripe'

Maximum height: undetermined
Maximum diameter: undetermined
Minimum temperature: 0°F (−18°C)
Light: full sun

'Goldstripe' is an American cultivar developed from a seedling of *Phyllostachys heterocycla* f. *pubescens*. The new shoot and branch tips are pale pink to cream colored. The new leaves are prominently white striped, fading to green by fall. The culm exhibits varying green and gold striping patterns.

Phyllostachys humilis

Maximum height: 20 ft. (6 m)
Maximum diameter: 1 in. (2.5 cm)
Minimum temperature: 0°F (−18°C)
Light: full sun

One of the smallest species in the genus, *Phyllostachys humilis* is leafy and establishes rapidly. It is excellent as a hedge plant, taking well to vigorous pruning, or left relatively unpruned. Young culms are an attractive dark brown, turning green with maturity, or sometimes an orange-yellow in strong sun. Its exact origins are unknown, but *P. humilis* is believed to be of Chinese origin. It is cultivated in Japan.

Phyllostachys iridescens

Maximum height: 40 ft. (12 m)
Maximum diameter: 2¾ in. (7 cm)
Minimum temperature: 0°F (−18°C)
Light: full sun

Native to China's Jiangsu and Zhejiang Provinces, and widely distributed elsewhere, *Phyllostachys iridescens* produces choice shoots. The internodes often have indistinct yellowish striae running along their length, particularly near the base. The cured culms are used for implement handles and construction, and this species is also planted for ornamental purposes. Because of the reddish culm leaf sheaths and the large, pendulous culm leaf blades reminiscent of a cock's comb, the new shoots are said to resemble red roosters in a bamboo grove. Unfortunately, at least some of the plants in circulation in the United States are misidentified and are not *P. iridescens*.

Phyllostachys makinoi

Maximum height: 60 ft. (18 m)
Maximum diameter: 2¾ in. (7 cm)
Minimum temperature: 0°F (−18°C)
Light: full sun

The new culms of *Phyllostachys makinoi* have a white powder on their surface, giving them a blue-green appearance. Like those of *P. viridis*, the culms have minute dimples, which are noticeable by running a fingernail along the surface of the culm. This species has a stiffly erect habit. The culm wood is very hard and dense, and it is used in house construction, furniture manufacture, and pulpwood for paper. The midseason shoots are suitable for the table. Although fairly cold tolerant, *P. makinoi* needs a warm climate, ample water, fertilizer, and mulch to thrive and achieve its maximum height. It is one of the most widely cultivated bamboos in Taiwan. The bamboo is named after Tomitaro Makino, a Japanese botanist working in Taiwan. It was introduced into Japan from Taiwan in 1913.

Phyllostachys mannii

Maximum height: 30 ft. (9 m)
Maximum diameter: 2 in. (5 cm)
Minimum temperature: −5°F (−21°C)
Light: full sun

Phyllostachys makinoi. Quail Botanical Gardens.

Phyllostachys mannii has culm wood that is hard, durable, resistant to cracking, and splits well for weaving. Although the shoots are edible, they are rather astringent. Introduced from China long ago, the species grows in the wild in India and Burma. It is named after Gustav Mann, who collected the species in 1889. It is likely that *P. mannii* and *P. decora* are conspecific.

Phyllostachys meyeri

Maximum height: 36 ft. (11 m)
Maximum diameter: 2¾ in. (7 cm)
Minimum temperature: 0°F (−18°C)
Light: full sun

Phyllostachys meyeri was introduced into the United States in 1908 by USDA plant explorer Frank N. Meyer. The midseason shoots are edible, though not choice. This species has an erect growth habit. The excellent culm wood is strong and splits well.

Phyllostachys nidularia

Maximum height: 33 ft. (10 m)
Maximum diameter: 1¾ in. (4.4 cm)
Minimum temperature: 0°F (−18°C)
Light: full sun

The culm nodes are very prominent and provide an attractive contrast to bamboos with less prominent nodes. The large culm leaf blades and exaggerated auricles have a distinctive appearance, and they are readily identifiable even while still tightly wrapped around the emerging shoot. Shoot initiation begins in early midseason. The shoots are excellent and are free from bitterness even in the raw state. The culm wood is not strong, but is used for shrimp traps in China "because of its color and sweet smell" (Zhu et al. 1994b).

Phyllostachys nidularia f. farcta

Maximum height: 33 ft. (10 m)
Maximum diameter: 1¾ in. (4.4 cm)
Minimum temperature: 0°F (−18°C)
Light: full sun

Characteristics are similar to the principal form, but the lower part of the culm is solid or nearly solid.

Phyllostachys nidularia f. glabrovagina

Common synonym: *Phyllostachys nidularia* 'Smoothsheath'
Maximum height: 33 ft. (10 m)
Maximum diameter: 1¾ in. (4.4 cm)
Minimum temperature: 0°F (−18°C)
Light: full sun

Characteristics are similar to the principal form, but without the hairs on the sheath scars and the base of the culm leaf sheath.

Phyllostachys nidularia, showing the distinctive, exaggerated auricles on the culm leaf embracing the new culm. Author's garden.

Phyllostachys nidularia 'June Barbara'

Maximum height: undetermined
Maximum diameter: undetermined
Minimum temperature: 5°F (−15°C)
Light: mostly sunny

A variegated cultivar started from seed in 1987, *Phyllostachys nidularia* 'June Barbara' is somewhat less cold hardy, and considerably less vigorous, than the principal form. The variegation, strongest on the new leaves, often exhibits a brushed effect, not unlike the variegation on *Sasa kurilensis* 'Shimofuri'. The green in the leaf color is a light, lime green, perhaps part of the reason for the plant's modest vigor. It is an attractive but slow-growing cultivar.

Phyllostachys nigra

Common names: black bamboo, kurochiku
Maximum height: 55 ft. (17 m)
Maximum diameter: 3¼ in. (8.3 cm)
Minimum temperature: 0°F (−18°C)
Light: mostly sunny

A beautiful, choice ornamental. The culms and branches of *Phyllostachys nigra* are at first dark green, turning eventually to a deep solid black. The small green leaves contrast strikingly with the jet-black culms, branches, and branchlets. This species has long been highly valued as an ornamental in China and Japan, and it is believed to be the first bamboo introduced into Europe, coming to England around 1827. Though widely cultivated in its native China, it is relatively rare in the wild.

Phyllostachys nigra is often smaller in habit than its maximum size would suggest. Growing conditions, as well as the presumed existence of various strains, may account for some of the size differences, as well as differences in the rate of color change and color depth. The plant prefers less intense sunlight and is less upright than most species of the genus. Its gracefully arching habit contributes to its considerable beauty, but also limits its landscaping applications. It bends readily under the weight of rain or snow—or the weight of its own foliage, particularly in older culms that bear greater leaf mass. Where a stiffly upright bamboo is required, *P. nigra* would not be the first choice. Although some might consider it a sacrilege, *P. nigra* can be topped and pruned to moderate its arching habit—or topped and pruned even more aggressively to make a highly attractive hedge.

The dried culms hold their color. The culm wood is thin, but hard, and is excellent for furniture and other craftwork. The late midseason shoots are edible. *Phyllostachys nigra* is one of the more popular and desirable ornamentals in Asia and the West.

Numerous cultivars are available. Some are clearly distinctive and unique. Others may be more a product of growing conditions, or of rather modest distinctions.

Phyllostachys nigra shoot. Author's garden.

Phyllostachys nigra. The new culm in the foreground has not yet turned the deep, rich black characteristic of mature culms. Author's garden.

Phyllostachys nigra 'Bory'

Common synonym: *Phyllostachys nigra* 'Boryana'
Common name: snakeskin bamboo
Maximum height: 60 ft. (18 m)
Maximum diameter: 4 in. (10 cm)
Minimum temperature: 0°F (–18°C)
Light: full sun

Generally larger, more erect, and more heat tolerant than the principal form. The culm is spotted with brown to purplish black spots, sometimes described as a snakeskin or leopard-skin pattern. With exposure to strong sun, the culms are yellow-green with brown spots. A distinctive ornamental, 'Bory' has the small leaves and attractive foliage array of typical *Phyllostachys nigra*. On seasoned culms, the muted spotting pattern gives the culms a distinctive appearance that lends itself to decorative construction and craftwork. Shoot initiation occurs late in the season.

Phyllostachys nigra 'Hale'

Maximum height: 20 ft. (6 m)
Maximum diameter: 1½ in. (4 cm)
Minimum temperature: –5°F (–21°C)
Light: mostly sunny

Phyllostachys nigra 'Hale' is purportedly a smaller and more cold hardy variant of the principal form. Conversely, it is also reported to be a larger cultivar than the type form that turns black more quickly. It is not clear if this cultivar is substantively different from the principal form, or if its reported characteristics are a response to different growing conditions. In the northeastern United States, with cold winters and hot summers, 'Hale' is reportedly smaller and more cold tolerant than the principal form. In the Pacific Northwest, with cool summers and mild winters, it reportedly grows as large or larger than the principal form.

Phyllostachys nigra var. *henonis*

Common synonyms: *Phyllostachys henonis*, *P. nigra* 'Henon'

Common names: Henon, hachiku
Maximum height: 65 ft. (20 m)
Maximum diameter: 5 in. (13 cm)
Minimum temperature: –5°F (–21°C)
Light: full sun

Unlike the culms and branches of *Phyllostachys nigra*, those of *P. nigra* var. *henonis* remain green. This variety readily grows much larger, and the growth habit is erect. *Phyllostachys nigra* var. *henonis* is no doubt the true biological species, but because the distinctive black-culmed variant, *P. nigra*, was described and named first, *P. nigra* var. *henonis*, the true species, has been relegated to the status of a variety. *Phyllostachys nigra* var. *henonis* fulfills several roles. It is a beautiful, large, landscape bamboo, and it has excellent properties for commercial applications. Its culm walls are thicker than those of *P. nigra*, but sustain the same profusion of delicate foliage.

In *The Cultivation of Bamboos in Japan*, published in 1899, Sir Ernest Satow lists three bamboos as typically capable of attaining great size: moso (*Phyllostachys heterocycla* f. *pubescens*), madake (*P. bambusoides*), and hachiku (*P. nigra* var. *henonis*). Although cited as less common than madake, hachiku was regarded as equally suitable to the same uses, including water pipes, scaffolding, and roofing poles, and it was regarded more highly than madake for bamboo ware and other utensils. At that time, it was not classified as a variety of *P. nigra*, but as a separate species, *P. henonis*.

In Japan, *Phyllostachys nigra* var. *henonis* is distributed in colder, more mountainous regions than *P. bambusoides* or *P. heterocycla* f. *pubescens*. Its late midseason shoots are somewhat bitter raw, but are very good after parboiling.

Phyllostachys nigra 'Megurochiku'

Maximum height: 60 ft. (18 m)
Maximum diameter: 4 in. (10 cm)
Minimum temperature: –5°F (–21°C)
Light: full sun

Generally similar to *Phyllostachys nigra* var. *henonis,* but the sulcus on older culms turns a dark purple-brown. At one time, 'Meguro-chiku' was a very rare bamboo, growing only on the Japanese island of Awaji, and was protected from collection. It has since made its way to bamboo nurseries, collectors, and growers, and is available from a number of sources.

Phyllostachys nigra f. *punctata*
Maximum height: 55 ft. (17 m)
Maximum diameter: 3¼ in. (8.3 cm)
Minimum temperature: 0°F (−18°C)
Light: mostly sunny

Similar to *Phyllostachys nigra,* but the black coloration is broken into irregular blotches. The degree of culm coloration may vary, sometimes eventually turning a more or less solid brownish black. Growing conditions or different strains may account for some of the variation. The reported distinctions vary, and *P. nigra* f. *punctata* is not always recognized as a separate form.

Phyllostachys nigra 'Shimadake'
Maximum height: 55 ft. (17 m)
Maximum diameter: 3¼ in. (8.3 cm)
Minimum temperature: −5°F (−21°C)
Light: full sun

Generally similar to *Phyllostachys nigra* var. *henonis,* with occasional brown or blackish vertical stripes of varying widths along the length of the culm internodes.

Phyllostachys nuda
Maximum height: 34 ft. (10 m)
Maximum diameter: 1¾ in. (4.4 cm)
Minimum temperature: −20°F (−29°C)
Light: full sun

One of the most cold hardy species of the genus, *Phyllostachys nuda* is an excellent small-leaved ornamental suitable for hedges and medium to tall screens, or as a specimen grove. Its new culms are very attractive, with gradations of dark purple-brown and olive tones, loosely covered with white powder. The thick culm wood is good quality and is often used for the legs of furniture. The early season shoots are fleshy and choice.

Phyllostachys nuda grows in extensive forests in eastern China and was introduced into the United States in 1908 by Frank Meyer. The name "nuda" alludes to the absence of auricles and fimbriae on both the culm and foliage leaf sheaths. Reportedly, in the West, the name "stone bamboo" is erroneously applied to *P. angusta.* According to C. S. Chao's *A Guide to Bamboos Grown in Britain* (1989), the Chinese common name "stone bamboo" actually belongs *P. nuda,* with its heavy thick-walled culms.

Phyllostachys nigra 'Megurochiku'. Author's garden.

Phyllostachys nuda f. localis
Maximum height: 34 ft. (10 m)
Maximum diameter: 1¾ in. (4.4 cm)
Minimum temperature: −20°F (−29°C)
Light: full sun

Similar to the type form, but the basal portion of the culm is spotted or densely blotched with brownish purple coloration.

Phyllostachys platyglossa
Maximum height: 30 ft. (9 m)
Maximum diameter: 2 in. (5 cm)
Minimum temperature: 0°F (−18°C)
Light: full sun

Although *Phyllostachys platyglossa* culms are suitable for fences and minor construction, the culm walls are thin and the wood is not particularly strong. The shoots, however, are considered choice, and this species makes an attractive landscape bamboo. It was introduced into the United States in 1984 from China's Zhejiang Province.

Phyllostachys praecox
Maximum height: 36 ft. (11 m)
Maximum diameter: 3 in. (7.5 cm)
Minimum temperature: 0°F (−18°C)
Light: full sun

Phyllostachys praecox has short internodes, and those near the base often have yellow-green striae running the length of the internode. Shoot initiation occurs very early in the

Phyllostachys nuda. Author's garden.

Phyllostachys platyglossa. Author's garden.

season. The shoots are considered exceptional. This bamboo is the main early season fresh vegetable in Shanghai and Zhejiang in China.

Phyllostachys praecox f. *prevernalis*
Maximum height: 36 ft. (11 m)
Maximum diameter: 3 in. (7.5 cm)
Minimum temperature: 0°F (−18°C)
Light: full sun

Similar to the type form, but the internodes are smaller in diameter toward the middle of their length.

Phyllostachys propinqua
Maximum height: 32 ft. (9.6 m)
Maximum diameter: 2 in. (5 cm)
Minimum temperature: −10°F (−23°C)
Light: full sun

In China, *Phyllostachys propinqua* is cultivated for shoot production. Shoot initiation occurs in late midseason. The hard culm wood is used for tool handles and small construction. It also splits well for weaving. Originally introduced into America in 1928 by F. A. McClure, the species was subsequently reintroduced from Germany, where it has proven its winter hardiness.

Phyllostachys robustiramea
Maximum height: 25 ft. (7.5 m)
Maximum diameter: 2¼ in. (6 cm)
Minimum temperature: 5°F (−15°C)
Light: full sun

Usually not very tall, *Phyllostachys robustiramea* has short internodes with longitudinal ribs and furrows. The shoots are suitable for the table.

Phyllostachys rubromarginata
Maximum height: 60 ft. (18 m)
Maximum diameter: 3½ in. (9 cm)
Minimum temperature: −5°F (−21°C)
Light: full sun

Phyllostachys rubromarginata internodes are long and slender, and the supranodal ridges are narrow, without prominence. The culm wood is tough and splits well. Shooting begins late in the season. The shoots have only slight bitterness prior to parboiling and are considered good quality for eating.

The upper culm leaf sheath margins are red. One of the Chinese names for the plant is "red-margined sheath bamboo," thus giving rise to its botanical name, *Phyllostachys rubromarginata*. It is reportedly tolerant of alkaline soils and strong winds. This species was the most vigorous and most productive of the bamboos studied in extensive tests in Alabama. It produced the largest tonnage of dry wood per acre, far exceeding the yield of loblolly pine (*Pinus taeda*). *Phyllostachys rubromarginata* is an excellent candidate for paper pulp production.

Because of the long internodes, the branching and foliage are less dense than in many other *Phyllostachys* species. Similarly, the culm diameter is generally smaller for a given height, giving it a graceful if less "massive" look. Some of the world's largest examples of this species grow in the American Southeast, where it achieves a size significantly exceeding that cited in Chinese literature. One of the more versatile bamboos, *P. rubromarginata* is an excellent choice for landscape use, shoots, culm wood, and paper pulp.

Phyllostachys stimulosa
Maximum height: 26 ft. (8 m)
Maximum diameter: 1½ in. (4 cm)
Minimum temperature: 0°F (−18°C)
Light: full sun

Phyllostachys stimulosa is a native of China's Zhejiang Province, and a recent introduction to America. The culm nodes are prominent, and the culms do not split well. Its shoots reportedly do not taste very good.

Phyllostachys violascens
Common synonym: *Phyllostachys bambusoides* 'Violascens'
Maximum height: 50 ft. (15 m)

Maximum diameter: 3 in. (7.5 cm)
Minimum temperature: 0°F (−18°C)
Light: full sun

At its best, *Phyllostachys violascens* is a striking ornamental. The culms display a varied array of striping patterns and colors as they age. New culms have olive-green to purple-brown coloration and streaking, which is variously predominant or secondary to the green coloration. As the culms age, the narrow, longitudinal color stripes become more distinct. The green and purple-brown colorations change to lighter green, yellow, straw yellow, and brownish crimson in varying degrees.

The degree of striping and coloration varies from culm to culm, and some descriptions appear to be at odds with other descriptions, suggesting that the new culms are a deep blackish violet, changing to yellow-green or yellow with age. Some authorities have suggested that two or more species or forms are being described as the same taxon, but the highly variable and progressively changing coloration of the culms, particularly when observed at different stages, may account for the variations.

New shoots appear early in the season. A third center branchlet at the node occurs more frequently than it does in most species of the genus. *Phyllostachys violascens* was once considered a variant of *P. bambusoides*, but it is now regarded as a separate species.

Phyllostachys viridiglaucescens
Maximum height: 40 ft. (12 m)
Maximum diameter: 2¾ in. (7 cm)
Minimum temperature: −5°F (−21°C)
Light: full sun

The most common bamboo grown in west-central Europe, *Phyllostachys viridiglaucescens* was introduced into France in 1846. It is, for no apparent substantive reason, far less popular or common in the United States. A desirable and versatile bamboo, *P. viridiglaucescens* has an erect growth habit and very straight

culms. Shooting begins early in the season. The shoots are good tasting and have only slight bitterness even when raw. The culm wood has excellent mechanical properties. The species name is derived from the character of the leaf undersides, which are pubescent and, purportedly, more distinctly blue-green than those of others in the genus, though the color difference does not seem particularly notable.

Phyllostachys viridis
Common synonyms: *Phyllostachys mitis, P. sulphurea* 'Viridis'
Maximum height: 55 ft. (17 m)
Maximum diameter: 3¾ in. (10 cm)
Minimum temperature: 0°F (−18°C)
Light: full sun

A large timber bamboo with excellent tasting shoots, *Phyllostachys viridis* is one of the latest shooting species of the genus. Its stance is sinuous rather than rigidly erect. Minute dimples on the surface of the culm are visible with a hand lens, and they can be felt by running a fingernail along the surface. The culm wood is hard and strong and can be readily split for weaving. The species spreads slowly when grown in areas with relatively cool summers, such as the Pacific Northwest.

Phyllostachys viridis 'Houzeau'
Common synonym: *Phyllostachys sulphurea* 'Houzeau'
Maximum height: 55 ft. (17 m)
Maximum diameter: 3¾ in. (10 cm)
Minimum temperature: 0°F (−18°C)
Light: full sun

Differing from the principal form with its yellow sulcus, *Phyllostachys viridis* 'Houzeau' developed from the spontaneous mutation of a rhizome cutting from a USDA introduction of *P. viridis*. It was named after Jean Houzeau, a Belgian involved with bamboo introductions, studies, and writings in the early part of the 20th century.

Phyllostachys viridis 'Robert Young'

Common synonym: *Phyllostachys sulphurea*
Maximum height: 55 ft. (17 m)
Maximum diameter: 3¾ in. (10 cm)
Minimum temperature: 0°F (−18°C)
Light: full sun

Most *Phyllostachys* plants with multicolored culms carry the accent color in the sulcus of the internode. *Phyllostachys viridis* 'Robert Young' is among those with accent striping outside of the sulcus, along the ungrooved portion of the culm. The irregular green striping first appears as a darker color of green on the lighter, sulfur green culm. After a time, the culm changes to sulfur yellow and then to old gold, but the striping remains dark green. An occasional leaf blade shows cream-colored stripes.

A highly desirable ornamental, 'Robert Young' also has the excellent shoot and culm-wood properties of the principal form. Propagules of *P. viridis* sometimes spontaneously generate new instances of 'Robert Young'. The cultivar was named after Robert Young, a horticulturist and bamboo researcher with the USDA. (See photo on page 73.)

Phyllostachys vivax

Maximum height: 70 ft. (21 m)
Maximum diameter: 5 in. (13 cm)
Minimum temperature: −5°F (−21°C)
Light: full sun

A choice, hardy, ornamental, timber bamboo, *Phyllostachys vivax* establishes and grows rapidly. The species name alludes to the plant's vigorous vegetative growth. This species is the most cold hardy of the large timber bamboos. It shoots in early midseason. *Phyllostachys vivax* generally resembles *P. bambusoides*, but its culm walls are much thinner, the wood is inferior, and the culms are less straight. However, *P. vivax* establishes and attains a large size far more quickly than *P. bambusoides*, and its shoots are excellent for eating and are free of bitterness even when raw. For a *Phyllostachys*,

it has large, broad leaves, giving it a bit of a tropical look. In the landscape, it is complemented by nearby smaller-leaved forms of *Phyllostachys*. For shoot production, or as a hardy, ornamental, timber bamboo, *P. vivax* is an outstanding selection.

Heavy rains and wind can fracture new culms of this lushly foliaged bamboo. Fracture is a greater risk if the adverse conditions occur just after the new culms have fully leafed out, but before the culms have sufficiently hardened. If this is a problem, the culms can be topped slightly to reduce the burden.

Phyllostachys vivax f. *aureocaulis*

Maximum height: 70 ft. (21 m)
Maximum diameter: 5 in. (13 cm)

Phyllostachys vivax shoot. Author's garden.

Phyllostachys vivax. Hakone Gardens.

Pleioblastus 337

Minimum temperature: −5°F (−21°C)
Light: full sun

Another choice ornamental timber bamboo, *Phyllostachys vivax* f. *aureocaulis* differs from the principal form by having yellow culms with random green stripes. Highly attractive, it retains the vigor of the principal form.

Pleioblastus

Similar to *Arundinaria,* and at one time classified within that genus, *Pleioblastus* includes hardy dwarf, shrub, and even small arborescent bamboos with leptomorph rhizomes. Within the genus are groups with shared characteristics, and some botanists have assigned sections or subgenera to them. The generic name is derived from the Greek words *pleios* and *blastos,* meaning many buds—a reference to the number of branch buds. Each node bears from three to seven principal branches. The leaves are arranged near the tips of the culms and branches. Largely of Japanese origin, *Pleioblastus* is widely distributed in Japan and China.

The genus encompasses a wide variety of variegated species and forms, providing the landscaper with a broad palette of colors and textures. The leaves are generally smaller and more slender than those of other shrub bamboos, such as *Sasa, Sasaella,* and *Indocalamus.* Although many *Pleioblastus* bamboos can be grown to the size of substantial shrubs, and some have an arborescent habit, the genus has become virtually synonymous with dwarf or groundcover bamboos. For most groundcover species of *Pleioblastus,* the slender culms and branches are overshadowed by proportionately larger leaves, thus the persistent or late-shedding culm leaves are generally not conspicuous. If grown as a groundcover, they benefit from an annual winter clipping, keeping their height in check and fostering spring growth of fresh-looking new culms, branches, and leaves.

Pleioblastus akebono

Common synonym: *Pleioblastus argenteostriatus* 'Akebono'
Maximum height: 1½ ft. (46 cm)
Maximum diameter: ¼ in. (0.6 cm)
Minimum temperature: 5°F (−15°C)
Light: full shade

Pleioblastus akebono is a highly attractive dwarf bamboo. Its leaves are sometimes nearly all white when they emerge in the spring, turning greener as the season progresses. The green coloration looks as if it had been finely brushed on the white leaves, greener toward the leaf stem, whiter to all white toward the leaf tip. This species grows slowly and prefers shade and humidity.

Pleioblastus amarus

Maximum height: 16 ft. (5 m)
Maximum diameter: ¾ in. (2 cm)
Minimum temperature: 0°F (−18°C)
Light: partial shade

The new culms of *Pleioblastus amarus* are covered with a dense white powder. The nodes may bear up to seven principal branches. The species is widely distributed in the Chang River Valley of China, where it is used for umbrella handles, flag poles, and similar items. The shoots are extremely bitter and are not harvested for food.

Pleioblastus argenteostriatus

Maximum height: 3 ft. (1 m)
Maximum diameter: ¼ in. (0.6 cm)
Minimum temperature: 5°F (−15°C)
Light: partial shade

Pleioblastus argenteostriatus is a variegated dwarf bamboo with varying amounts of cream-yellow striping in the leaves. Although it performs best with more shade, this species is reasonably tolerant of sun. An attractive bamboo, it is enhanced by clipping or mowing in early spring to refresh its foliage.

Pleioblastus chino

Maximum height: 12 ft. (4 m)
Maximum diameter: ¾ in. (2 cm)
Minimum temperature: 5°F (−15°C)
Light: partial shade

In the landscape, *Pleioblastus chino* and its various forms are typically treated as ground-cover or small shrub bamboos, but they can grow larger, into tall shrubs or hedges. The species and its forms are vigorous and have relatively deep running rhizomes. If allowed to grow larger, *P. chino* can spread aggressively.

Pleioblastus chino f. angustifolius

Maximum height: 10 ft. (3 m)
Maximum diameter: ¾ in. (2 cm)
Minimum temperature: 5°F (−15°C)
Light: partial shade

Similar to the type form, but with white-striped leaves, *Pleioblastus chino* f. *angustifolius* is somewhat less variegated than some of the other cultivars and forms of the species.

Pleioblastus chino f. elegantissimus

Maximum height: 6 ft. (1.8 m)
Maximum diameter: ½ in. (1.25 cm)
Minimum temperature: 5°F (−15°C)
Light: partial shade

A form of the species with very fine, white, often discontinuous stripes.

Pleioblastus chino 'Kimmei'

Maximum height: 10 ft. (3 m)
Maximum diameter: ¾ in. (2 cm)
Minimum temperature: 5°F (−15°C)
Light: partial shade

Similar to the type form, but the leaves have several yellow-white stripes, and the culms are yellow with light green stripes. Some of the plants in circulation in the garden trade in the

Pleioblastus akebono. Author's garden.

Pleioblastus chino var. *vaginatus* f. *variegatus,* grown as a tall shrub. Bamboo Sourcery.

United States are actually *Semiarundinaria yashadake* f. *kimmei.*

Pleioblastus chino 'Murakamianus'

Maximum height: 10 ft. (3 m)
Maximum diameter: ¾ in. (2 cm)
Minimum temperature: 5°F (−15°C)
Light: partial shade

The white-striped leaves of 'Murakamianus' are strongly but variably variegated. On average, three-quarters of the leaf is white, but it may vary from all white to nearly all green. This cultivar is reasonably tolerant of sun, but prefers filtered light.

Pleioblastus chino var. vaginatus f. variegatus

Maximum height: 10 ft. (3 m)
Maximum diameter: ½ in. (1.25 cm)
Minimum temperature: 5°F (−15°C)
Light: partial shade

Pleioblastus chino var. *vaginatus* f. *variegatus* has smaller, narrower leaves than the type form. Its delicate white striping is stronger than that of *P. chino* f. *elegantissimus,* but not nearly as bold as *P. chino* 'Murakamianus'. Although generally grown as a groundcover, it can be grown as a hedge, or even as a specimen plant.

Pleioblastus fortunei

Common synonyms: *Pleioblastus variegatus,*
    P. variegatus 'Fortunei'
Common name: dwarf whitestripe
Maximum height: 4 ft. (1.2 m)
Maximum diameter: ¼ in. (0.6 cm)
Minimum temperature: 5°F (−15°C)
Light: partial shade

A choice groundcover or shrub bamboo, *Pleioblastus fortunei,* commonly known as dwarf whitestripe, has crisp, green and white, striped

Pleioblastus fortunei. Author's garden.

leaves. Unlike many variegated bamboos, *P. fortunei* holds its variegation well through the summer's stronger sunlight. One of the earliest bamboos to come to Europe, it was introduced into Belgium in 1863.

Pleioblastus gauntlettii

Maximum height: 2½ ft. (0.8 m)
Maximum diameter: ¼ in. (0.6 cm)
Minimum temperature: 0°F (−18°C)
Light: partial shade

Believed to be a native of Japan, *Pleioblastus gauntlettii* is named after the British firm Messrs. Gauntlett Ltd., which listed this bamboo in its catalog. Most likely, *P. gauntlettii* is an incorrect name, though its correct name is uncertain. The small, erect culms bear leaves 7 in. (18 cm) long by ¾ in. (2 cm) wide.

Pleioblastus gramineus

Maximum height: 12 ft. (4 m)
Maximum diameter: ¾ in. (2 cm)
Minimum temperature: 5°F (−15°C)
Light: mostly sunny

One of the taller, somewhat arborescent *Pleioblastus* species, *P. gramineus* has very slender grasslike leaves, giving this bamboo its species name. Attractive in spite of its persistent culm leaves, the plant has a fountainlike growth habit. Native to the Ryukyu Islands of Japan, *P. gramineus* is reportedly tolerant of salt air. Although thin walled, the culms make excellent garden stakes. This species is sometimes used for bonsai.

Pleioblastus gramineus f. monstrispiralis

Common synonym: *Pleioblastus gramineus* 'Rasetsu-chiku'
Maximum height: 15 ft. (4.5 m)
Maximum diameter: 1 in. (2.5 cm)
Minimum temperature: 5°F (−15°C)
Light: mostly sunny

As with the principal form, the rhizome system of *Pleioblastus gramineus* f. *monstrispiralis* is leptomorph with amphipodial culm initiation. Many of the culms that tiller, arising from sympodial branching, grow in a pronounced spiral. It is indigenous to remote southern islands in Japan's Kagoshima Prefecture.

Pleioblastus hindsii

Maximum height: 20 ft. (6 m)
Maximum diameter: 1¼ in. (3.2 cm)
Minimum temperature: 5°F (−15°C)
Light: mostly sunny

Native to southern China, and introduced into Japan centuries ago, *Pleioblastus hindsii* is an attractive and distinctive arborescent species. Its leaves and culms are a deep olive green. Although its leaves are wider than those of *P. gramineus* and *P. linearis,* they are nonetheless very slender, with an unusually narrow and extended leaf tip. The leaves are considerably thicker and more leathery than those of most other bamboos. The new leaves are initially quite erect, particularly toward the top of the plant. The culm leaves are persistent.

Introduced into England around 1875, *Pleioblastus hindsii* is named for R. B. Hinds, a British surgeon and avid plant collector. It is reportedly quite tolerant of salt air. In China and Japan, *P. hindsii* is grown as an ornamental. In southern Japan, it grows up to 20 ft. (6 m) tall, and its excellent shoots are harvested as a delicacy. Because some shooting often occurs throughout the growing season, *P. hindsii* can be a source of fresh shoots when others are unavailable.

Identification of the species is somewhat muddled. In the United States and England, and probably elsewhere, other bamboos have long ago been erroneously introduced as *Pleioblastus hindsii.* One example that I have seen reportedly originated from USDA plant introduction number 75147. Presumably other than the authentic item, its leaves were wider, thin, and pliable rather than thick and leathery, and far less erect. This particular "hindsii" seems rather dull, with modest horticultural merit—a considerable contrast from other, presumably authentic, examples.

Pleioblastus humilis

Maximum height: 7 ft. (2.1 m)
Maximum diameter: ¼ in. (0.6 cm)
Minimum temperature: 0°F (−18°C)
Light: partial shade

A green-leaved bamboo typically used as a groundcover, but capable of growing much taller, *Pleioblastus humilis* spreads rapidly and is effective in erosion control. In larger areas, it can be refreshed by yearly mowing. It is indigenous to Japan.

Pleioblastus juxianensis

Maximum height: 10 ft. (3 m)
Maximum diameter: 1⅛ in. (3 cm)
Minimum temperature: 10°F (−12°C)
Light: mostly sun

A somewhat arborescent *Pleioblastus*, this species has leaves up to 6¼ in. (16 cm) long and 1 in. (2.5 cm) wide. The culms are used in making umbrellas and other small constructions.

Pleioblastus kongosanensis f. akibensis

Maximum height: 6 ft. (1.8 m)
Maximum diameter: ⅜ in. (1 cm)
Minimum temperature: 0°F (−18°C)
Light: mostly sunny

Pleioblastus kongosanensis f. *akibensis* is a green, dwarf bamboo with hairy culms. It is indigenous to central and southern Japan.

Pleioblastus kongosanensis 'Aureostriatus'

Maximum height: 6 ft. (1.8 m)
Maximum diameter: ¼ in. (0.6 cm)
Minimum temperature: 0°F (−18°C)
Light: partial shade

A dwarf bamboo, *Pleioblastus kongosanensis* 'Aureostriatus' has green leaves with occasional gold stripes.

Pleioblastus linearis

Maximum height: 18 ft. (5.5 m)
Maximum diameter: 1 in. (2.5 cm)
Minimum temperature: 5°F (−15°C)
Light: full sun

Introduced into the United States from Taiwan, and native to Japan's Ryukyu Islands, *Pleioblastus linearis* is one of the larger, somewhat arborescent species of *Pleioblastus*. Its leaves are long, very slender, and grasslike, and its branches are densely ramified with abundant leaves, giving the plant a plumed appearance. It is reportedly tolerant of salt air. The culms are used in fences and for making fish traps. In Okinawa, the culms with attached branches and leaves are used for roofing.

Pleioblastus nagashima

Maximum height: 6 ft. (1.8 m)
Maximum diameter: ¼ in. (0.6 cm)
Minimum temperature: 0°F (−18°C)
Light: partial shade

Pleioblastus nagashima is generally grown as a green groundcover bamboo. Its distribution extends into Kyushu, slightly more southerly than many of the Japanese *Pleioblastus*.

Pleioblastus oleosus

Maximum height: 16 ft. (5 m)
Maximum diameter: 1¼ in. (3.2 cm)
Minimum temperature: 0°F (−18°C)
Light: full sun

Another somewhat arborescent species, *Pleioblastus oleosus* is distributed in the Zhejiang, Fujian, Jiangxi, and Yunnan Provinces of China.

Pleioblastus pygmaeus

Common synonyms: *Arundinaria pygmaea,*
    Bambusa pygmaea, Sasa pygmaea
Maximum height: 2 ft. (0.6 m)
Maximum diameter: ⅛ in. (0.3 cm)
Minimum temperature: 5°F (−15°C)
Light: partial shade

Pleioblastus pygmaeus is a small, green, dwarf

bamboo. Its exact origins and nature are somewhat vague. Plants from various sources demonstrate different characteristics, and *P. pygmaeus* may actually include several related species or forms. There has been no documented record of its flowering, thus making classification by traditional methods all the more problematic.

A common groundcover in the nursery trade, *Pleioblastus pygmaeus* may be found under a variety of names, such as *Arundinaria pygmaea, Bambusa pygmaea,* and *Sasa pygmaea.* Confusing matters further, some non-specialist nurseries sell any small, green-leaved, leptomorph bamboo as "Pygmy bamboo." Some forms are more desirable than others, but in general, it is an attractive, if not spectacular, utilitarian groundcover.

Pleioblastus pygmaeus var. *distichus*

Common synonym: *Pleioblastus distichus*
Common names: dwarf fernleaf, distichus
Maximum height: 2 ft. (0.6 m)
Maximum diameter: 1/8 in. (0.3 cm)
Minimum temperature: 5°F (−15°C)
Light: partial shade

One of the smallest bamboos, *Pleioblastus pygmaeus* var. *distichus* is an attractive, all-green groundcover with very small leaves. The leaf blades are arranged tightly in two ranks, resembling a fern. This arrangement is called *distichus* and is the source of the plant's taxonomic and common names. It can be used for bonsai, in a rock garden, as a groundcover, or even as a lawn, trimmed with a lawnmower. It looks best when periodically clipped or mowed, fostering dense growth and a compact habit.

Pleioblastus shibuyanus 'Tsuboi'

Maximum height: 8 ft. (2.4 m)
Maximum diameter: 1/2 in. (1.25 cm)
Minimum temperature: 0°F (−18°C)
Light: partial shade

A distinctive, variegated groundcover or shrub bamboo, *Pleioblastus shibuyanus* 'Tsuboi' has relatively small leaves that create an interesting effect as the variegated white striping blends into the green. It has a robust and aggressive rhizome system for the size of the plant. As groundcover, shrub, hedge, or container plant, 'Tsuboi' is a choice ornamental.

Pleioblastus simonii

Common name: medake
Maximum height: 20 ft. (6 m)
Maximum diameter: 1½ in. (4 cm)
Minimum temperature: 0°F (−18°C)
Light: mostly sunny

Native to China and Japan, *Pleioblastus simonii* is one of the larger arborescent species of *Pleioblastus.* With its straight culms and erect habit, it is commonly used as a hedge bamboo,

Pleioblastus pygmaeus var. *distichus*. Author's garden.

Pleioblastus shibuyanus 'Tsuboi'. Author's garden.

but its persistent and prominent culm and branch leaves give it a bit of a tattered look. It is commonly planted as an ornamental in China. The straight culms are thin walled but strong, without prominent nodes, and are ideal for garden stakes. In China, the culms are used to make fishing rods and cages. The shoots are reportedly edible, but somewhat bitter.

Pleioblastus simonii was introduced into France in 1862 by the French consul to China, Mr. Simon, for whom the species is named. In many climates, *P. simonii* does not shoot until mid to late summer, providing little time for the shooting and branching to be completed before the onset of winter's cold. It is not considered an aggressive runner. *Pleioblastus simonii* is reportedly very tolerant of salt air.

Pleioblastus simonii 'Variegatus'
Maximum height: 20 ft. (6 m)
Maximum diameter: 1½ in. (4 cm)
Minimum temperature: 0°F (−18°C)
Light: mostly sunny

'Variegatus' is a variegated form of *Pleioblastus simonii*. The leaf shape and coloration vary considerably on the same culm, from wide to narrow, and all green to variegated with white striping. The new culm leaves are initially attractively variegated, but soon fade, and look increasingly scruffy with the passage of time. The variegation on the foliage leaves also diminishes over time. The cultivar is more aggressive than the type form and, to my taste, is not a particularly attractive variegated bamboo.

Pleioblastus viridistriatus
Common synonym: *Pleioblastus auricomus*
Maximum height: 6 ft. (1.8 m)
Maximum diameter: ½ in. (1.25 cm)
Minimum temperature: 0°F (−18°C)
Light: full shade

A striking ornamental groundcover for

Pleioblastus viridistriatus. Author's garden.

shaded environments, *Pleioblastus viridistriatus* produces new leaves that are vivid chartreuse with darker green stripes. As the season progresses, the coloration becomes less vivid, and when grown in the sun, the leaves are far less colorful, darkening to green with somewhat darker green striping. In late winter or early spring, *P. viridistriatus* should be clipped or mowed to remove most of the older leaves and make way for the showy new foliage.

Leaf size varies, but can range up to 8 in. (20 cm) long and 1½ in. (4 cm) wide on larger plants. Although the plant can reach a height of 6 ft. (1.8 m) in sunny conditions, it loses much of its appeal, and *Pleioblastus viridistriatus* is at its best in shady conditions as a groundcover or small shrub.

Pleioblastus viridistriatus f. *chrysophyllus*

Maximum height: 6 ft. (1.8 m)
Maximum diameter: ½ in. (1.25 cm)
Minimum temperature: 0°F (−18°C)
Light: full shade

Similar to the type form, except the leaves are uniformly chartreuse with no striping.

Pseudosasa

Pseudosasa is a genus of generally medium-sized to tall, shrublike Asian bamboos with leptomorph rhizomes and a solitary (or sometimes up to three in some species) principal branch at each node. Some of the largest species are arborescent. At the other end of the spectrum, *Pseudosasa owatarii* is a small shrub at its largest, and it is more often encountered as a groundcover bamboo less than 1 ft. (30 cm) tall. *Pseudosasa* culm leaves are coriaceous and persistent, or very late shedding. The foliage leaf blades are palmately arranged toward the top of the culms and tips of the branches. *Pseudosasa* is composed of some three dozen species.

Pseudosasa amabilis

Common synonym: *Arundinaria amabilis*
Common names: Tonkin cane, tea stick bamboo
Maximum height: 50 ft. (15 m)
Maximum diameter: 2½ in. (6.3 cm)
Minimum temperature: 10°F (−12°C)
Light: full sun

The famous Tonkin cane bamboo is highly regarded for its outstanding mechanical properties. It is still widely known by its earlier and longstanding botanical name, *Arundinaria amabilis*. The culms are strong, stiff, and resilient, with only a slight taper. The nodes are not prominent. In a mature stand, the culms are free of branches for one-half to two-thirds of their height. When grown and processed properly, the top-graded, cured culms are entirely free of branch scars.

Pseudosasa amabilis requires a warm temperate or cool tropical environment. It does not propagate well from rhizome cuttings and can be very slow to establish. If conditions are not ideal, the plants may not produce the highest quality culms that have made the species so notable. Introductions can certainly be successful, however, since it is virtually unknown in natural stands, and the cultivated stands of *P. amabilis* from China's Guangdong Province and Guangxi are the source of its reputation. The common name Tonkin cane suggests that the species may have had origins in northern Vietnam.

Traditional uses for the species include poles for supporting hop plants, rug poles, fences, and handicraft. It is the only bamboo used for making the finest split-cane fly fishing rods.

Pseudosasa cantori

Maximum height: 16 ft. (5 m)
Maximum diameter: 1⅛ in. (3 cm)
Minimum temperature: 10°F (−12°C) estimated
Light: partial shade

Native to the southern coastal provinces of Guangdong and Fujian, *Pseudosasa cantori* inhabits partially shaded, broad-leaved wood-lands at elevations below 1600 ft. (500 m). The culm wood is used in making furniture.

Pseudosasa japonica

Common names: arrow bamboo, yadake
Maximum height: 18 ft. (5.5 m)
Maximum diameter: ¾ in. (2 cm)
Minimum temperature: −5°F (−21°C)
Light: partial shade

One of the larger, somewhat arborescent pseudosasas, *Pseudosasa japonica* is a widely dis-tributed garden ornamental. Each node gener-ally has no more than a single principal branch. The culms are erect, and the ascendant branches bear drooping leaves up to 1 ft. (30 cm) long and 2 in. (5 cm) wide. Introduced into Europe in 1850, *P. japonica* made its way to the United States by 1860, one of the earliest species introduced into America. Reportedly tolerant of wind and salt air, *P. japonica* is a cold-hardy bamboo that grows as far north as the Japanese island of Hokkaido. A hedge 300 ft. (90 m) long was planted at the Rosewarne Experimental Horticultural Station in Corn-wall, England, as a barrier against the strong Cornish gales. In a controlled trial of 400 spe-cies of hedging plants for sheltering purposes, *P. japonica* was one of eight selected as most suitable.

Because the culm and branch leaves are persistent, and the branches ramify each year, mature, unkempt stands of *Pseudosasa japonica* can look scruffy and unattractive, but when well maintained, the upright culms and lush foliage are very attractive and distinctive. It has the largest leaves of any widely available, semi-arborescent, hardy bamboo. In the landscape, it is effective as a tall hedge, as a specimen plant, where it makes an elegant tall fountain, or as a container plant. To maintain its appear-ance, older culms should be removed from the grove or clump.

During culm harvesting, the branches can be removed cleanly and easily by simply pulling them downward. The round, slender culms are thin walled, but relatively strong, with long internodes. The nodes are uninflated and have no groove or flattening above them. Because of all these characteristics, the culms are suitable for making arrows, hence its com-mon name—arrow bamboo. If you already have a sufficient supply of arrows, the culms also make excellent garden stakes.

Pseudosasa japonica 'Akebono'

Maximum height: 18 ft. (5.5 m)
Maximum diameter: ¾ in. (2 cm)
Minimum temperature: −5°F (−21°C)
Light: partial shade

Similar to the type form, but the leaves have white variegation that is predominant toward the tip. Some leaves may be nearly all white, others nearly all green. The plant may not reli-ably maintain its variegation.

Pseudosasa japonica 'Akebonosuji'

Maximum height: 18 ft. (5.5 m)
Maximum diameter: ¾ in. (2 cm)
Minimum temperature: −5°F (−21°C)
Light: partial shade

Similar to the type form, but the leaves are variegated with yellow stripes. The leaf colora-tion in 'Akebonosuji' is reportedly somewhat more stable than in 'Akebono'. *Pseudosasa japon-ica* 'Variegata', cultivated in Europe, is said to be similar, but often reverts to the green type form.

Pseudosasa japonica 'Tsutsumiana'

Maximum height: 18 ft. (5.5 m)
Maximum diameter: ¾ in. (2 cm)
Minimum temperature: −5°F (−21°C)
Light: partial shade

Similar to the type form, but the internodes are swollen near their base, resembling a green onion. This plant requires some effort to dis-play its ornamental features, including thin-

Pseudosasa japonica with a groundcover bamboo. Hakone Gardens.

ning away less characteristic culms and removing the culm leaves to expose the swollen
internodes.

Pseudosasa owatarii

Maximum height: 3 ft. (1 m)
Maximum diameter: ¼ in. (0.6 cm)
Minimum temperature: 0°F (–18°C)
Light: partial shade

    Pseudosasa owatarii is an attractive, small-
leaved, dwarf species that often grows only a
few inches (8 cm or so) high. An excellent
specimen for bonsai, it is endemic to the southern Japanese island of Yakushima. *Pleioblastus
pygmaeus* is sometimes confused with *Pseudo-*

Pseudosasa owatarii. Author's garden.

sasa owatarii, but *P. owatarii* has shinier, more
tapering leaves, in more of a palmate arrangement, rather than the distichus (fernlike) arrangement of *P. pygmaeus* leaves.

Pseudosasa usawai

Maximum height: 16 ft. (5 m)
Maximum diameter: ¾ in. (2 cm)
Minimum temperature: 10°F (–12°C)
Light: mostly sunny

    Pseudosasa usawai is endemic to Taiwan and
widely distributed throughout the island,
where it grows in thickets in forests and open
grasslands. It is not as steadfastly hardy as the
more common *P. japonica.*

Qiongzhuea

Qiongzhuea is a genus of considerable historical
note and modern taxonomic debate. Its name
is derived from the Chinese vernacular name
Qiong, the name of a mountain range where a
distinctive indigenous bamboo was said to
have grown, and *zhu,* a word for bamboo. The
genus is very closely related to *Chimonobambusa,* and some taxonomists regard *Qiongzhuea*
as a section within *Chimonobambusa,* not as a
separate genus (Wen 1994). Evidence supports
both treatments, and thus does not definitively
validate either. In addition to the controversy
of its status as a separate genus, the genus assignment of some individual species is in question (Clark 1995).

    Qiongzhuea bamboos are native to central
China, where they occupy the understory of
forest habitats. In its natural environments,
Qiongzhuea generally shoots in the spring and
summer, whereas *Chimonobambusa* generally
shoots in the fall and winter. The elevation
range of *Qiongzhuea* extends higher than that
of *Chimonobambusa,* ranging from 2800 to 8500
ft. (850 to 2600 m). Extreme low temperatures
reach 5°F (–15°C), and average yearly humidity is approximately 85 percent. *Qiongzhuea*
culms are cylindrical with prominent or tumid
nodes, and unlike in *Chimonobambusa,* the

lower nodes are devoid of aerial roots or spines.

Qiongzhuea tumidissinoda

Common synonyms: *Chimonobambusa tumidinoda, C. tumidissinoda, Qiongzhuea tumidinoda*
Maximum height: 20 ft. (6 m)
Maximum diameter: 1¼ in. (3.2 cm)
Minimum temperature: 10°F (−12°C)
Light: partial shade

Qiongzhuea tumidissinoda is a very distinctive and attractive ornamental bamboo. The species name is derived from its tumid, or exceptionally swollen, nodes. The nodes are said to have the shape of two dishes placed face to face. The culms are used as walking sticks.

Qiongzhuea tumidissinoda is the subject of history, myth, and fable in Chinese culture, dating back to at least the Han Dynasty in the first or second century B.C. Various stories

Qiongzhuea tumidissinoda showing the smooth, exceptionally swollen node. Author's garden.

involve sages and ambassadors and their travels with the Qiongzhu stick, which was offered to the court of the Han Dynasty. The source of the Qiongzhu stick reportedly remained a mystery until the Sung Dynasty in the 12th century A.D., when it was "found" high on a mountain slope, above the Chang River, in northeastern Yunnan. Its natural distribution includes Guizhou, northeastern Yunnan, and southwestern Sichuan, at an altitude range of 5000 to 6900 ft. (1500 to 2100 m). The shoots are exceptionally choice edibles, both fresh and dried. Demand for the shoots has encouraged overharvesting in the plant's native locations (Bareis, e-mail communication; Wen 1994).

Because *Qiongzhuea tumidissinoda* is regarded as a unique cultural plant, the Chinese government has restricted its trade. Its narrow distribution range, its habitat in the isolated high mountain mists, and the secretive attitude of government officials and local monks alike contribute to its aura of protected mystery. The Yi people of what is now southwestern Sichuan have been exporting Qiongzhu walking sticks to the outside world since the Han Dynasty. Protective of their isolation and their industry, the Yi have also fostered this secretive aura (Lancaster 1997).

A bamboo with such distinctive characteristics would typically have been taxonomically described a century or more ago, but this plant escaped botanical description until 1980, when *Qiongzhuea tumidinoda* (note the species spelling) was described and published. Ironically, the species publication was not in accord with taxonomic requirements and was subsequently disallowed. The authors of the 1980 publication corrected the errors and republished the taxon in a valid form in 1996, but by that time, it had already been published validly, though for some reason as *Chimonobambusa tumidissinoda* rather than *Chimonobambusa tumidinoda*, hence its current identity as *Q. tumidissinoda*. Of course, some taxonomists regard the entire genus *Qiongzhuea* as merely a section within the genus *Chimonobambusa,* thus the name *C. tumidissinoda* is also used. The unusual nature of this bamboo continues to manifest itself in many ways.

By a combination of accident, luck, and cunning, Britain's Peter Addington was able to bring this protected plant to England from China in 1987. *Qiongzhuea tumidissinoda* flourishes in conditions of abundant rainfall, moderate sun, high humidity, and acid soil, forming dense thickets in its native environment. In England, it found a highly amenable environment, where it flourishes, and has developed a reputation as vigorous and exceptionally fast running. Excess sun causes the delicate sprays of foliage to turn yellowish green. Shade fosters a rich, deep green.

Raddia

A genus of attractive, tropical, herbaceous bamboos, *Raddia* exhibits nocturnal "sleep" movements, with leaf blades that fold upward along the culm at night. This curious phenomenon typically begins at sunset and progresses over a four-hour period, reversing itself at dawn. The sleep movements also occur when a plant is under moisture or temperature stress. The genus inhabits low-altitude forest understories in Brazil and countries to the north. *Raddia* can be found growing in sandy soil alongside cacti, or in scrub forest with bromeliads.

Some of the species have an attractive, fernlike leaf pattern. Bamboo gardeners and collectors tend to regard herbaceous bamboos as a relatively recent phenomenon in cultivation, but *Raddia guianensis* was cultivated in France, as a greenhouse plant, nearly a century and a half ago. There are approximately five described species and at least one additional undescribed species.

Raddia brasiliensis

Maximum height: 1½ ft. (46 cm) estimated
Maximum diameter: ⅛ in. (0.3 cm) estimated

Minimum temperature: 32°F (0°C)
Light: partial shade

Raddia brasiliensis has larger leaves and is less delicate than *R. distichophylla*. Its leaf color is a lighter green. As with all raddias, the leaves fold upward at night.

Raddia distichophylla

Maximum height: 1 ft. (30 cm) estimated
Maximum diameter: ⅛ in. (0.3 cm) estimated
Minimum temperature: 32°F (0°C)
Light: full shade

Raddia distichophylla is among the most attractive of the herbaceous bamboos. Its multiple pairs of deep green leaves give it a delicate fernlike appearance. And adding to the drama,

Raddia distichophylla. Author's garden.

as with all of the genus, the leaves fold upward at night.

Rhipidocladum

Rhipidocladum is a New World genus of bamboos with pachymorph rhizome systems and a tight clumping habit. The thin-walled, weak culms begin erect, then arch and droop, or they climb or clamber on nearby supports. The culm leaves have a distinctly triangular profile. The plants prefer humid growing conditions, and the native habitats range from sea level to 9500 ft. (2900 m), from northwestern Argentina and central Brazil to northeastern Mexico. The genus name is derived from the Greek, *rhipis,* fan, and *klados,* branch, referring to the characteristic fanlike branching pattern. There are approximately 23 known species, 17 of which have been described and classified.

Rhipidocladum pittieri

Maximum height: 30 ft. (9 m)
Maximum diameter: ⅜ in. (1 cm)
Minimum temperature: 32°F (0°C) estimated
Light: mostly sunny

An arching, clambering bamboo, *Rhipidocladum pittieri* is distributed from southern Mexico to Costa Rica, where it can be seen drooping over bluffs, cliffs, and embankments.

Rhipidocladum racemiflorum

Maximum height: 45 ft. (14 m)
Maximum diameter: ½ in. (1.25 cm)
Minimum temperature: 25°F (–4°C)
Light: mostly sunny

A clambering bamboo, *Rhipidocladum racemiflorum* depends on trees to support its slender culms, manifold branches, and tufts of small leaves. It is one of the most widespread species in the genus. Where growing conditions are amenable, *R. racemiflorum* makes a delicate and highly attractive ornamental.

Sasa

Sasa is a genus of cold-hardy, robust, shrublike bamboos with leptomorph rhizomes. They have a single branch per node, which typically approximates the diameter of the culm itself. The leathery culm and branch leaves are usually persistent. The foliage leaves are generally broad and large. *Sasa* bamboos are often aggressive runners. They are endemic to Asia, primarily Japan for the majority of the species, though Korea and China are also native ground. *Sasa* densely covers large expanses of grasslands or forest understory in northern Japan. Although they are distributed as far south as Hainan Island in the South China Sea, sasas are primarily associated with northern climates. *Sasa* is the northernmost naturally distributed bamboo genus, extending to 50°N latitude on Sakhalin Island, an island colonized by both Russia and Japan, then ceded to Russia in 1875. The genus ranges from sea level to approximately 8900 ft. (2700 m). Most sasas prefer shade.

Historically, *Sasa* has been used as a catchall term to signify small, shrublike, rather than arborescent, bamboos. The Japanese *sasa* is thought to derive from the Chinese *hsai-chu,* meaning small bamboo. Although many sasas are attractive plants, nearly all species suffer from some withering of the leaf tips or margins. One ornamental species, *S. veitchii,* has strongly withered leaf margins, giving the plant a desirable, variegated look. In the plant's native environments, the weight of winter snow bends the flexible culms to the ground, covering the leaves and buds, and protecting them from cold winds and desiccation. With the spring snowmelt, the culms become upright, and the evergreen leaves begin to photosynthesize again. The genus's lengthy flowering cycle has been variously placed between 60 and 100 years or more. Sasas are generally monocarpic, recovering from mass flowering primarily by the growth of seedlings.

Sasa species.

A taxonomically problematic group, *Sasa* once comprised more than 400 species, but less than 10 percent are still regarded as valid. Over the course of some 30 years, Sadao Suzuki's studies of the sasa group of bamboos—*Sasa, Sasamorpha*, and *Sasaella*—resulted in major taxonomic revisions. The results of the studies are reflected in his 1978 work, *Index to Japanese Bambusaceae*.

Because the flowers are so similar throughout the genus, species distinctions have been largely based on vegetative characteristics. Unfortunately, habitat and seasonal changes create significant vegetative differences in the same species. These differences have often been mistaken for indications of a new species. In his studies, Suzuki found that certain vegetative characteristics were usually stable, such as the presence or absence of hairs on the culm leaf sheath or lower blade surface, and could serve as bases for distinguishing species. Other characteristics, such as the presence or absence of fimbriae or the presence or absence of hairs on the upper surface of the leaves, were merely variations among individual plants and their immediate habitat, and were not bases for distinguishing species. Once the unstable attributes were excluded, the number of species decreased dramatically.

Some controversy remains, however, regarding taxonomic ranking. For example, some taxonomists treat the sasamorpha group as a separate genus, while others treat it variously as a subgenus or as a section within *Sasa*. More than two decades have elapsed since Suzuki's landmark work, and further realignment of the sasa group is likely.

Sasa kagamiana

Maximum height: 6 ft. (1.8 m)
Maximum diameter: ¼ in. (0.6 cm)
Minimum temperature: 0°F (−18°C)
Light: full shade
    A shrublike bamboo with leaves up to 1 ft. (30 cm) long and over 2 in. (5 cm) wide.

Sasa kagamiana ssp. yoshinoi

Maximum height: 2 ft. (0.6 m)
Maximum diameter: ⅟₁₆ in. (0.2 cm)
Minimum temperature: 0°F (−18°C)
Light: full shade
    An infrequently occurring dwarf subspecies that is endemic to the Pacific side of southwestern Honshu in Japan.

Sasa kurilensis

Maximum height: 10 ft. (3 m)
Maximum diameter: ¾ in. (2 cm)
Minimum temperature: −5°F (−21°C)
Light: full shade
    Sasa kurilensis is one of Japan's most prevalent bamboos. The name is derived from one of its native habitats, the Kuril Islands, a group of Russian islands northeast of Japan. Also distributed in northeastern Korea and Russia,

Sasa kurilensis 'Shimofuri'. Author's garden.

the species extends as far as 50°N, to Russia's Sakhalin Island, where it thrives in a cold, wet, snowy environment. Its leaves are up to 10 in. (25 cm) long and 3 in. (7.5 cm) wide.

Sasa kurilensis shoots are popular in northeastern and central Japan. Although the shoots are seldom grown commercially, they are gathered in the wild, and licenses are sometimes issued to protect against overharvesting. The shoots are relatively small in diameter, but usable shoots are commonly harvested at a length of 8 in. (20 cm), and they are often salt pickled in the manner of other Japanese vegetables.

Sasa kurilensis 'Shimofuri'

Common synonym: *Sasa kurilensis* 'Simofuri'
Maximum height: 11 ft. (3.5 m)
Maximum diameter: ¾ in. (2 cm)
Minimum temperature: −5°F (−21°C)
Light: full shade

A distinctive and highly attractive ornamental, *Sasa kurilensis* 'Shimofuri' is similar to the type form, but its leaves are variegated with fine white stripes, giving the appearance that the variegation was applied with a brush stroke. The leaves are up to 10 in. (25 cm) long and 2 in. (5 cm) wide. 'Shimofuri' needs partial shade to look its best, and it is not well suited to hot, dry environments. This cultivar originated from the flowering of the species in Japan in the early 1970s. It was introduced into Germany and America in the 1980s as either "Simofuri" or "Shimofuri."

Sasa megalophylla

Maximum height: 6 ft. (1.8 m)
Maximum diameter: ⅓ in. (0.8 cm)
Minimum temperature: 0°F (−18°C)
Light: full shade

Broadly distributed throughout most of Japan, *Sasa megalophylla* has leaves up to 11 in. (28 cm) long and 3 ⅛ in. (8 cm) wide.

Sasa nipponica 'Nippon-Kisuji'

Maximum height: 3 ft. (1 m)
Maximum diameter: ⅛ in. (0.3 cm)
Minimum temperature: 0°F (−18°C)
Light: full shade

Sasa nipponica 'Nippon-Kisuji' is a sasa of moderate height. Its leaves roll rather than wither during dry cold weather. The leaves are striped with yellow.

Sasa oshidensis

Maximum height: 6 ft. (1.8 m)
Maximum diameter: ¼ in. (0.6 cm)
Minimum temperature: 0°F (−18°C)
Light: partial shade

A vigorously growing shrub bamboo, reportedly with greater tolerance for heat and sun than many others in the genus.

Sasa palmata

Maximum height: 7 ft. (2.1 m)
Maximum diameter: ½ in. (1.25 cm)
Minimum temperature: −5°F (−21°C)
Light: full shade

One of the largest-leaved bamboos of the genus, with leaves up to 15 in. (38 cm) long and 3½ in. (9 cm) wide, *Sasa palmata* is widely distributed in the Western world. It was introduced into England in 1889, and the United States in 1925. Potentially very invasive, the species covers vast areas of land in mountainous regions of its native Japan, growing in the wild from the country's southernmost areas to its northernmost islands. It is also found on the Korean island of Cheju-do in the south, and Russia's Sakhalin Island in the north. Although *S. palmata* is very cold hardy, its thick, pea green, leathery leaves give it a tropical appearance. Like in many *Sasa* bamboos, the leaf tips and margins show withering from winter cold. *Sasa palmata* is an aggressive runner, particularly in cool climates, where it grows tallest and is most vigorous. It is an excellent container plant. In warmer climates it needs shade to look its best.

Sasa senanensis

Maximum height: 7 ft. (2.1 m)
Maximum diameter: ½ in. (1.25 cm)
Minimum temperature: −5°F (−21°C)
Light: full shade

A hardy bamboo similar to *Sasa palmata*, *S. senanensis* can be distinguished from *S. palmata* by the hairy undersides of its leaves. *Sasa senanensis* is widely distributed in the mountainous regions of Japan, reaching as high as the lower alpine zone. It reportedly flowers frequently.

Sasa shimidzuana

Maximum height: 6 ft. (1.8 m)
Maximum diameter: ¼ in. (0.6 cm)
Minimum temperature: 0°F (−18°C)
Light: full shade

The leaves of this species are up to nearly 1 ft. (30 cm) long and 2 in. (5 cm) wide.

Sasa tsuboiana

Maximum height: 6 ft. (1.8 m)
Maximum diameter: ¼ in. (0.6 cm)
Minimum temperature: −5°F (−21°C)
Light: full shade

Native to the central and southern regions of Japan, where it reaches elevations of up to 4100 ft. (1250 m), *Sasa tsuboiana* is among the most attractive of the sasas. Its distinctively dark green, glossy leaves are up to 11 in. (28 cm) long and 2½ in. (6.3 cm) wide. Unlike *S. palmata*, this species grows in mounded clumps, and it is less invasive. It is named after Isuke Tsuboi, a Japanese bamboo cultivator.

Sasa veitchii

Common name: kumazasa
Maximum height: 5 ft. (1.5 m)
Maximum diameter: ¼ in. (0.6 cm)
Minimum temperature: 0°F (−18°C)
Light: full shade

Sasa veitchii is an unusual ornamental bamboo. The attractive dark green leaves wither at the margins as winter approaches, giving the appearance of having beige-white variegation rimming a dark green leaf. This species is somewhat smaller-leaved than many others of the genus, though its leaves still measure up to 10 in. (25 cm) long and 2¼ in. (6 cm) wide. Somewhat invasive, height and vigor can be reduced by cutting the plant to the ground in the spring.

When grown in a small container with only a few culms, the withered leaf margins may simply give the impression of an unhealthy plant. In a larger container, as a groundcover, or as a mounded shrub, however, the pseudo-variegation can be strikingly attractive, particularly in the winter months, when the landscape may be looking a bit dull. The best landscaping strategy may be cutting it to the ground in the spring, enjoying the fresh, new, green foliage through summer, and appreciating the green and beige variegated display in the winter.

Sasaella

Sasaella is similar to *Sasa*, but has smaller leaves, more upright culms, and one to three branches per node. In landscaping, because of their larger form, *Sasa* bamboos are generally employed as shrubs, while *Sasaella* bamboos serve as groundcovers as well as shrubs.

Endemic to Japan, *Sasaella* is distributed from about 31°N to 41°N latitude, centered primarily on Honshu, the main central island of Japan. *Sasaella* is not distributed nearly as far north as *Sasa*.

The genus *Sasaella* was established in 1929 to separate a group of bamboos from the catchall genus *Arundinaria*. A taxonomically problematic group, *Sasaella* once comprised some 120 species, but only a dozen or so are still regarded as valid. Because *Sasaella* flowers show very little difference in structure throughout the genus, species distinctions have largely been based on vegetative characteristics. As with *Sasa*, however, habitat and seasonal changes create significant differences within the same species of *Sasaella*, and taxonomically irrelevant vegetative differences have often been mistaken for new species. In his extensive studies of *Sasaella,* Suzuki (1978) isolated stable vegetative differences and extensively revised the genus. Once the unstable attributes were excluded, the number of species decreased dramatically, to the present dozen or so.

Sasaella bitchuensis

Maximum height: 6 ft. (1.8 m)
Maximum diameter: ⅜ in. (1 cm)
Minimum temperature: 0°F (−18°C)
Light: full shade

Native to the eastern side of Honshu, *Sasaella bitchuensis* has densely hairy culm leaf sheaths.

Sasaella hidaensis var. muraii

Maximum height: 6 ft. (1.8 m)
Maximum diameter: ¼ in. (0.6 cm)
Minimum temperature: 0°F (−18°C)
Light: partial shade

From Japan, *Sasaella hidaensis* var. *muraii* is a green-leaved groundcover with somewhat small leaves for the genus. It has an attractive form.

Sasaella masamuneana

Maximum height: 6 ft. (1.8 m)
Maximum diameter: ¼ in. (0.6 cm)
Minimum temperature: 0°F (−18°C)
Light: partial shade

The green-leaved form of the much more popular variegated forms.

Sasaella masamuneana 'Albostriata'

Maximum height: 6 ft. (1.8 m)
Maximum diameter: ¼ in. (0.6 cm)
Minimum temperature: 0°F (−18°C)
Light: partial shade

Sasaella masamuneana 'Albostriata' is an at-

Sasaella masamuneana 'Albostriata'. Author's garden.

tractive, vigorous, variegated, dwarf bamboo. The first of the glossy leathery leaves to appear are strongly variegated with cream-white striping. Later leaves may be much less variegated. 'Albostriata' benefits from an early spring trimming to refresh its foliage and emphasize the bright variegation.

Sasaella masamuneana 'Aureostriata'
Maximum height: 6 ft. (1.8 m)
Maximum diameter: ¼ in. (0.6 cm)
Minimum temperature: 0°F (−18°C)
Light: partial shade

The characteristics are similar to *Sasaella masamuneana* 'Albostriata', but the variegation is golden yellow, rather than cream-white.

Sasaella ramosa
Maximum height: 6 ft. (1.8 m)
Maximum diameter: ¼ in. (0.6 cm)
Minimum temperature: −5°F (−21°C)
Light: mostly sunny

Typically much smaller than its stated maximum height, the green-leaved *Sasaella ramosa* is generally no more than 1½ ft. (46 cm) tall. Given the right soil and climate, it is a highly aggressive and dominant runner, and must be planted with care. In the garden trade, it is one of the plants often erroneously labeled *Sasa pygmaea*.

Sasaella sasakiana
Maximum height: 10 ft. (3 m)
Maximum diameter: ⅜ in. (1 cm)
Minimum temperature: 0°F (−18°C)
Light: mostly sunny

One of the larger bamboos of the genus, *Sasaella sasakiana* has three branches at each node.

Sasaella shiobarensis
Maximum height: 6 ft. (1.8 m)
Maximum diameter: ⅓ in. (0.8 cm)
Minimum temperature: 0°F (−18°C)
Light: partial shade

A green groundcover or shrub bamboo, *Sasaella shiobarensis* is native to Japan, in northern and central Honshu.

Sasamorpha
A small genus consisting of approximately six species, *Sasamorpha* includes bamboos with large leaves and leptomorph rhizome systems. The plants are generally similar in appearance to *Sasa* bamboos, but differ in that *Sasamorpha* culms have a more erect habit and the nodes are not prominently swollen. *Sasamorpha* is distributed in Japan, Korea, and China, at a latitude range of 28°N to 44°N. Some authorities do not recognize *Sasamorpha* as a separate genus and include the group as a section or subgenus within *Sasa*.

Sasamorpha borealis
Maximum height: 6 ft. (1.8 m)
Maximum diameter: ¼ in. (0.6 cm)
Minimum temperature: −10°F (−23°C)
Light: full shade

Native to Hokkaido, one of Japan's more northerly islands, *Sasamorpha borealis* is among the more cold hardy of the sasa variants.

Schizostachyum
An Old World tropical genus with a pachymorph rhizome system, *Schizostachyum* is distributed from southern China through Southeast Asia and the Pacific Islands. Except for one known clambering species, these bamboos have culms with an erect growth habit with drooping tips. The nodes bear many short branches. The thin-walled culms are light for their size and are used for rafts, roofing, water containers, musical instruments, and numerous other craft items. There are some 45 known species.

Schizostachyum brachycladum
Maximum height: 50 ft. (15 m)
Maximum diameter: 4 in. (10 cm)
Minimum temperature: 32°F (0°C) estimated
Light: full sun

Distributed in southern China and the Asia-Pacific, the yellow-culmed forms of *Schizostachyum brachycladum* are exceptional ornamentals. Some variants have solid yellow culms. Others have green-striped culms as well as leaves with yellow striping. The short branches do not emerge until mid-culm, forming a crown for the erect, tightly clumped culms. The culms of the green form are used as cooking vessels for rice. The culms are also used for musical instruments and other handicraft.

Semiarundinaria

This genus consists of arborescent or shrublike leptomorph bamboos. Many new species were added to the genus *Semiarundinaria* between about 1925 and 1950, later to be excluded. The genus is now generally regarded as originating exclusively from Japan. *Semiarundinaria fastuosa*, the type species for the genus, has been reported growing in the wild in mainland China and Taiwan, but these may be early introductions from Japan. Some botanists regard *Semiarundinaria* as a cross between *Phyllostachys* and *Pleioblastus*.

After *Phyllostachys*, *Semiarundinaria* is the most common genus of medium-sized temperate bamboos. Though somewhat similar, the two genera can be readily distinguished. *Phyllostachys* culms have a pronounced sulcus running the full length of the internode on the branching side. *Semiarundinaria* culms are mostly round, with a partial sulcus or flattening of the internode, primarily just above the node. *Semiarundinaria* culm leaves are deciduous, though they cling slightly longer than those of *Phyllostachys*, hanging from the middle of their base before dropping completely. *Phyllostachys* culm leaves hang briefly from the edge of their base, rather than the middle, before dropping. The culm leaf sheaths of *Semiarundinaria* are harder and thicker than those of *Phyllostachys*. This genus also has three principal branches, as compared to two in *Phyllostachys*. The foliage leaves of *Semiarundinaria* are gen-

erally broader and deeper green than those of *Phyllostachys*.

Semiarundinaria fastuosa

Maximum height: 34 ft. (10 m)
Maximum diameter: 1½ in. (4 cm)
Minimum temperature: –5°F (–21°C)
Light: full sun

Long a popular ornamental bamboo, *Semiarundinaria fastuosa* is the tallest and stateliest of the genus. It is steadfastly erect, making it a good choice in narrower confines where arching culms would be intrusive. Native to Japan,

Semiarundinaria fastuosa, with the culm leaf hanging by the center of the sheath base before falling away, characteristic of the genus. Author's garden.

it is distributed in Taiwan and mainland China and was introduced into Europe in the 1890s.

When exposed to sun, the green culms and branches of this species gradually turn a brick red or purple-brown color. The culm internodes are slightly grooved just above the branches. The culms are not particularly strong, but the shoots are edible and distinctively flavored. *Semiarundinaria fastuosa* is valued in the landscape as a specimen or tall hedge. A dense screen can be achieved in narrow confines by hedging back the branches. In subsequent years, the branches ramify and produce more foliage leaves, creating a dense erect screen requiring very little depth. Under most conditions, *S. fastuosa* is not an aggressive runner. It is reportedly tolerant of high pH soils and salt air.

Semiarundinaria fastuosa var. viridis

Maximum height: 34 ft. (10 m)
Maximum diameter: 1½ in. (4 cm)
Minimum temperature: −5°F (−21°C)
Light: full sun

Similar to the type form, but the culms and branches are a more vivid dark green, and they remain so even with exposure to the sun. Even with age, the culms retain their vivid dark green color better than a typical green-culmed phyllostachys.

Semiarundinaria fortis

Maximum height: 26 ft. (8 m)
Maximum diameter: 1½ in. (4 cm)
Minimum temperature: 0°F (−18°C)
Light: full sun

The attractive *Semiarundinaria fortis* is cultivated in Europe, but is relatively rare in America. It is also relatively rare even in Japan, its country of origin.

Semiarundinaria kagamiana

Maximum height: 34 ft. (10 m)
Maximum diameter: 1½ in. (4 cm)
Minimum temperature: 0°F (−18°C)
Light: full sun

Some botanists regard *Semiarundinaria kagamiana* as a variant of *S. fastuosa*. It is native to Japan, but the specifics of its natural habitat are unknown. The culms are initially green, changing to purple tones.

Semiarundinaria makinoi

Maximum height: 16 ft. (5 m) estimated
Maximum diameter: ¾ in. (2 cm)
Minimum temperature: 0°F (−18°C)
Light: mostly sunny

Semiarundinaria makinoi is an attractive bamboo that is reportedly among the smaller of the genus. The culms are initially green, turning reddish brown with age. Some authorities indicate that it is synonymous with *S. kagamiana*, and further compounding the confusion, some authorities regard *S. kagamiana* as a variant of *S. fastuosa*. Some of the variations and conflicting information regarding characteristics of these bamboos are likely attributable to environmental factors and perhaps, in some instances, the absence of established groves.

Semiarundinaria okuboi

Common synonym: *Semiarundinaria villosa*
Maximum height: 25 ft. (7.5 m)
Maximum diameter: 1½ in. (4 cm)
Minimum temperature: 0°F (−18°C)
Light: full sun

An attractive plant, *Semiarundinaria okuboi* is one of the few large-leaved temperate-climate bamboos that thrive in heat and strong sunlight. It is also one of the few broad-leaved temperate bamboos that have a somewhat arborescent habit, and the capability of achieving significant height.

Its role in the landscape is diminished only by the propensities of its rampantly spreading rhizome system. Numerous rhizomes run fast, long, and deep. A rhizome barrier that would be easily sufficient for a much larger *Phyllosta-*

chys bamboo may not be adequate to contain *Semiarundinaria okuboi,* particularly if the soil is loose and loamy, or if the barrier depth is marginal. If its spread can be kept in bounds, *S. okuboi* is an excellent plant for the landscape. It is also an excellent container plant. Its broad leaves contrast nicely with smaller-leaved phyllostachys.

Semiarundinaria yashadake

Maximum height: 25 ft. (7.5 m)
Maximum diameter: 1½ in. (4 cm)
Minimum temperature: 0°F (−18°C)
Light: full sun

Once classified as a variety of *Semiarundinaria fastuosa, S. yashadake* has more slender culms and a less upright habit, fewer branches, and broader leaves. So far, the plants sold as *S. yashadake* in the garden trade in the United States have been significantly shorter than the indicated maximum height. The species name has its roots in the Sanskrit word *Yaksa.* In Japanese, Yasha is the name of a female demon.

Semiarundinaria yashadake f. kimmei

Maximum height: 25 ft. (7.5 m)
Maximum diameter: 1½ in. (4 cm)
Minimum temperature: 0°F (−18°C)
Light: full sun

A very attractive ornamental, similar to the type form, but the culms are yellow with a vertical green stripe on the internode. In the sun, the culms may seasonally take on pink and red tones. The dark green leaves have occasional cream-colored striping.

Shibataea

The shrublike bamboos of genus *Shibataea* have leptomorph rhizomes and unusually short branches, usually with only one to two internodes. The culm nodes have three to seven main branches, which do not further ramify. There are no secondary branches. Leaf-bearing nodes have one, or rarely two, leaves. The internodes are flattened on the branching side. In the landscape, *Shibataea* bamboos make excellent shrubs, low hedges, or tall groundcovers. Their short branches give them a look not normally associated with bamboos.

The genus consists of approximately 10 species. It is endemic to eastern China, though one species, *Shibataea kumasaca,* grows in the wild in southern Japan. The genus name is derived from the name of the Japanese botanist and bamboo researcher K. Shibata.

Shibataea chinensis

Maximum height: 2 ft. (0.6 m)
Maximum diameter: ⅛ in. (0.3 cm)
Minimum temperature: −5°F (−21°C)
Light: partial shade

Shibataea chinensis is native to China's Zhejiang, Anhui, Jiangsu, and Jiangxi Provinces, where it is cultivated as an ornamental hedge. This species is somewhat similar to *S. kumasaca,* but it is smaller and reportedly not as sensitive to alkaline conditions.

Shibataea kumasaca

Maximum height: 7 ft. (2.1 m)
Maximum diameter: ¼ in. (0.6 cm)
Minimum temperature: −5°F (−21°C)
Light: partial shade

The most widely cultivated and popular species of the genus, *Shibataea kumasaca* was introduced into Britain in 1861 and into America in 1902. This attractive plant is rather unique in appearance for a bamboo, with its squat broad leaves on short branches and compact growth habit. It prefers very acidic soil, and easily shows leaf burn if grown in alkaline or even only slightly acidic conditions. The rhizomes are relatively shallow and moderately spreading, making control easier than many of the tall shrub bamboos. It is more tame in this regard than most species of *Pleioblastus.* In a clump, the leaves generally obscure the culms,

Shibataea kumasaca. Author's garden.

and the plant is excellent material for trimming into hedges or mounds.

Shibataea kumasaca f. *albostriata*

Maximum height: 7 ft. (2.1 m)
Maximum diameter: ¼ in. (0.6 cm)
Minimum temperature: −10°F (−23°C)
Light: partial shade

Similar to the type form, but with white-striped leaves. The plants now in cultivation originated from plants collected in Japan's Aichi Prefecture in 1967.

Shibataea kumasaca f. *aureostriata*

Maximum height: 7 ft. (2.1 m)
Maximum diameter: ¼ in. (0.6 cm)

Shibataea kumasaca. The characteristic short, broad leaves on short branches are unusual for a bamboo. Author's garden.

Minimum temperature: −10°F (−23°C)
Light: partial shade

Similar to the type form, but with yellow-striped leaves. *Shibataea kumasaca* f. *aureostriata* was introduced into Germany from Japan as early as 1865.

Shibataea lancifolia

Maximum height: 7 ft. (2.1 m)
Maximum diameter: ¼ in. (0.6 cm)
Minimum temperature: −5°F (−21°C)
Light: partial shade

Distributed in the Zhejiang and Fujian Provinces of China, *Shibataea lancifolia* has much longer and narrower leaves than the more widely known *S. kumasaca.*

Sinobambusa

Somewhat resembling *Semiarundinaria, Sinobambusa* bamboos are arborescent or tall and shrublike, with leptomorph rhizomes, long slender internodes, and usually three, but occasionally five to seven, main branches. The cylindrical internodes are compressed or flattened for a distance above the node. Culm leaves are promptly deciduous, leaving a corky sheath scar that is as prominent as the supranodal ridge.

Sinobambusa bamboos are naturally distributed in the southern and southeastern provinces of China, the islands of Hainan and Taiwan, and northern Vietnam, at a latitude range of 18°N to 30°N. Naturalized introductions include Japan, India, and Hawaii. There are approximately 24 known species.

In the field, *Sinobambusa* can be distinguished from *Semiarundinaria* in that *Sinobambusa* culm leaves abscise promptly and completely, whereas those of *Semiarundinaria* cling for a time by the base of the sheath before dropping. As a group, sinobambusas are attractive bamboos, but they are less hardy than *Semiarundinaria* or *Phyllostachys.*

Sinobambusa intermedia

Maximum height: 16 ft. (5 m)
Maximum diameter: 1 in. (2.5 cm)
Minimum temperature: 10°F (−12°C)
Light: mostly sunny

The young culms of *Sinobambusa intermedia* have a pronounced, white powdery coating. At mid-culm, the internodes are up to 24 in. (60 cm) long. The foliage leaves are up to 8 in. (20 cm) long and 1 in. (2.5 cm) wide.

Sinobambusa tootsik

Common name: Chinese temple bamboo
Maximum height: 30 ft. (9 m)
Maximum diameter: 1½ in. (4 cm)
Minimum temperature: 10°F (−12°C)
Light: mostly sunny

Perhaps the most widely cultivated species of the genus, *Sinobambusa tootsik* is native to China, and it was introduced into Japan during the Tang Dynasty, more than a millennium ago. An ornamental often planted around temples and monasteries, it has slender culms, long internodes, and many secondary branches bearing attractive foliage leaves. It has a slender graceful form, with tufts of foliage. *Sinobambusa tootsik* spreads vigorously under ideal conditions, but is intolerant of dry cold winters.

Sinobambusa tootsik f. albostriata

Maximum height: 30 ft. (9 m)
Maximum diameter: 1½ in. (4 cm)
Minimum temperature: 10°F (−12°C)
Light: mostly sunny

Similar to the type form, but with strongly variegated, cream-colored striping on the foliage leaves.

Thamnocalamus

Indigenous to the Himalayas and Africa, *Thamnocalamus* is a genus of relatively hardy bamboos with pachymorph rhizome systems. The identity and taxonomy of many of the clumping mountain bamboos—including *Thamnocalamus*, *Drepanostachyum*, and *Himalayacalamus*—has been problematic. While it is unlikely that the rugged *T. tessellatus* of South Africa would be confused with the delicate clumping bamboos of the Himalayas, other species, such as *T. spathiflorus*, have a more delicate appearance. *Thamnocalamus* can be distinguished from *Drepanostachyum* and *Himalayacalamus* by the presence of distinct leaf tessellation and by branch buds that are much taller than they are wide. The culm leaf blades of *Thamnocalamus* bamboos are generally erect rather than reflexed (bent backward).

Thamnocalamus spathiflorus

Common synonym: *Thamnocalamus aristatus*
Maximum height: 20 ft. (6 m)
Maximum diameter: ¾ in. (2 cm)
Minimum temperature: 5°F (−15°C)
Light: partial shade

A very attractive ornamental, *Thamnocalamus spathiflorus* is native to Nepal, Bhutan, and northwestern India. The name *T. aristatus* was given to a bamboo from the same area, and appears to be identical to the species given the name *T. spathiflorus* some 30 years earlier (Chris Stapleton, personal communication). Thus, the name *T. aristatus* is unnecessary, and bamboos identified as such should be renamed *T. spathiflorus*. The plants in circulation in the United States that have been called *T. aristatus* may be the more delicate variety of the species, *T. spathiflorus* var. *crassinodus*. *Thamnocalamus spathiflorus* is a polymorphic species, and its various subspecies and varieties are associated with specific geographic regions.

Although some reports indicate that the culms are brittle and not widely used, other reports indicate that they are strong and used for a variety of purposes, including fishing poles, mats, and baskets. The swollen nodes, however, make them less desirable for weaving than the culms of *Himalayacalamus* species, which if available, are harvested in their stead.

In the United States, some of the bamboos

Thamnocalamus spathiflorus, showing the upright culm leaf blades and swollen nodes.
Bamboo Sourcery.

sold as *Thamnocalamus spathiflorus* were misidentified and are likely *Fargesia murielae*. The confusion arose as a result of T. R. Soderstrom's efforts to change the name of *F. murielae* to *T. spathaceus*. As far as is known, the erroneously identified plants flowered gregariously in the 1990s, late in the flowering cycle with other *F. murielae* plants. Unlike those of *F. murielae,* the culm leaf blades of *Thamnocalamus spathiflorus* are upright, not reflexed (bent backward).

Thamnocalamus spathiflorus var. *crassinodus*

Common synonym: *Fargesia crassinoda*
Maximum height: 18 ft. (5.5 m)
Maximum diameter: ¾ in. (2 cm)
Minimum temperature: 5°F (−15°C)
Light: partial shade

Thamnocalamus spathiflorus var. *crassinodus* is distinguished from the principal form by its smaller leaves and more strongly swollen culm nodes. It is a delicate and attractive ornamental. As mentioned above, plants in circulation in the United States under the name *T. aristatus* may be *T. spathiflorus* var. *crassinodus*. As of this writing, a definitive assessment has not yet been made.

Thamnocalamus tessellatus

Common name: bergbamboes
Maximum height: 20 ft. (6 m)
Maximum diameter: 1¼ in. (3.2 cm)
Minimum temperature: 0°F (−18°C)
Light: mostly sunny

The only bamboo indigenous to South Africa, *Thamnocalamus tessellatus* grows in many areas of the country, sometimes covering vast areas of land. It is known by the Afrikaans name, bergbamboes. A South African mountain, Bamboesberg, is named after the bamboo that covers it. This mountain bamboo grows in open clumps, up to 10 ft. (3 m) tall in dry areas and 20 ft. (6 m) tall in moister areas. At one time, the culms were used in Zulu shields, and forest peoples used them for the shafts of arrows and spears. The culm and branch leaves are a striking bright, creamy white in the first season, but they persist and can look a bit dingy and tattered in subsequent seasons. The culms turn a deep green. If exposed to strong sunlight, they take on purple tones.

Thyrsostachys

Thyrsostachys is a genus of Old World tropical bamboos with slender erect culms, persistent culm leaves, and a pachymorph rhizome system. The foliage leaves are much smaller and delicate than is typical for tropical bamboos. There are two known species.

Thyrsostachys oliveri

Maximum height: 82 ft. (25 m)
Maximum diameter: 2½ in. (6.3 cm)
Minimum temperature: 25°F (−4°C)
Light: full sun

Native to Burma and northern Thailand,

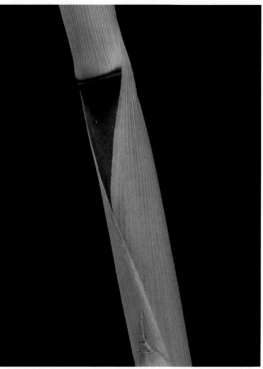

Thamnocalamus tessellatus, displaying the striking white culm leaves on a new culm. Author's garden.

Thamnocalamus tessellatus. Quail Botanical Gardens.

Thyrsostachys oliveri. Quail Botanical Gardens.

and cultivated in the Chinese provinces of Yunnan and Guangdong, *Thyrsostachys oliveri* is an attractive ornamental with towering upright culms and tufts of foliage. The culms are used for poles, construction, and handicrafts, and the new shoots are suitable for the table.

Thyrsostachys siamensis

Maximum height: 40 ft. (12 m)
Maximum diameter: 3 in. (7.5 cm)
Minimum temperature: 25°F (–4°C)
Light: full sun

Thyrsostachys siamensis is native to Thailand and Burma and cultivated in Yunnan Province. The foliage leaves are exceptionally delicate and slender, particularly for a tropical bamboo. The culms are thick walled but very slender. They have a variety of uses, such as fishing poles, for tools and construction, and as a source for paper pulp. This species, however, is more commonly planted as an ornamental.

Yushania

Yushania is a genus of shrublike mountain bamboos with pachymorph rhizomes. Because some of the rhizome necks are exceptionally elongated, these bamboos do not form a dense clump, but exhibit a spreading habit. *Yushania* plants have rhizomes of varying neck lengths. New rhizomes arising from the lower buds closer to the rhizome neck have long, rootless rhizome necks that may be more than a foot (30 cm) long. New rhizomes arising from the upper buds closer to the culm have shorter rhizome necks. In succeeding years, this growth habit produces small clumps spaced apart from other small clumps.

Yushania species have been previously placed in various other genera, including *Arundinaria*. Nomenclature remains less than clear, and the same plant may carry multiple species names. At present, there are some 84 known species of *Yushania*.

Ranging in elevation from 6000 to 12,000 ft. (1800 to 3700 m), *Yushania* consists of temperate-climate, moderately hardy bamboos with tessellated leaves. They can be distinguished from other montane genera growing in the same general area in that their culms are less prominently ridged than those of *Borinda*, and their branches are fewer and more upright. Whereas the young culms of *Thamnocalamus* are always smooth below the nodes, *Yushania* culms are usually rough. In their native environments, *Yushania* bamboos may form dense thickets that can prohibit trees or other vegetation from regenerating. The plants are often browsed heavily by livestock and other animals, and so their maximum height may seldom be achieved in natural environments.

Yushania alpina

Common synonym: *Arundinaria alpina*
Common name: African alpine bamboo
Maximum height: 55 ft. (17 m)
Maximum diameter: 5 in. (13 cm)
Minimum temperature: 25°F (–4°C)
Light: full sun

Previously known as *Arundinaria alpina*, *Yushania alpina* is found at elevations of 8000 to 10,000 ft. (2400 to 3000 m) in its native habitat in equatorial Africa. In the 1940s and 1950s, much of the bamboo forest land was cleared to plant fast-growing, exotic, softwood trees. In spite of the loss, this species still covers some 385,000 acres (156,000 hectares) of land in Kenya. It is Kenya's only bamboo, and *Y. alpina* forests are a habitat for elephants and buffalo, as well as a food source for monkeys. The culms are used by the local peoples for water pipes, furniture, weaving, crafts, and construction.

Yushania anceps

Common synonyms: *Arundinaria anceps*,
    A. jaunsarensis, *Yushania jaunsarensis*
Maximum height: 12 ft. (4 m)
Maximum diameter: ¾ in. (2 cm)

Thyrsostachys siamensis, small clump. Quail Botanical Gardens.

Yushania anceps. Bamboo Sourcery.

Minimum temperature: 10°F (−12°C)
Light: partial shade

Native to India, and introduced into Britain in 1865, *Yushania anceps* is the most well known example of the genus in the Western world. In *The Bamboo Garden*, published in 1896, A. B. Freeman-Mitford recounts that *Arundinaria anceps* was found at an estate sale of a deceased nurseryman, with no records to indicate its origin. Of its naming, the author stated, "Its nationality being uncertain, and the species showing no one conspicuous feature by which it may specially be recognized, and which would lead to the choice of a descriptive name, —though it is obviously as a whole perfectly distinct, —I have ventured to name it Anceps, the 'Doubtful' Arundinaria." Later that same year, native Indian plants were given the name, *A. jaunsarensis*. Since "anceps" was the earliest naming, it has taxonomic precedence. The change in genus name from *Arundinaria* to *Yushania* came in 1974.

In its native India, *Yushania anceps* is distributed primarily in cool temperate to subalpine climate zones. At one time, this species reportedly formed dense undergrowth covering more than 50 square miles (130 square kilometers) in one area of India. The culms are traditionally used to weave baskets and mats.

Yushania anceps 'Pitt White'

Maximum height: 30 ft. (9 m)
Maximum diameter: 1¾ in. (4.4 cm)
Minimum temperature: 10°F (−12°C)
Light: partial shade

A much larger cultivar of *Yushania anceps*, from the gardens at Pitt White in Dorset, England.

Yushania chungii

Maximum height: 10 ft. (3 m)
Maximum diameter: ½ in. (1.25 cm)
Minimum temperature: −4°F (−20°C)
Light: mostly sunny

Among the hardiest of the genus, *Yushania chungii* is native to China's Sichuan Province, in a wide elevation range from 5900 to 12,500 ft. (1800 to 3800 m). The native habitat of this attractive shrub bamboo encompasses a broad spectrum, from riverbanks and valley floors to steep slopes and various spruce, pine, oak, and beech forests. Although widespread in pine forests where soils are typically acidic, it is also reportedly tolerant of alkaline soils. Frequently an understory shrub, *Y. chungii* grows even more vigorously in openings in the forest canopy. It is a major food source for the giant panda.

Yushania maculata

Maximum height: 11 ft. (3.5 m)
Maximum diameter: ⅝ in. (1.5 cm)
Minimum temperature: 0°F (−18°C) estimated
Light: mostly sunny

Yushania maculata is native to Sichuan and Yunnan Provinces, at an elevation range of 5900 to 11,500 ft. (1800 to 3500 m). In Yunnan, it is found as an understory plant in pine forests. It shoots in late summer in its native habitats.

Yushania maling

Common synonym: *Arundinaria maling*
Maximum height: 15 ft. (4.5 m)
Maximum diameter: 2 in. (5 cm)
Minimum temperature: 5°F (−15°C)
Light: mostly sunny

The most common temperate bamboo in eastern Nepal, *Yushania maling* is also native to Sikkim, West Bengal, and western Bhutan. It is often a dominant plant in the forest understory, forming dense thickets. The shoots are suitable for the table. The leaves are used for animal fodder. Although not ideal, the culms are sometimes used to make baskets and fences.

Yushania maling. Quail Botanical Gardens.

Bamboos for Special Situations

THE FOLLOWING LISTS may help you find bamboo selections to meet your gardening and landscaping requirements. The lists are far from exclusive. Many other bamboos, some less commonly available, may also work as well or even better for your particular needs. Treat these lists as a point of departure rather than a point of conclusion.

Let us say you want a bamboo that is suitable for full shade. Those listed here are possibilities, but you should then look further in chapter 9, in the entries for the genus as well as the particular species, for more detailed information. For example, both *Fargesia murielae* and *Pleioblastus viridistriatus* are listed as bamboos for full shade, but *F. murielae* grows poorly, if at all, in warm soils and hot climates, and it curls its leaves in bright, hot sun. *Fargesia murielae* is a tall bushy shrub with broadly arching culms and delicate foliage. It can reach a height of 15 ft. (4.5 m). *Pleioblastus viridistriatus* is usually grown as a groundcover. It needs shade to maintain the distinctive chartreuse leaf variegation. Although both species are recommended for full shade, other cultural requirements are not the same, and they fulfill very different landscaping needs.

Use these lists as a quick guide, then explore further to find the bamboos that are right for you and your garden.

Tropical and Subtropical Bamboos

TIMBER BAMBOOS
Bambusa dolichoclada 'Stripe'
Bambusa lako
Bambusa membranacea
Bambusa oldhamii
Bambusa tulda
Bambusa vulgaris
Bambusa vulgaris 'Vittata'
Dendrocalamus asper
Dendrocalamus brandisii
Dendrocalamus giganteus

Dendrocalamus hamiltonii
Dendrocalamus latiflorus
Gigantochloa apus
Gigantochloa atroviolacea
Gigantochloa pseudoarundinacea
Guadua angustifolia
Thyrsostachys oliveri

MEDIUM-SIZED BAMBOOS
Bambusa beecheyana
Bambusa malingensis

Bambusa multiplex (most forms)
Bambusa pachinensis
Bambusa textilis
Gigantochloa albociliata

SMALL-SIZED BAMBOOS
Bambusa multiplex 'Fernleaf'
Bambusa multiplex var. *riviereorum*
Bambusa multiplex 'Stripestem Fernleaf'

Bambusa vulgaris 'Wamin'
Otatea acuminata ssp. *acuminata*
Otatea acuminata ssp. *aztecorum*

DWARF BAMBOOS
Raddia brasiliensis
Raddia distichophylla

Temperate-Climate Bamboos
TIMBER BAMBOOS
Phyllostachys bambusoides
Phyllostachys heterocycla f. *pubescens*
Phyllostachys makinoi
Phyllostachys nigra var. *henonis*
Phyllostachys viridis
Phyllostachys viridis 'Robert Young'
Phyllostachys vivax
Phyllostachys vivax f. *aureocaulis*

MEDIUM-SIZED BAMBOOS
Chusquea aff. *culeou*
Phyllostachys angusta
Phyllostachys atrovaginata
Phyllostachys aurea (all forms)
Phyllostachys aureosulcata (all forms)
Phyllostachys bissetii
Phyllostachys decora
Phyllostachys heteroclada
Phyllostachys nidularia
Phyllostachys nigra
Phyllostachys nuda
Phyllostachys platyglossa
Phyllostachys praecox
Phyllostachys propinqua
Phyllostachys violascens
Phyllostachys viridiglaucescens
Semiarundinaria fastuosa
Semiarundinaria fastuosa var. *viridis*
Semiarundinaria fortis

SMALL-SIZED BAMBOOS
Chusquea culeou
Chusquea culeou 'Caña Prieta'
Fargesia murielae

Fargesia nitida (all forms)
Fargesia robusta
Fargesia utilis
Hibanobambusa tranquillans 'Shiroshima'
Phyllostachys humilis
Pseudosasa japonica
Qiongzhuea tumidissinoda
Semiarundinaria makinoi
Thamnocalamus spathiflorus
Thamnocalamus spathiflorus var. *crassinodus*

SHRUB BAMBOOS
Indocalamus latifolius
Indocalamus longiauritus
Indocalamus tessellatus
Pleioblastus shibuyanus 'Tsuboi'
Sasa kurilensis 'Shimofuri'
Sasa palmata
Sasa tsuboiana
Sasaella masamuneana 'Albostriata'
Shibataea kumasaca
Yushania chungii

GROUNDCOVER BAMBOOS
Pleioblastus akebono
Pleioblastus argenteostriatus
Pleioblastus chino 'Murakamianus'
Pleioblastus chino var. *vaginatus* f. *variegatus*
Pleioblastus fortunei
Pleioblastus humilis
Pleioblastus pygmaeus
Pleioblastus pygmaeus var. *distichus*
Pleioblastus shibuyanus 'Tsuboi'
Pleioblastus viridistriatus
Pleioblastus viridistriatus f. *chrysophyllus*
Sasa veitchii
Sasaella masamuneana 'Albostriata'

Temperate-Climate Clumping Bamboos
Borinda boliana

Chusquea culeou
Chusquea culeou 'Caña Prieta'
Fargesia dracocephala
Fargesia murielae
Fargesia nitida
Fargesia robusta
Fargesia utilis
Thamnocalamus spathiflorus
Thamnocalamus spathiflorus var. *crassinodus*
Thamnocalamus tessellatus

Exceptionally Cold Hardy Bamboos
Fargesia dracocephala
Fargesia murielae
Fargesia nitida
Indocalamus tessellatus
Phyllostachys atrovaginata
Phyllostachys aureosulcata (all forms)
Phyllostachys bissetii
Phyllostachys decora
Phyllostachys nuda
Phyllostachys propinqua
Phyllostachys rubromarginata
Phyllostachys vivax
Sasa kurilensis
Sasa kurilensis 'Shimofuri'
Sasa palmata
Semiarundinaria fastuosa
Semiarundinaria fastuosa var. *viridis*
Shibataea kumasaca

Bamboos for Full Shade
Fargesia murielae
Fargesia nitida
Indocalamus latifolius
Indocalamus tessellatus
Pleioblastus akebono
Pleioblastus viridistriatus
Pleioblastus viridistriatus f. *chrysophyllus*
Sasa kurilensis
Sasa kurilensis 'Shimofuri'
Sasa palmata
Sasa tsuboiana
Sasa veitchii

Variegated Bamboos

Bambusa multiplex 'Silverstripe'
Hibanobambusa tranquillans 'Shiroshima'
Pleioblastus akebono
Pleioblastus argenteostriatus
Pleioblastus chino 'Murakami-anus'
Pleioblastus chino var. *vaginatus* f. *variegatus*
Pleioblastus fortunei
Pleioblastus shibuyanus 'Tsuboi'
Pleioblastus viridistriatus
Pleioblastus viridistriatus f. *chrysophyllus*
Sasa kurilensis 'Shimofuri'
Sasaella masamuneana 'Albostriata'
Sinobambusa tootsik f. *albostriata*

Bamboos for Houseplants

Bambusa multiplex (all forms)
Bambusa tuldoides 'Ventricosa'
Bambusa vulgaris 'Vittata'
Borinda fungosa
Chusquea coronalis
Chusquea cumingii
Chusquea pittieri
Chusquea tomentosa
Otatea acuminata ssp. *aztecorum*
Pleioblastus fortunei
Pleioblastus pygmaeus
Pleioblastus pygmaeus var. *distichus*
Pleioblastus viridistriatus
Pleioblastus viridistriatus f. *chrysophyllus*
Raddia distichophylla
Sasaella masamuneana 'Albostriata'
Yushania anceps

Bamboos for Bonsai

Bambusa multiplex var. *riviereorum*
Bambusa multiplex 'Tiny Fern'
Bambusa tuldoides 'Ventricosa'
Chimonobambusa marmorea
Chimonobambusa marmorea f. *variegata*

Pleioblastus akebono
Pleioblastus chino f. *elegantissimus*
Pleioblastus chino var. *vaginatus* f. *variegatus*
Pleioblastus fortunei
Pleioblastus gramineus
Pleioblastus pygmaeus var. *distichus*
Pleioblastus shibuyanus 'Tsuboi'
Pseudosasa owatarii

Bamboos for Borders and Low Hedges

Bambusa multiplex var. *riviereorum*
Phyllostachys humilis
Pleioblastus chino
Pleioblastus chino var. *vaginatus* f. *variegatus*
Pleioblastus fortunei
Pleioblastus pygmaeus
Pleioblastus pygmaeus var. *distichus*
Pleioblastus shibuyanus 'Tsuboi'
Sasaella masamuneana 'Albostriata'
Shibataea kumasaca

Bamboos for Tall Hedges and Screens

Bambusa multiplex (most forms)
Bambusa textilis
Gigantochloa hasskarliana
Hibanobambusa tranquillans 'Shiroshima'
Phyllostachys angusta
Phyllostachys atrovaginata
Phyllostachys aurea (all forms)
Phyllostachys aureosulcata
Phyllostachys bambusoides 'Allgold'
Phyllostachys bambusoides f. *castillonis*
Phyllostachys bambusoides f. *kawadana*
Phyllostachys bissetii
Phyllostachys decora
Phyllostachys heteroclada
Phyllostachys humilis

Phyllostachys nidularia
Phyllostachys nigra
Phyllostachys nuda
Phyllostachys platyglossa
Phyllostachys violascens
Phyllostachys viridiglaucescens
Pleioblastus simonii
Pseudosasa japonica
Semiarundinaria fastuosa
Semiarundinaria fastuosa var. *viridis*

Bamboos for Screens Two-Stories or Higher

Bambusa blumeana
Bambusa oldhamii
Bambusa textilis
Dendrocalamus asper
Dendrocalamus giganteus
Dendrocalamus latiflorus
Phyllostachys aureosulcata
Phyllostachys bambusoides
Phyllostachys bambusoides 'Allgold'
Phyllostachys bambusoides f. *castillonis*
Phyllostachys bambusoides f. *kawadana*
Phyllostachys makinoi
Phyllostachys nigra 'Bory'
Phyllostachys nigra var. *henonis*
Phyllostachys nigra 'Megurochiku'
Phyllostachys viridiglaucescens
Phyllostachys viridis (all forms)
Phyllostachys vivax
Phyllostachys vivax f. *aureocaulis*

Bamboos for Edible Shoots

Bambusa beecheyana
Bambusa blumeana
Bambusa longispiculata
Bambusa membranacea
Bambusa odashimae
Bambusa oldhamii
Chimonobambusa quadrangularis
Dendrocalamus asper
Dendrocalamus brandisii
Dendrocalamus giganteus

Dendrocalamus hamiltonii
Dendrocalamus latiflorus
Gigantochloa albociliata
Phyllostachys atrovaginata
Phyllostachys aureosulcata
Phyllostachys dulcis
Phyllostachys glauca
Phyllostachys heterocycla f. *pubescens*
Phyllostachys iridescens
Phyllostachys nidularia
Phyllostachys nuda
Phyllostachys platyglossa
Phyllostachys praecox
Phyllostachys propinqua
Phyllostachys rubromarginata
Phyllostachys viridiglaucescens
Phyllostachys viridis (all forms)
Phyllostachys vivax
Qiongzhuea tumidissinoda

Bamboos for Culm Wood

Bambusa burmanica
Bambusa dissimulator
Bambusa membranacea
Bambusa nutans
Bambusa textilis
Dendrocalamus asper
Dendrocalamus giganteus
Gigantochloa atroviolacea
Guadua angustifolia
Phyllostachys angusta
Phyllostachys bambusoides
Phyllostachys heterocycla f. *pubescens*
Phyllostachys makinoi

Phyllostachys meyeri
Phyllostachys nigra
Phyllostachys nigra 'Bory'
Phyllostachys nigra var. *henonis*
Phyllostachys propinqua
Phyllostachys rubromarginata
Phyllostachys viridiglaucescens
Phyllostachys viridis (all forms)

Bamboos for Erosion Control

Arundinaria gigantea ssp. *gigantea*
Arundinaria gigantea ssp. *tecta*
Bashania fargesii
Chimonobambusa marmorea
Phyllostachys aurea
Phyllostachys bissetii
Phyllostachys humilis
Pleioblastus chino (all forms)
Pleioblastus humilis
Pleioblastus pygmaeus
Sasa palmata
Sasaella masamuneana
Sasaella masamuneana 'Albostriata'
Sasaella ramosa
Semiarundinaria okuboi

Bamboos Tolerant of Alkaline Soils

Chusquea cumingii
Otatea acuminata ssp. *aztecorum*
Phyllostachys decora
Phyllostachys flexuosa
Phyllostachys glauca

Semiarundinaria fastuosa
Yushania chungii

Bamboos Tolerant of Water-Saturated Soils

Chusquea culeou 'Caña Prieta'
Chusquea uliginosa
Phyllostachys atrovaginata
Phyllostachys heteroclada
Phyllostachys nidularia

Bamboos Tolerant of Salt Air

Bambusa malingensis
Chusquea culeou
Chusquea culeou 'Caña Prieta'
Pleioblastus gramineus
Pleioblastus hindsii
Pleioblastus linearis
Pleioblastus simonii
Pseudosasa japonica
Semiarundinaria fastuosa
Semiarundinaria okuboi
Semiarundinaria yashadake

Mite-Resistant Bamboos

Bashania fargesii
Phyllostachys heterocycla f. *pubescens* (somewhat resistant)
Pleioblastus fortunei
Pleioblastus viridistriatus
Pleioblastus viridistriatus f. *chrysophyllus*
Semiarundinaria okuboi
Shibataea kumasaca

Botanical Gardens

IN THE UNITED STATES, bamboos are still regarded as rather unusual and problematic plants, and more often than not, they are absent from private and public gardens. Yet, many public gardens throughout the country do include bamboos, particularly, though not exclusively, gardens in southern and coastal regions. Exploring the gardens in your area may offer an excellent opportunity to view established stands of bamboo.

Many of the photographs in this book were taken at Quail Botanical Gardens and at Hakone Gardens. I want to extend my thanks for the assistance of these gardens in facilitating my photography.

Quail Botanical Gardens in southern California offers magnificent specimen clumps of tropical and subtropical bamboos, New World and Old World montane bamboos, and groves of selected temperate-climate bamboos. The American Bamboo Society was founded with the assistance of Quail Botanical Gardens, and the society's first quarantine greenhouse was located there. The greenhouse again made it possible to bring new bamboos to the United States. Quail Botanical Gardens has played a significant role in the rebirth of American bamboo culture. With a climate amenable to an exceptionally broad range of bamboos, the garden is an essential visit for any bamboo aficionado.

Quail Botanical Gardens
230 Quail Botanical Gardens Drive
Encinitas, California 92024
www.qbgardens.com

A traditional Japanese garden, Hakone Gardens contains almost exclusively temperate-climate bamboo species, and they are an integral part of the landscaping. The core of the garden was established in 1918. In 1987, construction began on a new garden devoted exclusively to bamboo and stone. For those captivated by bamboo and traditional Japanese landscaping, it is an excellent visit.

Hakone Gardens
21000 Big Basin Way
Saratoga, California 95070
www.hakone.com

Glossary

Adventitious: Occurring from an unusual or unexpected location. In the context of bamboos, the root system is adventitious, in that the roots do not primarily arise from a primordial root, but rather at the nodes of rhizomes and culms. In *Chusquea,* branch buds are adventitious, in that they arise in multiples independent of the typical location.

Aerial root: A root growing above ground level. Some bamboos have a tendency to produce aerial roots at their culm and branch nodes.

Albino: All white; lacking chlorophyll. An albino seedling will grow for a time, nourished by the nutrients stored in the seed, but without any food-producing mechanism, its demise is a certainty.

Amphimorph: A rhizome system that includes both pachymorph and leptomorph rhizomes. Amphimorph rhizome systems are rare among bamboos, and so far, have been confirmed in only three species: *Aulonemia fulgor, Chusquea fendleri,* and *C. scandens.* See also *leptomorph, pachymorph.*

Amphipodial: Strictly speaking, the term refers to plants with both a sympodial and monopodial branching habit. For example, *Shibataea kumasaca* has monopodial rhizomes and sympodial (tillering) culms. Amphipodial is often erroneously used in reference to rhizome type rather than branching habit. See also *amphimorph, leptomorph, monopodial, pachymorph, sympodial.*

Apical meristem: A group of actively dividing, undifferentiated cells at the growing tip of a stem or root. In bamboos, the sheath cells are the first to become differentiated at the growing tip.

Arborescent: Having the form and characteristics of a tree; treelike. The large timber bamboos are arborescent.

Auricle: The ear-like flaps that extend from the upper part of a sheath on both sides of the blade. Depending on the species, auricles may be prominent or entirely lacking. Regardless of species, auricles are entirely absent from rhizome sheaths.

Axis: A central stem along which plant parts are arrayed.

380

Bamboos: Grasses of the subfamily Bambusoideae. The woody species of the subfamily belong to the tribe Bambuseae. The herbaceous species belong to the tribe Olyreae.

Blade: The part of the leaf that is typically flat and green and is dedicated to photosynthetic activity. It may be prominent, reduced, modified, or absent, depending on the function and type of leaf.

Bract: A modified, protective leaf, such as is found within or just below the flowering parts of plants. In bamboo, the modified, sometimes scalelike leaves that protect the rhizomes, or those that protect new buds, may be called bracts.

Branch complement: A branch or bud grouping at a node. The number of branches in the complement and the nature of their array are identifying characteristics for bamboo.

Bud: A small, dormant protuberance on a stem or branch, from which a shoot, leaf, or flower may arise. In bamboo, the buds on rhizomes can produce a culm or other rhizomes. Buds on culms and branches can produce branches or leaves.

Bud complement: See *branch complement.*

Bulliform cells: Large cells in the epidermis of the leaf that collapse during water stress, causing the leaves to curl or roll tightly into the shape of needles, thus reducing the leaf surface area to a minimum.

Caespitose: Tightly grouped or clumped. Bamboos with short-necked, pachymorph rhizome systems have a caespitose habit. See also *diffuse, pluricaespitose.*

Caryopsis: Typically a hard, dry, one-seeded fruit that does not open; the characteristic seed of grasses. A cereal grain is a familiar example of a caryopsis.

Cilia: Small, fine hairs along the margin of a structure, usually forming a fringe.

Clade: An evolutionary group or lineage descended from a common ancestor.

Cladistics: An analytical methodology that focuses on the branching of lineages to determine evolutionary history, and on taxonomic groupings reflecting evolutionary lineage.

Cladogram: A branching diagram that depicts evolutionary lineages.

Clumping: See *caespitose.*

Conspecific: Of or belonging to the same species.

Coriaceous: Leathery and tough.

Cotyledon: A seed leaf. It may remain within the seed coat or emerge during germination and turn green. Monocots have a single seed leaf; dicots have a pair of seed leaves.

Culm: An aboveground stem on a grass plant. The term is commonly associated with bamboo. Relative to other grass plants, the culms of most bamboos are very large and woody.

Culm leaf: A large, overlapping leaf that encases an emerging culm, protecting it and providing temporary support while it lignifies. The sheath portion of the culm leaf is far larger than the blade. In common terminology, and in earlier technical literature, the culm leaf is sometimes called the "culm sheath." See also *foliage leaf.*

Culm sheath: See *culm leaf.*

Deciduous: Shedding or falling away at a specific season or period of growth. Culm leaves, for example, may be deciduous or may be persistent. See also *persistent.*

Dicot: Dicotyledon; a plant with a pair of cotyledons (seed leaves) in the seed. Dicots include trees and shrubs. Bamboos and other grasses are monocots. See also *monocot.*

Diffuse: Widely spaced; culms arising singly rather than in groups. This habit is associated with so-called running bamboos. It is also commonly and erroneously associated solely with bamboos that have leptomorph rhizome systems, but bamboos with long-necked pachymorph rhizomes may also have a diffuse habit. See also *caespitose, pluricaespitose.*

Extravaginal branching: New branches burst through the culm leaf near its base. This type of branching is characteristic of some *Chusquea* bamboos. See also *infravaginal branching, intravaginal branching.*

Fimbriae: Bristly, fringelike hairs that extend from the margins of the leaf sheath, usually from the auricles; also called oral setae. They range from prominent to entirely lacking, depending on the species.

Foliage leaf: The type of leaf that is responsible for nearly all of the bamboo plant's photosynthetic activity. To this end, the blade is the predominant part of the foliage leaf, whereas the sheath is typically much smaller and is scarcely apparent on casual observation. See also *culm leaf.*

Gregarious flowering: The simultaneous flowering of a given generation of bamboo. The flowering is termed gregarious when most or all of the same bamboo generation begin flowering.

Herbaceous: Not woody; having no persistent aerial parts. Virtually all of our familiar bamboos are woody, but many less well-known bamboo species are herbaceous. See also *woody.*

Infravaginal branching: Similar to extravaginal branching, except that the branches emerge horizontally or downward, breaking through at the base of the culm leaf sheath where it attaches to the culm. This type of branching is known only in the New World in some *Chusquea* species, and in the Old World in *Dinochloa* and *Nastus.* See also *extravaginal branching, intravaginal branching.*

Inflorescence: A flower cluster. Inflorescences have distinctive characteristics that help define genera, and in spite of other tools now available, they continue to play an important role in bamboo taxonomy.

Internode: The part of the culm between two nodes.

Intravaginal branching: New branches emerge through the mouth of the culm leaf, rather than bursting through it. The emerging branches push the culm leaf away from the culm, if the culm leaf has not already shed. This type of branching is characteristic of many bamboos, including *Phyllostachys.* See also *extravaginal branching, infravaginal branching.*

In vitro: Literally, "in glass"; used in reference to biological processes that are reproduced in a culture vessel or plate. In the context of bamboo, *in vitro* techniques are used to induce and study flowering, as well as for experimental and commercial propagation.

Lanceolate: Shaped like the head of a lance; much longer than wide, tapering at both ends.

Leaf: The primary photosynthetic organ. Most, but not all, leaves have a photosynthetic function. In the context of bamboos and other grasses, the sheath and blade are the primary parts of the leaf. All bamboos and other grasses have foliage leaves; woody bamboos have culm leaves as well. See also *culm leaf, foliage leaf.*

Leptomorph: A type of rhizome that typically runs laterally and does not turn upward to become a culm—although a leptomorph rhizome can under some circumstances become a culm. A leptomorph rhizome is usually hollow and smaller in diameter than the culms that originate from it. The rhizome neck is always short. Internodes are longer than wide. Nodes are sometimes prominent. Buds are arranged horizontally. Most buds remain dormant, but those that germinate may produce either culms or new rhizomes. Bamboo species with leptomorph rhizome systems are commonly associated with running bamboos. See also *amphimorph, pachymorph.*

Ligule: A small, tongue-like extension behind the sheath blade that extends upward from the tip of the sheath proper. Depending on the species, the ligule ranges from prominent to inconspicuous. The ligule helps keep moisture away from the newly forming culms and branches and prevents moisture from running down the culm or branch and collecting at the node. Woody bamboos, unlike herbaceous bamboos, also have an outer ligule, but it is always much smaller and is usually nearly invisible.

Lodicules: Small, scalelike flaps at the base of grass flowers, thought to be vestiges of petals or sepals.

Micropropagation: The culturing of cells from various parts of a plant in a specialized medium. Nutrients and hormones are manipulated so that the test tube–grown cultures differentiate into roots and shoots, and ultimately a complete plant that can be grown in soil.

Monocarpic: Flowering once, and then dying. Monocarpy is widespread among woody bamboos. Most pachymorph bamboos that are subject to gregarious flowering are monocarpic. As a group, leptomorph bamboos are more likely to survive gregarious flowering, but are typically severely weakened, and monocarpy occurs with some frequency as well.

Monocot: Monocotyledon; a plant with only a single cotyledon (seed leaf) in the seed. Bamboos, like other grasses, are monocots. See also *dicot.*

Monophyletic: A group of taxa that all descend from a common ancestor. See also *polyphyletic.*

Monopodial: A branching habit in which a single dominant stem, or axis, gives rise to secondary branches, or axes. The term was originally derived to describe rhizome branching habit. In monopodial rhizomes, each rhizome runs laterally, usually without turning upward to become a culm, and gives rise to secondary axes that either turn upward to become culms or constitute new, laterally running rhizomes that will, in turn, give rise to secondary axes of their own. Although it describes only the branching habit, exclusive of other structural characteristics, the term is loosely synonymous with leptomorph when applied to rhizomes—at least, one frequently encounters it as such in the literature. See also *amphipodial, sympodial.*

Montane: Of, or growing in, mountainous areas.

Morphology: The study of the form and structure of organisms, as opposed to the study of their functions.

Multicaespitose: See *pluricaespitose.*

Neck: Usually associated with the rhizome, the neck is a structural element of every segmented axis of the bamboo plant, including the culm, branches, and rhizome. Structurally, the neck permits creation of a new and larger axis. The highly compressed stacking of progressively larger internodes can create a new axis much larger than the axis from which it originated. This is well illustrated by the rhizomes and culms of lep-tomorph timber bamboos. The rhizomes are proportionally much smaller in diameter than the culms (new axes) they generate. The highly compressed internodes of the neck progressively increase in diameter to form the base of the culm.

Nectary: A gland associated with flowers that secretes nectar to attract insects. Most bamboos are wind pollinated, and so the flowers have no nectaries.

Nodal diaphragm: The portion of the node that separates the hollow internodes—in most bamboos, the internodes are hollow and the nodes are always solid.

Node: The point on a culm, branch, or other axis where leaves, shoots, branches, roots, or flowers are attached. In the context of bamboo, the nodes delimit the segments of the segmented structure.

Oral setae: See *fimbriae.*

Pachymorph: A type of rhizome that always turns upward and becomes a culm. It is nearly always curved and, at its maximum width, is slightly thicker than the above-ground culm it becomes. Rhizome nodes are not prominent. The internodes are wider than long, and usually solid. New rhizomes emerge from lateral buds on an existing rhizome. As with the original rhizome, these new rhizomes always turn upward and become culms. The neck of the rhizome can be either long or short. This rhizome structure is commonly associated with clumping bamboos, although many species with pachymorph rhizome systems do not exhibit a clumping habit. See also *amphimorph, leptomorph.*

Palmate: Three or more leaves or leaflets originating from an apparent common point, in the manner of a palm.

Persistent: Not deciduous; not shedding or falling away. Culm leaves, for example, may be persistent or may be deciduous. See also *deciduous.*

Phylogeny: The evolutionary history of a species or other, higher, taxonomic grouping.

Pluricaespitose: Arising in dispersed clumps. Species with pachymorph rhizome systems that have a combination of short and long rhizome necks display this culm and clump habit. Species with leptomorph rhizome systems and tillering culms also display this habit. For the leptomorph bamboos, this habit is sometimes termed amphipodial or (incorrectly) amphimorph. See also *caespitose, diffuse.*

Polyphyletic: A group of taxa that do not all descend from a common ancestor. See also *monophyletic.*

Primordium: The earliest stage of development, or the most rudimentary form of an organism or plant part.

Propagule: A new plant created from a parent plant.

Pruinose: A white, waxy, powdery coating. In the context of bamboos, for example, the young culms of some species are pruinose.

Pseudopetiole: An elongated constriction at the base of the foliage leaf blade, found in bamboos and a few other grasses; similar to the petiole in dicots. Although the pseudopetiole is attached to the sheath, rather than directly to a branch, the sheath is so tightly wrapped around the branch that it is barely distinguishable from it.

Pubescent: Covered with short, fine hairs.

Rhizome: An underground stem, or underground portion of a stem. The rhizome has the same or similar structure as the culm, the aboveground stem. It has nodes, internodes, leaves (here generally consisting of the sheath with no blade), and roots.

Root: The (usually) underground part of a plant that absorbs water and nutrients. It also serves to anchor the plant in the soil. It is the only bamboo axis that does not have a segmented structure—that is, unlike culms, branches, and rhizomes, roots have no nodes, internodes, or leaves.

Running: See *diffuse, pluricaespitose.*

Scandent: Climbing.

Sheath: The lower part of the leaf that tightly encircles the stem or branch. It is a very large and prominent part of the culm leaf, but a much smaller, and sometimes barely noticeable, part of the foliage leaf.

Sheath scar: A mark left around the lowermost part of the node where the sheath was attached.

Sport: A plant that is markedly different from the parent plant, generally as the result of a mutation.

Spikelet: The basic unit of a grass flower cluster.

Sulcus: A pronounced groove running the length of the internode, caused by the presence of a developing branch bud at the internode's base, grooving the culm as the internode elongates. A prominent sulcus is a distinguishing characteristic of the genus *Phyllostachys.*

Supranodal ridge: The uppermost part of the node. Varying among species, the supranodal ridge ranges from nearly indistinguishable to very prominent.

Sympodial: A branching habit in which each succeeding branch, or axis, becomes dominant. The term was originally derived to describe rhizome branching habit. In sympodial rhizomes, each new rhizome turns upward and becomes a culm. Although it describes only the branching habit, exclusive of other structural characteristics, the term is loosely synonymous with pachymorph when applied to rhizomes—at least, one frequently encounters it as such in the literature. See also *amphipodial, monopodial.*

Taxon: A taxonomic category or group (plural, taxa).

Tessellation: Fine cross-veining in leaves, creating a gridlike or checkered appearance that is visible on close examination. Not all bamboo leaves are tessellated. Tessellation is associated with greater cold hardiness. Most or all tropical bamboos have no leaf tessellation.

Thorn: A stiff, woody, modified branch that ends in a sharp point. Some tropical and semitropical bamboo species have thorns.

Tillering: Sending forth new shoots from the base of a stem. In the context of bamboos, tillering refers to new culms that arise from the basal buds of existing culms without an intervening rhizome. It is characteristic of some bamboo species with leptomorph rhizome systems. Although sometimes superficially similar, bamboos with pachymorph rhizome systems are not tillering, per se, but rather have an intervening (though unified) rhizome between the existing stem and new culm.

Unicaespitose: See *caespitose.*

Vascular bundle: Strands of conducting tissue. They are the means by which water, nutrients, and other substances are transported throughout a plant.

Whip: A culm generated from a whipshoot. These tend to be smaller, more curved, less erect, and have shorter internodes than culms emerging from buds on a rhizome. See *whipshoot.*

Whipshoot: A tip of a leptomorph rhizome that turns upward and grows into an above-ground culm. Whipshoots are relatively common with recently established plants but nearly absent from well-established plants.

Woody: Lignified, not herbaceous; having persistent aerial parts. Bamboo does not have true wood, which is derived from secondary growth. Virtually all of our familiar bamboos are woody, but many, less well-known bamboo species are herbaceous. See also *herbaceous.*

Bibliography

Adams, W. 1996. Are the Himalayan bamboos hardier than previously thought? *American Bamboo Society Northeast Chapter Newsletter* (September): 4.

Adamson, W. C., G. A. White, H. T. DeRigo, and W. O. Hawley. 1978. Bamboo production research at Savannah, Georgia, 1956–77. ARS-S-176, Agricultural Research Service, U.S. Department of Agriculture, Washington, D.C.

Alderman, A. 1995. Bamboo ground covers. *Fine Gardening.* 45: 54–57. Reprinted in *Pacific Northwest Bamboo* (Fall 1997): 20–21.

Anantachote, A. 1990. Flowering characteristics of some bamboos in Thailand. In *Bamboos: Current Research.* Proceedings of the International Bamboo Workshop, Cochin, India. Ottawa, Canada: International Development Research Centre. 66–75.

Austin, R., D. Levy, and K. Ueda. 1970. *Bamboo.* New York: Weatherhill.

Banik, R. L. 1995. *A Manual for Vegetative Propagation of Bamboos.* New Delhi, India: International Network for Bamboo and Rattan.

Banik, R. L., and A. N. Rao. 1996. Bamboo: Strategies for improvement. In *Bamboo, People and the Environment.* New Delhi, India: International Network for Bamboo and Rattan. 2: 101–119.

Bareis, K. 1996. Bamboo potential in the Pacific Northwest using an Asian agro-forestry model. In *Bamboo and the Pacific Northwest: The Proceedings of the Pacific Northwest Bamboo Agro-forestry Workshop,* edited by G. Cooper and T. Taylor. Portland, Oregon: The Pacific Northwest Chapter of the American Bamboo Society. 16–24.

Barnhart, E. 1983. New Alchemy bamboo hardiness report: 3/4/83 trials of hardy bamboo on Cape Cod at the New Alchemy Institute. *The Journal of the American Bamboo Society* 4 (1&2): 36–37.

Bell, M. 1998. *Phyllostachys. Pacific Northwest Bamboo* (Summer): 19–20.

Billings, D., and L. Houf. 1995. Banking on bamboo. *Missouri Conservationist.* Reprinted in *Pacific Northwest Bamboo* (August–October 1995): 12–13.

Bol, G. 1993. Foreword. In *The Bamboos,* by F. A. McClure. Cambridge, Massachusetts: Harvard University Press, 1963. Reprint, Washington, D.C.: Smithsonian Institution Press.

Brennecke, K. 1980a. Propagation of bamboo by vegetative fractions. *The Journal of the American Bamboo Society* 1 (1): 12–15.

———. 1980b. A survey of U.S.D.A. bamboo introductions. *The Journal of the American Bamboo Society* 1 (1): 2–11.

Breyer, S. 1993. Propagation of container grown bamboos by division of rhizomes with attached culms. *American Bamboo Society Newsletter* (June): 7–13.

But, P. P., L. Chia, H. Fung, and S. Hu. 1985. *Hong Kong Bamboos.* Hong Kong: The Urban Council.

Calderón, C., and T. R. Soderstrom. 1973. *Morphological and Anatomical Considerations of the Grass Subfamily Bambusoideae Based on the New Genus* Maclurolyra. Smithsonian Contributions to Botany (11). Washington, D.C.: Smithsonian Institution Press.

Campbell, J. J. N. 1985. Bamboo flowering patterns: A global view with special reference to East Asia. *The Journal of the American Bamboo Society* 6: 17–35.

Campbell, J. J. N., and Z. S. Qin. 1983. Interaction of giant pandas, bamboos, and people. *The Journal of the American Bamboo Society* 4 (1&2): 1–35.

Camus, E. 1913. *Les Bambusées.* Paris: Paul Lechevalier.

Cao, Q., S. Feng, and Y. He. 1996. Effects of mulching on the shoot production of *Phyllostachys praecox* stands. In *Bamboo, People and the Environment.* New Delhi, India: International Network for Bamboo and Rattan. 1: 101–108.

Chao, C. S. 1989. *A Guide to Bamboos Grown in Britain.* Kew, England: Royal Botanic Gardens, Kew.

Chapman, G. P., and W. E. Peat. 1992. *An Introduction to the Grasses (including bamboos and cereals).* Oxon, England: C A B International.

Chen, S. L., and L. C. Chia. 1988. *Chinese Bamboos.* Portland, Oregon: Dioscorides Press.

Chua, K. S., B. C. Soong, and H. T. W. Tan. 1996. *The Bamboos of Singapore.* Singapore: International Plant Genetic Resources Institute.

Clark, L. G. 1989. Systematics of *Chusquea* section *Swallenochloa,* section *Verticillatae,* section *Serpentes,* and section *Longifoliae* (Poaceae–Bambusoideae). *Systematic Botany Monographs* (27). Ann Arbor, Michigan: The American Society of Plant Taxonomists.

———. 1995. Foreword. The taxonomy and cultivation of *Chimonobambusa* Makino. *The Journal of the American Bamboo Society* 11 (1&2): 4–5.

———. 1997a. Bamboos: The centrepiece of the grass family. In *The Bamboos,* edited by G. P. Chapman. San Diego, California: Academic Press. 237–248.

———. 1997b. Diversity, biogeography and evolution of *Chusquea.* In *The Bamboos,* edited by G. P. Chapman. San Diego, California: Academic Press. 33–44.

———. 1999. Bamboo diversity and phylogeny: *Chusquea* and its allies. *Pacific Northwest Bamboo* (Winter): 13–14.

Clark, L. G., and R. W. Pohl. 1996. *Agnes Chase's First Book of Grasses.* 4th ed. Washington, D.C.: Smithsonian Institution Press.

Clark, L. G., W. Zhang, and J. F. Wendel. 1995. A phylogeny of the grass family (Poaceae) based on *ndhF* sequence data. *Systematic Botany* 20 (4): 436–460.

Clayton, W. D., and S. A. Renvoize. 1986. *Genera Graminum: Grasses of the World.* London: Her Majesty's Stationary Office.

Cooper, G. 1994. Is there a problem with bamboo mites? *Pacific Northwest Bamboo* (November–December): 2–3.

——. 1995. Bamboo quarantine: A surmise for its continued existence since 1918 to the present. *Pacific Northwest Bamboo* (August–October): 10.

——. 1996a. American bamboo industry—past, present and future: Comparison/contrast to China. In *Bamboo and the Pacific Northwest: The Proceedings of the Pacific Northwest Bamboo Agro-forestry Workshop,* edited by G. Cooper and T. Taylor. Portland, Oregon: The Pacific Northwest Chapter of the American Bamboo Society. 1–15.

——. 1996b. Moso to all. *Pacific Northwest Bamboo* (Summer): 23–24.

——. 1999. Guess who's coming to dinner? *Pacific Northwest Bamboo* (Summer): 37–38.

Crouzet, Y. *General Catalog: Nurseries of the Bambouseraie.* Anduze, France.

Crouzet, Y., and P. Starosta. 1998. *Bamboos.* Köln, Germany: Evergreen.

Cusack, V. 1997. *Bamboo Rediscovered.* Trentham, Australia: Earth Garden Books.

——. 1999. *Bamboo World: The Growing and Use of Clumping Bamboos.* East Roseville, Australia: Kangaroo Press.

Darke, R., ed. 1994. *The New Royal Horticultural Society Dictionary: Manual of Grasses.* Series editor M. Griffiths. Portland, Oregon: Timber Press.

Dart, D. L. 1999. *The Bamboo Handbook.* Belli Park, Australia: Nemea.

Davidson, P. 1997. Quarantine Greenhouse. *Pacific Northwest Bamboo* (Winter): 1.

DeRigo, H. T. 1993. Studies on the agronomic culture of phyllostachoid bamboos. *American Bamboo Society Newsletter* (December): 6–8.

DeRosa, C. 1996. Bamboo barriers. *American Bamboo Society Newsletter* (June): 11.

Ding, Y., D. Grosser, W. Liese, and W. Hsiung. 1992. Anatomical studies on the rhizome of some monopodial bamboos. In *Bamboo and Its Use: International Symposium on Industrial Use of Bamboo.* Beijing, China: International Tropical Timber Organization, Chinese Academy of Forestry. 143–150.

Ding, Y., G. Tang, and C. Chao. 1997. Anatomical studies on the culm neck of some pachymorph bamboos. In *The Bamboos,* edited by G. P. Chapman. San Diego, California: Academic Press. 285–292.

Dransfield, S. 1992. *The Bamboos of Sabah.* Sabah, Malaysia: Forestry Department.

Dransfield, S., and E. Widjaja. 1995. *Plant Resources of South-East Asia 7: Bamboos.* Leiden, The Netherlands: Backhuys Publishers.

Eberts, W. 1991. *Bambus.* Baden-Baden, Germany: Bambuscentrum.

Ehrensing, D. 1996. Non-wood fiber sources for pulp and paper production in the Pacific Northwest. In *Bamboo and the Pacific Northwest: The Proceedings of the Pacific Northwest Bamboo Agro-forestry Workshop,* edited by G. Cooper and T. Taylor. Portland, Oregon: The Pacific Northwest Chapter of the American Bamboo Society. 49–60.

Ellis, R. P. 1986. A review of comparative leaf blade anatomy in the systematics of the Poaceae: The past twenty-five years. In *Grass Systematics and Evolution,* edited by T. R. Soderstrom, K. W. Hilu, C. S. Campbell, and M. E. Barkworth. Washington, D.C.: Smithsonian Institution Press. 3–10.

Experimental Forest, College of Agriculture, National Taiwan University. 1980. *Bamboos of the Chitou Forest Recreation Area.* Taiwan: The Experimental Forest, College of Agriculture, National Taiwan University.

Fabel-Ward, R. D. 1980. Report on flowering and fruiting of *Arundinaria angustifolia. The Journal of the American Bamboo Society* 1 (4): 44–47.

Fadem, R. 1974. *Bamboo: Pacific Bamboo Gardens.* 3rd ed. San Diego, California: Pacific Bamboo Gardens.

Fairchild, D. G. 1903. *Japanese Bamboos and Their Introduction into America.* Reprint. American Bamboo Society, 1994.

Farrelly, D. 1984. *The Book of Bamboo.* San Francisco, California: Sierra Club Books.

Flatabø, G. 1995. Bamboo hardiness reports: Bamboos in Norway. *Temperate Bamboo Quarterly* (Spring–Summer): 38–40.

Freeman-Mitford, A. B. 1896. *The Bamboo Garden.* Reprint. American Bamboo Society, 1994.

Fu, M., and R. L. Banik. 1996. Bamboo production systems and their management. In *Bamboo, People and the Environment.* New Delhi, India: International Network for Bamboo and Rattan. 1: 18–33.

Gielis, J. 1995. European company has 25 bamboos in tissue culture. *Pacific Northwest Bamboo* (August–October): 23.

Gielis, J., I. Everaert, and M. De Loose. 1997. Genetic variability and relationships in *Phyllostachys* using random amplified polymorphic DNA. In *The Bamboos,* edited by G. P. Chapman. San Diego, California: Academic Press. 107–124.

Gielis, J., I. Everaert, P. Goetghebeur, and M. De Loose. 1996. Bamboo and Molecular Markers. In *Bamboo, People and the Environment.* New Delhi, India: International Network for Bamboo and Rattan. 2: 45–67.

Gielis, J., P. Goetghebeur, and P. Debergh. 1997. Morphological and biochemical aspects of flowering in bamboos—the development of model systems. In *The Bamboos,* edited by G. P. Chapman. San Diego, California: Academic Press. 179–186.

Griffiths, M. 1994. *The New Royal Horticultural Society Dictionary: Index of Garden Plants.* Portland, Oregon: Timber Press

Guala, G. F. II. 1993. Cyanogenesis in the bamboos: A phylogenetic perspective. *The Journal of the American Bamboo Society* 10 (1&2): 1–8.

Haubrich, R. 1980. Handbook of bamboos cultivated in the United States. Part I: The genus *Phyllostachys. The Journal of the American Bamboo Society* 1 (4): 48–92.

———. 1981. Handbook of bamboos cultivated in the United States. Part II: The giant tropical clumping bamboos. *The Journal of the American Bamboo Society* 2 (1): 2–20.

———. 1982. Preface to "The culture of moso bamboo in Japan, Part I," by J. Oshima. *The Journal of the American Bamboo Society* 3 (1): 2–28.

———. 1996. Timber bamboo. In *Bamboo and the Pacific Northwest: The Proceedings of the Pacific Northwest Bamboo Agro-forestry Workshop,* edited by G. Cooper and T. Taylor. Portland, Oregon: The Pacific Northwest Chapter of the American Bamboo Society. 61–63.

Hawke, R. G. 1992. A bamboo performance report. *Chicago Botanical Garden Plant Evaluation Notes* 3: 1–4.

Henderson, S. 1997. Building a bamboo farm. In *Proceedings: 1997 Pacific Northwest Bamboo Agro-Forestry Workshop.* The Pacific Northwest Chapter of the American Bamboo Society. Ch. 8H, 1–10.

Hitchcock, A. S. 1935. *Manual of the Grasses of the United States.* Second edition revised by A. Chase, 1950. Reprint. New York: Dover, 1971.

Hollowell, V. C. 1997. Systematic relationships of *Pariana* and associated neotropical taxa. In *The Bamboos,* edited by G. P. Chapman. San Diego, California: Academic Press. 45–60.

Hsiung, W. 1986. Growth pattern of monopodial rhizomes of bamboo plants. *The Journal of the American Bamboo Society* 5: 73–78.

———. 1991. Prospects for bamboo development in the world. *The Journal of the American Bamboo Society* 8: 168–178.

Hsiung, W., Z. Din, Y. Li, and P. Lu. 1985. Studies on branching pattern of monopodial bamboos. In *Recent Research on Bamboos.* Proceedings of the International Bamboo Workshop, Hangzhou, China. Ottawa, Canada: International Development Research Centre. 128–135.

Isagi, Y., T. Kawahara, and H. Ito. 1997. A computer-aided management system of *Phyllostachys* stands based on the ecological characteristics of carbon cycling. In *The Bamboos,* edited by G. P. Chapman. San Diego, California: Academic Press. 125–134.

Janssen, J. J. A. 1985. The mechanical properties of bamboo. In *Recent Research on Bamboos.* Proceedings of the International Bamboo Workshop, Hangzhou, China. Ottawa, Canada: International Development Research Centre. 250–256.

Janzen, D. H. 1976. Why bamboos wait so long to flower. *Annual Review of Ecology and Systematics* 7: 347–391.

Jaquith, N. 1994. A new name for *Phyllostachys purpurata. American Bamboo Society Newsletter* (April): 1.

———. 1997. Flowering bamboo presents an opportunity. In *Proceedings: 1997 Pacific Northwest Bamboo Agro-Forestry Workshop.* The Pacific Northwest Chapter of the American Bamboo Society. Ch. 1, 1–4.

Jaquith, N., and R. Haubrich. 1996. When bamboo flowers. *American Bamboo Society Newsletter* (April): 1–3.

John, C. K., R. S. Nadgauda, and A. F. Mascarenhas. 1995. Bamboos—Some newer perspectives. *Current Science* 68 (9 & 10): 885–896. Reprinted in *Temperate Bamboo Quarterly* (Spring–Summer 1995): 17–28.

Judziewicz, E. J., and L. G. Clark. 1991. An overview of the diversity of New World bamboos. *The Journal of the American Bamboo Society* 8: 117–122.

Judziewicz, E. J., L. G. Clark, X. Londoño, and M. J. Stern. 1999. *American Bamboos.* Washington, D.C.: Smithsonian Institution Press.

Judziewicz, E. J., and T. R. Soderstrom. 1989. *Morphological, Anatomical, and Taxonomic Studies in* Anomochloa *and* Streptochaeta *(Poaceae: Bambusoideae).* Smithsonian Contributions to Botany (68). Washington, D.C.: Smithsonian Institution Press.

Kawamura, S. 1927. On the periodic flowering of bamboo. *Japanese Journal of Botany* 3: 335–349.

Keng, P. C. 1948. Preliminary study on the Chinese bamboos. Technical Bulletin of the National Forest Research Bureau, Nanking 8: 1–21.

Koyama, H., and E. Uchimura. 1995. Seasonal change of photosynthesis rate and its relation to the growth of *Phyllostachys bambusoides.* In *Bamboo, People and the Environment.* New Delhi, India: International Network for Bamboo and Rattan. 1: 109–120.

Kumar, A. 1996. Mass propagation of tropical sympodial bamboos through macropro-liferation. In *Bamboo, People and the Environment*. New Delhi, India: International Network for Bamboo and Rattan. 1: 56–61.

Lancaster, R. 1997. Plants that should be better known: *Qiongzhuea tumidinoda*. *American Bamboo Society Newsletter* (April): 1–2.

Large and Small Bamboo (Take to Sasa). 1971. Japan: Hoikusha.

Lawson, A. H., 1968. *Bamboos: A Gardener's Guide to Their Cultivation in Temperate Climates*. London: Faber and Faber.

Lewis, D. 1993. *Bamboo on the Farm*. Redmond, Washington: Bamboo Gardens of Washington.

——. 1997. Bamboo shoot yields in henon bamboo grove. In *Proceedings: 1997 Pacific Northwest Bamboo Agro-Forestry Workshop*. The Pacific Northwest Chapter of the American Bamboo Society. Ch. 8L, 1–7.

——. 1998. *Hardy Bamboos for Shoots and Poles*. Seattle, Washington: Daphne Works.

Li, D.-Z. 1997. The *Flora of China* Bambusoideae project—Problems and current understanding of bamboo taxonomy in China. In *The Bamboos*, edited by G. P. Chapman. San Diego, California: Academic Press. 61–81.

Liese, W. 1985. Anatomy and properties of bamboo. In *Recent Research on Bamboos*. Proceedings of the International Bamboo Workshop, Hangzhou, China. Ottawa, Canada: International Development Research Centre. 196–208.

——. 1991. Progress in bamboo research. *The Journal of the American Bamboo Society* 8: 151–167.

——. 1999. Bamboo: Past–Present–Future. *American Bamboo Society Newsletter* (February): 1–7.

Liese, W., and G. Weiner. 1996. Ageing of bamboo culms: A review. In *Bamboo, People and the Environment*. New Delhi, India: International Network for Bamboo and Rattan. 1: 132–148.

——. 1999. Modification of bamboo culm structures due to ageing and wounding. In *The Bamboos*, edited by G. P. Chapman. San Diego, California: Academic Press. 313–322.

Lin, Q. 1996. Cultivation techniques for *Dendrocalamopsis oldhamii*. In *Bamboo, People and the Environment*. New Delhi, India: International Network for Bamboo and Rattan. 1: 50–53.

Linton, F. 1994. Did you know? *American Bamboo Society Newsletter* (February): 18–19.

——. 1995. The bamboo farm. *Temperate Bamboo Quarterly* (Spring–Summer): 32–34.

Londoño, X. 1996. Diversity and distribution of New World bamboos, with special emphasis on the Bambuseae. In *Bamboo, People and the Environment* (Abstract). New Delhi, India: International Network for Bamboo and Rattan. 2: 101–119.

Lucas, Susanne. 1993. The International Bamboo Association. *American Bamboo Society Newsletter* (August): 5–6.

——. 1998a. American bamboo gardens. *American Bamboo Society Newsletter* (October): 7–8.

——. 1998b. Looking at chusqueas with Lynn Clark—A Costa Rican field trip. *American Bamboo Society Newsletter* (December): 1–3.

Makita, A. 1992. Survivorship of a monocarpic bamboo grass, *Sasa kurilensis*, during the early regeneration process after mass flowering. *Ecological Research* 7: 245–254.

——. 1997. The regeneration process in the monocarpic bamboo, *Sasa* species. In *The Bamboos,* edited by G. P. Chapman. San Diego, California: Academic Press. 135–145.

Masman, W. 1995. *Bamboo Names and Synonyms.* Ruurlo, The Netherlands. Internet publication [http://www.rsl.ox.ac.uk/users/djh/ebs/synonyms.htm].

McClure, F. A. 1925. Some observations on the bamboos of Kwangtung. *Lingnan Agricultural Review* 3: 40–47.

——. 1953. Bamboo as a building material. Foreign Agricultural Service, U.S. Department of Agriculture, Washington, D.C.

——. 1957. Bamboos of the genus *Phyllostachys* under cultivation in the United States. Agricultural Handbook No, 114, Agricultural Research Service, U.S. Department of Agriculture, Washington, D.C.

——. 1966. *The Bamboos.* Cambridge, Massachusetts: Harvard University Press. Reprint. Washington, D.C.: Smithsonian Institution Press, 1993.

——. 1973. *Genera of Bamboos Native to the New World (Gramineae: Bambusoideae).* Edited by T. R. Soderstrom. Smithsonian Contributions to Botany (9). Washington, D.C.: Smithsonian Institution Press.

McNeely, J. A. 1996. Bamboo, biodiversity and conservation in Asia. In *Bamboo, People and the Environment.* New Delhi, India: International Network for Bamboo and Rattan. 2: 1–22.

Mejia-Sualés, T., and G. Castillo-Campos. 1996. Bamboos: A natural resource in Monte Blanco, Mexico. *Temperate Bamboo Quarterly* (Summer): 86–93.

Miles, C. 1998. Report on Tenino Farm Project. *Pacific Northwest Bamboo* (Winter): 26.

Miller, S. 1994. Spider (bamboo) mite population booms after hot, dry summer. *Pacific Northwest Bamboo* (November–December): 2.

Mitchell, G. 1989. Notes on bamboo survivability in the Pahrump Valley. *The Journal of the American Bamboo Society* 7 (1&2): 17–21.

Muller, L. 1995. Indonesian *Gigantochloa* selections and the Granny Smith apple. *American Bamboo Society Newsletter* (December): 3–6.

——. 1996a. Cultivated *Gigantochloa:* Escape from "death by flowering." *American Bamboo Society Newsletter* (February): 4–7.

——. 1996b. The forgotten bamboo macrocosm of South-East Asia. *American Bamboo Society Newsletter* (June): 8–10.

——. 1998. Giant cultivated *Gigantochloa* bamboos of Java, Bali, and South Sumatra. *American Bamboo Society Newsletter* (August): 3–4.

Nadgauda, R. S., C. K. John, M. S. Joshi, V. A. Parasharami, and A. F. Mascarenhas. 1997. Application of *in vitro* techniques for bamboo improvement. In *The Bamboos,* edited by G. P. Chapman. San Diego, California: Academic Press. 163–177.

Nelson, G. 1997. Evaluation of temperate bamboo species as forages for livestock. In *Proceedings: 1997 Pacific Northwest Bamboo Agro-Forestry Workshop.* The Pacific Northwest Chapter of the American Bamboo Society. Ch. 7, 1–9.

Ohrnberger, D. 1999. *The Bamboos of the World.* Amsterdam, The Netherlands: Elsevier.

Ohrnberger, D., and J. Goerring. 1983–1987. *The Bamboos of the World.* Germany. Reprint. Dehra Dun, India: International Book Distributors, 1990.

Oshima, J. 1931a. The culture of moso bamboo in Japan, Part I. Translated by S. Katsura. Edited by R. Haubrich. Reprint. 1982. *The Journal of the American Bamboo Society* 3 (1): 2–28.

——. 1931b. The culture of moso bamboo in Japan, Part II. Translated by S. Katsura. Edited by R. Haubrich. Reprint. 1982. *The Journal of the American Bamboo Society* 3 (2): 33–46.

Qui, F. 1982. *Phyllostachys pubescens* in China. *The Journal of the American Bamboo Society* 3 (3): 49–54.

Qui, F., and N. Ma. 1992. Selection of cold resistant economic bamboo species in China. *The Journal of the American Bamboo Society* 9: 8–16.

Rao, I. V. R., A. M. Yusoff, A. N. Rao, and C. B. Sastry. *Propagation of Bamboo and Rattan Through Tissue Culture.* The International Development Research Centre Bamboo and Rattan Research Network.

Rao, I. V. R., and A. B. Zamora. 1996. Enhancing the availability of improved planting materials. In *Bamboo, People and the Environment.* New Delhi, India: International Network for Bamboo and Rattan. 1: 6–17.

Recht, C., and M. F. Wetterwald. 1992. *Bamboos.* Translated by Martin Walters. Portland, Oregon: Timber Press.

Renvoize, S. A., and T. R. Hodkinson. 1997. Classification of *Phyllostachys.* In *The Bamboos,* edited by G. P. Chapman. San Diego, California: Academic Press. 95–106.

Restrepo, E. A., S. Mutis, D. M. Macías, and S. Vélez. 1990. *Tropical Bamboo.* Edited by Marcelo Villegas. New York: Rizzoli International Publications.

Riedelsheimer, M. 1994. The diverse clones of *Fargesia nitida.* Edited by Whitney Adams. *American Bamboo Society Newsletter* (August): 1–3.

——. 1995. *Fargesia*—Another word for challenge. *American Bamboo Society Newsletter* (June): 1–3.

Rivière, A., and C. Rivière. 1879. *Les bamboos.* Paris: Au Siège de la Société d'Acclimataxion.

Satow, E. 1899. *The Cultivation of Bamboos in Japan.* Reprint. American Bamboo Society, 1993.

Savile, D. B. O. 1986. Use of rust fungi (Uredinales) in determining ages and relationships in Poaceae. In *Grass Systematics and Evolution,* edited by T. R. Soderstrom, K. W. Hilu, C. S. Campbell, and M. E. Barkworth. Washington, D.C.: Smithsonian Institution Press. 168–178.

Saxena, S., and V. Dhawan. 1996. Commercialization of bamboo tissue culture. In *Bamboo, People and the Environment.* New Delhi, India: International Network for Bamboo and Rattan. 1: 62–74.

Shor, B. 1993. How ABS began. *American Bamboo Society Newsletter* (August): 1–3.

——. Bamboo Flowering. Unpublished compilation.

Shor, B., S. Tengwall, and R. S. Lowe. 1996. Thomas Edison and the light bulb. *American Bamboo Society Newsletter* (April): 10–11.

Shor, G. 1995. The bamboo quarantine system. *Pacific Northwest Bamboo* (August–October): 6.

——. 1998. *Chusquea culeou* and/or "breviglumis." *Pacific Northwest Bamboo* (Summer): 10–11.

——, ed. 1999. *American Bamboo Society: Bamboo Species Source List No. 19.* Albany, New York: American Bamboo Society.

Sigu, G. O. 1994. A need for conservation of *Arundinaria alpina* K. Schum in Kenya and its ecological significance. In *Bamboo in Asia and the Pacific.* Proceedings of the 4th International Bamboo Workshop, Chiangmai, Thailand. Bangkok, Thailand: Forestry Research Support Programme for Asia and the Pacific. 48–50.

Sineath, H. H., P. M. Daugherty, T. N. Hutton, and T. A. Wastler. 1953. *Industrial Raw Materials of Plant Origin: (V.) A Survey of the Bamboos.* Engineering Experiment Station of the Georgia Institute of Technology Bulletin XV (18).

Soderstrom, T. R. 1985. Bamboo systematics: Yesterday, today, and tomorrow. *The Journal of the American Bamboo Society* 6: 4–16.

Soderstrom, T. R., and R. P. Ellis. 1986. The position of bamboo genera and allies in a system of grass classification. In *Grass Systematics and Evolution,* edited by T. R. Soderstrom, K. W. Hilu, C. S. Campbell, and M. E. Barkworth. Washington, D.C.: Smithsonian Institution Press. 225–238.

Soderstrom, T. R., and R. P. Ellis. 1988. *The Woody Bamboos (Poaceae: Bambuseae) of Sri Lanka: A Morphological-Anatomical Study.* Smithsonian Contributions to Botany (72). Washington, D.C.: Smithsonian Institution Press.

Soldaat, E. 1997. Bamboo mites in Holland. *Pacific Northwest Bamboo* (Winter): 7.

St. Clair, T. R. 1999. A nomenclatural note. *American Bamboo Society Newsletter* (June): 7–8.

Stapleton, C. M. A. 1994a. The Bamboos of Nepal and Bhutan, Part 1. *Edinburgh Journal of Botany* 51 (1): 1–32.

———. 1994b. The Bamboos of Nepal and Bhutan, Part 2. *Edinburgh Journal of Botany* 51 (2): 275–295.

———. 1994c. The Bamboos of Nepal and Bhutan, Part 3. *Edinburgh Journal of Botany* 51 (3): 301–330.

———. 1994d. *The Bamboos of Bhutan.* Kew, England: The Royal Botanic Gardens.

———. 1994e. *The Bamboos of Nepal.* Kew, England: The Royal Botanic Gardens.

———. 1994f. The blue-stemmed bamboo *Himalayacalamus hookerianus. American Bamboo Society Newsletter* (June): 1–4.

———. 1995a. Flowering of *Fargesia nitida* in the UK. *American Bamboo Society Newsletter* (October): 1–4.

———. 1995b. Muriel Wilson's bamboo. *Bamboo Society Newsletter, European Bamboo Society Great Britain* (21). Reprinted in *American Bamboo Society Newsletter* (April 1995): 6–11.

———. 1996. Comments on the conservation of *Sinarundinaria. American Bamboo Society Newsletter* (December): 9–10.

———. 1997a. The morphology of woody bamboos. In *The Bamboos,* edited by G. P. Chapman. San Diego, California: Academic Press. 251–267.

———. 1997b. A new combination in *Cephalostachyum* with notes on names in *Neomicrocalamus* (Gramineae–Bambusoideae). Kew Bulletin 52 (3): 699–702.

———. 1998a. Form and function in the bamboo rhizome. *The Journal of the American Bamboo Society* 12: 21–36.

———. 1998b. New combinations in *Borinda* (Gramineae–Bambusoideae). Kew Bulletin 53 (2): 453–459.

———. 1998c. Seed germination. *Pacific Northwest Bamboo* (Summer): 17.

——. 1999a. *Bambusa fortunei* and *Bambusa variegata:* Competing basionyms for the white-variegated dwarf leptomorph bamboo currently placed in *Arundinaria, Pleioblastus,* or *Sasa. Bamboo Society Newsletter, European Bamboo Society Great Britain.* (31): 36–40.

——. 1999b. Sino-Himalayan bamboos on the US west coast. *American Bamboo Society Newsletter* (December): 1–6.

——. 1999c. *Yushania* vs. *Sinarundinaria:* Good news and bad. *Bamboo Society Newsletter, European Bamboo Society Great Britain.* (31): 42–43.

Stapleton, C. M. A., and V. R. Rao. 1996. Progress and prospects in genetic diversity studies on bamboo and its conservation. In *Bamboo, People and the Environment.* New Delhi, India: International Network for Bamboo and Rattan. 2: 23–44.

Sturkie, D. G., V. L. Brown, and W. J. Watson. 1968. Bamboo Growing in Alabama. Bulletin 987, Agricultural Experiment Station, Auburn University, Auburn, Alabama.

Sulthoni, A. 1996. Shooting period of sympodial bamboo species: An important indicator to manage culm harvesting. In *Bamboo, People and the Environment.* New Delhi, India: International Network for Bamboo and Rattan. 1: 96–100.

Sun, C., and G. Xie. 1985. Fibre morphology and crystallinity of *Phyllostachys pubescens* with reference to age. In *Recent Research on Bamboos.* Proceedings of the International Bamboo Workshop, Hangzhou, China. Ottawa, Canada: International Development Research Centre. 247–249.

Suzuki, S. 1978. *Index to Japanese Bambusaceae.* Tokyo, Japan: Gakken.

Taylor, A. H., and Z. Qin. 1997. The dynamics of temperate bamboo forests and panda conservation in China. In *The Bamboos,* edited by G. P. Chapman. San Diego, California: Academic Press. 189–203.

Tewari, D. N. 1992. *A Monograph on Bamboo.* Dehra Run, India: R. P. Singh Gahlot for International Book Distributors.

Turner, M. 1996. The care and feeding of large running bamboos in the Southeast. *American Bamboo Society Newsletter* (August): 10–11.

——. 1999. Spring weather and frozen shoots. *Pacific Northwest Bamboo* (Spring): 20–21.

——. 1999. The summer of '98 and other ramblings. *Pacific Northwest Bamboo* (Spring): 18–19.

Turtle, A. 1995a. Bamboo hardiness reports: Bamboos in Summertown, TN after –4°F winter low temperature. *Temperate Bamboo Quarterly* (Spring–Summer): 40–41.

——. 1995b. A note on David Bisset's bamboo. *American Bamboo Society Newsletter* (June): 16.

——. 1995c. Second annual bamboo lovers' conference; a report. *Temperate Bamboo Quarterly* (Spring–Summer): 4–7.

——. 1996a. Bambuseros, a year in the life of . . . . *Temperate Bamboo Quarterly* (Summer): 64–69.

——. 1996b. Bamboo Mecca–Kew. *Temperate Bamboo Quarterly* (Summer): 94–102.

——. 1996c. Handling big bamboo. *Temperate Bamboo Quarterly* (Summer): 103–110.

——. 1996d. An Indiana winter. *Temperate Bamboo Quarterly* (Summer): 130–132.

——, ed. 1996e. *Professional Bamboo Growers Conference Proceedings, October 1995, Savannah, Georgia.* Summertown, Tennessee: Earth Advocates Research Facility.

Turtle, S. 1999. Bambuseros in Costa Rica. *Temperate Bamboo Quarterly* (Spring): 6–11.

Valade, I., and Dahlan, Z. 1991. Approaching the underground development of a bamboo with leptomorph rhizomes: *Phyllostachys viridis* (Young) McClure. *The Journal of the American Bamboo Society* 8 (1&2): 23–42.

Valley, R. 1996. Northwest experiences in bamboo agro-forestry. In *Bamboo and the Pacific Northwest: The Proceedings of the Pacific Northwest Bamboo Agro-forestry Workshop*, edited by G. Cooper and T. Taylor. Portland, Oregon: The Pacific Northwest Chapter of the American Bamboo Society. 38–48.

Vélez, S. 1997. Bamboo architecture in Colombia. In *Proceedings: 1997 Pacific Northwest Bamboo Agro-Forestry Workshop*. The Pacific Northwest Chapter of the American Bamboo Society. Ch. 11, 1–5.

Walker, P. M. B., ed. 1989. *Cambridge Dictionary of Biology*. Cambridge, Massachusetts: Cambridge University Press.

Wang, C. P., Z. H. Yu, G. H. Ye, C. D. Chu, C. S. Chao, S. Y. Chen, C. Y. Yao, and H. R. Zhao. 1980. A taxonomic study of *Phyllostachys*, China. *Acta Phytotaxonomica Sinica* 18 (1): 15–19, 168–193.

Wang, D., and S. Shen. 1987. *Bamboos of China*. Portland, Oregon: Timber Press.

Wen, T. 1985a. Some ideas about the origin of bamboos. *The Journal of the American Bamboo Society* 6: 104–111.

——. 1985b. Three genera of Bambusoideae from China. In *Recent Research on Bamboos*. Proceedings of the International Bamboo Workshop, Hangzhou, China. Ottawa, Canada: International Development Research Centre. 18–23.

——. 1994. The taxonomy and cultivation of *Chimonobambusa* Makino. *The Journal of the American Bamboo Society* 11 (1&2): 8–80.

Were, J. M. 1990. *Arundinaria alpina* in Kenya. In *Bamboos: Current Research*. Proceedings of the International Bamboo Workshop, Cochin, India. Ottawa, Canada: International Development Research Centre. 32–33.

Widmer, Y. 1997. Life history of some *Chusquea* species in old-growth oak forest in Costa Rica. In *The Bamboos*, edited by G. P. Chapman. San Diego, California: Academic Press. 17–31.

Winkler, D. 1996. Forests, forest economy and deforestation in the Tibetan prefectures of West Sichuan. *Commonwealth Forestry Review* 75 (4): 296–301.

Wong, K. M. 1995a. *The Bamboos of Peninsular Malaysia*. Kuala Lumpur, Malaysia: Forest Research Institute.

——. 1995b. *The Morphology, Anatomy, Biology, and Classification of Peninsular Malaysian Bamboos*. Kuala Lumpur, Malaysia: University of Malaya.

Wu, B., and N. Ma. 1985. Bamboo research in China. In *Recent Research on Bamboos*. Proceedings of the International Bamboo Workshop, Hangzhou, China. Ottawa, Canada: International Development Research Centre. 18–23.

Yamamoto, K. 1997. *Bamboo in Kyoto*. Translated by P. L. Houser. Kyoto, Japan: Mitsumura Suiko Shoin Publishing Co.

Yat, Y. C., S. G. Cooper, T. J. Hansken, and C. C. Yat. 1984. Research on the raising of *Phyllostachys pubescens* seedlings. *The Journal of the American Bamboo Society* 5 (3&4): 79–86.

Young, R. A., J. R. Haun, and F. A. McClure. 1961. Bamboo in the United States: Description, culture, and utilization. Agricultural Handbook No. 193, U.S. Department of Agriculture, Washington, D.C.

Young, S. M. 1991. Bamboos in American botanical gardens past, present and future. *The Journal of the American Bamboo Society* 8 (1&2): 97–116.

Yoshida, K. 1999. *Bambusa textilis. American Bamboo Society Newsletter* (February): 8.

Zhang, G., and F. Chen. 1985. Studies on bamboo hybridization. In *Recent Research on Bamboos.* Proceedings of the International Bamboo Workshop, Hangzhou, China. Ottawa, Canada: International Development Research Centre. 179–184.

Zhang, W. Y., and N. X. Ma. 1991. Study on genetic breeding of bamboo plants in China. *Bamboo Abstracts* 4 (1): 1–12.

Zhu, S., W. Li, and X. Zhang. 1994a. *Substitute Bamboo for Timber in China: A Final Report of Project.* Beijing: Chinese Academy of Forestry.

Zhu, S., N. Ma, and M. Fu, principal eds. 1994b. *A Compendium of Chinese Bamboos.* China: China Forestry Publishing House.

Index

Pages with photographs appear in boldface.